Getting Started in

Stocks

The *Getting Started In* Series

Getting Started in
Stocks

THIRD EDITION

Alvin D. Hall

John Wiley & Sons, Inc.

New York • Chichester • Weinheim • Brisbane • Singapore • Toronto

This publication is designed to provide accurate and
authoritative information in regard to the subject
matter covered. It is sold with the understanding that
the publisher is not engaged in rendering legal, accounting,
or other professional services. If legal advice or other
expert assistance is required, the services of a competent
professional person should be sought.

ISBN: 0-471-17753-9

Printed in the United States of America

10 9 8 7 6 5 4 3

This book is dedicated to the memory of four dear friends

Richard Leigh Chittim
Isaac Henry Wing Professor of Mathematics Emeritus
Bowdoin College
Brunswick, Maine

Virginia Perkins White
Chapel Hill, North Carolina

Norman C. Robertson
Chicago, Illinois

and

John Davenport Neville
Richmond, Virginia

Contents

Acknowledgments

After more than 15 years of teaching the information contained in this book and after revising three editions, I still find it enlightening to put my spoken words in writing. My career in financial services training has continued to give me a platform on which to experiment with and refine the presentation of this information. My inquisitive students—now numbering in the thousands—have not been shy in asking me direct and probing questions that help me to clarify and expand topics, making this new edition more useful for the audience for whom it is intended.

Two other groups of people continue to be very helpful in enabling me to keep this book "on the money." First, I thank my friends in the financial services industry: John Keefe, Doug Carroll, and Julie Hahnke. They diligently read the added text, patiently listened to me read paragraphs over the phone, and bluntly asked those questions that led me to more creative and clear ways of explaining difficult subjects. Secondly, I thank my friends outside the securities industry: Roger Bakeman, Marvin Heiferman, Lotte Bruen, Michelle Kurland, and Betsy Stapleton. Their curiosity and questions about investing, as well as the overall stock market, were invaluable. They helped me anticipate many of the questions and concerns of the reader.

I truly appreciate the unending patience and understanding that Jacqueline Urinyi and Myles Thompson at John Wiley & Sons, Inc. have shown during my detailed revision and expansion of this new edition. I also thank them for their ongoing support and belief in my future projects.

Graphic designer Cindy Geist helped me create new figures and reprinted many of the illustrations originally created by Bryan Forman—an art director, beginning investor, and reader of this book—and Trudy Lundgren.

Robin Schoen, my public relations consultant, continues to apply her creativity and diligent work to expand the success of this book.

My most heart-felt thanks go to my friend Jonathan Drori, Executive Producer at the British Broadcasting Corporation (BBC), and to everyone—Nick Mirsky, Paul O'Connor, Michelle Kurland, Rebecca Lavender, Carol Mynott, David Bennett, John Parry, and Kathy Miller—whose hard work, professionalism, and creativity made the television series "Alvin Hall's Guide to Successful Investing" a joy and a success.

Investing in Stocks: The Fears, the Fantasies, the Facts

T his book is a practical tool for anyone interested in stocks. Often those who are inexperienced in investments are left feeling confused when an experienced investor or professional tries to explain what stocks are, how they work, and how to use them to make money. This book is written to make you—a newcomer to the stock market or a person simply looking for straightforward, clear information—feel knowledgeable.

Almost everyone knows the word *stocks*, and almost everyone has a story about a friend, relative, or acquaintance who has invested in the market. Usually it is the amount of money this friend made—or lost—that influences an individual's perceptions of investing in stocks. Individual attitudes toward investment in stocks are as varied as the stories people tell. Some stories are of sudden riches, usually told with considerable pride and relish. Others are of huge losses and are often murmured in hushed tones, if at all. The three profiles that follow illustrate the diversity of feelings and experiences that people have about investing in stocks.

The first concerns a woman who worked as a middle manager in a small manufacturing company and decided to begin investing in stock early in her career. She was not rich. Often she could save only a few hundred dollars each quarter to invest. She had a clear goal in mind: to build a portfolio of what she decided were high-quality stocks—those that paid dividends regularly and whose issuers produced good products. Working with a broker, she researched the companies that interested her and bought 5, 10, or 20 shares as her income permitted. When she could, she reinvested the dividends in more shares. Over a number of years and after several stock splits, her holdings increased nicely, and the dividends from these investments began to provide her with a little discretionary income. With a small amount of this extra money, she began buying a few of what she called her "fun stocks": small, somewhat risky companies whose products interested her. Today, her retirement income comes primarily from the portfolio of stocks that she built. Looking back over her years of investing in stocks, she gives the following advice to beginning investors: Buy quality. She readily admits that her "fun stocks" taught her how the stock market works, providing quick cash sometimes and harsh lessons at others. Her high-quality stocks, on the other hand, provided little action or excitement but have paid off handsomely in growth and steady dividends over the long run.

The second profile involves an art curator and author who saves diligently and invests his money only in art. His rationale is, "At least you have something to decorate the walls even if it loses its value." This person has never invested in a single stock. He is afraid of the market—a fear that comes from his boyhood. He remembers how his uncles, aunts, and cousins invested money in the market, certain that they were going to make a killing. More often than not, they got killed, losing all of their investment and then having to borrow money from relatives to cover their living expenses and losses. To him, stocks represent a sinkhole into which people pour fantasies of making it rich. Recently, however, some of his friends have done well investing in stocks and stock mutual funds, piquing his curiosity. He remains skeptical about investing, but he is interested in learning how stocks work and how his friends use them to make money.

The third profile is of a college professor and his wife, who runs a children's bookstore. Despite two incomes, they lived on a tight budget for several years in order to repay educational loans and save for a home. They now have some extra money, which they wish to invest. They are both intelligent people and are interested in stocks, but "don't want to have to read *The Wall Street Journal* every day. And don't want to have to watch and listen to those nightly business programs." Also, they have lots of questions typical of beginning investors:

- ✔ How do we know what stocks to buy?
- ✔ When should we sell?
- ✔ Should we use a full-service or a discount broker?
- ✔ What extra services can we expect from a full-service broker for the higher commissions we'll pay?
- ✔ Can we get our money out of the market quickly if we need it right away?
- ✔ What kinds of risks are we taking by investing in stocks?
- ✔ What are the chances we'll lose our hard-earned money?
- ✔ Can we protect ourselves against loss when we invest in stocks?

The fears, insecurities, and questions contained in the second and third stories are typical of beginning investors. For some, this lack of knowledge combined with the seemingly formidable mystique of the stock market leaves them paralyzed at the starting line. They are unable to make even the simplest decisions and thereby miss good investment opportunities. Others take a more cavalier position, jumping, usually wallet first, into the pit with the bulls and the bears, hoping to learn as they go along.

If you have little or no investment experience, this book will demystify the stock market. In clear and easy-to-understand prose, you will obtain the fundamental knowledge that enables you to understand:

1. The various types of stocks and their characteristics.
2. The financial rewards and risks associated with each.
3. Basic stock analysis—those fundamental and techni-

cal factors within a company, within the stock market, and within the overall economy that influence the performance of stocks.

4. Conservative and aggressive strategies to follow in achieving your financial goals.

5. How mutual funds provide an indirect and "managed" way for an individual to invest in stocks.

6. General methods of investing in the international markets.

This book is not written in technical language. I assume that you have chosen this text seeking information that is presented and explained in clear, easily understandable English. The highly technical jargon, shorthand speech, and buzzwords that many people fearfully associate with Wall Street are absent.

Nevertheless, you will have to learn some words and phrases that describe various investment instruments, their characteristics, and the stock market itself. The first time each of these terms is used it will be italicized and defined in the book's margin. When appropriate, I use a real-life example or illustration to expand and clarify the definition. The book contains a glossary of these and many other investment terms.

The text proceeds in five logical and cumulative steps designed to allow you to develop an overall knowledge of stocks, their markets, and their investment possibilities.

Step 1: *Setting your goals.* Having clearly defined goals as well as being aware of your time horizon and the limits of your risk tolerance are essential to successful investing in stocks or any other security. To say that you "want to make money from investing" is an insufficient delineation of your goals. Are you investing for the short term or the long term? For a child's education or your retirement? To generate cash immediately or to build capital? How much money can you afford to invest without adversely affecting your lifestyle? How much of a return would you accept as reasonable for your investment? How much capital are you able and willing to risk? These are questions that you must answer *before* making any investment.

Step 2: *Choosing the right type of stock.* When most people think of stocks, they think of only two types: common and preferred. But there are at least 10 different categories of common and preferred stocks. All represent a direct investment in a company and entitle stockholders to receive dividends. The distinct characteristic of each type of stock can affect its performance and investment return in the market. Among the categories of common and preferred stocks that you will learn about in this book are:

✔ Blue-chip stock.
✔ Income stock.
✔ Growth stock.
✔ Penny stock.
✔ Large-cap stock.
✔ Small-cap stock.
✔ Straight preferred stock.
✔ Cumulative preferred stock.
✔ Callable preferred stock.
✔ Convertible preferred stock.
✔ Adjustable rate preferred stock.

Step 3: *Formulating strategies.* How do you allocate your assets in order to achieve the goals you have set? There is a broad spectrum of relatively simple strategies, from very conservative to very aggressive, that beginning investors can use as models. This book discusses these strategies and shows how an individual stock or combination of stocks can be used to achieve your investment objectives. The models, of course, will be illustrative. You will find other securities that will enable you to accomplish the same goals.

Step 4: *Analyzing stock.* No whiz-bang computer program, accounting experience, or M.B.A. degree is necessary to analyze stock in which you wish to invest. The information you must have to make a sound investment decision can be contained in the security's prospectus, the company's financial statements, annual reports, and other publicly available documents. Both fundamental and technical analyses will be explained and illustrated. You will learn the meaning of such items as earnings per share, price-earnings (P-E) ratio, book value, the advance-decline theory, and the Dow Jones Industrial Average. I will show how this information fits into your investment decision-making process.

Step 5: *Reviewing alternatives*. Instead of purchasing individual stocks and building a portfolio, you may wish to invest in an existing portfolio managed by a professional. If this is the case, a stock mutual fund may be the right vehicle. Perhaps you want to participate in the profitable price movement of a stock without actually owning it. In this case, a stock-equivalent product, such as a warrant or option, may be suitable. At this last step, you will learn how to assess the benefits and risks of the various stock-derivative investment products compared with the actual stock itself. Stock equivalents, also referred to as stock-derivative products, have many of the investment dynamics of stocks but do not involve direct ownership of the stock itself. The investment instruments that will be explained are:

1. Stock mutual funds.
2. Rights.
3. Warrants.
4. Stock options (calls and puts).

International investing using stock is covered in this book. With the increasing globalization of the securities industry and the growing importance of the Pacific Rim, Latin America, Eastern Europe and various emerging markets, many investment opportunities exist abroad. This book describes how to use international and global mutual funds as well as American depositary receipts and American depositary shares—stock-equivalent investment instruments—to accomplish your investment goals using the world markets.

With this book, you will come to understand the many investment instruments that come under the heading "stocks." You will gain the skill necessary to assess the broad range of investment possibilities that stocks offer and understand the rewards and risks associated with each. The final decision to invest will be yours, but at the very least you will be well informed by having read this book.

Chapter

1

Setting Your Goals: Assessing Risks and Rewards

"I just opened an account at a brokerage house. I work hard to earn my money, and I want to start making it work better for me by investing." A friend who has reached a point in his career where he has some discretionary income recently made this statement. When asked exactly how he plans to achieve the goal of making his money "work better" using stocks, he replied confidently, "Always buy low and sell high."

My friend's initial statement is the reason that most people begin investing in stocks. They have discretionary income—money in excess of that required for their living expenses, savings, and the necessary insurance coverage and cash reserves for emergencies—and want this money to earn more than it would in an account at a commercial or savings bank. Indeed, this is a good reason for investing in stock. Historically, stocks have provided a better return than most other types of investment. However, my friend's old chestnut of a response to the question of how he will achieve his goal indicates that he has given little, if any, thought to *investment planning*. Therein lies the potential for failure and disappointment.

When many people find they have "extra" money, the normal human response is to spend it. If they manage to restrain that urge, the next response is to invest the money in a

investment planning defining an investment objective and establishing a systematic approach to achieve it.

get-rich-quick scheme. Both impulses often result in lost opportunities. Before making any investment, whether in real estate, art, antiques, bonds, or stocks, you must first evaluate your current and potential financial means, determine the goal or purpose of making the investment, and then design an investment strategy appropriate to these means to achieve the goals. Clearheaded assessment and planning are particularly important when you are considering investing in any securities that are inherently speculative, like stocks.

The six questions that follow are those that all people contemplating investing in stocks should ask themselves before they make their first purchase. Under each question we explore the issues and topics that must be considered.

HOW MUCH MONEY DO I HAVE TO INVEST?

What you *want* to invest may be quite different from what you *have* to invest. Investment planning starts with reviewing your assets, liabilities, and future cash needs. Through this process, you determine your *net worth*. Thoroughness must be your guiding rule. Your assessment must include the following considerations:

net worth
the difference between the total value of a person's assets and possessions (e.g., home, land, savings, investments) and the person's total indebtedness (e.g., mortgage, car loan, credit cards, student loans).

1. Income: salary, bonuses, and trusts.
2. Savings and other investments: bank accounts, certificates of deposit (CDs), real estate, annuities, mutual funds, stocks, bonds, and so forth.
3. Living expenses: the number of your dependents, food, utilities, housing costs, education costs, and vacations, for example.
4. Insurance coverage: medical, disability, and life insurance, among others.
5. Retirement plan: individual retirement accounts or plans provided by an employer.
6. Estate planning (a properly executed will is essential).
7. Discretionary income: that which is available after essential living expenses have been paid.

A review of your own budget may enable you to answer the "how much" question. If you are unable to assess your own financial position, seek the help of an objective, qualified investment professional or financial adviser. In addition to determining your net worth and capital available for investing, this process should enable you to establish what portion of this money should be liquid and what portion should be invested for the long term.

In the securities industry, much of the financial information enumerated above is requested on a brokerage firm's new account form. The broker uses it to create your *financial profile*, which becomes part of the information he or she considers when making investment recommendations.

HOW MUCH RISK AM I WILLING TO ACCEPT?

This is a complex question involving an understanding of the risk-to-reward relationship that is germane to all investing and an understanding of each person's investment temperament. The relationship between risk and reward is direct: the greater the risk, the greater the potential return from the investment; the lower the risk, the lower the return.

There are two types of returns that you can expect from investing in stocks: cash dividends and capital gains. *Cash dividends* are that part of a company's after-tax earnings that management decides to distribute to its stockholders. These payments are **not** automatic or guaranteed. This is true for both common and preferred stocks, as well as high-quality and low-quality stocks (see Chapter 2). A company's board of directors meets regularly (usually quarterly) to decide whether a dividend will be paid and, if so, the amount and when it will be paid.

Capital gains are the profits made from an increase in the market value of the securities. For the most part, the risk (or fall) of a stock's market value reflects the direct relationship between a company's performance and an investor's desire to own the stock. When investors believe

financial profile an assessment of an investor's assets, liabilities, investment objectives, and willingness to bear risk.

cash dividends part of a company's after-tax earnings that its board of directors decides, usually quarterly, to distribute to the shareholders.

capital gain the profit that results when the proceeds from the sale of a stock are higher than the stock's cost basis.

capital appreciation an increase in the market value of a stock or the overall market.

total return the yield or percentage return on an investment that considers both the income made from dividends and the capital gains made on the stock's appreciation.

diversification investing in different securities, different industries, or a mutual fund portfolio containing various securities in order to diminish the risk associated with investing in too few securities.

timing attempting to buy or sell a security at the optimum moment in its price movement.

that a company is developing well or is in a good position to do so, they buy the stock, hoping that the price will increase over time. An increase in the market value of a security is also called *capital appreciation*. The combination of the dividend income and the capital appreciation made on an investment constitutes your *total return*.

If you are seeking dividend income or capital gains from stock, you must be willing to accept some of the risks associated with this investment. Remember that all stocks are risky investments—and some are riskier than others. The biggest risk you face is the loss of the capital that you have invested because the company's stock becomes worthless. This is known as "capital risk." This risk is not just one risk; it takes several forms. Each is always present in the marketplace to a greater or lesser degree, depending on the type of stock. Through *diversification* and *timing*, you can reduce the potential impact of these risks on your investments. The various forms of capital risk are:

1. *Business risk.* The company in whose stock you invest may not generate the sales and earnings growth that you expected. Also, the management of the company may not be able to bring the company to the next stage of development. As a result, the price of the security may remain low or even fall. At worst, the business may fail, and the stock will be worthless. Business risk plagues both new businesses and old businesses—for example, Singer, International Harvester (now known as Navistar), and Apple Computer.

2. *Stock-specific risk.* Also known as unsystematic risk, this is the risk associated with "putting too many eggs in one basket." If you buy only one stock—IBM or Philip Morris, for example—and the value of the stock drops 30 percent in one day, then you have lost 30 percent of your capital. You can protect yourself against this type of risk by investing in the stocks of a broad range of companies, industries, or geographical areas, or by investing in different types of securities. This is known as diversification. In theory, diversification protects you because when one security's price is falling, another in the portfolio may be rising. The net result is that the two price movements offset each other. For an individual investor trying to accomplish this or his or her own, diversification has its drawbacks. It requires time spent analyzing stocks and actively managing the portfolio. It can also be costly because of the money spent on transaction fees.

3. *Liquidity or marketability risk.* When you are ready to liquidate or close out a securities position, you may discover that it is difficult to accomplish this. There may be too few investors in the market. This is known as a *thin market.* In this situation, you could incur high transaction fees closing out the position, which in turn would produce a lower-than-expected return or a greater-than-expected loss.

4. *Interest rate risk.* This risk affects all fixed-income securities—preferred stocks and *bonds.* The market price of these securities fluctuates inversely to changes in interest rates. When interest rates fall, the prices of outstanding fixed-income securities rise. Conversely, when interest rates rise, the prices of outstanding fixed-income securities fall. The changes result from the forces of supply and demand. Fixed-income investors always seek securities that pay the highest *yield* commensurate with the level of risk they are willing to accept. When interest rates are falling, there will be greater demand for the older, already outstanding securities that pay high dividends or interest. When interest rates are rising, investors want to sell the low-yield securities they own and buy the newer securities that pay the better yield. During periods of interest rate volatility, this risk is most acute. For example, when you purchase a new issue, fixed-rate preferred stock, you run the risk that interest rates may rise shortly after you have bought the issue. The result would be an immediate loss, because the market value of the preferred would decline.

The early 1990s showed that common stock prices can be affected by interest rate changes. During this time interest rates were at an all-time low. Passbook savings accounts were yielding between 2 percent and 3 percent per year and certificates of deposit (CDs) paid only slightly better. Seeking higher yields in exchange for a little more

thin market also called an illiquid market; a market in which there are few buyers or sellers of a security and that is characterized by increased price volatility.

bond a long-term debt security issued by a corporation, a municipality, or the U.S. government in which the issuer promises to pay the holder a fixed rate of interest at regular intervals and to repay the face value of the security at maturity.

yield the percentage or rate of return that an investor makes on capital invested in a security or in a portfolio of securities.

risk, investors transferred their savings and rolled over their CDs into mutual funds. As a result, mutual fund managers had more cash available to invest in securities. This increased demand from the fund managers for shares in which to invest this money as well as to set up new funds drove stock prices higher and higher. If interest rates were to increase, many investors would pull their money out of these mutual funds and invest it in safer instruments, such as CDs. The resulting lower demand for mutual fund shares and the resulting decreased demand for stocks by mutual fund managers could cause common stock prices to decline.

5. *Systematic risk.* Also known as market risk, this is the risk associated with the movement of the overall market. If the entire market declines, as it did on October 19, 1987, when the Dow Jones Industrial Average dropped 508 points, or 22.6 percent of its value, the value of all shares in your portfolio will likely decline. Diversification cannot protect you against this risk. *Hedging* is the protective strategy to use. (This is explained more thoroughly in Chapter 8.)

hedging

protecting against or limiting losses on an existing stock position or portfolio by establishing an opposite position in the same security.

6. *Inflationary or purchasing power risk.* Inflation erodes the purchasing power of money over time. The great attraction of investing in common stock is that this risk is minimized. Historically, stocks have kept pace with inflation better than any other type of securities investment.

7. *Political risk.* This risk is most prominent when investing in the stock of companies located in politically unstable areas, such as Central America and Eastern Europe. Continued instability can severely reduce the productivity of the company whose stock you own. At worst, the country could decide to nationalize all businesses, in which case your investment would be lost.

8. *Taxation risk.* Changes in the rates at which dividend income and capital gains are taxed could change the demand for stocks, making them more or less attractive as investment vehicles.

To a beginning investor, it might seem ironic that for only two potential ways of earning money from stock—dividends and capital gains—there are so many risks. This is why the next step in investment planning—determining your attitude toward your money, in particular your discretionary income—is important. Some individuals do not want to invest in anything where their capital is at risk. Others are all too ready to take unnecessary risks without the opportunity for commensurate rewards. Most people fall somewhere between these two extremes. Once you know your attitude toward your money and understand the risks associated with investing in securities, the next step is setting your investment goal.

My friend's goal of wanting to make his money work for him is far too general. Each investor must have clearly defined objectives before entering the stock market if he or she is to have a reasonable chance of achieving them. The ways that people with virtually the same financial profiles may want their money to work for them are as varied as their individual lifestyles and ambitions. For example, a person whose goal is to generate current income from investing may purchase stocks that pay high dividends, such as utilities and blue chips. Another person's goal may be to build a portfolio of securities that will provide income for retirement. This person might invest in stocks whose market values and dividend payments are expected to increase over the long term. A third person may want to speculate in the market, buying and selling stock whose prices fluctuate broadly over the short term. The investment goal is important because it becomes the measure against which the performance of the selected investments is judged.

The most common investment objectives are income, conservative growth, aggressive growth, and speculation.

Income. Investors with this goal want to make current income from their investments. Typically, they use this money for some or all of their living expenses. Stocks that provide high dividend income, including high-yielding common and preferred stocks, are suitable for this objective. Most investors automatically assume that this objective is synonymous with conservative, safe investments.

junk bond
low-quality (rated BB by Moody's, Ba by Standard & Poor's (S&P), or lower), high-risk long-term debt security. To avoid the negative associations of the word "junk," more and more firms use synonyms such as high-yield bond, noninvestment-grade bond, and below investment-grade bond.

volatility
the relative amount or percentage by which a stock's price rises and falls during a period of time.

wealth building an investment strategy designed to increase one's net worth over time.

This is not necessarily true. Some very risky securities—*junk bonds* (a.k.a. high-yield bonds) or low-quality preferred stock, for example—provide high current income. If you are not interested in these kinds of speculative, income-producing securities, specify preservation of capital as a dual objective. If you want both income and preservation of capital, invest in securities that are relatively secure and stable—that is, those that are free from extreme price *volatility*. Suitable securities are those whose prices are relatively stable but still pay reasonable dividends, such as blue-chip companies.

Conservative Growth. Investors with this goal seek to build an investment portfolio that will make money over the long term by capital appreciation—hence, the use of the word "growth." Having taken a long-term view, these people do not want too much risk. They should understand that the security may not pay high dividends currently and its price will fluctuate over time. The overall expectation, however, is that the market value of the stock and its dividend payments will increase. This objective is also known as *wealth building*.

Aggressive Growth. Securities that are expected to produce large short-term and long-term capital gains are suitable for investors with this objective. Current income from dividends is of little or no interest, and preservation of capital is a lower priority. Securities suitable for this objective are highly speculative. The high risk could yield high profits—or result in substantial losses.

Speculation. This is the objective of a person who buys and sells stocks often solely to profit from short-term price fluctuations. Most beginning investors are encouraged to "invest" in the market rather than speculate. The word "investing" suggests a longer-term view than does "speculation," which implies a total focus on short-term profits. Speculators do not expect to hold the securities for long periods.

Speculators are important to the functions of the market for all investors because their presence increases both the liquidity and the efficiency of the market. Another view is that their presence brings undue volatility to the market, pushing stock prices up quickly in response to good news or driving prices down on bad news. Clearly speculation is the riskiest objective you can have.

Understanding your tolerance for risk and setting investment goals appropriate to that tolerance is not a simple task, and it is not static. As your financial means change, you will want to adjust your investment goals.

ARE STOCKS APPROPRIATE INVESTMENT VEHICLES FOR ME?

In order to answer this question, you must have a basic understanding of the characteristics of stocks, bonds, and other investment instruments. This knowledge, provided in Chapter 2, must go beyond simply being able to compare the characteristics of various instruments. You must also know the alternative products (mutual funds, options, and others) through which you can invest in stocks and bonds. And, to restate two points already made, you need a clear understanding of your investment goals and risk tolerance, in light of your age, the amount of money you have in savings, and other characteristics.

It is safe to say that either alone or as part of a portfolio of other securities, stocks can be an appropriate investment vehicle for accomplishing a broad range of investment objectives. However, investing in stocks is not suitable for all people, especially those whose primary objective is preservation of capital. Price fluctuation is an inherent characteristic of these securities. The stocks of even the most stalwart and successful companies (IBM, for example) can be subject to wide price fluctuations—a winner one day, a loser the next. If you do not want your money at risk, you will most likely find the stock market's volatility gut-wrenching and will not be able to sleep at all, day or night.

At the other end of the risk spectrum are people who speculate in the stock market. They buy and sell constantly, seeing each rise and fall in a stock's price as an opportunity to make money. For these individuals, the market's volatility is as exhilarating as a ride on a giant roller coaster.

Most investors fall somewhere between these two extremes of the risk spectrum. They are willing to accept a moderate amount of risk in order to get a better-than-average, long-term return on their investment. For these people, investing in stocks is usually part of a mix of other investments—for example, money market or cash-equivalent securities, bonds, real estate, and annuities. Too often this combination of investments is totally arbitrary. Most investors give little thought to how a well-planned mix of investments can enable them to minimize certain risks and optimize their chances of obtaining their investment goals. The planned and systematic division of money among various types or classes of investments with an eye toward achieving the optimal effective mix given a person's financial objectives is known as *asset allocation*.

 asset allocation the systematic placement of investment dollars into various classes of investments, such as stocks, bonds, and cash equivalents.

Successful asset allocation is not a simple process. Its implementation requires evaluating and analyzing a good deal of information. The explanation presented here is designed to give you an overview and fundamental understanding of the process. At all times, keep in mind that there is neither a perfect asset allocation model for each economic condition nor a common approach to determining the optimal asset mix. The goal here is to present a basic approach that will enable you to understand the importance of asset allocation in your investment decisions.

Figure 1.1 outlines the four basic steps involved in asset allocation, proceeding from the general to the particular. Your first step is to determine the classes of assets in which to invest. By tradition, the three classes of assets usually are: (1) *cash equivalents*—safe, short-term investments such as money market funds and treasury bills; (2) stocks or equity securities; and (3) bonds or fixed-income securities. Other classes, such as international stocks and commodities (listed in the footnotes of Figure 1.3) enable the investor to refine his or her allocation.

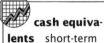 **cash equivalents** short-term investments that are virtually like cash because of their high liquidity and safety.

The second step is to determine the amount of money to invest in each class. This decision involves more than assigning various percentages to each class in re-

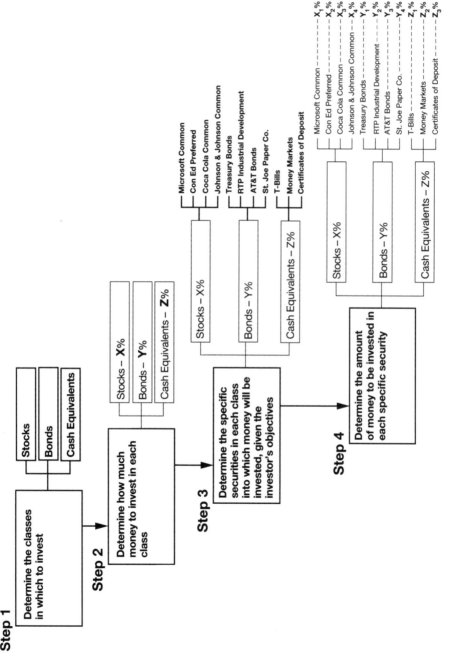

FIGURE 1.1 The four steps of asset allocation.

11

sponse to the bullish (buy stock) or bearish (sell stock) sentiments of market strategists. You must research such information as the historical performance of the various classes during certain economic conditions and the risk-to-reward relationship that influences the returns from investments. Always keep in mind the investment objective that the asset mix is designed to achieve.

Clearly, there are economic conditions under which stocks will potentially provide greater returns than can be obtained from other investments. During periods when low interest rates result in low returns from fixed-income securities, people tend to invest more of their money in stocks, hoping that the total returns—from both dividends and capital gains—will exceed the returns from bonds. During periods of high inflation, usually characterized by high interest rates, stocks are less attractive investments; fixed-income securities are preferred because their fixed yields are higher.

There is no perfect asset mix for all investors. A rule of thumb used by many investment advisers recommends that the percentage of your total investment assets allocated to stocks (or stock mutual funds) should be equal to 100 percent *minus* your age. If you are 35 years old, for example, 65 percent of your investment assets should be in stocks or stock mutual funds. Using this asset allocation model, your investment portfolio will become more conservative as you get older because the percentage invested in stocks will decline. How often you adjust the percentages of money invested in the various asset classes is a decision that you must make. Again, there is no perfect frequency and there are no optimum percentages. Your decision will be based on your expectations for the future performance of the various assets and your risk tolerance as you grow older.

The scenario described above is one example of flexible asset allocation—where the investor changes the mix of assets in response to changes in the performance of a particular class of assets, changes in interest rates, or changes in one's personal situation. There is also the traditional, static, or robot asset allocation mix; it consists of 55 percent stocks, 35 percent bonds, and 10 percent cash equivalents. (See Figure 1.2 and footnote 6 in Figure 1.3.) The advantage of the static model is that your role in the

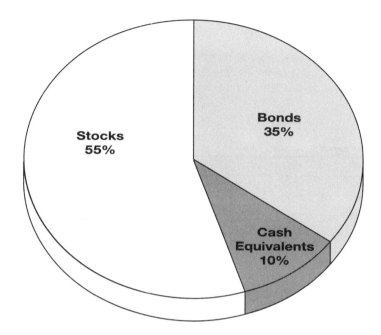

FIGURE 1.2 Traditional, static asset allocation mix.

initial decision-making process is essentially passive. However, you still have to choose the specific stocks, bonds, or mutual funds in each of the asset classes.

During the fourth quarter of 1996 when interest rates were low, *The Wall Street Journal* published the asset mixes recommended by the investment strategists at 14 brokerage firms. As Figure 1.3 shows, the percentage of assets recommended for stock investments ranged from 40 percent to 70 percent. (The average was approximately 58 percent.)

At Step 3 in the asset allocation model (Figure 1.1), you identify the securities that belong in each class. When categorizing equities for this purpose, consider which stocks provide steady dividend income, which ones offer long-term capital appreciation, and which ones offset the risks associated with other types of securities in the mix.

In Step 4, you determine the amount of money to allocate to each specific issuer's stocks and bonds.

The information contained in Figure 1.3 stops at the second step. The variations in three-month, one-year, and

Who Has the Best Blend?

Performance of asset-allocation blends recommended by 14 major brokerage houses in periods ended Dec. 31, 1996. Figures do not include transaction costs. Houses are ranked by 12-month performance. Also shown is the mix each house now recommends.

BROKERAGE HOUSES	PERFORMANCE			RECOMMENDED BLEND		
	THREE-MONTH	ONE YEAR	FIVE YEAR	STOCKS	BONDS	CASH
Lehman Brothers	7.1%	17.8%	76.1%	65%	35%	0%
Goldman Sachs	6.6	17.4	80.9	60	25	10[1]
PaineWebber	6.4	15.8	75.5	54	35	11
First Boston	6.4	15.7	N.A.	60	30	10
Raymond James	6.5	15.6	64.2	60	15	15[2]
Prudential	6.2	15.3	74.3	70	25	5
Dean Witter	6.3	15.0	76.1	65	20	15
Bear Stearns	6.2	15.0	N.A.	55	35	10
Edward Jones	5.8	15.0	N.A.	65	25	10[3]
Smith Barney	5.8	14.3	71.1	50	40	10
Salomon Brothers	5.9	13.9	66.0	45	35	20
A.G. Edwards	5.7	13.8	67.3	60	30	10
Everen	5.1	13.1	67.5	62	33	5[4]
Merrill Lynch	4.7	11.5	67.8	40	50	10[5]
AVERAGE	6.1	14.9	71.5	58	31	10

BY COMPARISON:

Robot blend[6]	6.2	15.0	73.2	
Stocks	8.1	23.6	104.8	
Bonds	4.7	4.9	44.4	
Cash	1.3	5.4	25.1	

[1] Recommends 5% in commodities
[2] 45% in U.S. stocks, 15% international, 10% in real estate
[3] 55% in U.S. stocks, 10% international
[4] 47% in U.S. stocks, 15% international
[5] 26% in U.S. stocks, 14% international
[6] Always 55% stocks, 35% bonds, 10% cash

NA = Not applicable (not in study for full period)
Sources: Company documents, Wilshire Associates Carpenter Analytical Services

FIGURE 1.3 Asset allocation recommendations from 14 brokerage firms during the fourth quarter of 1996. Reprinted by permission of *The Wall Street Journal*, © 1996 Dow Jones & Company, Inc. All rights reserved worldwide.

five-year performance documented in the chart show how choosing the right investments influences the return from each asset mix. At this point, you might wonder which allocation has provided the better performance over time: the traditional, static asset mix (now called the "robot blend" by *The Wall Street Journal*) or the recommendations of the strategists. According to *The Wall Street Journal*, several individual strategist's recommendations have outperformed the traditional mix, but the average five-year return among all of the analysts is surprisingly close to that of the robot blend.

Few individual investors successfully accomplish asset allocation on their own. It is a complex process requiring diligent, careful analysis of financial information about the overall economy and the securities of specific companies. Individuals who build their own portfolios sometimes use the services of a professional investment adviser or financial planner to help them establish the appropriate asset mix and select individual securities. Small investors would be wise to follow the recommendations of their mutual fund or pension fund managers.

In light of the information presented during this discussion of asset allocation and its importance in helping investors achieve their investment goals, perhaps the question posed at the beginning of this section should be revised from "Are stocks appropriate investment vehicles for me?" to "How much money should I invest in stocks?"

HOW DO I SELECT
THE APPROPRIATE STOCK?

Many investors interpret this question to mean: "How can I evaluate a company's health and intrinsic value—its operating strength, sales, earnings, profitability, and growth potential—to determine if it is worthy of my investment?" The answer to this question is simple: Once you have identified the company in which you may want to invest, research and analyze information about that company and its financial performance.

Much of the information used to judge a company's health and value can be found in three places: the *prospec-*

prospectus
a summary of the registration statement that all companies must file with the Securities and Exchange Commission before issuing securities; it contains audited financial information, the company's business history, its officers, and its future business plans.

tus for the security, and the company's unaudited quarterly reports and audited annual reports that publicly held companies must file with the Securities and Exchange Commission (SEC). At the very least, read the first and third items carefully. Under the SEC's rules, a prospectus must fully and fairly disclose information about a company's financial history and its management, thus providing investors with enough information to judge the merits of investing in a security. If the stock has been issued and outstanding for a while, it is very difficult to obtain a prospectus; the annual report, an audited status report on the current condition of the company, is the next best choice. An annual report can often be obtained by writing to the company's investor relations department, usually located at its corporate headquarters. (The various ways in which this information can be analyzed are covered in Chapter 5.)

This kind of research and analysis is more easily discussed than performed; it often requires more time than most beginning investors want or can afford to spend. Standard & Poor's and Value Line have subscription services, updated quarterly, that provide a detailed summary of each publicly held company's performance history, current financial condition, and future prospects. These services also evaluate the risk and timeliness of investing in each company's stock they cover. (See Figures 5.1 and 5.2.) Many public libraries subscribe to the Standard & Poor's and Value Line publications as well as other investment newsletters. Both companies also offer their stock reports in other formats as well as through various on-line computer services and the Internet.

Specifically, Standard & Poor's Stock Reports are available (1) in a CD-ROM format that is updated every two weeks, (2) through CompuServe and in a format that can be downloaded and printed using Adobe software, (3) through Telescan, (4) through S&P-On-Demand (800-546-0300), and (5) through an Internet site (http://www.stockinfo.standardpoor.com) through which you can access and print the reports. Fees vary depending upon whether you subscribe to S&P services or simply want to print a single stock report page.

In addition to its traditional printed subscription service, Value Line offers its stock analysis sheets (1) on computer disks published monthly (weekly updates are available to subscribers via modem every Friday at 12:00 noon Eastern Standard Time), and (2) through Compu-Serve in a format that can be downloaded and printed. You can get individual company analysis sheets through CompuServe. The costs for Value Line's analysis varies depending on whether you subscribe to other services or just want to print a single page.

Investment advice and analysis are also provided through periodic newsletters from corporations (such as Kiplinger) and from prominent investment advisers (such as Elaine Garzarelli, Ned Davis, and Martin Zweig). The cost of the advice is usually the price of the subscription. However, newsletters that provide more up-to-the-minute information cost more. Keep in mind that these newsletters, particularly those published by individual advisers, rise and fall in popularity based on the current performance of the stocks they recommend. The subscription fee for a particular newsletter also varies depending on popularity and success.

A full-service brokerage house typically has a research department that follows selected individual stocks or market sectors (e.g., technology, communications, health care, entertainment, etc.). Not only do the brokerage firm's analysts compile and evaluate information about an individual stock from the reports that the company must file with the SEC, they also talk directly to the company's senior management via periodic conference calls. The information they glean is used to estimate the company's future growth and earnings potential, and to make buy, hold, or sell recommendations to the firm's clients. If you have an account at one of these firms, your registered representative uses this research, in combination with your stated investment objectives, to recommend securities to you as a client. Your broker will usually send the firm's research reports to you on request at no cost. This research is not free, however; its costs are factored into the commissions that investors pay when buying and selling securities.

WHEN IS THE BEST TIME TO BUY OR SELL STOCKS?

A friend pulled most of her money out of the stock market in early 1996 and placed the cash in a money market account. She believed that the market was at an all-time high and that there would be a sharp decline in the near future. Over a year later, she is still waiting on the sidelines for that big correction (i.e., drop) so that she can go back into the market and pick up some "bargains"—stocks that are undervalued.

Timing concerns all investors. Anyone interested in buying stocks wants to know how to identify an upcoming price rise and buy shares just before it occurs. Once they have bought the stocks and have watched the price rise, investors then want to know how they can foresee a price decline and sell off the shares before it occurs. Timing is usually the domain of *technical analysis*, which seeks to identify the conditions under which the price movement of a stock or the market is likely to change direction. These conditions, called "buy signals" and "sell signals," are more suggestive than prescriptive. Most investors try to confirm their probability by reviewing other factors.

As my friend's strategy reveals, however, the timing of her purchases (or sales) and the selection of stocks (the "bargains") are interrelated. Determining the true worth of a company or of the market is the domain of *fundamental analysis*. It enables investors to estimate when the real value of a company will be reflected in the market price of its stock. At times, a company's outstanding shares will be undervalued or overvalued compared to what an analyst has determined is the business's fundamental worth. An investor would buy an undervalued stock or sell short an overvalued stock, hoping to profit by liquidating the position when the price of the stock moves back in line with the company's real value. Although fundamental analysis and technical analysis are separate disciplines, they are often used together to decide not only which security to buy based on fundamental values but also the best time to buy based on technical factors.

technical analysis using charts of a stock's past price and volume movements to predict its future short-term price movements.

fundamental analysis evaluating a company's financial statements, sales, earnings, and management as a means of predicting the future long-term price movement of its stock.

Two types of timing affect the decision to buy or sell: timing related to the overall market and timing related to individual stocks. My bargain-hunting friend is primarily concerned with market timing. She believes that during a sharp market decline, the prices of most stocks will fall in concert, and during a market rise, the prices of most stocks will appreciate. In short, the overall trend of the market is reflected in the price movements of most stocks. Further, she believes that by waiting to purchase selected securities after the market has fallen to a particular low, she will be able to acquire them at prices that are below their real worth. In technical jargon, this condition is known as an *oversold market*: The market price of the security is well below the real worth of the company. When the market value of the security has been driven up well above the fundamental value of the company, the condition is known as an *overbought market*.

Using the overall market movement as the only indicator to time the purchase or sale of stocks is not a fail-safe strategy. Certainly it is true that stock prices tend to follow the market's trend (known as the "herd instinct"), but using an index or average as the only buy or sell indicator ignores the fact that each individual stock moves on its own as well; its price rises and falls in response to information about that company. Each stock presents its own timing opportunities within the market's overall trends. These arise primarily from investors' responses to reports of a company's current and future earnings, its dividends rate, and positive or negative news about the company. Additionally, business cycle developments and economic cycle developments—recession, inflation, deflation—can affect the fundamental value of a company and the market price of its stock.

Timing must take into account whether an investor's goals are long-term or short-term. In the first case, timing is a less critical issue. A long-term investor's focus is usually on fundamental factors: the increased value of an investment over time. This individual must understand that reversals are a normal part of the market's cyclical movement and must be prepared to wait them out. When you make long-term investments, try to avoid emotional, short-term responses to the periodic reversals of the mar-

oversold market a technical term used to describe a stock (or market) whose price has fallen quickly and sharply, far below its "real" value; usually an indication of an impending price rise.

overbought market a technical term used to describe a stock (or market) whose price has risen quickly and unexpectedly; usually an indication of a future price decline.

ket; otherwise you will lose through higher transaction costs, lost opportunities, and lost profits.

For short-term investors—traders or speculators—timing is everything. The old adage, "He who hesitates is lost," is most applicable. In a volatile market, a delay can quickly turn a gain into a loss—or you can suddenly find yourself on the wrong side of the market. Short-term trading is inappropriate for most beginning investors because commissions costs are high and market expertise is critical. Still, most beginning investors confuse speculating with investing. They think that to invest in stocks they must speculate (i.e., trade stocks frequently). A possible reason for this confusion exists in an observation made by Benjamin Franklin: "Inside every investor is a speculator struggling to get out."

WHEN AND HOW SHOULD I REEVALUATE MY HOLDINGS AND INVESTMENT STRATEGIES?

The answer to this question depends on whether you are a speculator or a long-term investor. Speculative investing must be monitored closely—weekly, daily, or even hourly. It also requires discipline. The basic philosophy is to cut losses and let profits run. Many speculators and traders set limits—15 percent, 20 percent, or 25 percent—on the amount that the price of a stock can move against them before they liquidate the position. Regardless of any justification that they may have for wanting to hold an unprofitable position, disciplined traders get out of the market at the predetermined loss they are willing to incur on the investment. Speculators do not try to recover their losses by waiting for the price of the stock to rebound; they simply cut their losses.

While speculators try to cut their losses quickly, they try not to take their profits too quickly. The old adage about "letting profits run" is also one of their principles. The combination of the two philosophies results in the large gains made on the fewer winning positions exceeding the small losses on the larger number of unprofitable positions. In fact, historical analysis of speculators' trades has revealed a surprising fact: The number of losing trades often outnumbers the profitable trades. To reiterate a point made earlier, successful speculation requires discipline and is usually not suitable for beginning investors.

Long-term investors must be disciplined in reviewing their financial holdings periodically—at least annually. Too often they relegate this responsibility to their broker, who is generally unaware of significant changes in a client's personal or financial circumstances. Many events can prompt a reevaluation of a person's situation—births, deaths, marriage, divorce, illness, job promotion, loss of job, inheritance, and others. Age is an important consideration, especially if a person believes that investments in equities always outperform other investments over time. The conventional wisdom is that younger investors should place more money in growth-oriented common stocks. (Remember the rule-of-thumb asset allocation mix recommended by many financial advisers: stocks should make up a percentage of your total investment assets equal to 100 percent *minus* your age.) Investors approaching retirement should shift more investment dollars into stable, income-producing securities. But there are no absolute percentages governing the amount that should be invested in each type of security at different ages.

A reevaluation takes you back to Step 1 of the decision process, asking the question, "What are my investment objectives in light of these changes?" Remember that you are not trying to outsmart the market. You are simply refining or redirecting your long-term needs in light of new information. You may discover that your objectives have changed. For example, if there has been a birth in the family, it may be time to start considering long-term investing for the child's education. You may find that the objectives are the same but some securities in the portfolio have changed. If you originally established a portfolio of only blue-chip stocks, you may discover that some of the companies' stocks have become speculative due to changes in the economy, increased competition, or changes in the company's future earnings potential. In this case, it may be time to liquidate certain positions and acquire others. Or you may find that the investment climate has changed. Interest rates may be so low that buying preferred stocks offers no real gain, especially when compared to the rate of inflation. Common stocks, which are less sensitive to fluctuations in interest rates, may provide a better total return. An investment review, either regularly or when and if personal or family circumstances change, is essential to achieving your investment goals.

Chapter

Common Stock and Preferred Stock

When you buy a corporation's stock—either common or preferred—you become part owner of that company. This ownership is also referred to as having equity in a company; hence, stocks are called *equity securities*. As an "owner" of the company, you are entitled to share in the company's earnings through dividend payments and to benefit from the company's growth through the increase in the market value of the stock you own.

The percentage or proportion of this ownership depends on how many of the company's shares you own. If, for example, the company has 100,000 shares outstanding and you own 1000 of them, then you are a 1 percent (1000 ÷ 100,000) shareholder of that company. If another investor owns 5000 of the same company's outstanding shares, that person owns 5 percent (5000 ÷ 100,000) of the company.

Bonds, in contrast, do not represent ownership in a company. When you buy a corporation's bond, you become a creditor of the company, in effect, loaning money to the company by purchasing the bond. The company, in turn, promises to pay you interest on this loan at regular intervals—usually semiannually. The company also agrees to repay the principal or face value of the bond on a designated date in the future when the bond matures. On this date, all interest payments stop. Bonds, therefore, have a

> **equity securities** securities representing ownership in a business and the right to receive dividends.

fixed term. Stocks, on the other hand, have an indefinite life, and dividend payments can continue for as long as you own the company's shares.

A company issues either stocks or bonds when it wishes to raise capital from public investors. This new money is usually earmarked for specific purposes, such as the research and development of new products, building new plants, acquiring new equipment, increasing production, or improving and developing new product distribution and sales systems. The decision to issue either stocks or bonds depends on the financial condition of the company and the general economy at the time. Some factors typically considered are the cost of borrowing money (interest rates), the amount of debt that the company is already carrying, and, especially for stock, the amount of control that the owner or board of directors of the company is willing to relinquish in exchange for the capital it receives from investors. A company that chooses to issue an equity security issues common stock first because this security is part of each company's capitalization.

common stock an equity security that usually gives the holder the right to receive dividends and vote on company issues.

capitaliza-tion that part of a company's funds raised by issuing stocks and bonds.

authorized shares the maximum number of common and preferred shares that a company is authorized to issue by its corporate charter.

COMMON STOCK

Common stock is the most widely traded of all corporate securities. It offers investors great liquidity. On the New York Stock Exchange (NYSE), more than 500 million shares are traded on average each day. On NASDAQ, the average daily trading volume exceeds 600 million. This trading volume is made possible by two factors: the public's demand for common stock and, one of the primary characteristics of common stock, the ease with which ownership can be transferred from one investor to another.

In the United States, each publicly traded incorporated business is required to declare at least one class of common shares as part of its initial *capitalization*. The number of common shares is usually specified in the incorporation documents that the company files with a division of the Secretary of State's office. Once the business is incorporated, these shares are referred to as *authorized shares*. At this point, these shares have not been issued and do not trade. Only after they have been registered with the Securities and Exchange Commission and then distributed or sold to the public are these shares considered to be *issued and outstanding* and can then trade in the stock market.

When a company "goes public"—that is, issues common shares to public investors—it does not issue all of its authorized stock. The reason is that the company wishes to retain the ability to split its stock, issue options to its management and employees, and issue additional shares to the public at a later date if and when it needs to raise more money.

> **issued and outstanding** authorized shares that have been distributed to investors and that may trade in the market.

Rights of Common Stockholders

Common shareholders are granted certain rights or privileges by the issuing corporation. Many of these benefits, along with ease of transferability, make common stock an attractive investment.

Right to Receive Dividends. All common shareholders have the right to receive dividends, if dividends are declared. These dividends are usually paid quarterly in cash, although a company may choose to pay a stock dividend, giving investors additional shares in the company in lieu of cash. A company does not pay dividends automatically. All dividends must be declared by the company's board of directors. A company is not required to pay dividends regularly in the same way that it is legally required to pay interest on bonds when the payment is due. If the board decides not to declare a dividend, the common shareholders receive nothing during that quarter. Common stockholders cannot demand dividend payments even when the company is profitable.

Cash dividends are declared from the earnings that remain after the company has paid the required interest on any outstanding bonds, paid its taxes, and paid dividends on its preferred shares (if any of these securities are outstanding). The amount or percentage of these earnings that is paid to common shareholders depends on the company's cash reserves, its needs, its reputation, and the philosophy of the board of directors regarding dividend

blue-chip stock the shares of stable, profitable, and well-known public companies that have a long history of consistent growth and dividend payments.

income stock the shares of companies that make regular and substantial dividend payments to investors.

growth stock stocks of new, expanding companies whose market values are expected to appreciate rapidly.

payments. Older, more mature companies—those whose shares are called *blue-chip* or *income stocks* such as Exxon, AT&T, General Electric, and Dow Chemical—and utilities tend to make regular and substantial dividend payments, partly because these companies have established a reputation for such payments. The main reason, however, is that since these are mature, well-established companies, the price of their stock tends to remain relatively stable, offering potential investors little opportunity for capital appreciation. These companies make their common stock attractive by providing investors with substantial current income through dividend payments.

Companies in new, expanding industries—those whose shares are called *growth stock*, such as technology and biotechnology companies—usually pay low dividends, if they pay any at all. Microsoft, for example, pays investors no dividends, although it is a highly profitable company. These companies typically retain the earnings that would be paid to common stockholders as dividends and reinvest them in the company, usually in research and new product development. As the company grows and becomes more profitable, the market price of its stock generally increases, benefiting stockholders. Overall, growth stocks tend to increase in price faster than income stocks—sometimes two or three times as fast. Investors interested in capital appreciation find growth stocks attractive.

Some significant risks are associated with investing in growth stocks. Although their prices tend to rise faster than those of income stocks, they also tend to decrease faster, thereby increasing investors' chances of losing money. And because growth stocks pay little or no dividends, investors must be aware of the amount of time that their capital will have to remain invested in the company before it achieves the desired price appreciation. During this time, investors receive little, if any, current income from the investment.

A company's board of directors may choose to pay a stock dividend instead of a cash dividend. This decision allows the company to save the cash or earnings that would have been used to pay the dividends.

A stock dividend may not satisfy the needs of persons seeking current income from their investment in common stock, but there are certain benefits to investors. First, stock dividends are not taxed at the time they are distributed. You pay taxes only after the stock is sold, which may be years after the date you received it. In contrast, you must pay tax on cash dividends in the year the company pays them. Second, as a result of a stock dividend, you own more of the company's shares at a lower *cost basis* per share.

To demonstrate this point, we use an illustration of a "Corporate Dividend News" table (Figure 2.1) from *The Wall Street Journal*. In the section of Figure 2.1 headed "Stock," Arrow Financial has declared a 10 percent stock dividend payable to all common shareholders. Let's consider an investor who already owns 100 shares that were purchased at $22 per share. (Commission costs are not included in these examples.) The total value of the investment is $2200. After the stock dividend is paid, the investor will own 110 shares of Arrow Financial (10 percent more than before). Her cost basis for tax purposes will now be $20 per share. This new cost basis is computed by taking the total value of the original investment ($2200) and dividing it by the total number of shares the stockholder will own after the stock dividend. The stock will now provide a gain if the investor sells it at any price higher than $20 per share, the new cost basis.

Stock dividends have one particularly confusing feature that must be clarified. While a stock dividend results in an investor's owning more shares of a company's outstanding stock, the percentage of the total outstanding shares that the individual owns remains exactly the same. Each stockholder receives the same dividend percentage; however, the actual number of shares received depends on the amount of stock the individual owned when the dividend was paid. Continuing with the example, if another investor owns 1000 shares of Arrow Financial, he will receive 100 additional shares through the stock dividend. Each investor simply owns the same proportion as before, but of a larger number of outstanding shares.

Many investors are confused about when they must own the stock in order to be eligible to receive a cash or stock dividend. Four key dates must be understood in order to clarify this confusion; in chronological order, they

cost basis
the price, for tax purposes, paid for a security, including commissions and markups.

CORPORATE DIVIDEND NEWS

Dividends Reported September 27

REGULAR

Company	Period Amt.	Payable date	Record date
Abington Svgs Bk	Q .10	10 – 24 – 96	10 – 10
Adobe Systems	Q .05	10 – 16 – 96	10 – 2
Ameron Intl Corp	Q .32	11 – 19 – 96	10 – 24
ApplchnPwr 7.40%pf	Q 1.85	11 – 1 – 96	10 – 11
Binks Mfg	Q .10	11 – 1 – 96	10 – 18
Central Hudson G&E	Q .53	11 – 1 – 96	10 – 10
Community Svgs FL	Q .20	11 – 1 – 96	10 – 15
Delmarva Pwr & Lt	Q .38½	10 – 31 – 96	10 – 11
Digital Eq dep pfA	Q .555	10 – 15 – 96	10 – 1
FoxMeyer Hlth $5pf	Q 1.25	10 – 15 – 96	10 – 8
Graco Inc	Q .12	11 – 6 – 96	10 – 4
Homestake Mining	Q .05	11 – 22 – 96	11 – 1
Kaufman&BroadHome	Q .07½	11 – 27 – 96	11 – 13
New York Bncp	Q .20	10 – 24 – 96	10 – 10
Pacific Telesis Gp	Q .31½	11 – 1 – 96	10 – 9
Pier 1 Imports	Q .04	11 – 19 – 96	11 – 5
Ralston-Ral Purina	Q .30	12 – 6 – 96	11 – 18
Roosevelt Finl pfA	Q .81¼	11 – 15 – 96	11 – 5
Rouge Steel Co	Q .03	10 – 25 – 96	10 – 11
SBC Communications	Q .43	11 – 1 – 96	10 – 10

IRREGULAR

Company	Period Amt.	Payable date	Record date
Aetna Inc 6.25% CIC Votpf	Q 1.1894½	11 – 15 – 96	10 – 25
Aetna Inc.	Q .20	11 – 15 – 96	10 – 25
Scotland Bancorp Inc	Q .07½	10 – 25 – 96	10 – 14

FUNDS - REITS - INVESTMENT COS - LPS

Company	Period Amt.	Payable date	Record date
Burnham Fund clA	Q h.13	10 – 8 – 96	9 – 30
CommonSnsGrw&Inco II B	Q .0435	10 – 15 – 96	9 – 30
CommonSensGwthInco	Q .06¾	10 – 15 – 96	9 – 30
CommonSense MunlBd	M h.05½	10 – 31 – 96	10 – 31
Evrgreen Am Ret Y	Q h.12	9 – 30 – 96	9 – 27
Evrgreen Balance A	Q h.145	9 – 30 – 96	9 – 27
Evrgreen Balance B	Q h.12	9 – 30 – 96	9 – 27
Evrgreen Balance Y	Q h.154	9 – 30 – 96	9 – 27
Evrgreen Found A	Q h.133	9 – 30 – 96	9 – 27
Evrgreen Found B	Q h.105	9 – 30 – 96	9 – 27
Evrgreen Found Y	Q h.142	9 – 30 – 96	9 – 27
Evrgreen Found C	Q h.105	9 – 30 – 96	9 – 27
Evrgreen Gth&Inc A	Q h.031	9 – 30 – 96	9 – 27
Evrgreen Gth&Inc Y	Q h.043	9 – 30 – 96	9 – 27
Evrgreen Tot Ret B	Q h.258	9 – 30 – 96	9 – 27
Evrgreen Tot Ret Y	Q h.27	9 – 30 – 96	9 – 27
Evrgreen Value A	Q h.085	9 – 30 – 96	9 – 27
Evrgreen Value B	Q h.046	9 – 30 – 96	9 – 27
Evrgreen Value Y	Q h.099	9 – 30 – 96	9 – 27
Gabelli Eqty Inco	Q h.07	9 – 30 – 96	9 – 27
Hancock Pat Select	M .1031	10 – 28 – 96	10 – 10
LL&E Royalty Tr	M .0519	10 – 15 – 96	10 – 7
Monmouth REIT	Q .12½	12 – 16 – 96	11 – 15
Utd Mobile Homes	Q .15	12 – 16 – 96	11 – 15
VK AC Corp Bd B	M h.036	10 – 15 – 96	9 – 30
VK AC Corp Bd A	M h.04	10 – 15 – 96	9 – 30
VK AC GlblGovtSecC	M h.039	10 – 15 – 96	9 – 30
VK AC GlblGovtSecA	M h.044	10 – 15 – 96	9 – 30
VK AC GlblGovtSecB	M h.039	10 – 15 – 96	9 – 30
VK AC GvtSecs A	M h.058	10 – 15 – 96	9 – 30
VK AC GvtSecs B	M h.052	10 – 15 – 96	9 – 30
VK AC GvtSecs C	M h.052	10 – 15 – 96	9 – 30
VK AC HiIncoBd A	M h.049	10 – 15 – 96	9 – 30
VK AC HiIncoBd B	M h.04½	10 – 15 – 96	9 – 30
VK AC HiYld Muni A	M .06¼	10 – 31 – 96	10 – 31

Company	Period Amt.	Payable date	Record date
VK AC HiYld Muni B	M .054¼	10 – 31 – 96	10 – 31
VK AC HiYld Muni C	M .054¼	10 – 31 – 96	10 – 31
VK AC LMGovt A	M .05½	10 – 31 – 96	10 – 31
VK AC LMGovtB	M .047	10 – 31 – 96	10 – 31
VK AC TexMunlSec A	M h.04½	10 – 31 – 96	10 – 31
VK AC USGovtIncA	M h.04⅝	10 – 31 – 96	10 – 31
VK AC USGovtIncB	M h.04⅛	10 – 31 – 96	10 – 31
VK AC USGovtIncC	M h.04⅛	10 – 31 – 96	10 – 31

STOCK

Company	Period Amt.	Payable date	Record date
Arrow Financial	10%	11 – 1 – 96	10 – 11
FoxMeyer Hlth pfA	s	10 – 15 – 96	10 – 8

s-Dist of.02625 of a pfd A shr for each pfd A shr held.

| Imperial Bancorp | s | 10 – 18 – 96 | 10 – 11 |

s-3-for-2 stock split.

INCREASED

Company	Period	New Amount	Old Amount	Payable date	Record date
First Mutual Bncp	Q	.08	.07	10 – 18 – 96	10 – 10
Golden Enterprises	Q	.12	.11¾	10 – 30 – 96	10 – 7

FOREIGN

Company	Period	Amt.	Payable date	Record date
Banco de Galicia	–	19%	10 – 8 – 96	10 – 4
Hghvld Steel ADR	–	r.8576%	10 – 18 – 96	8 – 23

r-Revised amount.

INITIAL

Company	Period Amt.	Payable date	Record date
Biomet Inc	A .10	11 – 22 – 96	10 – 25
EXEL Limited new	Q .25	10 – 25 – 96	10 – 11
Gabelli ABC Fund	n.47	9 – 30 – 96	9 – 27

n-Includes $.15 from inco and $.32 from cap gains.

| Monmouth Captl Corp | A .05 | 12 – 16 – 96 | 11 – 15 |

A-Annual; b-Payable in Canadian funds; h-From income; k-From capital gains; M-Monthly; Q-Quarterly; S-Semi-annual.

* * *

Stocks Ex-Dividend October 1

Company	Amount	Company	Amount
AT&T Corp	s	CorpusChristi Bcsh	.07½
s-.324084 of a shr of Lucent Tech for each shr held.		Falcon Products	.025
		Fisher Scientific	.02
Amer Govt Inco	.03	Gnrl Chemical Grp	.05
Amer Govt IncoPort	.03½	Genl Gwth Props	.43
Amer Muni IncoPort	.062¾	Highlander Inco Fd	.094
Amer Muni Term I	.04¾	Knight-Ridder new	.20
Amer Muni Term III		Mapco Inc	s
Amer Muni Term Tr	.0542	s-2-for-1 stock split.	
Amer Muni Term II	.0517	Meridian Indust Tr	.29
Amer Opport Inco	.037	Miller Industries	s
Amer Select Port	.08½	s-2-for-1 stock split.	
AmStratIncPort II	.08¼	MinnMunilnco Port	.063⅛
AmStratIncPort III	.08¼	MinnMuniTrm II	.0492
AmStratIncPort	.08	MinnMuniTrm	.0509
Americas Inco Tr	.05¼	St John Knits	.02½
Amwest Insur Grp	.11	WMC Ltd ADR	†.3498
Baxter Intl	s	†-Approximate U.S. dollar amount per American Depository Receipt/Share before adjustment for foreign taxes.	
s-1/5th shr of Allegiance Cp for each shr held.			
Call Rlty Corp	.45		
Cedar Fair LP	.62½		
Contl Holmes Hlding	.05		

FIGURE 2.1 "Corporate Dividend News" column showing Arrow Financial's announcement of a 10 percent stock dividend. "Corporate Dividend News" published daily in *The Wall Street Journal*. Reprinted by permission of *The Wall Street Journal*, © 1996 Dow Jones & Company, Inc. All rights reserved worldwide.

are the declaration date, the ex-dividend date, the record date, and the payable date. Investors generally become aware of them in a slightly different order.

The *declaration date* is the day that the decision of the company's board of directors is announced to the public. This announcement notes the frequency with which it is paid ("Q" in Figure 2.1 stands for "quarterly"), the amount of the dividend that will be paid, the payable date, and the record date. All of these items are set by the corporation's board of directors.

The *payable date* is the date that the corporation will pay the dividend to shareholders who are entitled to receive it. Typically, a shareholder receives the dividend check on the payable day. The *record date* is, in lay terms, the cutoff date that the company sets to determine who is eligible to receive the dividend. In short, an investor who owns the stock as of this date will receive the dividend. The list of eligible stockholders is compiled by the *registrar* or *transfer agent*, who is responsible for maintaining a complete and accurate record of who owns a company's stock, including names and addresses. (Today, the registrar and transfer agent are usually the same bank or trust company.) When the record date is announced, the company instructs its registrar to compile a list of all individuals who own the common stock at the close of business on the record date. These persons, usually referred to as *holders of record*, are eligible to receive the dividend when it is paid. (A company can act as its own transfer agent or it can hire an outside firm.)

Logically, there must be a date in the schedule on or after which a person buying the stock will not be eligible to receive the dividend. And logically, this date must be before the record date. This date is known as the *ex-dividend date*. (See the bottom right-hand section of Figure 2.1.) It is the first date that anyone buying the stock will not be eligible to receive the dividend that has been declared. In effect, the stock is now trading without (*ex* in Latin) the dividend. This date is not set by the company. It is set by the stock exchange for securities that trade there or by the National Association of Securities Dealers for stocks that trade in the over-the-counter market.

 declaration date the day that the board of directors announces the terms and amount of a dividend payment.

 payable date the date on which the cash or stock is paid to the investor who purchased the stock before the ex-dividend date.

 record date the deadline date, set by the board of directors, on which an investor must be recorded as an owner of the stock in order to be eligible to receive the dividend payment.

registrar a firm, usually a commercial bank or trust company appointed by the issuer of a security, that is responsible for keeping an accurate list of all stockholders' names and addresses.

transfer agent usually a commercial bank or trust company responsible for canceling old certificates and issuing new certificates; also responsible for mailing dividends and other important information and documents to the shareholders.

holder of record the person whose name appears as the owner of the security on the company's records, usually as of the record date.

Voting Rights. Common stock is sometimes referred to as voting stock because the right to vote is traditionally a characteristic of this security. Because of this right, common stockholders have the greatest control over the management and policies of a company. They decide a broad range of issues, including changes in the corporate charter, the authorization or issuance of new stock, reorganizations, mergers, and, perhaps most important, the election of the company's board of directors, which is responsible for setting the management direction of the company, reviewing overall performance, and determining the dividend that the company will pay to its common stockholders.

Most elections and policy decisions occur at the company's annual meeting, which most investors do not attend. As a result, most shareholders vote by *proxy*. When it is time for the shareholders to vote, the company that issued the common stock sends proxy materials—a voting card and information about the persons nominated to directorships or about the issues being decided—to either the customer (if the stock is held in the customer's name) or the brokerage firm (if the stock is held in "street name"—the name of the brokerage firm holding it on the customer's behalf). In the latter case, the brokerage firm or its authorized agent distributes the proxy materials to the customer who, in turn, checks his or her choices, signs the proxy form, and returns it to the firm (or agent), which places votes in accordance with each customer's choices. If the customer does not return the proxy, the brokerage firm will usually vote in accordance with the recommendations of the current management.

Most companies give their common shareholders one of two voting methods: the *statutory method* or the *cumulative method*. The specific voting method is determined by the company's owner or its board of directors when the business is first incorporated, before it issues shares to the public. Importantly, once the common stock has been issued, the voting method can be changed only with a majority vote of the shareholders.

In order to understand the difference between the

two methods, consider the following scenario. There are three positions open on a company's board of directors, and 10 people are running for these positions. You own 100 shares. Under the statutory voting method, you can cast 100 votes for each of the positions being filled. You must choose three candidates and cast 100 votes for each of those three. This is the only way you can cast your votes. You cannot pool the votes, casting all 300 for one candidate; nor can you split your votes, giving 50 votes to one candidate, 250 to a second candidate, and none to the third. This method, the oldest and the most common, clearly gives control to stockholders in direct proportion to the amount of stock they own.

Under the cumulative voting method in the same situation (you own 100 shares and are voting in an election for three positions on the board of directors), you can pool or split your votes as you wish. You can cast all 300 votes for one candidate, 150 votes each for two of the candidates, or 200 for one candidate and 100 for another. But you are limited to casting your votes for no more than the number of positions being decided.

Clearly the cumulative voting method is advantageous to small shareholders. By banding together and agreeing to place all of their votes behind one individual, for example, small shareholders have a better chance of electing someone to the board of directors who represents or is sympathetic to their interests and concerns. Under the statutory method, the people owning the most shares—usually family members and their handpicked board members—control the company. Exactly the same voting methods are used to decide issues involving the firm's management, such as whether the company should issue new shares or split its stock.

The right to vote can be banded together in another way called a *voting trust*. This is usually established when a company has been in financial difficulty for a period of time and board members want to concentrate voting power so that they can make changes in corporate policy quickly. The board sets up a voting trust at a commercial bank and asks common stockholders to deposit their shares into the trust. The bank serves as the trustee

ex-dividend date the day, set by the National Association of Securities Dealers, or an exchange, that the bid price of the stock is reduced by the dividend amount. Anyone purchasing the stock on that day or later will be ineligible to receive the cash dividend.

proxy a form by which an investor votes in absentia or transfers voting authority to another party.

statutory voting method a procedure whereby a shareholder must divide his or her total votes equally among the directorships being decided; the standard voting method in most corporations.

cumulative voting method a procedure whereby a shareholder can place his or her votes on director-ships in any combination he or she chooses.

voting trust a trust, usually having a maximum life of 10 years, established to control the voting shares of a corporation.

voting trust certificate (VTC) negotiable certificates showing that common shares have been deposited into a voting trust and that shareholders have forfeited their right to vote.

of the account. In exchange for each common share deposited in the account, the bank issues a *voting trust certificate* (VTC) to each shareholder that gives the holder all the rights and privileges of a common stockholder except the right to vote. This privilege now belongs to the trust, which is controlled by the board of directors.

Voting trusts are established for a fixed period of time—anywhere from 5 to 10 years. Once investors deposit shares into a voting trust, they cannot withdraw them until the trust is dissolved. This restriction does not adversely affect the marketability of the voting trust certificates. They have the same liquidity and ease of transferability that the common shares have. If investors did not deposit all of the shares into the voting trust, then a broker must be careful when purchasing the company stock for a customer to determine whether the customer wants to buy the common stock or the voting trust certificates.

In recent years, voting rights offered to common shareholders have become more complicated. The old rule of "one share, one vote" used by the New York Stock Exchange does not always apply. Many companies have issued two classes of common shares: one class with voting rights and another class with partial or no voting rights. When these two types exist, the full-voting shares are usually issued to the owner of the company and his or her family members who wish to retain control of the company, and the limited- or nonvoting shares are issued to the public. The example most often cited is the Ford Motor Company, which has two classes of common outstanding, Class A and Class B. Class A, which trades on the New York Stock Exchange and represents more than 90 percent of the company's total outstanding shares (both A and B), has only limited voting rights. Class B controls 40 percent of the total votes although it makes up less than 10 percent of all outstanding common shares and does not trade publicly. It is held by the Ford family and key board members, thereby ensuring the family's strong influence over the company.

Other companies issue classes of shares with weighted rights or super voting rights. The various classes are arbitrarily labeled Class A common, Class B common, or Class C common. There is no consistent practice among companies in labeling the different groups; hence, there is no consistency in the voting characteristics among the classes. Remember that the structure of the voting rights is determined by the company and its board of directors when the stock is issued. If the right to vote is important to you, then it is important to be aware of the various classes of shares and their voting rights that some companies have outstanding.

Right to Maintain Proportionate Ownership in the Company. Under many companies' charters, existing common stockholders have the right to maintain their proportionate ownership of the outstanding stock when new shares are issued. If, for example, you own 10 percent of a company's outstanding common shares and the company issues 500,000 additional shares, you automatically have the right to purchase 10 percent, or 50,000, of the new shares. This privilege is known as the *preemptive right*. Under its terms, a company must offer all new common shares to existing stockholders first. The distribution to existing stockholders of the privilege to purchase these additional shares is handled through a process known as a *rights offering*, which is discussed in detail in Chapter 8.

preemptive right an entitlement giving existing stockholders the right to purchase a proportional amount of new common shares before they are offered to other investors.

Limited Liability and Last Claim to the Company's Assets in a Liquidation. If a company in which you own stock goes bankrupt or the investment proves bad, your total loss as a common stockholder is limited to the amount that you paid for the security. Neither the corporation, the banks from which it borrowed money, the companies to which it owes money, nor the bondholders have any claims on your personal assets.

Additionally, if a company goes bankrupt, you have a claim against the company's remaining assets; however, yours is the last behind the claims of all other types of securities holders and creditors. The priority of claims when a company is dissolved is:

rights offering an offering of new shares to existing shareholders. The method and terms by which preemptive rights are distributed to existing shareholders are explained in the prospectus that accompanies the offering.

par value for common stock, an arbitrary value assigned to the stock at the time it is issued.

market value the price of a stock determined by expectations of the company's growth and earnings by investors.

IPO abbreviation for initial public offering, a company's first-time issuance of common stock to the public.

1. Wages and taxes.
2. Secured bondholders.
3. General creditors and unsecured bondholders.
4. Preferred stockholders.
5. Common stockholders.

In practical terms, there are usually no assets left when the common stockholders' claims are finally reached.

Valuation of Common Stock

Two terms—*par value* and *market value*—often confuse new investors as to the real value of common stock. The par value of common stock is set at the time the company files its incorporation papers or the stock is authorized. It is an arbitrary value that is virtually meaningless to investors. Originally, it represented the value of the company's assets underlying each share. Today, par value serves some arcane bookkeeping purposes for the issuing company. For example, some states' incorporation fees are based on this value. To avoid excessive fees, a company puts a low par value or even no par value on its stock. Both Exxon and McDonald's common shares, for example, have no par value. Therefore, the par value of common stock has no relation to a stock's issue price, potential earnings, dividend policy, or market value.

When a company issues common shares to the public for the first time, the issuance is called an *IPO* or initial public offering. The issue price or public offering price of new shares is set by the underwriter who helps the company price the issue and sell it to the public. In setting the price of a new issue, the investment banker considers the amount of capital that the company wishes to raise, the number of shares being offered to the public, the company's earnings record, and the anticipated dividends, as well as the price and earnings of the stock of similar companies. It also considers the indications of interest that it receives from sending out a preliminary prospectus, or *red herring*, for the issue.

Throughout the underwriting process, the investment banker does a delicate balancing act. At the same time that the underwriter wants to get the issuer the maximum proceeds or capital from the sale of the new issue, the firm also wants to establish an offering price that is attractive to investors, thereby achieving the complete sale of the issue. Often, the public offering price of a new issue is established as much by the underwriter's considerable intuitive judgment, based on the information and facts it is evaluating, as by hard financial data.

Once the underwriter and the issuer have sold the new shares to the public at the offering price, their market value in the secondary or aftermarket is determined primarily by investors' expectations of the company's growth and increase in earnings. If investors lose confidence in a stock due to lower-than-expected growth or reduced dividends and begin to sell it, the market price will decline. Conversely, if they view the company's prospects favorably and start to buy its shares, the price will rise.

There are actions that companies can legally take to influence the value of their stock in the secondary market. If a company feels the price of its stock is too high and wants to increase the marketability of its shares to investors in a broader economic range, it may initiate a *stock split*. The board of directors meets to set the terms of the stock split. The specifics (i.e., the ratio of the split, the record date, and the payable date) are announced by the company and are published in the "Stock" section of the "Corporate Dividend News" column (see Figure 2.2) of *The Wall Street Journal*. In this figure, we see that Microsoft has announced a two-for-one stock split. The additional shares will be distributed on December 6 to all persons who were shareholders of record on November 22. Let's say, for example, that the price of Microsoft shares closes at $150 per share on the day before the split occurs. An investor who owns 100 shares (total value $15,000) before the split will own 200 shares afterwards. The shares will have an adjusted market value of $75 per share ($150 ÷ 2). For shareholders, there is no change in the total value of their investment in the company or in the percentage of ownership in the company's stock. Each investor's equity is simply spread over more shares.

 red herring
jargon for the preliminary prospectus, which is used to get an indication of the public's interest in a security before the price is set and the security is issued.

 stock split
an increase or decrease in the number of a company's authorized shares that results in no change in the total value of the investor's holdings.

CORPORATE DIVIDEND NEWS

Dividends Reported November 12

Company	Period Amt.	Payable date	Record date
REGULAR			
Albany Intl clA	Q	.10	1– 3–97	12– 6
Allstate Corp	Q	.21¼	12–30–96	11–27
AquilaGas Pipeline	Q	.01¼	12– 6–96	11–21
Boatmens Bncshs	Q	.42	1– 1–97	11–30
Cleveland Cliffs	Q	.32½	12–27–96	12– 12
Coastal Corp	Q	.10	1– 1–97	11–29
Coastal Corp pfA	Q	.29¾	12–15–96	11–29
Coastal Corp pfB	Q	.45¾	12–15–96	11–29
Coastal Corp pfH	Q	.53⅛	12–15–96	11–29
Community Bks PA	Q	.20	1– 2–97	12–17
Elbit Ltd	Q	.06	1–20–97	1– 6
Everest Reinsurance Hldgs ..	Q	.03	12–19–96	12– 4
ExpeditorsIntl Wash	S	n.08	12–16–96	12– 2
n-On pre-split shares.				
1st West VA Bncp	Q	.19	12–16–96	11–29
Gainsco Inc	Q	.01½	1–15–97	12–31
GreenPoint Finl	Q	.20	12– 5–96	11–22
HBO & Co	Q	.02	1–20–97	12–31
Hastings Mfg	Q	.10	12–16–96	11–25
Hecla Mining pfB	Q	.87½	1– 1–97	12–11
Horizon Bancorp TX	Q	.04	12– 5–96	11–25
Household Intl	Q	.39	1–15–97	12–31
Huntco Inc clA	Q	.03½	12– 9–96	11–27
Intl Paper Co	Q	.25	12–16–96	11–22
La-Z-Boy Inc	Q	.19	12–10–96	11–22
Lake Ariel Bncp	Q	.17	12–13–96	11–15
Loctite Corp	Q	.30	1– 2–97	12– 6
Minn Mng & Mfg	Q	.49	12–12–96	11–22
Nobel Insur Ltd	Q	.05	12– 4–96	11–20
Noma Indust clA	Q	b.03	11–29–96	11–22
Noma Indust clB	Q	b.02⅞	11–29–96	11–22
Nuveen (John) Co	Q	.21	12–16–96	12– 1
Pillowtex Corp	Q	.05	12–16–96	12– 2
Schawk Inc cl A	Q	.06½	12–30–96	12– 16
ScientificTech	Q	.04	12– 3–96	11–20
Sphere Drake Hldgs	Q	.04	12– 2–96	11–22
TNP Enterprises	Q	.24½	12–15–96	11–27
Tech Electro Ind Inc Uts	Q	.09	12–31–96	11–30
Terra Industries	Q	.04	12–12–96	11–27
IRREGULAR				
Midcoast Energy Res Inc	Q	.08	12– 2–96	11–22
Resource Bcshs Mtg	Q	.03	12–13–96	11–29
FUNDS - REITS - INVESTMENT COS - LPS				
Capstead Mtge pfB	M	.10½	11–29–96	11–22
Fortis Securities	M	.061	12–16–96	11–25
Liberty All-Star	Q	k.31	1– 6–97	11–21
STOCK				
Brightpoint Inc	S		12–16–96	11–25
s-3-for-2 stock split.				
Chefs Intl	S		12– 6–96	11–22
s-1-for-3 reverse stock split.				
DSP Communications	S		12– 2–96	11–13
s-2-for-1 stock split approved.				
Dell Computer Corp	S		12– 6–96	11–25
s-2-for-1 stock split.				
Emerson Electric	S		3–10–97	2–21
s-2-for-1 stock split.				
ExpeditorsIntl Wash	S		12–11–96	11–25
s-2-for-1 stock split.				
FDP Corp	S		12–10–96	11–26
s-3-for-2 stock split.				
Financial Industries Corp	S		11–19–96	11–20
s-5-for-3 stock split approved.				
1st West VA Bncp		4%	12–16–96	12– 2
Microsoft Corp	S		12– 6–96	11–22
s-2-for-1 stock split.				
Murphy Oil Corp	S		12–31–96	12– 2
s-1 shr of Deltic for every 3.5 Murphy shrs held.				

Company	Period	Amount	Payable date	Record date
Sigma-Aldrich		s	1– 2–97	12–16
s-2-for-1 stock split.				
INCREASED				
		--Amounts--		
		New	Old		
Auto Data Proc	Q	.11½	.10	1– 1–97	12–13
Bandag Inc	Q	.25	.22½	1–21–97	12–20
Bandag Inc clA	Q	.25	.22½	1–21–97	12–20
Emerson Electric	Q	.54	.49	12–10–96	11–22
Hon Industries	Q	.14	.12	11–29–96	11–21
KN Energy Inc	Q	.27	.26	12–31–96	12– 16
Litchfield Finl	A	.05	.04	12–31–96	12–16
Sigma-Aldrich	Q	p.12½	.11	1– 2–97	12–16
p-Payable on pre split shares.					
SunTrust Banks	Q	.22½	.20	12–16–96	12– 2
Trustmark Corp	Q	.14	.12	12–16–96	12– 2
FOREIGN					
Unilever NV	–	†1.3173		12–20–96	11–18
Unilever PLC ADR	–	†.8472		12–30–96	11–26
INITIAL					
Rentrak Corp	–	s		11–25–96	11–18
s-1 shr of BlowOut Entertainment Inc for every 8.34 shrs					
held. Subj to SEC effectiveness.					
SPECIAL					
Lake Ariel Bncp	–	.05		12–13–96	11–15

A-Annual; b-Payable in Canadian funds; h-From income; k-From capital gains; M-Monthly; Q-Quarterly; S-Semi-annual; t-Approximate U.S. dollar amount per American Depositary Receipt/Share before adjustment for foreign taxes.

* * *

Stocks Ex-Dividend November 14

Company	Amount	Company	Amount
Allergan Inc	.13	MuniVest NY Insd	.060916
Amer Israeli Paper	4.20	MuniVest PA Insd	.060203
Apex Municipal Fd	.056830	MuniYield AZ Fund	.060205
Avon Products	.29	MuniYld CA Insd II	.074701
BergenBrunswig clA	.12	MuniYield CA Insd	.072511
CPI Corp	.14	MuniYield CA Fd	.078926
Carlisle Cos	.24½	MuniYield FL Insd	.071754
Cipsco Inc	.52	MuniYield FL Fd	.075914
Corporate HiYld	.122256	MuniYield Fund	.085115
Corporate HiYld II	.103955	MuniYield Insd II	.07444
Deluxe Corp	.37	MuniYield Insd	.078287
Duke Rlty Inv pfA	.65722	MuniYield MI Insd	.073012
Dyersburg Corp	.01	MuniYield MI Fd	.077313
Garan Inc	.20	MuniYield NJ Fund	.075977
Garan Inc	.20	MuniYield NJ Insd	.074691
Goodyear Tire&Rub	.28	MuniYield NY Insd	.077587
H&Q Life Sciences	1.64	MuniYld NY Ins II	.069314
H&Q Hlthcare Inv	4.49	MuniYld NY Ins III	.067957
Harris Corp	.38	MuniYield PA Fund	.075435
Hyperion 1997 Term	.03333	MuniYield Quality	.075636
Hyperion 1999 Term	.03958	MuniYield Qlty II	.077454
Hyperion 2002 Term	.04⅜	Olsten Corp	.07
Hyperion 2005 Inv	.05	PartnerRe Ltd	.15
Hyperion Total Ret	.07½	Phelps Dodge Corp	.50
Inco Opp Fd 1999	.041667	Ralston-Rai Purina	.30
Inco Opp Fd 2000	.05	Rockwell Intl	.29
Ingersoll-Rand Co	.20½	Sr High Inco Port	.078561
Kollmorgen Corp	.02	Smucker (JM) clA	.13
Libbey Inc	.07½	Smucker (JM) clB	.13
Louisiana-Pacific	.14	SunAmerica Inc new	.10
MonarchMachineTool	.05	Superior Surgical	.11
MuniAssets Fund	.070407	Taur MuniCA Hld	.058251
Muni Advantage Fd	.0665	Taur MuniNY Hld	.058549
Munienhanced Fd	.060389	Unilever NV	†1.317344
MuniInsured Fd	.042305	WaldenRes 9.16%pfB	.57¼
MuniVest CA Insd	.068445	Walden Resid Props	.46½
MuniVest FL Fd	.066242	Worldwd Dollarvest	.122375
MuniVest Fund	.052923	t-Approximate U.S. dollar
MuniVest Fund II	.074231	amount per American Depos-
MuniVest MI Insd	.066154	itary Receipt/Share before
MuniVest NJ Fd	.065003	adjustment for foreign taxes.

FIGURE 2.2 "Corporate Dividend News" column showing Microsoft's announcement of a two-for-one stock split. "Corporate Dividend News" published daily in *The Wall Street Journal.* Reprinted by permission of *The Wall Street Journal,* © 1996 Dow Jones & Company, Inc. All rights reserved worldwide.

Stock splits can be quite profitable for an investor who buys and holds shares over the long term. Figure 2.3 illustrates the results of stock splits if you had bought 100 shares of Microsoft in December 1986 when the stock was trading at $48.

The overall impact of a stock split is usually beneficial to shareholders because this action tends to be viewed positively by the market. First, the company's board of directors often increases the amount of the dividend per share, thereby increasing investors' yield or return on the investment. Second, the stock's lower price tends to increase demand for the security because it is now affordable for a larger pool of investors, especially small investors.

The type of stock split just described is called a "positive stock split" and is used more frequently by companies than a "negative" or "reverse stock split," in which the company reduces the number of shares outstanding. In Figure 2.2, Chefs International has announced a one-for-three reverse stock split. A company takes this action

Date	Action	# of Shares Customer Owns	Total Market Value
Dec. 1986	Cust buys	100	*4800[1]
Aug. 1987	2 for 1 stock split	200	
Apr. 1990	2 for 1 stock split	400	
Jun. 1991	3 for 2 stock split	600	
Jun. 1992	3 for 2 stock split	900	
May 1994	2 for 1 stock split	1800	
Dec. 1996	2 for 1 stock split	3600	*270,000[2]

1. In December 1986, Microsoft's market price was approximately $48 per share.
2. In December 1996, after 6 stock splits, Microsoft's market price was approximately $75 per share.

FIGURE 2.3 Benefits of stock splits: Since going public in 1986, Microsoft has split its stock six times. The chart above shows the number of shares and their value in December 1996 if a person had bought 100 shares in December 1986.

when the price of its shares is too low, and it is in danger of being delisted by a stock exchange or NASDAQ.

Another action that a company may take to influence the price of its stock in the market is to buy back stock that it has already issued to the public. It can repurchase the stock through a *tender offer*—a formal offer to purchase stock from investors at a fixed price (usually the current market price or a slight premium to the current market price)—or it can buy its stock in the open market. The stock that the company buys back after it has already been issued is called *treasury stock*. It is no longer part of the company's issued-and-outstanding shares and therefore has none of the rights and privileges of such shares. Treasury stock receives no dividends, has no voting rights, has no preemptive rights, and is not considered when the company calculates its earnings per share.

Most investors are unaware of the existence of treasury stock; however, it can have an impact on the return on their investment. By repurchasing its own stock in the open market, a company reduces the number of shares outstanding. Hence, dividends are spread over fewer shares, resulting in an increased return for investors.

What does a corporation do with the shares of treasury stock? It may simply hold them. After repurchasing them at a relatively low market price, it may hold them for a while before reissuing them to the public at a higher price in order to raise additional capital. It may distribute the treasury stock to key employees as part of their bonus plan or to any employee as part of the company's Employee Stock Option Plan (ESOP). Once distributed, these shares again become part of the company's issued-and-outstanding common stock, receiving all the benefits and privileges of such stock.

tender offer
a limited-time offer by a company to purchase its own shares or another company's outstanding shares, usually at a premium to their current market value.

treasury stock stock that has been repurchased by the corporation that issued it.

Classification of Common Stock

All incorporated businesses are required to issue at least one class of common stock. Some corporations, such as General Motors (GM) and Food Lion (shown in Figure 2.4), issue more than one class of common shares. As discussed earlier in this chapter, differential voting rights are

NEW YORK STOCK EXCHANGE

52 Weeks Hi	Lo	Stock	Sym	Div	Yld %	PE	Vol 100s	Hi	Lo	Close	Net Chg
75 ½	50	GenElec	GE	2.04	3.1	14	8931	67 ⅝	66 ⅝	66 ⅞	+ ⅝
8 ⅝	3 ⅞	GenHost	GH	.34	5.0	32	114	6 ¾	6 ⅝	6 ¾	...
16 ⅛	7 ¾	GenHouse	GHW	.32	2.0	12	64	15 ⅞	15 ½	15 ⅞	+ ⅜
57 ¾	35 ⅜	GenMills	GIS	1.28	2.2	21	1836	57 ⅜	56 ¼	57 ⅛	+½
50 ½	**30 ⅜**	**GenMotor**	**GM**	**1.60**	**4.2**	**...**	**8471**	**38 ⅛**	**37 ½**	**37 ¾**	**+ ¼**
45 ⅞	40 ¾	GenMotor pf		3.75	8.4	...	X8	45	43 ¾	44 ½	+ ¼
60 ¼	55	GenMotor pf		5.00	8.6	...	X3	58 ¼	58 ¼	58 ¼	- ½
47	**27 ⅞**	**GenMotor E**	**GME**	**.64**	**1.6**	**20**	**2461**	**41**	**39 ¾**	**40 ¾**	**+1**
82 ⅝	82 ⅛	GenMotor E pf			...	...	1473	83 ¼	80 ¾	83	+ ⅞
47 ⅞	38 ½	GenPubUtil	GPU	2.60	5.3	10	550	48 ⅝	47 ⅞	48 ⅝	+ ⅞
99 ⅞	69	GenRe	GRN	1.68	1.8	14	1416	95 ¼	92 ⅜	95 ¼	+3 ⅛
59 ⅜	31 ⅜	GenSignl	GSX	1.80	4.5	...	282	40 ¾	39 ⅞	40 ⅛	+ ⅛
6 ⅞	3	Genesco	GCO		...	100	847	4	3 ⅞	4	...
14 ¾	8	GenevaSteel	GNV		...	5	133	13 ⅜	13 ⅜	13 ⅜	- ⅛
5 ¼	1 ½	GenRad	GEN		...	...	139	2 ⅞	2 ⅝	2 ⅝	- ¼
42 ⅜	33 ⅛	GenuinePart	GPC	1.45	3.6	15	535	40 ⅝	40	40 ⅛	+ ⅛
16 ⅜	4 ⅞	GeorgiaGulf	GGC		...	5	1650	15 ¼	14 ⅞	15	- ⅛
48 ½	25 ⅜	GenPacific	GP	1.60	3.7	10	1995	43 ¼	42 ⅜	42 ¾	- ½
5	1 ⅛	Flowint	FLOW		...	14	87	2 9/16	2 ⅜	2 ⅜	...
14	5 ⅞	FlowMole	MOLE		...	23	2351	14 ¾	14	14 ⅝	+⅞
17	**11 ⅛**	**FoodLion A**	**FDLNA**	**.15**	**.9**	**31**	**1137**	**17**	**16 ⅜**	**16 ⅞**	**+ ⅜**
17	**10 ¾**	**FoodLion B**	**FDLNB**	**.15**	**.9**	**32**	**1064**	**17 ⅛**	**16 ⅝**	**17**	**+ ¼**
8 ½	4 ¾	FoothillBcp	FOOT	.16	2.4	6	9	6 ¾	6 ¾	6 ¾	+ ½

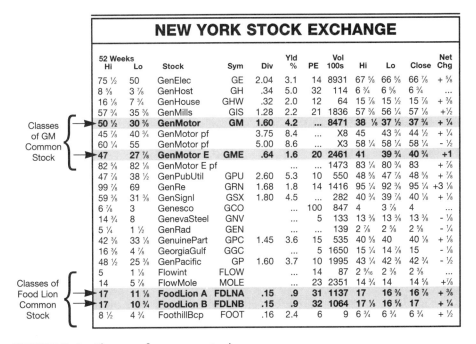

Classes of GM Common Stock (GenMotor; GenMotor E)

Classes of Food Lion Common Stock (FoodLion A; FoodLion B)

FIGURE 2.4 Classes of common stock.

usually the distinction between or among various classes. However, this is not uniformly true; there can be other differences. Each class can have a different annual dividend rate, or each can be backed by a different division or subsidiary of the issuing corporation. Investors should carefully read the prospectus of each class of common to find out the exact privileges granted.

If the prospectus is unavailable, another source of information is Standard & Poor's Corporation Records, a reference service that contains detailed information about more than 12,000 publicly held companies. The "Stock Data" section from each corporation's financial coverage contains, among other useful information, a description of the privileges and features of each class of common stock that the company has issued.

Class is a way of distinguishing the different issues of common stock distributed by one company, but the common stocks of different companies are often categorized based on different investment features, such as dividend payment history, potential for capital appreciation, and reactions to the economy and business cycles. Growth stocks, income stocks, and cyclical stocks are examples of these groupings, some of which are defined below. Keep in mind that these categories are not necessarily mutually exclusive. One analyst's growth stock may be another analyst's blue-chip stock.

Blue-chip stock. Named after the most valuable chips in a poker game at a casino, these are shares of the largest and most successful public companies. These companies have shown the ability to maintain and grow profits over a long period of time and through different market conditions. They also tend to pay dividends consistently, and increase these payments as earnings increase.

Countercyclical stock. The prices of these companies' shares move opposite to the business cycle. When the economy is contracting, these stocks increase in price. When the economy expands, their prices fall.

Cyclical stock. The market value of these securities moves directly with any anticipated rise or fall of the economy—in an exaggerated fashion. As the economy strengthens, sales grow by some multiple of the growth of the economy. The company's profits soar and therefore the price of its common stock rises. When the economy contracts or a recession occurs, sales of the company's products contract even more rapidly and profits shrink or disappear. As a result, the price of the company's stock falls. The term "cyclical stock" is almost a synonym for the common shares issued by companies that produce durable goods and companies in the home-building industries.

Defensive stock. This is the stock of a company that is affected less adversely than most during a recession or a downturn in the economy. The demand for the company's products remains relatively strong even in a worsening economy. Examples are stock issued by utility companies, food companies, and pharmaceutical companies.

Emerging-growth stock. This is the common stock of a young company that the market has only recently begun to recognize the growth and earnings potential of its sector and/or industry. Such a company has no track record of steady growth of sales or earnings, and pays no dividends. It does, however, have an interesting, commercially viable product.

Established-growth stock. McDonald's, Coca-Cola, and Microsoft are classic examples of established-growth companies. Typically, stock issued by such a company has traded in the market for several years, showing steady increases in earnings. Often there have been several stock splits during this period. The company remains in a growth position because it continues to build market share for its products. Established growth companies may or may not pay dividends. (Remember, dividend payments must be declared by the company's board of directors.) If the established growth company does pay a dividend, then it usually increases the dividend in tandem with increases in earnings.

Income stock. Utility companies shares are, for most investors, synonymous with the phrase "income stock." These companies pay a high percentage of their earnings to their shareholders as dividends. In the old days, these shares were often referred to as "widow and orphan" stocks because of the reliability and size of the dividend payments.

Interest-sensitive stock. Bank and utility stocks are the classic interest-sensitive stocks. Utilities borrow large amounts of money to fund their activities. When interest rates rise, the cost of borrowing increases and utility companies' profits decline. When interest rates fall and remain low, it costs the company less to finance its operations; hence its business activities produce more profits. The interest sensitivity of bank stocks is a bit more complex. Like utilities, banks borrow large amounts of money. As interest rates rise, the bank's cost of funds increases more rapidly than its income from assets. At the same time, fewer businesses are willing to pay the higher interest rates. The cost increase combined with a decline in the demand for loans causes bank profits to decline. Hence the price of the bank's stock declines. When interest rates fall, the bank's cost of funds decreases and business borrowing increases. The bank's profits go up and its stock prices increase. In summary, a high-interest-rate environment tends to be bearish for the price of bank stock. Conversely, a low-interest-rate environment tends to be bullish for the price of bank stock.

Lettered stock. This is common stock that is not freely or easily transferable because it has been issued privately by a company and has not been registered with the Securities and Exchange Commission. These securities are most often sold to sophisticated investors with substantial financial resources. The persons agree, usually in writing, not to resell the securities except under certain circumstances and only after holding them for a designated period of time.

Penny stock. Technically, penny stock is a common stock whose market value is less than $5 per share. Many penny stocks trade at less than $1 per share. These shares are issued by small companies that may have a new product or idea that shows growth potential. Characteristically these issues have few assets other than the potential of the idea. These securities are very risky.

Special-situation/Turnaround stock. This is stock of a company involved in a restructuring, merger/acquisition, or bankruptcy. Typically, the stock of the company involved is selling below its true or fair market value. Investors expect the price of the stock to rise over time; however, there is no guarantee or even good odds that this will indeed occur. Hence, investing in special-situation stocks is quite risky.

These groupings can prove bewildering to beginning investors. In Figure 2.5, these and other types of common stock are categorized under two headings intended to

Reflecting the State of the Company's Growth	Reflecting Reactions to the Economy
Blue Chip stock	Cyclical stock
Income stock	Counter-cyclical stock
Established-growth stock	Defensive stock
Emerging-growth stock	Interest-sensitive stock
Penny stock	
Special Situation stock	

FIGURE 2.5 Categories of common stock.

clarify these groupings: stocks that reflect the state of the company's growth and stocks that reflect the company's reaction to the general economy or business cycles.

PREFERRED STOCK (OR PREFERENCE SHARES)

Preferred stock gets its name from two characteristics in which it has preference over (is senior to) common stock:

1. A company must pay dividends to its preferred shareholders before it can pay any dividends to its common shareholders.
2. If the company goes bankrupt, preferred shareholders' claims on the company's assets are considered before those of the common shareholders.

Although preferred stock is categorized as an equity security, it has features that are similar to both common stock and bonds (debt securities). Like common stock, it represents ownership in the corporation; however, the owners of preferred shares are more like silent partners. Typically they have no voting rights and therefore no voice in the management of the company. (Some companies permit limited voting by preferred shareholders or grant them voting rights under certain circumstances. These are usually detailed in the prospectus for the security.) Preferred shareholders have no preemptive rights. The company is not required to offer new preferred shares to existing shareholders before the securities are sold to the public.

Like owners of common stock, preferred shareholders have the right to receive dividends. Usually paid quarterly, these dividends must be declared by the company's board of directors; however, the amount or percentage is typically fixed when the security is issued to the public. The dividend payments remain the same for as long as the security is outstanding. In this way, a preferred stock is like a bond on which the interest rate is set at the time the security is issued and remains the same throughout its life. Unlike a bond, however, a preferred share does not have a maturity date; it has an indefinite life.

The amount or percentage of the dividend that an investor receives is based on the par value of the preferred. Most preferred shares have traditionally been issued with a par value of $100. Today, many preferred issues are assigned a $25 par value in order to make them attractive to a broader range of investors. Like the interest on a bond, the amount of the annual dividend is a percentage of par value. A "10 percent preferred" with a $100 par value pays investors $10 annually (10 percent of $100) or $2.50 quarterly. (This same stock is also referred to as a "$10 preferred.") Par value is important to preferred stock in the same way it is important to bonds. It is not, as with common shares, an arbitrary value of no importance to investors.

Because the dividend rate on preferred stock is fixed, the forces that affect its issue price and market price are different from those that affect common shares. Most new issue preferred shares are sold to the public at par value; $25 is the most usual issue price and par value for preferred stock today. The amount or percentage of the fixed dividend reflects the financial health of the issuer, as well as the prevailing interest rates at the time the security is issued. The preferred rates are usually higher due to the increased risk associated with corporate securities as compared with, for example, the risk of U.S. government securities. If investor confidence flags severely, as it did with several commercial banks in poor financial condition in early 1990, a corporation may be forced to offer dividend rates that are substantially higher than prevailing interest rates in order to sell its new issue preferred.

Although the market price of preferred stock is generally considered to be fairly stable, it is sensitive to interest rate changes. As interest rates rise, the market value of outstanding preferred stock with a fixed dividend rate declines. Conversely, as interest rates fall, the market value of outstanding preferred shares rises. The following example illustrates this point.

You own a portfolio consisting of 10 percent (or $10) preferred shares, each having a current market value of $100. (The securities are trading at their par value.) Interest rates in the broad market decline to 5 percent—half of the rate on the preferred that you own. Because the outstanding preferred pays a higher dividend rate than investors can earn by purchasing newly issued, fixed-rate securities, they will be willing to pay a *premium* for the already outstanding preferred. In theory, the market price on the outstanding preferred would nearly double, because the 10 percent rate is twice as attractive as the 5 percent current rate. Consequently, the preferred should trade at close to $200 per share, twice its par value.

 premium
the amount by which the market value of a preferred stock exceeds its par value.

If, on the other hand, interest rates rise, the outstanding preferred would be less attractive to investors. They could purchase new issue preferred stock that would pay a better annual dividend. The subsequent lower demand for the outstanding preferred would result in a decrease in its market price. It would sell at a *discount*.

A change in interest rates is not the only factor that influences the price of preferred stock. Investor confidence is another. The market value of an issuer's outstanding preferred will trade at lower prices in response to flagging investor confidence. If a company is experiencing financial difficulty, its board of directors may choose to suspend all dividend payments or make only partial payments to its preferred shareholders. Current stockholders may begin to sell their shares at the same time that new

 discount
the amount by which the market value of a preferred stock is below its par value.

buyers, also wary, choose to purchase the shares of other companies. The resulting decreased demand will cause the price of the security to decline.

Remember that the market value of common stock is determined by investors' expectations regarding a company's performance and earnings growth. Common shares offer investors two ways to make money: (1) participation in the company's earnings growth through increasing dividends payments, and (2) participation in the company's increasing worth through the rise in the market value (capital appreciation or capital gains) of its common shares. These growth opportunities are generally not available to purchasers of preferred stock. This is one of the trade-offs that preferred shareholders make in exchange for both their preferential status and their fixed dividend payments. Nonetheless, preferred stock is considered safer than common stock. It is suitable for investors seeking safety of principal and predictable dividends. It is, however, somewhat less liquid than common stock because there is less preferred stock issued by companies.

Features or Types of Preferred Stock

When a company first issues preferred stock, it usually gives the shares certain features designed to increase the marketability of the security to investors, to enable it to respond to changes in the investment or economic environment, or to satisfy investor demands. These features are disclosed to the customer in the prospectus when the company issues the shares. The preferred stock may be:

1. Cumulative.
2. Callable.
3. Convertible.
4. Adjustable rate (commonly referred to by the acronym ARP—adjustable rate preferred).

A preferred issue may have none of the above characteristics, in which case it is called a "plain-vanilla" preferred. On the other hand, a preferred issue may have a combination of these features. For example, a preferred issue may be a cumulative callable preferred, or cumulative convertible preferred. Remember, the corporation issuing the stock, along with its underwriters, determines what features its preferred issue will have.

When people speak of a "type" of preferred, they are usually referring to one of these features. The four most frequently issued "types" of preferred are discussed in detail below.

Cumulative Preferred. If a company fails to pay dividends on *cumulative preferred*, the missed payments accumulate as arrearages. The shareholder has the right to receive all the accumulated back dividends before any dividends can be paid to common shareholders. In most cases, these arrearages are paid. However, if a company fails to pay them or offers only a partial settlement, cumulative preferred shareholders have no legal recourse. Today, most preferred stock is issued with the cumulative feature. Issues without this feature are known as "noncumulative preferred."

 cumulative preferred if dividend payments are missed, holders of these shares have a right to receive all back dividends before any dividend payments can be made to common shareholders.

Callable Preferred. A *call feature* gives the issuing company the right, at its option, to recall its outstanding preferred stock and repay the stock's par value to shareholders. Sometimes the company pays investors a slight premium over par value when the stock is called. A company will most likely exercise this call provision when interest rates in the general market are significantly lower than the dividend rate it is paying on an outstanding preferred issue. Suppose, for example, that Chrysler issued preferred stock with a 14 percent dividend rate in 1982. If it were to issue the same stock today, it could issue it with a 9 percent dividend rate because interest rates have fallen significantly since that time. Clearly, the 5 percent difference would represent a significant savings for Chrysler. If the outstanding preferred had a call provision, Chrysler would most likely issue new shares with the lower dividend rate and use

 call feature a provision that permits the issuer to repurchase preferred stock, usually at a premium to its par value.

the proceeds to "call" the outstanding, high-dividend preferred.

Calling a high-dividend preferred represents a savings to the issuer. Conversely, it represents a loss of income for investors. If the Chrysler shares had a $25 par value, an investor owning the 14 percent preferred would have received a $3.50 per share dividend annually (14 percent of $25). A person who bought the new issue would receive only $2.25 per share annually (9 percent of $25). The premium that a company offers shareholders when it calls its preferred is small compensation for the loss of income.

Clearly, investors and issuers have opposite opinions on callable preferred stock. Investors do not like having their high-dividend preferred called when interest rates drop. During periods of high interest rates, the public is more willing to purchase a company's non-callable preferred. The issuing company, on the other hand, wants to retain the right to call the issue and save money, if and when interest rates fall. The compromise is preferred stock with *call protection*. When issuing new preferred, the company makes the shares non-callable for the first five years of its life. (The length of the call protection varies, although five years is standard.) Afterward, the shares are callable at a premium over its par value as compensation to holders of the called issue. The premium is usually highest in the first year of the call. It then drops or, to use an industry phrase, "is scaled down" each subsequent year until it reaches par value.

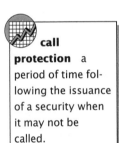

call protection a period of time following the issuance of a security when it may not be called.

The following example illustrates this concept. On July 1, 1995, a company issues preferred stock at $25 per share. (Remember that preferred is issued at its par value.) The issue has a five-year no-call provision; thus, it cannot be called until after July 1, 2000. At that time, the shares are callable at a 5 percent premium over its par value, or $26.25. The provisions of the call state that in each subsequent year after the initial call, the premium will drop by 1 percent. On July 1, 2001, the premium drops to 4 percent, or $26. On July 1, 2002, the premium drops to 3 percent, or $25.75. By the year 2005 and in all subsequent years, an investor who tenders shares in response to the call receives only par value ($25) for the stock. This compromise allows companies to take advantage of changes in interest rates. At the same time, investors know that they will receive the fixed dividend for the minimum period specified in the terms of the call protection.

A call provision can affect the market price of a preferred stock when interest rates fall. Combining the two examples used earlier, we can illustrate when and how this occurs. Let's postulate that Chrysler issued 14 percent preferred ($25 par value) with a five-year call protection. By July 1, 2000, Chrysler could distribute new preferred at 9 percent due to a drop in interest rates. The outstanding 14 percent shares would be very attractive to investors, who would be willing to pay a premium for the high dividend rate. If there were no call provisions on the shares, their theoretical market price at this time would rise to a little more than $44. It would be unwise to purchase the preferred at this price when it is callable at $26.25 per share. If this did happen, you would have an immediate loss of approximately $17.75. While stock might trade above the call price if interest rates drop early in the call protection period, as the end of this time approaches, the market price of the preferred would move closer and closer to the call price. Once the company can issue a call, the preferred will not trade above its call price. The call price therefore acts as a ceiling on how far the market price of preferred stock can rise in response to a decline in interest rates.

Convertible Preferred. *Convertible preferred* stock gives shareholders the right to convert their shares into another security—usually the common stock of the same issuer. The terms and conditions of the conversion are set by the issuer when the security is first sold (i.e., issued) to the public. For example, a company issuing new $25 par value convertible preferred sets the *conversion ratio* at 2:1. This means that whenever you choose, you can convert one share of preferred stock into two shares of common stock. This ratio is fixed. It does not change with the mar-

convertible preferred preferred stock that shareholders can convert into a fixed number of common shares.

conversion ratio the number of common shares that an investor receives when converting a preferred stock.

ket value of the preferred or of the common stock. It will, however, be changed if the common stock splits or the issuer pays a stock dividend.

The choice to convert is purely yours. When is it advantageous to convert? The example that follows illustrates such an opportunity.

You purchase a $100 par value convertible preferred stock with a conversion ratio of 10:1. For every preferred that you own, you will receive 10 common shares when and if you convert. If the market price of the preferred is $100 per share at the same time that the market value of the common is $10 per share, the securities are described as trading at *parity*. This means that the market value of the convertible preferred equals the total market value of the 10 shares of common stock. In this case, $100 would be the parity price of the preferred if $10 is the market price of the common stock (10 shares × $10 = $100). "Parity price" and "market price" are not synonymous. They are the same only when the preferred and common are trading at parity, which is not often. Usually convertible securities trade at a slight premium over the parity price of the common stock.

parity when the total market value of the common shares into which a security can be converted equals the market value of the convertible security.

Because convertible preferred stock can be turned into common stock, the prices of these two securities tend to move in tandem. Given the many different forces at play in the market, the prices do not always move at the same time or in the same direction. Sometimes the preferred's market price may be above the parity price. When this occurs, the preferred is said to be trading at a premium. At other times, the market price of the preferred may be below parity with the common, trading at a discount. For holders of a convertible preferred, the price disparity presents an opportunity to profit.

Continuing with our example, the market price of the preferred drops to $85 per share on word that interest rates are increasing at the same time that the market price of the common rises to $11 per share based on reports of increased sales and earnings for the company. Based on the price of the preferred, the common would have to be trading at $8.50 ($85 ÷ 10) in order to be at parity. However, its market price is $11 per share. If you owned or bought the preferred, you could convert into the common, acquiring the common at a cost basis of $8.50, and then sell the stock at its market price of $11. You would have a $2.50 per share profit on each share of the 10 common shares.

Explained from another point of view, the market price of 10 shares of common would be $110 ($11 × 10 shares). The total parity price of the common upon conversion would be $25 higher than the market price of the preferred, $85. The $25 difference represents the total profit you would make by converting the preferred and then selling the common shares at their current market price.

In reality, the price disparity between an issuer's convertible preferred and its common stock exists for only a short period of time—seconds in fact. *Arbitrage* by professional traders who watch the market closely for these opportunities causes the two prices to return quickly to parity. Hence, it is rare that a preferred would trade at a discount to parity. It is also virtually impossible for individual investors to profit from the situation illustrated above. Professional arbitrageurs are always there first.

arbitrage
the simultaneous purchase and sale of securities in different markets in an attempt to profit from short-term price disparities.

Still, convertible preferred stock is advantageous because it allows you to convert to common shares when their capital appreciation and dividend payments exceed your return from the fixed-rate preferred stock. Convertibility offsets the fact that *straight preferred* does not offer much growth potential to investors.

straight preferred a synonym for "nonconvertible preferred."

The conversion feature is also beneficial to the issuer. Because the shareholders have the potential to participate in the company's growth, convertible securities often have a lower fixed dividend rate when compared to other preferred stock.

Adjustable Rate Preferred. *Adjustable rate preferred* (ARP) shares do not pay a fixed dividend. Instead, as the name suggests, the dividend rate is reset periodically. The new rate is usually reset at a slight premium to some standard rate (such as the discount rate on 90-day U.S. govern-

adjustable rate preferred a preferred stock whose dividend is adjusted periodically to reflect changing interest rates.

ment Treasury bills) or a rate determined by a formula adopted by the issuer. Some adjustable rate preferred issues have provisions that permit the issuer to adjust the dividend rate every 49 days. Given this frequency, the reset rate usually reflects short-term interest rates instead of long-term rates. This type of ARP is known as a *money market preferred*.

Another recent variation on this theme is the *auction rate preferred*. Like money market preferred, the rate is reset every 49 days; however, the issuer proposes dividend rates, which the shareholders (usually large institutions) may accept or reject. If the shareholders reject the offer, the corporation has two options: raise the rate to a level that the holders will accept (which can sometimes be quite high if investors have lost confidence in the company) or buy back the issue at its par value.

ARPs, especially money market ARPs, have a distinct advantage for investors. Because the rate is reset every 49 days, the interest rate risk associated with preferred stock is minimized. The market price of the stock still moves in opposite directions to changes in the interest rates. The degree of its movement is decreased by the fact that every 49 days, when the rate is adjusted to the prevailing market rate, the preferred trades again at par value. In short, investors can sell adjustable or auction rate preferred every 49 days at the security's par value.

money market preferred adjustable rate preferred whose dividend is adjusted to reflect short-term interest rates.

auction rate preferred adjustable rate preferred shares whose dividend is adjusted periodically by the issuer offering a rate to which the shareholders must agree.

Issues of Preferred Stock

A preferred stock with features and a dividend rate different from other outstanding preferred by the same issuer is not referred to as being a different class, as common stock is. It is simply a different issue. Most companies have only one issue or class of common stock outstanding, but many have several issues of preferred stock trading in the market at the same time, as Commonwealth Edison does (Figure 2.6). Among the preferred issues the utility company has outstanding are $1.90 preferred, $2.00 preferred, and $8.40 preferred. If you checked

NEW YORK STOCK EXCHANGE

52 Weeks Hi	Lo	Stock	Sym	Div	Yld %	PE	Vol 100s	Hi	Lo	Close	Net Chg
8 5/8	3 3/4	ChockFull	CHF	.24t	3.1	15	102	7 3/4	7 5/8	7 3/4	+ 1/8
17 5/8	9 1/8	Chrysler	C	.60	4.2	48	2847	14 1/2	14 1/8	14 1/4	- 1/4
29	9	CircuitCty	CC	.10	.6	11	640	17 1/4	16 7/8	17	- 1/8
70 7/8	35 3/4	Circus	CIR		...	24	1035	66 3/4	64 1/2	66 3/4	+1 7/8
109 3/4	62	Citicorp	CCI	1.80	1.7	14	15699	105 3/8	103 5/8	104	+ 5/8
95 1/2	**82 5/8**	**Citicorp pf**		**6.00**	**6.4**	**...**	**5**	**93 3/4**	**93**	**93 3/4**	**+ 3/4**
100 1/2	**93 1/4**	**Citicorp pf A**		**7.00**	**7.1**	**...**	**2**	**99**	**99**	**99**	**...**
103 1/2	**70 1/4**	**Citicorp pf B**		**9.28e**	**10.3**	**...**	**1**	**90**	**90**	**90**	**+3 7/8**
24 5/8	**17**	**Citicorp pf C**		**2.28**	**10.0**	**...**	**42**	**23 1/8**	**22 5/8**	**22 7/8**	**+ 3/8**
45 5/8	32 1/8	Clorox	CLX	1.44	3.8	15	1478	39 1/2	38 3/8	38 5/8	- 1 1/8
28 5/8	14 7/8	ClubMed	CMI	.30	1.3	8	90	22 5/8	22 1/8	22 5/8	+ 1/8
55 1/2	37 1/8	CocaCola	KO	.96	1.8	27	7967	54 7/8	54 1/8	54 3/4	+ 1/2
19 3/4	12 1/4	CocaColaEnt	CCE	.05	.3	29	1424	19	18 1/4	19	+ 1/2
77 3/8	56	ColgatePalm	CL	1.80	2.4	17	698	76 3/4	76 1/4	76 3/8	...
22 1/4	16 1/8	CommerclMtls	CMC	.52	2.5	12	12	20 7/8	20 5/8	20 3/4	...
19 3/8	4 1/2	Commodoreint	CBU		...	14	3875	18 3/8	17 5/8	17 7/8	- 1/2
40	27 1/4	ComwEd	CWE	3.00	7.71	78	2616	39 3/8	39 1/8	39 1/4	- 1/4
40	**28 5/8**	**ComwEd pf A**		**1.42**	**3.5**	**...**	**6**	**40 5/8**	**40 3/8**	**40 5/8**	**+ 3/8**
22 1/4	**19**	**ComwEd pf B**		**1.90**	**9.2**	**...**	**36**	**20 7/8**	**20 3/4**	**20 3/4**	**- 1/8**
23 1/8	**19 1/8**	**ComwEd pf C**		**2.00**	**9.0**	**...**	**3**	**22 1/8**	**22 1/8**	**22 1/8**	**...**
26 1/4	**24**	**ComwEd pf D**		**2.37**	**9.2**	**...**	**6**	**25 3/4**	**25 1/8**	**25 5/8**	**+ 1/8**
30	**26 1/8**	**ComwEd pf E**		**2.87**	**9.8**	**...**	**8**	**29 5/8**	**29 5/8**	**29 5/8**	**+ 1/8**
95 1/4	**84**	**ComwEd pf F**		**8.40**	**9.1**	**...z4050**		**91 7/8**	**91 1/2**	**19 7/8**	**+ 1 7/8**
37 3/8	29 1/8	ComwEngy	CES	2.92	8.9	15	106	32 7/8	32 1/4	32 7/8	+ 3/4

Issues of Citicorp Preferred Stock — Citicorp pf through Citicorp pf C

Issues of Commonwealth Edison Preferred Stock — ComwEd pf A through ComwEd pf F

FIGURE 2.6 Various issues of preferred stock from Commonwealth Edison.

Standard & Poor's Corporation Records, you might find that each issue has a distinct combination of features. For example, one issue might be a straight cumulative preferred, another might be a cumulative convertible preferred, and still another might be an auction rate callable preferred.

Preferred Stock Today

Until this point, this discussion of preferred stock has presented the basic or classic concepts that have always been associated with this security. Many outstanding preferred issues have these characteristics, but many of the shares issued today have new features that represent significant changes. Three of these are important to investors who are considering purchasing these securities.

In theory, preferred stocks have an indeterminate life,

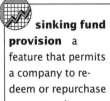

sinking fund provision a feature that permits a company to redeem or repurchase an outstanding preferred issue or bond using money that it has deposited into an escrow account.

but this is becoming less and less true. Today most preferred stock is issued with a *sinking fund provision*. This provision, which many bonds have, allows the issuer to retire the shares after a period of time, usually 8 to 10 years after they were issued. During each year the preferred is outstanding, the corporation deposits money into an escrow account that will be used to retire the preferred.

The second characteristic is that fewer companies are issuing preferred shares with fixed par values of $100, $50, or even $25. Companies are issuing no par value preferred. In this case, the dividend is a fixed dollar amount, not a fixed percentage of the par value.

And finally, fixed-rate preferred is being replaced increasingly by adjustable and auction rate preferred. This feature allows the issuer to reset the dividend periodically based on the prevailing interest rate and the financial condition of the company. The percentage or amount of the dividend is usually reset every quarter.

Individual investors are no longer the largest purchasers of preferred shares. Tax breaks have made it very attractive for one company to invest in the preferred stock of another corporation. Under the Internal Revenue Service's corporate dividend-received exclusion rule, 70 to 80 percent of the dividend amount that a domestic company receives from investing in an equity security of another domestic corporation is excluded from taxation. The exact percentage excluded depends on the percentage of a company's stock the investing corporation owns, and not all dividends are excludable. To be eligible for this deduction, the Internal Revenue Service requires a 46-day holding period for the investing corporation. Hence, the 49-day readjustment period for adjustable rate preferred is designed to make the stock eligible for the dividend-received exclusion. If the investing corporation does not like the new rate, it can sell the preferred it is holding and still qualify for the exclusion on the dividends received. For a corporation, this type of tax benefit is available on few other investments.

SUMMARY

Common stock and preferred stock are both negotiable equity securities, but in many ways they are different. Preferred stock is increasingly being given features, like the sinking fund provision, that are closer and closer to those of a bond. Nonetheless, it is each distinct feature or combination of features that makes common and preferred suitable for investors with a broad range of investment objectives. As we explore the ways these investments are analyzed and used, you may want to refer back to this chapter to clarify any points that may be confusing.

Chapter

The Basics of Buying and Selling Stocks

Buying stocks is what most people think of as investing (or speculating) in the stock market. The securities industry jargon for buying stock includes the phrases "establishing a *long position*" and "going long [the stock]." You buy securities when you believe the price will, over time, rise above the price originally paid for the stock and produce a profit. In general, the shorter the period of time during which you expect to profit, the more speculative, or risky, the investment is considered to be. When you sell stocks that you own, the action is called *selling long*; you are liquidating a long stock position.

Another way of speculating in stocks is by *selling short*. You use this strategy when you are bearish on a stock—that is, you believe the price of a stock will decline. Through a broker, you borrow shares, from either another investor or a brokerage firm, and sell them in the market. (The process whereby the firm borrows and lends the securities is unimportant to you as an investor.) Your objective is eventually to buy back the same number of borrowed shares at a lower price than you originally received when you sold them and then return the shares to the lender. This strategy is called a "short sale" because you do not own (i.e., have borrowed) the securities that you have sold. When you eventually buy back the borrowed

long position phrase denoting ownership of a security, which includes the right to transfer ownership and to participate in the rise and fall of its market value.

selling long selling securities or liquidating stock positions that an investor owns.

selling short
strategy investors use to profit from a price decline; involves selling securities that the investor does not own, with the intent of replacing the securities at a lower price.

 covering
eliminating a short position by buying the shares that have been sold short and delivering them to the lender.

stock and close the short position, this transaction is known as *covering* a short sale.

To illustrate selling short, let's say you believe that Digital stock, which is trading at $45 per share, is about to decline. In order to profit from this situation, you sell short 100 shares of the stock at $45, receiving proceeds of $4500. (Commissions are deducted from the sale price.) Digital then declines to $30 per share, and you cover the short position, paying $3000 to repurchase the 100 shares. (Commissions are added to the purchase price.) Having sold short the stock at $45 per share and then bought it back at $30 per share, you have a gross profit of $1500.

Selling short is a complex and risky strategy. When you sell short, you want the stock's price to decline. If the price rises, you are subject to unlimited potential loss. (Short sales are explained in more detail in Chapter 4.) It is important for you, as a beginning investor, to have a clear and basic understanding of the jargon used for buying (going long, covering a short sale) and selling (selling long, selling short) stocks so that you will understand some of the investment strategies discussed in this chapter.

INVESTMENT ACCOUNTS

Opening an account at a brokerage firm is a simple procedure. You begin by filling out a new account form. Typically, you must provide at least the following information on this form: your name, address, social security or tax identification number, confirmation that you are of legal age, citizenship, the name of your bank (or other brokerage firm if appropriate), name of your employer, and your investment objectives. If you are married, the firm may request the name, address, social security number, and employer of your spouse. Additional information, such as your approximate net worth or annual income, may be requested in order to fulfill the firm's requirements for opening a new account. This additional information varies slightly among brokerage firms, but each firm requires potential customers to provide sufficient information so that it can "know the customer." In general terms, this means the broker handling the account, and the firm, must be familiar with a customer's financial means, fiscal responsibility, and investment objectives in order to transact business properly with the client. This information is also used by the broker to make recommendations suitable to the investor.

A new account form is required for all customer accounts. Cash accounts and margin accounts are the two most common types used to trade securities.

Cash Account

Most investors trade stocks using a *cash account*. In this account, you can buy any stock by depositing 100 percent of the shares' market value or you can sell long (liquidate) stocks that are fully paid. When stocks are bought or sold in a cash account, settlement typically occurs three business days after the date of the transaction. This is known in the securities industry as *regular way settlement*. On the settlement date (the due date) you must pay for the purchased stocks in full. If you sold long stocks, the certificates must be delivered to the broker on or before that date, at which time the sales proceeds are released to you. In many cases, the firm already has the certificates, which it has been holding for you.

Should you fail to pay for the stock or deliver the certificates on the settlement date, the brokerage firm may liquidate the position. Following this forced liquidation, the firm freezes your account for at least 90 days. This means that you can trade in the account only by depositing "good funds"—cash, a certified or guaranteed check, or federal funds—before any trade will be executed.

If the forced liquidation results in a loss, you are liable. In order to recoup the loss, the firm may demand additional cash from you, legally attach any *cash balances* that you may have in other accounts, or liquidate other securities positions already in the account.

You cannot use the proceeds from the sale of shares

cash account an account in which an investor buys securities by paying for them in full or sells securities fully paid.

regular way settlement the normal settlement method for stock transactions, occurring three business days after the trade date.

 cash balances cash deposits in an account at a brokerage firm that are uninvested or awaiting investment.

to pay for an earlier purchase of the same shares. You must first pay for the purchase before any proceeds from the sale can be withdrawn or used. For example, a customer buys 200 Duracell common shares at $20 per share on Monday. Regular way settlement on this purchase will occur on the following Thursday—three business days after the trade date. By Wednesday, the second business day after the purchase, the price of Duracell has risen to $27 per share, and the investor sells the 200 shares. The customer has a $1400 profit ($7 × 200 shares). In order to receive the profit, the investor must first deposit $4000 in the account on the Thursday following the purchase in order to settle the initiating transaction. The sales proceeds will be credited to the account on the settlement date of the closing transaction—the following Monday. To reiterate, investors are prohibited from buying stocks, selling them profitably before settlement, and then using the proceeds to meet the cash deposit required to settle the initial transaction.

Some of the transactions that you can make in a cash account include:

1. Buying fully paid stock.
2. Selling fully paid stock.
3. Buying rights (see Chapter 8).
4. Buying warrants (see Chapter 8).
5. Buying options (see Chapter 8).

In the last three cases, the positions can also be liquidated in a cash account.

When you buy shares in a cash account, you can request that the stock certificate be issued in your name, or that the shares can be held in *street name*. If you want a certificate issued in your name, the transfer agent prints your name on the certificate and sends it to you for safekeeping. Not only can this process take several weeks, but many brokerage firms now charge customers a fee to issue a stock certificate. Therefore, if you plan to sell the shares quickly, you would be ill-advised to have a certificate issued in your name.

 **street name** industry term describing securities owned by an investor but registered in the name of the brokerage firm.

If your securities are held in street name, the securities are placed at a *depository* in the name of your brokerage firm. No stock certificates are issued; instead all record of your ownership exists as a computer entry. The depository is responsible for the safekeeping of these records. When securities are held in street name, the name of the individual investor is unknown to the corporation that issued the shares. The issuing corporation's records show your brokerage firm (or the depository) as the *holder of record*; however, your name appears in the brokerage firm's records as the *beneficial owner* of the shares. Unless you request otherwise, virtually all firms automatically hold securities in street name.

Many investors believe it is safer to have the stock certificate issued in their names because it proves they own the stock. This is not true. A person who is the beneficial owner of a stock held in street name receives the same legal protection, benefits, and privileges as a person whose stock is in customer name. The brokerage firm must promptly credit all dividends to investors' accounts and promptly forward all corporate communications—proxies and annual reports, among others—to investors.

There are advantages to leaving securities in street name. The process of selling the securities is simplified, in part because the firm does not have to get your signature on the certificates. Since the securities are in its name, the firm simply sells them on your behalf when you tell your broker to do so. A security held in street name is also less likely to be lost or damaged because the firm keeps them at a central depository, such as the Depository Trust Company (DTC). Replacement of a lost or damaged stock certificate is costly.

Perhaps the only investor who benefits from having securities issued in his or her name is a large investor who uses the services of several brokers. The advantage here is that he or she can choose to initiate a trade through one broker and liquidate the position through another.

Many companies, especially those trading on international exchanges such as the Tokyo Stock Exchange, do not issue stock certificates at all. Instead, ownership of

depository
a place, usually a bank or trust company, where securities are held and where the day-to-day movement of securities is handled by computer. The Depository Trust Company in New York is the primary and largest repository of securities in the U.S. and is the central depository facility for most brokerage firms and banks.

holder of record the name of the owner of a security as it is recorded in the records of the transfer agent or issuer.

beneficial owner the investor who owns securities held in street name.

book entry only securities for which no certificates are issued or available to the customer.

shares in the company is in *book entry only* form. The number of shares that an investor owns is listed in the computer records of the registrar or transfer agent for the issuing company. When the shares are bought or sold, no certificates change hands. The change of ownership is simply recorded in the registrar's records. The issuance of book-entry-only securities reduces the amount of paperwork associated with stock transactions and provides better safeguards for the securities. In the United States, this form of ownership is being accepted only slowly by people who invest in stocks. In the debt markets, particularly Treasury bills, Treasury bonds, and municipal bonds, book-entry-only ownership is more widespread.

Margin Account

margin account an account in which an investor buys (or sells short) securities by depositing part of their market value and borrowing the remainder from the brokerage firm.

In a *margin account*, you do not pay in full for stocks that you buy or sell. Under current Federal Reserve Board rules, you must deposit half (50 percent) of the stock's market value at the brokerage firm when you establish the position. The remainder you borrow from the brokerage house. If, for example, you have $3000 to invest and use a cash account, you can buy only $3000 worth of securities. If you buy the securities on margin, you can purchase $6000 of securities. This *leverage* enables you to double the purchasing (or selling) power of every dollar invested in stocks. It also doubles the returns you can make for each dollar invested.

leverage the purchase (or sale) of a large amount of stocks using a small amount of the investor's money. The rest of the money is borrowed from the brokerage firm.

The risks associated with margin trading are also increased by leverage. You lose twice as fast because there is less money backing the position. Moreover, you must also pay interest on the loan from the brokerage firm. A greater profit is necessary for you to break even.

Trading stocks on margin is more speculative than trading them fully paid. The mechanics of trading stocks on margin are set forth in detail in Chapter 4, but there are some basic concepts that beginning investors need to understand at this point. Any stock can be bought or sold in a cash account, but not all stocks can be traded on margin. Common and preferred stocks that are "marginable" include:

1. All stocks listed on an exchange.

2. All NASDAQ National Market Issues (NMS)—the approximately 4000 largest, most active over-the-counter (OTC) stocks trading on the NASDAQ Stock Market.

3. All other over-the-counter stocks (NASDAQ Small-Cap Issues and the "Pink Sheets" stocks) contained on the Federal Reserve Board's margin list.

All other stocks can be bought or sold only in a cash account, where you must deposit 100 percent of their market value.

When you buy or sell shares on margin, the certificates are always held in street name. They cannot be issued in your name because the brokerage firm has a lien (margin loan) against the value of the securities. The firm does this to protect itself. If the market value of the securities declines and you fail to deposit the additional money requested by the firm—a *maintenance call*—in order to maintain adequate equity in the account, the broker can liquidate the securities without your signature. You are liable for all losses resulting from this forced liquidation.

Some transactions involving stock and equity derivatives can be performed only in a margin account. These include:

1. Buying stocks on margin.

2. Selling stocks short.

3. Writing uncovered stock options (see Chapter 8).

TRADING STOCKS

Sizes of Trades

Stock trades are described as round lots or odd lots. A *round lot trade* in stock is usually for 100 shares or multiples thereof. This is the most common trading unit on the stock exchange floor and in the over-the-counter market. However, there are some preferred stocks and even fewer common stocks on exchanges that trade in round lots of 10 shares. The technical term for these stocks is *cabinet stocks*.

 maintenance call a demand from a brokerage firm that an investor deposit sufficient funds in a margin account to restore it to the minimum margin requirement.

 round lot trade a trade involving 100 shares of stock.

 cabinet stock exchange listed stock that trades in 10-share round lots and does not have an active trading market.

Because they do not trade frequently and their prices are usually high—like Berkshire Hathaway class A shares, whose price is over $31,000 per share—the exchange established smaller round lot units for these stocks.

Any trade for 1 to 99 shares of a stock (or for 1 to 9 shares of cabinet stock) is called an *odd lot trade*. Many small investors trade in odd lots because they lack the funds to buy round lots. Frequently, a brokerage firm will group odd lots together in order to form a round lot, and then execute the trade. As a percentage of dollars invested, commission costs on these transactions are higher.

odd lot trade
a stock trade involving between 1 and 99 shares.

The Trading Markets: Exchange and Over-the-Counter

As beginning investors soon discover, there is not just one stock market in which all securities are bought and sold. Stocks and bonds trade in two markets: on a *stock exchange* or in the *over-the-counter (OTC) market*. Collectively these markets are called the secondary or *aftermarket*. When new issues are distributed or sold to the public, this activity takes place in the *primary market*. Although the impact of these distinctions is of little import to most people's investment decisions, this is nonetheless important information to know.

stock exchange an auction market in which exchange members meet in a central location to execute buy and sell orders for individual and institutional customers.

Exchange-Listed Stocks. Commonly referred to as *listed stocks*, these are the approximately 5600 common and preferred stocks that trade on the floors of the exchanges in the United States. The seven largest exchanges are:

over-the-counter (OTC) market a decentralized, negotiated market in which many dealers in diverse locations execute trades for customers over an electronic trading system or telephone lines.

1. New York Stock Exchange.
2. American Stock Exchange.
3. Chicago Stock Exchange.
4. Pacific Stock Exchange.
5. Philadelphia Stock Exchange.
6. Boston Stock Exchange.
7. Cincinnati Stock Exchange.

Generally, listed stocks are the outstanding shares of the best-capitalized and most widely held U.S. companies (such as AT&T, IBM, and 3M) and large foreign companies (such as Glaxo-Wellcome, Hanson PLC, Gucci, Telefonos de Mexico [TelMex], and Deutsche Telekom). Approximately 4000 of these and other companies' common and preferred stocks trade on the New York Stock Exchange, the largest equities exchange in the United States.

A company's stock trades on an exchange for two reasons: (1) the company and its shares meet the exchange's listing requirements, and (2) the company wants the prestige of having its securities traded in the same place as those of the biggest and best corporations in the country. The criteria for being listed on an exchange include consideration of the following items:

✔ A company's aggregate before-tax earnings.
✔ The number of publicly held shares.
✔ The number of shareholders.
✔ The stock's trading volume.
✔ The price of the security.
✔ A national interest in trading the security.

Each exchange sets its own listing requirements. Hence, the same stocks do not trade on all of the exchanges, although there is some overlap.

When you place an order to buy or sell a listed stock, the broker or registered representative records your instructions on an order ticket, which the firm transmits electronically to the floor of the exchange. There, a *floor broker* receives the order, takes it to the *trading post* where the stock trades, and executes it with the *specialist* or another floor broker. Once the transaction is completed, the price at which the order is executed is reported on the *ticker*. Confirmation and the details of the execution are sent by computer to the brokerage firm and the registered representative, who notifies you. A written *confirmation* of the execution is sent to you on the next business day.

When buying or selling listed securities, the brokerage

 aftermarket a collective term for the markets— exchange and over-the-counter—in which stocks are bought and sold after they are issued to the public. Proceeds from trades in this market go to the investors.

 primary market the market, either exchange or over-the-counter, in which securities are first issued to the public, with the proceeds going to the issuing corporation.

 listed stock a company whose stock meets the listing requirements of one of the exchanges and has been accepted by the exchange to trade on its floor.

floor broker
an exchange member and an employee of a member firm who executes buy and sell orders on the trading floor of an exchange.

trading post
the designated place on the exchange floor where a particular stock trades.

specialist
an exchange member firm located at the trading post, responsible for maintaining a fair and orderly market in the stock(s) assigned to it.

ticker the electronic display that continuously shows the stock symbols and prices at which each successive order is executed; also called the ticker tape or the consolidated tape.

firm always acts as an *agent* or middleman between you and the buyers and sellers on the exchange floor. Specialists and floor brokers are prohibited from trading directly with the public. As compensation for its role in executing the order, the brokerage firm charges its customers a *commission*. When you buy stock, the brokerage firm adds the commission to the purchase price of the securities. When you sell shares, the commission is deducted from the proceeds that you receive. The amount of the commission must be disclosed to you on the written confirmation.

Over-the-Counter Stocks: NASDAQ and the Pink Sheets. If a company's common or preferred stock does not trade on an exchange, then it is said to trade in the over-the-counter (OTC) market. The OTC market is not a centralized market; there is no trading floor on which orders are executed. Across the United States and around the world, thousands of brokerage firms trade by telephone or use an interdealer electronic computer system known as *NASDAQ* (National Association of Securities Dealers Automated Quotation system) to buy and sell securities out of their own inventories. Approximately 16,000 stocks trade in the OTC market.

Today, however, the term "over-the-counter" is being redefined by NASDAQ. Describing itself in advertisements as "The NASDAQ Stock Market" and featuring the names of some of the largest companies in America (e.g., Microsoft, MCI, Intel) that trade over its electronic system, NASDAQ is presenting itself as being on par with and more forward-thinking than the traditional stock exchanges. NASDAQ would also prefer that the phrase "over-the-counter" be used only in reference to the non-NASDAQ traded stocks that are listed on the *Pink Sheets* (see Figure 3.3).

From the more traditional point of view, the over-the-counter market for stocks is a tiered market, consisting of three distinct segments. The approximately 4000 best-capitalized and most-active OTC companies' stocks are known as *NASDAQ National Market Issues*. (See Figure 3.1.) Of the stocks in this group, nearly 1000 meet the NYSE's listing requirements. However, the companies' boards of directors have chosen to keep their stock trading

NASDAQ NATIONAL MARKET ISSUES

	52 Weeks Hi	52 Weeks Lo	Stock	Sym	Div	Yld %	PE	Vol 100s	Hi	Lo	Close	Net Chg
	11	5¼	Lindbrg	LIND	.28	3.1	8	10	9	9	9	...
s	44½	21	LindsayMfg	LINZ	.20	.6	15	932	36½	36	36	−¼
s	50¼	21¾	LinrTch	LLTC	.20f	.6	19	11712	33¾	31¼	33⅛	+1⅝
n	6¼	5	LionBrew	MALT		...	...	151	5¼	5	5¼	+¼
	26⅛	11⅞	LiposmeCo	LIPO		...	dd	9763	13¼	11⅞	12⅞	+13/16
	48¾	26¾	LiposmeCo pf	LIPOZ	1.94	6.5	...	26	30	28	30	+2
	33½	26½	LiqBox	LIQB	.44	1.6	12	17	28¼	27	27	−1¼
	16¾	11½	LitchFnl	LTCH	.04r	.3	14	104	13	12½	12½	−¼
	40	30¼	Littelfuse	LFUS		...	23	1279	35⅝	35	35⅝	+⅜
	5½	2⅜	LiuskiInt	LSKI		...	dd	103	4	3⅞	4	+3/16
	6⅞	2⅜	LIVE Entn	LIVE		...	10	264	4½	4	4⅛	+⅛
n	13	7 7/16	Livent	LVNTF		...	...	126	8¾	8⅜	8¾	...
	17½	9⅛	LoJack	LOJN		...	21	731	11	10⅜	10⅞	+7/16
	15¼	9	LodgeNetEntn	LNET		...	dd	1855	12¼	11¾	11⅞	−5/16
n	28⅛	18	Loehmanns	LOEH		...	...	562	20⅝	20⅜	20⅝	...
	41¾	16⅜	LoewenGp	LWNG	.12e	.4	dd	6582	27¼	26¾	27¼	+7/16
n	8¾	4¼	LogalEdSftwr	LOGLF		...	...	22	4¾	4½	4¾	...
s	23½	9½	LoganRdhous	RDHS		...	28	67	16½	15¾	16	−¼
	14⅜	3	LogicDvc	LOGC		...	19	77	3⅞	3⅝	3⅝	−⅛
n▼	22¼	9⅝	LogicWorks	LGWX		...	52	703	10⅜	9½	9⅞	−½
	15	7¼	♣LomakPete	LOMK	.03e	.2	32	591	12½	12	12½	+¼
	12¾	8	LondonInt	LONDY	.19e	1.6	...	9	12	11⅝	11⅝	...
	18½	13	LndnPac	LPGLY	1.16e	8.3	...	26	14⅜	14	14	−¼
	45	29⅝	LoneStarStk	STAR		...	25	4602	32	31	31⅝	+¼
	15⅜	7½	LoneStrTech	LSST		...	19	869	14½	14⅛	14⅜	−⅛
	33¼	20⅞	LI Bncp	LISB	.40	1.4	15	3207	28¾	28¼	28⅜	+1/16
	29½	14½	LonghrnStk	LOHO		...	20	1165	16	15¼	15½	...
	4½	2	LoronixInfo	LORX		...	dd	1297	4⅛	3½	4⅛	+⅝
	1¾	½	LotteryEnt	LOTO		...	dd	125	11/16	19/32	19/32	−3/32
	23½	16 15/16	LufkinInd	LUFK	.60	3.1	13	55	19⅝	19	19⅝	+⅝
n	30	7	Lumisys	LUMI		...	...	729	10½	10	10⅛	...
s	50	18½	♣LunarCp	LUNR		...	37	100	37	34¾	37	+1½
	25⅛	10¼	LundInt	LUND		...	11	16	13⅛	13⅛	13⅛	−⅝
n▼	29¼	5⅞	Lycos	LCOS		...	...	868	6⅛	5¾	5 13/16	−⅛
			-M-M-M-									
	12⅜	6⅝	MACC Private	MACC		...	...	6	10	9¾	9¾	−¼
s	27	22¼	MAF Bcp	MAFB	.32	1.3	9	137	25¼	24¼	25¼	+½
	38	27 7/64	MaicHldgs	MAIC	stk	...	10	54	31¾	31	31¾	+¾
	23¾	13	MARC Inc	MARC	.40	2.0	15	8	20	20	20	...
n	24⅝	23⅝	MCI Cap QUIPS	MCICP	.17p	...	...	1757	24⅝	24⅛	24⅝	+¼
	31⅛	22⅜	MCI Comm	MCIC	.05	.2	28	33392	25½	24⅜	25⅜	+¾
	32¼	14½	MDL InfoSys	MDLI		...	21	1271	30½	29½	29⅞	+⅝
n	33¼	20½	META Gp	METG		...	...	175	24¾	24¼	24¾	...
	16¼	13	MFB Cp	MFBC	.06e	.4	20	150	14½	14⅛	14½	...
	8	5¼	MFRIInc	MFRI		...	13	243	7⅛	7	7	+¼
s	39¼	18½	♣MFS Comm	MFST		...	dd	12077	33¼	30⅞	33¼	+1¾
	65⅞	37½	MFS Comm dep pf	MFSTP	2.68	4.7	...	552	57½	55	57½	+1½
	6⅝	3⅝	MGI Pharma	MOGN		...	dd	77	5¾	5½	5¾	...
	4 33/64	1⅝	MH Meyerson	MHMY		...	9	149	3⅛	3	3	−⅛
	19½	6¼	MIDCOM	MCCI		...	...	419	12½	11½	12⅛	+1⅛
	4	1⅜	MK Gold	MKAU		...	...	84	1¾	1 11/16	1 11/16	...
	8¾	2⅞	MK Rail	MKRL		...	dd	569	6⅛	5¾	5 55/64	+7/64
	25¼	20⅞	MLF Bcp	MLFB	.76f	3.2	12	30	24⅛	23⅞	24⅛	...
	6⅞	2⅝	♣MRS Tch	MRSI		...	dd	709	3⅛	2⅞	3	...
sx	40¼	5 9/32	MRV Comm	MRVC		...	59	4613	21¾	18	20	+1¾
	27¾	15	MSB Bcp	MSBB	.60	3.5	29	68	17	15¾	17	...
	22⅛	15¼	MSCarr	MSCA	.02p	...	23	337	21½	21	21	...
	13½	4	MS Fnl	MSFI		...	11	33	5	4⅞	4⅞	...
	3⅞	1⅜	MTI Tch	MTIC		...	dd	342	2½	2 5/16	2½	+⅛
	17⅞	12⅝	♣MTL Inc	MTLI		...	10	291	17¾	17¼	17⅝	+⅛
s	22½	13⅞	MTS Sys	MTSC	.32	1.6	12	218	19¾	19¼	19¾	...
	16	3¼	M Wave	MWAV		...	dd	33	4⅜	3⅝	3⅝	−⅛
	72¼	43	MacDermd	MACD	.60	.8	14	1	71	71	71	+2½
	1 15/16	¾	MaceSecurity	MACE		...	dd	16	1 5/16	1 5/16	1 5/16	...
	6	1⅞	Macheezmo	MMRI		...	17	34	2⅞	2⅝	2⅝	−¼
n	16¼	7	MackieDsgn	MKIE		...	14	21	9⅞	9 9/16	9⅝	+¼
	14¼	11¾	MacmIBl g	MMBLF	.60	...	...	37	13⅜	13⅛	13⅛	...
s	63¾	14⅛	♣Macromedia	MACR		...	22	9143	17½	16⅛	17⅜	+1¼
n▲	1 15/16	6 49/64	Macronix ADR	MXICY	p	...	...	154	11⅜	11⅛	11⅜	+1/16
	48⅝	10	MadgeNetwks	MADGF		...	...	5715	12⅞	11⅛	12⅝	+1½
s	27½	21½	MadsnGas	MDSN	1.27	5.8	16	235	22	21½	22	...
	15¼	6⅞	MagainPharm	MAGN		...	...	1093	8¾	7⅞	7⅞	−¼
	15⅜	2⅜	MagalSecSys	MAGSF	stk	...	...	5130	9⅛	7⅛	8¼	+15/16
	14⅞	6⅞	MagicSftwr	MGICF		...	28	561	12	11½	11½	−¼
	24½	10¼	MichaelStr	MIKE		...	dd	2487	11¼	10¾	11	+⅛
x	30½	21	MichFnl	MFCB	.70	3.1	13	8	22¾	22¾	22¾	+¼
	32½	12	Micrel	MCRL		...	22	1157	18¼	16¾	18	+¾
	40¼	8¾	MicrionCp	MICN		...	15	898	11¾	9⅛	11	+1½
	21	11¼	MicroBioMd	MBMI		...	52	301	18¾	18	18¾	−¼
n	8	2½	McrCompTch	MCTI		...	...	362	2 11/16	2½	2 9/16	+1/16
	21¼	8¼	MicroFocus	MIFGY		...	12	64	11¼	11	11⅛	+⅛
	18⅝	5⅝	♣MicroLinear	MLIN		...	8	962	7	6¾	6⅞	−⅛
	56⅞	14	♣MicroWarhse	MWHS		...	26	3753	24	21¾	23	+¾
	16¼	7¼	MicroAge	MICA		...	dd	1012	12⅞	12⅜	12¾	+5/16
	45	19¾	MicrochpTch	MCHP		...	32	21717	35¼	31½	33¾	+1⅞
n	20½	8¾	Microcide	MCDE		...	...	303	11¼	10	11	+1
	34½	5½	Microcom	MNPI		...	12	1517	8	7⅜	7½	−⅜
	31¼	4⅜	Microdyne	MCDY		...	77	424	5⅛	4½	4⅝	...
	5⅝	1⅞	Microelectro	MPIX		...	dd	201	4 5/16	4⅛	4 3/16	+1/16
	4	1 7/16	♣Microfluidic	MFIC		...	dd	536	1¾	1 9/16	1 11/16	+⅛
	18⅝	8¾	Micrografx	MGXI		...	dd	1104	11⅞	11⅜	11½	−⅛
	12⅝	2¾	Microlog	MLOG		...	16	277	7⅝	7⅛	7⅛	−⅜
	29⅞	8¾	MicronElec	MUEI		...	32	4462	13⅜	12½	13⅜	+¾
	5⅜	2	Micronics	MCRN		...	dd	166	2½	2⅜	2⅜	−⅛
	53¾	18¾	♣MicrosSys	MCRS		...	62	189	22¾	22	22¼	−½
	8⅝	3	MicroToMain	MTMC		...	14	215	4	3⅝	4	+7/16
	14⅜	7⅜	♣Microsemi	MSCC		...	11	394	9⅞	9 9/16	9¾	+⅛
	125⅞	79⅞	Microsoft	MSFT		...	35	60016	120⅞	117⅜	120⅝	+2¾
	18	5½	MicrotekMed	MTMI		...	22	283	14⅛	13¾	14	−⅛
	25½	5	Microtest	MTST		...	17	432	9¼	8¾	9⅛	+⅛
	22½	11¼	Microtouch	MTSI		...	30	819	17½	15¾	15¾	...
n	20½	9⅝	Micrware	MWAR		...	...	9	16	15⅞	15⅞	+⅛
n	15	2⅜	MicrwPwr	MPDI		...	dd	1110	2⅞	2½	2⅝	...
	19¼	15¾	MidContinent	MCBS	.40	2.3	...	47	17⅝	17½	17½	−½
	18⅞	15⅜	MidAmInc	MIAM	.64	3.4	16	53	18⅝	18½	18 9/16	−1/16
	41 25/64	34¼	MidAmInc pf	MIAMP		...	...	25	41¼	40¾	41¼	+¼
	14¼	5⅜	Middleby	MIDD		...	22	20	7	6¾	7	−⅛
	19¼	15½	MidsexWtr	MSEX	1.10	6.7	12	54	16½	16	16½	...
	9⅜	1⅝	Midisoft	MIDI		...	dd	156	3¾	3⅜	3⅜	−¼
	19½	6¾	MidlandFnl	MDLD	.15	1.8	dd	130	8¾	8½	8½	−¼
	10½	3⅜	♣MikohnGamg	MIKN		...	dd	211	8	7½	7½	−½
	2½	¾	MilesHm	MIHO		...	dd	1025	2½	2⅜	2 15/32	−1/32
s	17¼	8⅝	MilgrayElec	MGRY		...	8	10	10¾	10¾	10¾	...
n	24⅝	10½	MillenmPharm	MLNM		...	...	413	15⅜	14⅜	14¾	−¾
	35¼	23¾	MillerHrm	MLHR	.52	1.6	18	1339	33¼	32	33	+15/16
	6⅝	2	MillerBldg	MTIK		...	dd	98	6⅜	6⅛	6⅛	−¼
	51¼	28	MillicmInt	MICCF		...	...	197	39	38⅜	39	+¼
▼	17⅛	11⅝	MiltonFed	MFFC	.52f	4.5	16	5	11½	11½	11½	−¾
n	13	7⅞	MindSprngEnt	MSPG		...	...	129	10½	9⅝	10½	+¾
	55	41	MineSftyAp	MNES	1.12f	2.4	17	3	47¼	47¼	47¼	+2¼
	33¾	7¾	MiniMed	MNMD		...	81	746	25	23	25	+2
	23⅝	9½	Minntch	MNTX	.10	.9	18	1046	11½	10¾	11½	+⅞
	7 11/16	4 11/16	MirmrMng	MAENF		...	...	406	5⅜	4 15/16	5⅜	+11/32
	25⅛	17¾	MissChem	MISS	.40	1.9	8	886	21	20¼	20¾	+⅝
	34	22	MS ValyBcsh	MVBI	.50f	1.5	13	1	33	33	33	+¾
	8	3⅝	MitchamInd	MIND		..	11	195	6¼	5⅞	5⅞	−5/32
	191½	151¾	Mitsui	MITSY	2.78e	1.5	...	7	180¾	180¾	180¾	+3¾
	9⅞	5⅞	MityLite	MITY		...	13	71	7¾	7½	7¾	+¼
n	9½	4½	♣Mizar	MIZR		...	8	91	4⅞	4¾	4⅞	−⅝
	25¼	20½	MoblGsSv	MBLE	1.12f	4.9	9	69	22¾	21¾	22¾	+½
	6	2 13/16	MobileMini	MINI		...	26	592	3 3/16	2⅞	3⅛	+1/16
	36⅜	9⅞	MoblTelcm	MTEL		...	dd	7225	13¼	11⅞	13	+⅞
	29¼	8	MblMedia	MBLM		...	dd	5057	9¼	8⅜	8⅝	+⅜
	12	9⅛	ModnCtrls	MOCO	.24	2.1	17	66	11½	11	11¼	−¼
	33	22½	ModineMfg	MODI	.68	2.6	13	473	26¼	25½	26	−¼
	6¼	1⅞	ModtechInc	MODT		...	33	100	6¼	6 15/64	6¼	+⅝
	20	12½	MohawkInd	MOHK		...	33	2052	18	17¼	17¾	...
n	13¾	7¼	MlclrDvc	MDCC		...	...	8	8	8	8	−½
	10	4¾	MolclrDyn	MDYN		...	dd	129	6⅝	6¼	6¼	−⅜
s	37	27¼	♣Molex	MOLX	.06	.2	21	1355	30½	29½	30¼	+¾
s	34¾	25⅜	♣Molex A	MOLXA	.06	.2	21	1078	29½	28½	29½	+½
	41¼	21¾	MoltenMetal	MLTN		...	cc	509	28¼	26½	27¼	−1
	14¼	8	♣MonacoCoach	MCCO		...	16	21	11½	10¾	11½	...
	7⅞	1⅝	MonacoFin A	MONFA		...	dd	130	1 13/16	1 11/16	1 13/16	+⅛
	6¼	2¾	MonrchCasino	MCRI		...	25	4	2¾	2¾	2¾	−½
	34¾	18	♣MondaviCp A	MOND		...	18	1740	29	27¾	28¾	+½
s	29	13	MoneyStr	MONE	.10	.4	20	5282	24¾	24	24¼	−⅛
	6⅜	4⅞	♣MonmthRE	MNRTA	.50	8.7	19	32	5⅞	5⅝	5¾	−⅛
	20½	12 73/512	MonroMufflr	MNRO	stk	...	18	30	19½	18¾	19½	+¼

FIGURE 3.1 A listing of NASDAQ National Market Issues from *The Wall Street Journal*. Notice that two of the largest companies whose shares trade on NASDAQ—MCI and Microsoft—are shown in the listings. Reprinted by permission of *The Wall Street Journal*, © 1996 Dow Jones & Company, Inc. All rights reserved worldwide.

confirmation
a notice sent from the broker to the customer on the day after the trade date that gives the details of the execution of an order.

agent a registered person who acts as the intermediary in the purchase or sale of a security and charges a commission for the service; a synonym for "broker."

commission
the fee charged by a broker or agent for executing an order for a customer.

in the NASDAQ market, preferring the way trading is conducted over the NASDAQ system to the way trading is conducted on an exchange. The listing requirements for a company's stock to be placed in the National Market Issues group are similar to those for equity securities trading on a stock exchange, including shareholder approval to issue additional shares, prohibitions against shareholder disenfranchisement, annual shareholder meetings, and an independent board of directors. As Figure 3.1 shows, the NASDAQ National Market Issues listings in the financial press are identical to the listings for NYSE-traded stocks.

The second tier of OTC stock is listed under the heading *NASDAQ Small-Cap Issues* (see Figure 3.2). There are approximately 1400 stocks in this tier. These companies' stocks do not meet the listing requirements for inclusion in the National Market Issues tier. In fact, the requirements to be included in this group are significantly lower than those in the first group. These companies are considerably less capitalized (having fewer assets and revenues), have fewer shares outstanding, and have a lower price per share. In short, stocks in this group are more speculative.

The lowest level of OTC stocks—all of which are non-NASDAQ stocks—are listed on the Pink Sheets. (See Figure 3.3.) Published daily by the National Quotation Bureau in Cedar Grove, New Jersey, the Pink Sheets list in alphabetical order the company's name, the last reported price of its stock (when available), and the name of the brokerage firm (or firms) that makes a market in the stock. In many cases, there will be no price for a stock on the Pink Sheets because it has not traded recently. A broker must call the *market maker* at the telephone number provided on the sheet to find out the current and accurate market price of the stock.

Although the stocks of many large companies trade over the counter, overall the market is one of growth stocks. This is especially true of the NASDAQ Stock Market. Generally, the listing requirements for stocks to trade OTC are more lenient than those of the exchanges. The NASDAQ Small-Cap Issues and the Pink Sheets stocks'

NASDAQ SMALL-CAP ISSUES

FIGURE 3.2 A listing of NASDAQ Small-Cap Issues from *The Wall Street Journal*. Reprinted by permission of *The Wall Street Journal*, © 1996 Dow Jones & Company, Inc. All rights reserved worldwide.

NQB's "Pink Sheets"® and "Yellow Sheets"™

Section I

August 2, 1996
Vol. 84 Issue 151

Published daily, except New York Stock Exchange holidays by:

National Quotation Bureau, Inc.

▲ AN INFOBASE HOLDINGS COMPANY

150 Commerce Road, Cedar Grove, N. J. 07009-1208

Telephone 201-239-6100   FAX 201-239-2908   Listing Department 800-LIST-OTC

A & A FOODS LTD	ANAFF	WK VOL- 351 H-	9/16	L- 1/2	17/32	21/32	
A & W BRANDS INC		CARR SECS CORP NY		800 221 2243			
A A IMPORTING CO INC	*ANTQ	CARR SECS CORP NY		800 221 2243			
		HERZOG HEINE GEDULD NJ		212 962 0300			
		A G EDWARDS & SONS ST L		800 325 8197	.001		W/O
		CARR O .08F HRZG O .10F					
M-AAON INC	AAON	WK VOL- 583 H- 5 1/4		L- 4 3/4	4 3/4	5 1/8	
M-ABC BANCORP	ABCB	WK VOL- 116 H- 19		L- 18	18 1/4	19	
A B C INVESTMENT CO		CARR SECS CORP NY		800 221 2243			
M-ABC RAIL PRODUCTS CORP	ABCR	WK VOL- 1826 H- 22 3/4		L- 22 1/8	21 7/8	22 1/8	
A.B.E. INDUSTRIAL HOLDING	*ABEH	HRZG O .05F					
M-AB ELECTROLUX CLASS B ADR	ELUXY	WK VOL- 411 H- 51 1/4		L- 50 3/8	49 3/4	50	
		CS FIRST BOSTON NY		212 909 3441			
ABN AMRO HOLDING NV ADR	*ARBLY	CS FIRST BOSTON NY		212 909 3441			
		HERZOG HEINE GEDULD NJ		800 221 3600			
		MERRILL LYNCH PFS NY		212 449 4093			
		ARNHOLD&S BLEICHROEDER NY		212 943 7518			
M-ABR INFORMATION SVCS INC	ABRX	WK VOL- 8184 H- 49		L- 42	52	52 1/2	
ABS INDUSTRIES INC		HERZOG HEINE GEDULD NJ		800 966 7022			
		TROSTER SINGER CORP J CY		800 222 0890			
		PARAGON CAPTL CRP BCA RTN		800 521 8877			
M-ABT BUILDING PRODS CORP	ABTC	WK VOL- 872 H- 21 3/4		L- 21 1/4	21	21 3/4	
M-ACC CONSUMER FINANCE CORP	ACCI	WK VOL- 2480 H- 6 7/8		L- 6	6 3/4	7	
M-ACC CORP	ACCC	WK VOL- 18625 H- 56		L- 50 5/8	55 1/4	56	
M-ACE CASH EXPRESS INC	AACE	WK VOL- 162 H- 14 1/4		L- 13	12 1/2	13 1/4	
M-ACM GOVT INCOME FUND INC	ACG	TAMAR SECS INC CLEVELAND		216 595 0496	9 3/8	9 7/8	
M-ACM GOVT SECS FUND INC	GSF	TAMAR SECS INC CLEVELAND		216 595 0496	8 3/8	8 7/8	
M-ACM GOVT SPECTRUM FND INC	SI	TAMAR SECS INC CLEVELAND		216 595 0496	6	6 1/2	
ACNB CORP	*ACNB	FAHN B 15 3/4F O 16 3/4F FBWA B 15 1/2F O 17F					
		FJMC B 15 3/4F O 16 3/4F HILL B 15 3/4F O 17F HOPR B 16F O 17F					
		JANY B 16F RYAN B 16F O 17F					
ACR GROUP INC	ACRG	WK VOL- 1244 H- 1		L- 1	7/8	1	
ACS INDUSTRIES INC	*ACSC	KOONCE SECS INC BTHSDA,MD		800 368 2802			
		CARR SECS CORP NY		800 221 2243			
M-ACT MANUFACTURING INC	ACTM	WK VOL- 1157 H- 14 7/8		L- 12 3/8	15	15 1/2	
M-ACT NETWORKS INC	ANET	WK VOL- 9894 H- 27		L- 23 3/4	21 3/4	22 1/2	
ACTV INC	IATV	WK VOL- 3390 H- 3 11/16		L- 3 1/16	3 7/8	4 11/16	
M-ADAC LABORATORIES	ADAC	WK VOL- 27974 H- 20 1/2		L- 18 3/8	20	20 1/4	
ADA FINANCIAL SVC CORP	*ADAF	CARR B .02F					
M-A.D.A.M SOFTWARE INC	ADAM	WK VOL- 665 H- 3 3/8		L- 3	3 1/8	3 3/8	
M-ADC TELECOMMUNICATNS INC	ADCT	WK VOL- 35074 H- 44 1/4		L- 41	43 3/4	44 1/4	
M-ADE CORP	ADEX	WK VOL- 3876 H- 10		L- 9	8 1/4	9	
ADI TECHNOLOGIES INC	*ADIKF	HERZOG HEINE GEDULD NJ		800 225 3271			
ADM TRONICS UNLTD INC	ADMT	WK VOL- 1721 H- 5/16		L- 19/64	9/32	5/16	
AEG AKTIENGESELLSCHFT ADR	*AEGXY	CS FIRST BOSTON NY		212 909 3441			
		HERZOG HEINE GEDULD NJ		800 225 3271			

Explanatory Notes

* Designates a Non-NASDAQ over-the-counter security

BW   Bid Wanted

M   Included on Federal Reserve list of marginable securities

OW   Offer Wanted

UNS Unsolicited

VJ   In bankruptcy or receivership or being reorganized under the Bankruptcy Act, or securities assumed by such companies.

W/O Work out price

The Nasdaq Stock Market BID, ASKED quotes are as of 4 PM the prior day. WK VOL number of securities traded for the prior week, updated each Mon. H (high) L (low) closing trade prices for the week are also provided for all Nasdaq securities. If there was no trading, no H or L information is shown.

The Pink Sheets, an interdealer quotation system for equities, are only available to registered brokers, dealers or financial institutions.

The offers to buy or sell contained herein do not constitute solicitations in any state in which such solicitation would be unlawful. These offers are not solicitations (a) to any person to whom the solicitation would be unlawful or (b) by any dealer in any state in which such dealer is not licensed.

The information provided herein by registered brokers and dealers is subject to SEC and NASD regulatory requirements and while this information is obtained from reliable sources, we do not guarantee its accuracy.

FIGURE 3.3 The Pink Sheets listing. The Pink Sheets list the bid and ask prices of certain over-the-counter stocks, mostly low-priced, thinly traded domestic issues and foreign issues (ADRs). The sheets are published and distributed to brokerage firms each business day and are named for the color of the paper on which the information is printed. The Yellow Sheets, referred to in the heading on the page, show the price quotes for corporate bonds that trade over the counter. Reproduced with permission of National Quotation Bureau, Inc. All rights reserved.

requirements involve lower price per share, lower after-tax earnings and net worth for the company, and fewer outstanding shares. As a result, the majority of the companies whose shares trade in this market are newer, smaller, and less well capitalized. Many investors will interpret this description as meaning that the over-the-counter stocks are riskier. Although this is often true, many larger, well-capitalized companies like MCI, Apple Computer, Intel, McCormick Spice Company, and Microsoft choose to keep their stocks in this market. This is done because the listing fees in the OTC market are lower than those of the stock exchange and some companies' managements prefer the OTC's market maker system (explained later) over the exchange's specialists system.

Customer orders are executed differently in this market. As with listed issues, a registered representative records your order on an order ticket. The ticket is sent to the trading desk within the brokerage firm where a trader "shops"—using a computer-based order routing and execution system—among the stock's market makers for the highest *bid price* if you wish to sell the security or the lowest *asked price* if you want to buy the security. Market makers are brokerage firms that buy and sell out of their own inventories. Here, again, your firm acts as an agent in the transaction executing your order on your behalf with a market maker. It adds commission to the asked price you pay when buying stock and deducts the commission from proceeds it receives for selling the stock for you.

If your firm is a market maker for the stock that you wish to buy or sell, then it can execute the trade out of its own inventory of the security. In this case, the firm is not acting as an agent; it is acting as a *dealer* or "principal" in the trade. A market maker's or dealer's role in the over-the-counter market is similar to that of a specialist on the exchange; however, the exchange specialist cannot trade or deal with the public and carries no accounts for the public. A market maker can deal with the public. Like a department store, the over-the-counter market maker buys securities into its inventory and then sells them out of it. The firm charges a *markup* on the asked price of the

 NASDAQ
acronym for National Association of Securities Dealers Automated Quotation system, the electronic trading system that enables brokers and dealers that trade NASDAQ-listed stocks to get real-time quotes and execute orders directly with each other.

 Pink Sheets
sheets listing the bid and ask prices of certain over-the-counter stocks, mostly low-priced and foreign issues; named for the color of the paper and published each business day by the National Quotation Bureau.

NASDAQ National Market Issues the approximately 4000 most active and best capitalized OTC stocks that meet NASDAQ's listing requirements and trade on the NASDAQ Stock Market.

NASDAQ Small-Cap Issues the second tier of stocks that trade on the NASDAQ Stock Market, consisting of approximately 1400 companies whose shares are less active, lower-priced, and more speculative. Listing requirements for these stocks are much lower than those for NASDAQ National Market Issues.

stock when you are buying. When you sell OTC stocks, the market maker deducts a *markdown* from the bid price.

The amount of the markups or markdowns is disclosed to you, the customer, on only the NASDAQ National Market Issues. The markups and markdowns on other OTC stocks—those on the Pink Sheets or listed under the NASDAQ Small-Cap Issues heading—are not disclosed to you. You would therefore not know the profit that the dealer is making on the transaction. Your confirmation for a trade in these stocks would show a "net price." It must also disclose that the firm "acted as a principal in the transaction and is a market maker in the security."

A brokerage firm is prohibited from acting as both a broker (agent) and a dealer (principal or market maker) in the same OTC trade. Hence, for executing a customer's order, a firm can charge the customer either a commission or a markup (or a markdown) but never both.

The National Association of Securities Dealers (NASD), the regulatory body of the over-the-counter market, does not set a minimum or maximum limit on commissions, markups, or markdowns. In general terms, the regulation simply states that all markups, markdowns, and commissions must be "fair and reasonable" considering the circumstances of the transaction and the services provided. Full-service brokerage houses that offer customers research and investment advice charge higher fees than do discount firms, which offer few services beyond order execution.

New Issue Stock

When a company issues stock to the public for the first time, the issuance is called an *initial public offering (IPO)*. If the same company later issues more shares to the public, these new shares are simply referred to as a *new issue*. In both cases, the proceeds from the sale of the stock go to the issuing company, which uses the services of an *underwriter* (also known as an investment banker) to set the *public offering price* and promote the sale of the stock to the public.

Typically you can purchase a new issue only from a brokerage firm that is a member of the underwriting group. These are the only firms that have the new shares to sell. If you do not have an account at one of these firms, it will be extremely difficult (if not impossible) for you to buy even a few shares of a new issue.

No commission is added to the stock's public offering price when you buy a new issue. This is a *net transaction*. The underwriter's compensation is built into the issue price. Investors purchasing a new issue must receive a copy of the issuing company's prospectus at or prior to receiving confirmation of the trade. Most initial public offerings occur in the over-the-counter markets because most start-up companies do not meet the strict listing requirements of the exchanges.

Once the new shares are issued (sold) to the public, investors immediately begin to trade (sell and buy) the shares in the secondary or aftermarket—that is, on the floor of the exchange or in the over-the-counter market. The profits from trades in these markets do not go to the issuing company; instead they go to the investors.

If, immediately after issuance, the price of the shares in the secondary market exceeds their public offering price, the stock is described as a *hot issue*. For example, in 1995 both Gucci and Pixar went public. Gucci's initial public offering price was $22 per share. At the end of the first day of trading, the stock's closing price was $26\frac{3}{4}$, a one-day gain of nearly 22 percent for anyone lucky enough to have bought the stock at the offering price. Pixar, the company that did the animation for the movie *Toy Story*, also issued shares in 1995 at $22 per share. On the first day of trading, investor demand for the shares, spurred by the popularity of the movie, caused the market price to soar to $42 per share, a one-day gain of 90 percent.

Nearly a year later, Gucci shares had continued their upward movement, trading at $62 per share. However, during the same period of time, Pixar's price had declined to $13. In both cases, investors lucky enough to buy shares at the initial public offering price had an immediate and substantial gain. Yet, this immediate surge in the secondary market price of a new issue does not necessarily

 market maker an NASD member firm that disseminates bid and asked prices at which it stands ready to buy stock into and sell stock from its inventory at its own risk; synonymous with "dealer."

 bid price the price at which a market maker offers to purchase an OTC stock from an investor who wishes to sell.

 asked price the price at which a market maker offers to sell stock to a buyer; also known as the "offer price."

 dealer a NASD member firm that makes a market in an OTC stock; also called a "principal" or a "market maker."

markup the amount or percentage added to the asked price when a customer buys an OTC stock from a firm acting as a principal or market maker in the transaction.

markdown the amount or percentage subtracted from the bid price when the customer sells OTC stock to a market maker or principal firm.

initial public offering (IPO) the first time that a company issues or sells its stock to the public.

new issue securities offered for sale by the issuer in the primary market (for example, an initial public offering).

indicate the value of the company or how it will perform later in the market. More often than not, the initial price increase of a hot issue is caused by keen investor interest in or hype about a new growth industry, as opposed to the strength of the individual company.

Most new issues, however, do not become hot issues. More commonly, all of the shares are sold at their offering price in the primary market, and then the price declines slightly once they begin trading in the secondary market. This price decline is caused by speculators (also known as flippers) who immediately sell off their shares if the stock does not become a hot issue.

New issues can fail to attract enough interest for underwriters to be able to sell the issuing company's shares. In this case, the underwriter may delay the issuance or withdraw the shares from the market. Anyone who bought shares of the failed offering gets his or her entire investment back from the underwriter.

Knowing the difference between the exchange market and the over-the-counter market (especially NASDAQ) and how trades are executed in each enables you to understand better the information that is disclosed on the confirmation. Additionally, this knowledge helps clarify how a stock's liquidity in the market affects the cost of a trade—both the price at which an order is executed and the commissions, markups, or markdowns on a transaction. [**Note:** On most confirmations, the broker's fees are simply called commissions regardless of whether they are markups, markdowns, or commissions.]

Types and Uses of Orders

Most investors use only a few of the many types of orders available. The three most frequently used orders are market orders, limit orders, and stop orders, Knowing how each of these orders is executed, the results that each order can produce, and the risks associated with each is key to using them effectively.

Throughout this discussion, keep some basic facts in mind. If no time limit is specified on an order, it is a *day* order. If it is not executed or cancelled by the end of the trading session in which it was placed, it expires. If you want an order to stand in the market longer, then the notation GTC—good 'til canceled—must be placed on the order. An order with the GTC notation is also called an *open order* and theoretically can remain unexecuted in the market for years. However, brokerage firms usually require a GTC order to be renewed or confirmed monthly or quarterly.

Market Order. Investors use *market orders* most frequently to buy or sell stocks. When you call your broker and say, "Buy 200 shares of Motorola" or "Sell 100 shares of Home Depot," you are placing a market order. You specify both the stock and the number of shares but not a price or time. The stock is bought or sold at the market price of the security when the order reaches the exchange floor or the over-the-counter trading desk.

Figure 3.4 shows that ABC stock is trading close to $35 per share (indicated by the bullet on the line graph). If you enter a market order to buy or sell ABC, it would be executed near $35 per share.

An investor placing a market order knows that it will be executed promptly—usually within a few minutes (or even seconds given the new computerized trading systems) after it is placed—unless there is a thin market for the stock. In this case, execution may take much longer. It is understood that a buy market order will be executed at the lowest available price and a sell market order will be executed at the highest available price at the time.

A broker cannot and does not guarantee a specific execution price on a market order. This point confuses many investors who call their brokers, request a price quote on a stock, and then place the order to buy or sell. They are usually surprised to find out that the order is not executed at the price that the broker quoted over the phone. Investors must keep in mind that the broker or account executive does not execute the order directly, but only writes the order ticket and places the order. The order is then executed at the best price available when it reaches the trading floor (for exchange-traded stocks) or

 underwriter a brokerage firm that assists the issuer of a new security in setting the offering price and in marketing the securities to the public; also known as an investment banker.

 public offering price the price at which a security is sold to the public by its underwriters.

net transaction a trade, such as the purchase of a new issue, in which the buyer or seller is not charged a commission or additional fee.

 hot issue a newly issued stock that immediately begins trading in the secondary market at a price higher than its public offering price.

day order
an order to buy or sell securities without a time notation; if it is not executed or canceled, it expires at the end of the trading session during which it was placed.

open order
remains valid until it is executed or canceled; same as a good 'til canceled (GTC) order.

market order
an order to buy or sell stock immediately at the best available market price.

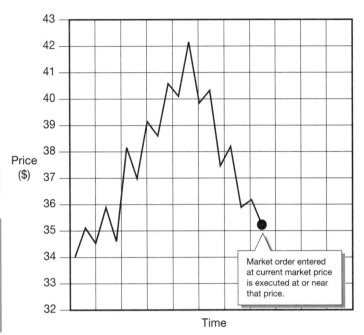

Market order entered at current market price is executed at or near that price.

FIGURE 3.4 Price movement and current market price of ABC common stock.

trading desk (for over-the-counter stocks). In the short time between the phone conversation with your broker and the order reaching the trading area for execution, the price of an actively or heavily traded stock will most likely have changed.

Many investors still believe that all orders are sent to a floor broker, who yells and gesticulates in a crowd of other floor brokers in an attempt to get an execution. For most customer orders, this image is no longer true. Today most investors' market orders are routed through computerized order-routing and reporting systems. The New York Stock Exchange's system is known as Super-DOT (Designated Order Turnaround). Customer orders are electronically routed to the specialist, who executes the order. NASDAQ's system is called SOES—an acronym for Small Order Execution System. This system automatically executes customer orders at the best available price quotes shown in the NASDAQ system.

Limit Order. When you place a *limit order*, you specify the price at which you want the order executed. It is understood that the order will be executed only at the stated limit price or better. The limit price is never the same as the stock's current market price. It is always "away from the market"—either above (on sell limit orders) or below (on buy limit orders) the current price. You believe the stock will move to the specified price within a reasonable period of time, and when it does you want your order to be executed. The length of time that a limit order stands in the market after it has been entered depends on whether it is or is not marked GTC. If no time is specified when the order is placed, the order is a day order and will be canceled at the end of the trading session if it is not executed. The following examples illustrate how buy limit and sell limit orders are used and executed in the market.

> **limit order**
> an order to buy stock (buy limit) at a specified price or lower, or to sell stock (sell limit) at a specified price or higher.

Buy Limit Order. A buy limit order is used to buy stock at a price that is below its current market price. Perhaps you observe that ABC common stock is trading at $34 per share. You want to purchase the stock but only if the price is $32 or lower. You believe that the price will decline to this point during the next few weeks before rising due to the increased demand resulting from the attractive low price, so you enter the following buy limit order: "Buy 100 ABC at $32 GTC." Note that this order is placed "away from"—specifically below—the stock's current price, as Figure 3.5 illustrates.

Once you have placed the order and your broker has entered it, neither of you have to do anything else. The computerized system "minds" or monitors the order and the market for you. If and when the price declines to or below the limit price, the order will be executed and the stock purchased at $32 or lower. The risk for you is that the buy limit order may not be executed at all. If the stock does not trade down to at least $32, the limit price, the order will not be executed.

No investor would ever place a buy limit order above the current market. Because the stock's price would already be below the limit price, the order would be executed immediately, defeating the purpose of a limit order.

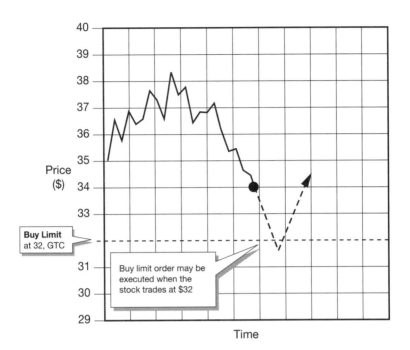

FIGURE 3.5 Strategic placement of a buy limit order. The line chart shows the price fluctuation of ABC stock, with the bullet indicating the current market price of $34. The dotted line shows the price decrease and subsequent rally anticipated during the next few weeks. The horizontal line of dashes indicates a buy limit order having been placed at $32, below the stock's current market price.

Sell Limit Order. A sell limit order is used to sell stock at a price that is higher than its current market price. For example, you own 100 shares of ABC, which is trading at $37 per share. You believe the stock will reach a peak price of nearly $40 per share during the next few days and then decline. Wanting to sell near the high, you enter the following sell limit order: "Sell 100 ABC at $39 GTC." As Figure 3.6 shows, the sell limit price is entered above the stock's current market price.

If and when the stock's price rises to or above the limit price, the order will be executed and the stock sold at $39 or higher; your objective will be accomplished. If the price never rises to the limit price, the order will not be executed. This is your risk.

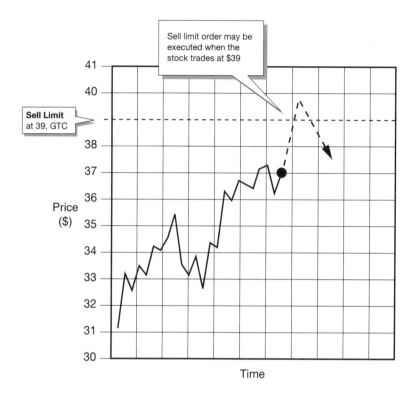

FIGURE 3.6 Strategic placement of a sell limit order. The line chart shows the price fluctuation of ABC stock, with the bullet indicating the current market price of $37. The dotted line shows the price increase and subsequent price decline expected to occur. The horizontal line of dashes shows a sell limit order having been placed at $39, above the stock's current market price.

No investor would place a sell limit order below a stock's current market price. An order entered at this position would be executed immediately because the stock's market price would already be above the order's limit price. The objective of the order would be negated.

An investor who enters a limit order knows that if the order is executed, the stock will be bought or sold at the limit price 99.99 percent of the time. The danger is that the limit order will not be executed if the security's market price does not reach the limit price. For a buy limit order, the stock must trade down to at least the limit price. For a sell limit order, the stock must trade up to at least the limit price. Part of the skill in using a limit order is determining how far "away from the market" to set the limit price.

Stop Order. Also called a stop-loss order, a *stop order* is used primarily to limit losses on profitable stock positions. As with a limit order, you enter a stop order at a specified price, called a "stop price," that is away from the stock's current market price. You expect the stock to rise or fall to the stop price within a reasonable period of time. The primary difference between a stop order and a limit order becomes clear in the execution of this order. When the stock's market price reaches a stop order's specified price, the order automatically becomes a market order and is then executed at the security's market price at that time. In short, the specified price serves as a "trigger," changing the stop order to a market order. With a stop order, you know that if the market trades at or passes through the stop price, the order will be executed.

The risk is that the order may not be executed at the stop price. Remember, the stop price is only a "trigger," prompting the order to be entered as a market order. In fact, it may be executed at a price that is not advantageous—above or below the stop price. You do not learn the price at which a stop order has been executed until the confirmation is received. The examples and figures that follow demonstrate the effective use of both sell stop orders and buy stop orders. (Stop orders can be used only on stock exchanges. They are not accepted in the over-the-counter market, including NASDAQ.)

Sell Stop Order. A sell stop order is used to protect profits on a long stock position. Assume that you originally purchased 200 shares of ABC stock at $35. The price subsequently has risen to $50 per share, yielding a $3000 gross profit. However, you are concerned that the price may decline quickly and wipe out much of your gain. To protect the profits, you place a sell stop order below the stock's current market price, as shown in Figure 3.7.

stop order
an order that becomes a market order to buy (buy stop) or to sell (sell stop) when the stock trades at a specified price, known as the stop price. Also called a "stop-loss order."

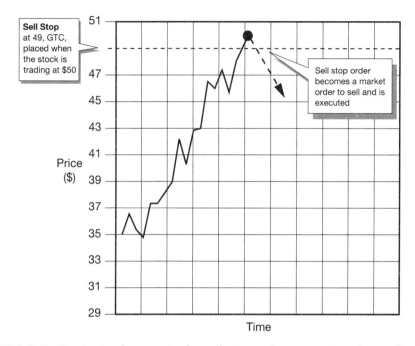

FIGURE 3.7 Strategic placement of a sell stop order protecting the profits on a long stock position. The line graph shows that ABC stock has risen from $35 to the current price of $50 per share, indicated by the bullet. You believe that a price decline may occur, indicated by the dotted line continuing from the current price on the graph, and wish to protect the $3000 profit you have made on the long stock position. You place a sell stop order at $49, below the current market price.

If the stock price declines to $49 or lower, the sell stop order will become a sell market order and will be executed at the prevailing market price. If the stock is sold at $49 (the stop price), you have effectively limited the reduction of your gain to $200 ($1 × 200 shares), leaving a gross profit of $2800. To put it another way, you have protected approximately $2800 of the original $3000 profit on your long stock position. While the order can be executed at a price higher or lower than the stop price once the market reaches the specified price, in most cases a sell stop order is executed at the stop price.

You do not have to wait until the price reaches its peak before entering a protective sell stop order. You can place the order when you purchase the stock to limit your losses if an unanticipated downturn occurs. Or you can enter successively higher sell stop orders as the market price of the stock rises, canceling those that were entered when the stock was trading at a lower price. This strategy will provide you with continual protection.

Buy Stop Order. A buy stop order is used to protect profits on a short stock position. As illustrated in Figure 3.8, you have sold short 100 shares of ABC stock at $50 per share and the price has declined to $34, yielding a $1600 profit. Concerned that a price rise might cause you to lose the

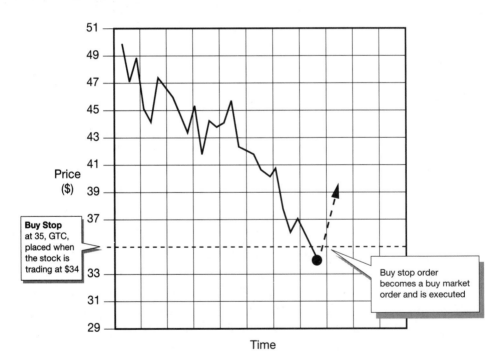

FIGURE 3.8 Strategic placement of a buy stop order protecting the profits on a short stock position. The graph shows that the 100 shares you sold short at $50 per share have declined to $34, indicated by the bullet. The dotted line indicates the anticipated price rise that would adversely affect your gains. In order to protect the profits (or limit the losses), you place a buy stop order at $35, above the current market price.

gain, you place a buy stop order at $35, above the current market price of the stock. If the market price of ABC stock rises from $34 to $35 per share, the buy stop order will become a market order to buy and will be executed at the stock's then-current market price. If the stock were bought in at $35, you would be left with a gross profit of $1500, having limited the losses to $100 ($1 per share).

Using the same strategies described for a sell stop order, you can enter a protective buy stock order when a short position is first established or enter them successively as the stock price declines to protect your position against an unexpected upturn.

Stop orders have some of the same risks as limit orders. If the market does not reach the stop price, the order will never be executed. This is not a major concern, however. Because stop orders are used largely to protect profits, they would remain unexecuted only if the stock were moving in a profitable direction for you.

A greater risk is that the stop order may be executed at a price significantly lower (in the case of a sell stop order) or higher (in the case of a buy stop order) than the stop price. Remember that unlike limit orders, stop orders become market orders when the stock reaches the specified price. If the stock price is moving quickly and many investors have entered stop orders at a given price, the market price at which the stop order may be executed can differ significantly from the stop price. This would be caused by the increased buying or selling that result from the execution of a large number of stop orders standing in the market at a specific price.

Perhaps the greatest risk in using a stop order is that the order may be executed on one of the small reversals that occur in the normal price movement of a stock. As all of the graphs have shown, a stock's price action is characterized by a series of small rises and falls. If an order's stop price is placed too close to the stock's current market price, the order may be executed during one of these small, insignificant reversals, thereby prematurely liquidating the position that you sought to protect. This could cost you profits as well as additional commissions if you choose to reestablish your original stock position.

In addition to protecting existing stock positions by liquidating them, stop orders can be used to establish new positions. Technical analysts enter buy and sell stop orders in anticipation of a significant short-term rise or decline in a stock value. A technician will place a buy stop order above a resistance level so that he or she can purchase the stock during the early phase of a significant price rise. He or she enters a sell short stop order below a support level in order to sell short at the beginning of a short-term decline. (This subject is discussed in Chapter 6.)

Figure 3.9 summarizes how market orders, limit orders, and stop orders are placed in relation to a stock's current market price or trading range.

In conclusion, when you enter stop or limit orders, which will be executed only if and when the stock trades at the specified price, keep the following four points in mind:

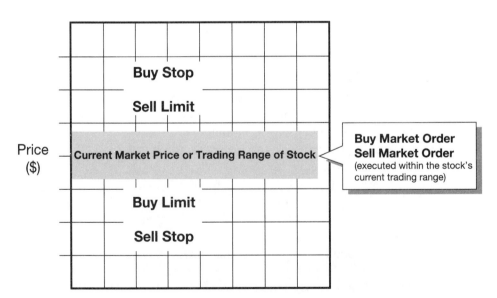

FIGURE 3.9 Summary of a strategic placement of market, limit, and stop orders. Market orders to buy or sell are executed within the market's trading range. Sell limit and buy stop orders are placed above the current market. Buy limit and sell stop orders are placed below the current market price.

1. Unless a time notation is specified for these orders, they are considered day orders and will be canceled at the end of the trading day if they are not executed.

2. No execution will occur unless the stock trades at or through the limit price or the stop price.

3. The stop or limit prices should be chosen with care so that they are not executed prematurely.

4. If the market is moving quickly, these orders may be executed at prices that are different from the specified limit price or stop price.

Investment Strategies

"What is the best way to invest in stock?" and "Do I really have to read *The Wall Street Journal* every day?" These are two of the questions asked most frequently by beginning investors. The answers, especially to the first question, often surprise many people interested in the stock market. There is no perfect or best investment strategy for everyone. Even among the strategies used most frequently by beginning investors, some are only more or less speculative than others. And the frequency with which a person must follow the market—that is, read the financial news—is a function of the speculative characteristics and time frame of an investment. Usually the more speculative and short-term the strategy is, the more closely it must be followed.

This chapter presents the most common beginning investment strategies, starting with those considered least speculative (and uncomplicated) and then proceeding to the most speculative:

1. Buy and hold, with dividend reinvestment.
2. Dollar-cost averaging.
3. Constant-dollar plan.
4. Constant-ratio plan.
5. Buying on margin.
6. Short selling.

The strategy that you choose should be in keeping with your investment objectives, financial means, time horizon, and risk tolerance. Additionally, consider how often you want to read or monitor the financial news.

BUY AND HOLD

The merits of buying high-quality stocks and holding them for the long term are seldom addressed. Yet this strategy can produce substantial returns, without your having to read the financial press every day or even every month. In fact, it is the passive management aspect of this investment strategy that is attractive to many people. It also minimizes timing risk—deciding when is the "best" time to buy or sell an investment. The success of the buy-and-hold strategy depends on three key elements: (1) the long-term trend of the stock market, (2) the characteristics of the stocks chosen, and (3) dividend reinvestment.

Price Appreciation

Historically, the stock market has moved upward, continually increasing in value over time. Clearly there have been market crashes (October 1929), bear markets (January 1973–December 1974), market breaks (October 1987), and market corrections (October 1989 and July 1996), when the prices of all securities plummeted precipitously. Following each decline, however, the market recovered and moved still higher. Anyone who owned shares or a portfolio of stocks that reflected the broad movement of the market has seen their value steadily increase through the highs and lows of the market. By simply being in the market during a period of sustained growth, such as the 1980s and early 1990s, a person would have seen the value of his or her investments increase. The buy-and-hold strategy puts you in a position to profit from this long-term upward trend of the stock market.

Selecting the stocks to buy and hold is somewhat more tricky. Look for shares of companies that have a high degree of financial strength (including good profit margins and steady earnings growth), are industry leaders or pacesetters in product sales and development, and are taking steps to improve their current market share and ensure long-term growth. The stocks that meet this description are generally blue-chip stocks, income stocks (particularly shares of public utilities and telephone companies), and established-growth stocks. A typical conservative, income-oriented investor might place more money in income stocks, while a slightly more aggressive, although still conservative, investor might invest more in established growth stocks. The key factor is that the stocks in these categories have the potential to increase in price and pay higher dividends over the long term. For an investor who buys and holds, these features certainly increase the likelihood that the strategy will be successful.

Dividend Reinvestment

One particularly beneficial aspect of the buy-and-hold strategy is the compounding effect that a *dividend reinvestment plan* can have on your return. Commonly referred to by the acronym DRP (pronounced "drip"), the plan is offered to existing stockholders by over 1000 companies, such as Procter & Gamble, American Express, Exxon, NationsBank, William Wrigley Jr. Company, Kemper, SmithKline Beecham, and British Petroleum. Instead of receiving dividends in cash, you can direct the company to use the money to buy additional common shares for you. Shortly after you buy a company's stock, you can call the shareholders' relations department of the corporation and request information about the company's dividend reinvestment plan. The corporation will send correspondence welcoming you as a shareholder and inviting you to participate in its dividend reinvestment plan.

dividend reinvestment plan a plan whereby a company's existing shareholders choose to have their cash dividend payments automatically reinvested in additional shares of the company's stock.

Through the plan, you can buy whole or fractional shares. Traditionally, a bank, acting as trustee for the company, holds the shares on your behalf. Every quarter the company sends you a statement showing the number of shares that were purchased by you through your brokerage firm and the number of shares held in the DRP on your behalf. At any time, you can request that certificates for the shares in the plan be issued in your name.

Most companies charge no brokerage fees for dividend reinvestment transactions; many, however, do assess a nominal handling fee. Usually you elect to participate in a dividend reinvestment plan when you first buy the company's stock, but you can elect to participate in the plan at any time while holding the shares. Over the long term, this essentially passive investment feature can increase your holdings in a company and thereby result in increased returns if the value of the stock appreciates.

The example that follows demonstrates the benefits of a dividend reinvestment plan for the small investor. In 1981, a friend bought 50 shares of Du Pont common stock at a market price of $30 per share. His total original investment was $1500 (excluding commissions). At the time of this purchase, he elected to participate in the company's dividend reinvestment plan. He did not invest any outside monies in the stock; he simply bought and held the original 50 shares and through the plan used his dividends to buy additional shares. In 1986, he decided to sell all of the stock, when its price had risen to $98 per share. As a result of dividend reinvestment, his equity ownership had increased to 96 shares. The gross proceeds from the sale were $9408 (96 shares × $98).

What was the investor's percentage return on his investment? Most investors would simply divide the profit made on the transaction by the amount of the original investment. As the following calculation shows, he made a 527 percent profit on the original $1500 investment.

$$\frac{\$9408 - \$1500}{\$1500} = \frac{\$7908}{\$1500} = 527\%$$

This calculation gives a sense of the gross return on the original investment, but it is not an accurate measure of return. The technically correct way to measure the return would be to compute the year-by-year return, taking into account both the compounding effect of the dividend reinvestment and any taxes that the investor must pay. (This is a complex formula that can be found in many advanced texts on yield or portfolio analysis.) Applied to our example, this formula shows that the combined dividend payment and capital appreciation on the stock provided a total return (exclusive of any tax considerations) of approximately 44 percent per year.

Not all companies offer dividend reinvestment plans. You can find out which companies have such plans by referring to Standard & Poor's *Directory of Dividend Reinvestment Plans*, Moody's *Annual Dividend Record*, or Evergreen Enterprises' *Directory of Companies Offering Dividend Reinvestment Plans*, among other publications. The terms of reinvestment plans vary from company to company, although the following provisions are typical:

1. The company (the issuer) pays or absorbs all brokerage fees and other costs associated with reinvesting the dividend.

2. The additional common shares acquired through the plan may be purchased at a slight discount from the stock's current market price.

3. Participants in the plan may "round up" fractional shares to full shares by depositing additional funds in the plan when the dividend is reinvested.

4. Participants may be permitted to invest additional money in the plan beyond the amount of the dividend. (Typically, this additional money can be added only at the time of the dividend reinvestment and the company sets minimum and maximum limits on the amount.)

5. Occasionally dividends from a company's preferred stock may be reinvested in the same company's common stock.

6. The shares that the investor acquires through dividend reinvestment can be sold through the plan without commissions, provided the individual has not taken physical delivery of the shares.

Dividend reinvestment offers small investors an easy way to build wealth. It works best when the company has a solid history of dividend payments and steady price appreciation.

Dividend reinvestment plans do have some disadvantages, particularly in the area of taxation. First, dividends are considered taxable income to the investor in the year in which they are paid out, even if they have been used to buy additional shares of a company's stock under a dividend reinvestment plan. The investor in the Du Pont example was taxed on the dividends paid each year, although he reinvested the money. And he paid taxes on the gross profits when he sold all of the shares accumulated under the plan. Second, the investor must keep records of the market price at which each additional share is purchased. When the shares are eventually sold, the amount of the investor's gain will not be simply the difference between the purchase price of the original shares and the later sale price of the accumulated shares, as the example implied. The Internal Revenue Service requires investors to compute the average cost basis of the total number of shares purchased during the holding period. The gain or loss is then the difference between the average cost of all shares and their sale price. If a person sells only some of the shares acquired through dividend reinvestment, different tax rules apply. A tax specialist should be sought for advice in this and similar situations. Despite these complex tax implications, dividend reinvestment plans provide a convenient and easy way for investors, particularly small investors, to build ownership in a company over a long period of time.

Stock Splits

Keep in mind that not all companies offer dividend reinvestment plans or pay dividends. Even without these, the number of shares that a long-term, buy-and-hold investor owns can increase through periodic stock splits. As discussed in Chapter 2, when the price of a stock becomes "too expensive" (this is a subjective valuation), the company's board of directors may vote to split the stock. In the case of a positive stock split, the number of shares that you own increases (see Figure 2.3) without your having to make any additional

investment in the company. If the price of the stock continues to increase after the split, then you own more shares on
which to make money. The decision to split a company's
stock is completely at the discretion of the company's board
of directors. There is no predetermined market price or time
at which a stock split occurs.

Price appreciation, dividend reinvestment, and stock
splits can result in substantial gains for the investor who
follows the buy-and-hold strategy. This largely passive,
long-term strategy should not be thought of as synonymous with what some people jokingly call the "buy-and-
neglect" strategy. Investing by neglect—buying small
amounts of different stocks, throwing the certificates in a
drawer, and forgetting that you own them—has been
known to provide some investors (or, depending on the
degree of negligence, their heirs) with surprising gains;
however, profits from this strategy are more the apoc-
ryphal exception than the rule.

From a practical point of view, an investor has (and
should use) the opportunity to review a company's performance, financial stability, earnings growth, dividends, the
objectives of the management, and prospects for future
growth every quarter. All reporting corporations are required by the Securities and Exchange Commission (SEC)
to send quarterly reports to their stockholders. If a company has a number of bad quarters in a row, sell and switch
to another company. There is, after all, no reason to stay on
the *Titanic* just because you bought a first-class ticket.

The buy-and-hold strategy is not a glamorous approach to investing. It will provide no great cocktail party
stories about one-day killings in the market. In fact, some
people might call it boring. Nonetheless, it has proved to
be one of the most convenient ways for small investors to
get started in stocks. Investors using this strategy must
maintain a long-term view of the market and stay the
course through the usual declines or reversals of the market. In a real sense, you are on autopilot after making the
initial decision. You do not have to follow the financial
news daily, weekly, or even monthly. Minimum vigilance
is required—just enough to monitor any changes in the
long-term prospects of the company that may warrant

selling the stock and investing in shares of a more suitable company.

A common practice among many buy-and-hold investors is to recoup their initial investment at some point. Usually after the price of the stock has increased substantially or after the shares have split and increased in value, some investors sell enough shares to get back the money they used to make the initial purchase. Other investors sell enough shares to recoup their initial investment plus any interest the money would have earned in a bank savings or money market account. The sales proceeds are typically returned to the investor's bank savings account where the money earns interest with little or no risk to principal. The logic and advantage of this practice are clear and simple. The initial money invested has been returned (with or without interest) to a safe, risk-free bank account. The remaining stock position is supported totally by the profits made on the original investment. If the stock's price declines, or the company goes bankrupt, then the investor feels that he or she has lost only the profits. Having recouped the original investment and placed it in a bank, the investor is realistically in the same position he or she would have been if the original money had simply been deposited in a bank.

DOLLAR-COST AVERAGING

dollar-cost averaging a strategy whereby a person invests the same amount of money at regular intervals in a stock or a mutual fund without regard for the price fluctuations of the security.

Dollar-cost averaging is a long-term strategy whereby you invest the same amount of money in a stock or mutual fund at regular intervals—monthly, quarterly, or semiannually. You buy the security without considering its market price at the time of each purchase. Consistency in the amount invested and the regularity of the payments is essential to the success of dollar-cost averaging in order to minimize pricing and timing risk.

Dollar-cost averaging works on the following simple principles: When the price of the security declines, the fixed investment amount buys more shares. Hence, your purchasing power expands. When the price of the security rises, the fixed investment amount buys fewer shares.

Consequently, your purchasing power contracts. Over the long term, you will discover that the cost of each share is lower than the average price per share during the investment period.

At first reading, this explanation of dollar-cost averaging sounds like a form of investment alchemy. After all, how can securities bought over a period of time cost less than their average price? The simple example that follows illustrates the mechanics and benefits of dollar-cost averaging.

You invest $200 on the first of each month, purchasing odd-lot shares of a particular company or mutual fund. As is characteristic of the market, the price fluctuates and is therefore different each time you buy the stock. Figure 4.1 shows the security's price per share on the first of each month and the number of shares purchased at that time. The investment period is 12 months.

You can see the benefit of this strategy by comparing the average cost per share over the period of investment

Month	Dollars Invested	Price Per Share	Number of Shares Bought
1	$200	$25.00	8.00
2	200	22.00	9.09
3	200	20.00	10.00
4	200	26.00	7.69
5	200	19.00	10.50
6	200	18.00	11.11
7	200	24.00	8.33
8	200	28.00	7.14
9	200	31.00	6.45
10	200	35.00	5.71
11	200	30.00	6.67
12	200	32.00	6.25
Total # of Payments	**Total $ Invested**	**Average Price Per Share**	**Total # of Shares Bought**
12	$2,400	$25.83 ($310 ÷ 12)	97

FIGURE 4.1 Example of 12-month investment period using dollar-cost averaging.

with the average price per share over the same period. Over 12 months, you invested $2400 ($200 × 12) and purchased 97 shares. The average price per share of the stock during this period was $25.83. This value is computed by adding the price per share for each month and dividing the total by the number of periodic investments made:

$$\$310 \div 12 = \$25.83$$

The average cost per share for this period was $24.74. This is computed by taking the total amount invested regularly during the 12-month period and dividing it by the number of shares purchased:

$$\$2400 \div 97 = \$24.74$$

Each share cost $1.09 less than the average price per share during the same period. Given that the price of a security always fluctuates, dollar-cost averaging virtually guarantees that your cost basis will always be lower than the average price per share.

The fact that the average cost is lower than the average price does not mean that you have a guaranteed gain. Such a guarantee would indeed be investment alchemy. If a stock's price trend is downward, for example, the average cost will still be lower than the average price; however, you would have an overall loss on the price of the stock. An examination of the first six months of the period illustrated in Figure 4.1 illustrates this point. The market price at the beginning of this period is $25.00 per share. In the sixth month, it is $18.00, a decrease of $7.00 per share. The average price per share during the six months is $21.67 ($130 ÷ 6). The average cost per share, however, is $21.28 ($1200 ÷ 56.38), $.39 lower than the average price. Dollar-cost averaging works in both a declining market and a rising market, and its benefits are enhanced when it is combined with a dividend reinvestment plan. However, the strategy offers no guarantees that you will make a profit on the investment or be protected against a loss.

There are several disadvantages to this method of

investing. First, dollar-cost averaging can limit your prof-its during a rising market. If the price of a stock increases sharply with only small reversals or declines, then the av-erage cost per share will most likely be higher than the market price of the stock when the strategy was started. In this case, dollar-cost averaging limits your gain. You would have had a greater profit by purchasing all of the shares at the outset.

This disadvantage is of minimal concern to most investors, however, for two reasons. First, dollar-cost av-eraging is primarily a means for a person with modest capital to begin investing regularly in the market. Typi-cally, this person is able to buy only a few shares at one time. Wealth building is usually the long-term objective. Second, the relationship between the initial cost and the average cost varies according to the market price fluctu-ation during the investment period. In Figure 4.1, the average cost ($24.74) is lower than the market price of the stock when the plan was initiated ($25.00). For each investor, the specific benefits of dollar-cost averaging will be somewhat different, depending on the length of the investment period, the fluctuations in the security's price during this time, and the amount of money in-vested.

Taxation is the second potential problem facing an investor who uses dollar-cost averaging. As with the buy-and-hold strategy, the taxable gain or loss is based on the average cost of the shares over the period of the invest-ment, which could be 5 years, 10 years, or more. If this strategy is combined with dividend reinvestment, then calculating the cost basis for tax purposes becomes even more complicated. Investors should keep all year-end statements that they receive from their brokerage houses or mutual funds. These statements usually show the aver-age cost of the shares purchased over the 12-month pe-riod.

Like the buy-and-hold strategy, dollar-cost averaging starts from the basic premise that the price or value of stocks has tended to increase over the long term. The suc-cess of this strategy depends on your discipline in adher-ing to the following principles:

1. Invest over a long period of time. Dollar-cost averaging should be continued for $7\frac{1}{2}$ to 10 years. This recommendation is based on the cyclical history of the market. Over the past 100 years, there have been about 40 recessions—that is, severe market corrections—or a downturn about every $2\frac{1}{2}$ years. If you continue to invest through about three of these corrections, the benefits of dollar-cost averaging tend to be maximized.

2. Invest at regular intervals; monthly or quarterly is preferable.

3. Invest regardless of the price of the stock.

4. Choose high-quality stocks or mutual funds. A company or fund with a history of regular dividend payments and the potential for capital appreciation is a good choice. Dividend reinvestment can enhance the benefits of dollar-cost averaging.

In addition, you should have sufficient fortitude so that you can stick to the plan through highs and lows, and sell out at the peak. Thus, the money allocated for dollar-cost averaging should be wealth-building funds, not committed funds.

Periodically, review the financial statements and other information of the relevant company to ascertain whether it is still in keeping with your stated investment objectives.

 constant-dollar plan an investment method in which a person maintains a fixed-dollar amount of a portfolio in stocks, buying and selling shares periodically to maintain the fixed-dollar amount.

CONSTANT-DOLLAR PLAN

Under the *constant-dollar plan*, you invest a fixed-dollar amount of a portfolio in stock. You then maintain the same level of investment in stock regardless of the extent of the increase or decrease in the price of the stock. If the price of the stock rises, you sell enough to reduce the total value of your shares to the constant-dollar amount and invest the sale proceeds in fixed-income securities. Traditionally, the fixed-income securities in which the money would be invested is bonds, but this narrow interpretation is no longer true. Depending on the economic climate, you may choose to put your money in certificates of deposit (CDs) or in cash-equivalent securities or keep it as cash in a money market account. If the price of the stock declines, you buy enough shares to return the total value of the stock to the constant-dollar amount. The funds used to buy these common shares do not come from the sale of the fixed-income securities. You must use money from other sources.

The benefit of this plan is that it forces you to take profits when a stock's price rises. Thus, the tendency of most investors to buy more shares in response to a price rise, and therefore buy at the peak price, is mitigated. Conversely, when the price of a stock declines, this plan dictates that you buy more shares, thereby allowing you to take advantage of the expanded purchasing power of your money. You are also *averaging down*: lowering the overall cost basis of the total shares in the portfolio. Throughout the term of this investment plan, the percentage of your portfolio invested in stocks and other investments will vary, as shown in Figure 4.2. When stock prices rise, prompting you to sell, the percentage of the portfolio invested in stock will decrease, and other investments will increase. When stock prices fall, prompting you to buy, the percentage invested in stock will increase, and other investments will decrease. The graphs at the top and bottom of the figure illustrate these relationships.

averaging down a strategy in which an investor lowers the average price paid per share of stock by purchasing more shares when the price declines.

Figure 4.2 illustrates how the constant-dollar plan works for an investor maintaining $50,000 of a portfolio in stocks and the remainder in bonds or other fixed-income securities. At the time the portfolio is established, the individual determines that he will restore the portfolio to the constant-dollar amount when the price of the stock rises or falls by 20 percent of his original investment. Hence, when the value of the shares increases $10,000 (20 percent), he sells some of them, returning the total value of the stock position to $50,000. The proceeds of the sale are reinvested in bonds. When the stock's value declines $10,000 (20 percent) below $50,000, the investor buys enough shares to restore the total value of the position to $50,000.

The success of this plan is based on the observation that over the long term, the price of stocks rises. As this price appreciation occurs, the constant-dollar plan forces

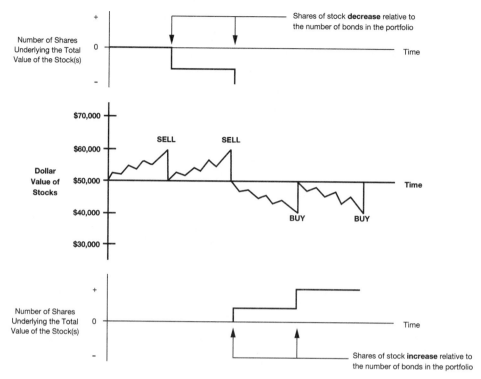

FIGURE 4.2 Constant-dollar plan.

you to take profits from speculative investments (stocks) and transfer them to less speculative securities (bonds, preferred stocks, certificates of deposit).

The investor in Figure 4.2 establishes a $100,000 portfolio, in which $50,000 will be constantly maintained in stocks and $50,000 in bonds. Assume that the prices of the stocks steadily appreciate. Each time the price reaches the constant-dollar level and activates the sell signal, the customer transfers the equity that exceeds the constant-dollar amount into bonds, with interest rates that are probably lower than the total return he is making on the stocks. In a prolonged bull market, an investor using the constant-dollar plan does not maximize profits. In fact, the overall or total return from the investment portfolio will be lower than if the money were left in stocks. However, the transfer of profits made on speculative investments (stocks) into safer vehicles (bonds) is an overriding investment objective of the relatively cautious investor who relies on the constant-dollar plan.

Selecting the stock or mutual fund that will enable this plan to work most effectively is not easy. Stocks with relatively stable prices are not the optimum choices for the constant-dollar plan. Instead, look for companies whose stock has good potential for long-term appreciation and whose market price tends to fluctuate.

Determining the constant-dollar value of the portfolio to maintain in stocks depends as usual on the degree of risk that you are willing to accept. If you are conservative and averse to risk, invest more money in fixed-income and cash-equivalent securities than in stocks. If your objective is focused more on growth, maintain a larger dollar amount of the portfolio in stocks. Additionally, your decision will be influenced by market conditions. If interest rates are low, stocks are a preferable investment because they offer an opportunity for growth.

Unlike the situation prevailing under the buy-and-hold and dollar-cost averaging strategies, price risk and timing risk become significant factors in the constant-dollar plan. For example, should you sell stocks after only a small price rise or wait for a bigger rise and more profits? Should you buy more shares after a brief decline or wait for a bigger price dip? This dilemma can be handled in two ways, both of them totally arbitrary. You can set percentages (e.g., 20 percent, 25 percent, 30 percent) or dollar values (e.g., $2500, $5000, $7000) of price increases and decreases that will serve, respectively, as automatic sell and buy signals. For example, if the price of a stock declines 20 percent, purchase enough shares to restore the stock's value to the constant-dollar amount. Or, instead of using percentage of gain or loss as signals, set intervals of time (e.g., quarterly, semiannually). At the beginning or end of each period, review the status of your investments in the portfolio and take the appropriate buy or sell action. Usually an investor selects one parameter—percentage, dollar value, or time—to prompt a review of the investment portfolio.

Setting the parameters discussed above reduces, or at least mitigates, price and timing risk. You no longer have to figure out whether the stock's price is going higher or lower or what is the best time to buy or sell. The review and reinvestment decisions are automatically made when the stock reaches the designated percentage or dollar value or at a designated period of time. These parameters also mitigate emotional risk—the risk that you might react inappropriately to a temporary sharp decline or rise in the market between review periods.

The most significant risk that remains is reinvestment risk. When, at the predetermined level, you sell the appreciating stock and buy fixed-income securities, you could be investing in a security that will provide a lower return than the stock. On the other hand, when the price declines, you could be buying more shares of a company or mutual fund whose suitability in view of your investment objectives has changed. Stock selection and a periodic review of the holdings are as essential to the success of this strategy as is the price fluctuation of the shares.

CONSTANT-RATIO PLAN

constant-ratio plan an investment method in which a person maintains a fixed ratio between stocks and bonds throughout the investment period, with regular adjustments made to compensate for different levels of price increases and decreases.

The *constant-ratio plan* is similar to the constant-dollar plan except that you maintain a fixed percentage of the portfolio invested in stocks and a fixed percentage invested in bonds—for example, 50 percent of the value of a portfolio in stocks and 50 percent in fixed-income securities. Another investor, following the recommended static asset allocation mix, would maintain 55 percent of the portfolio's value in stocks, 35 percent in bonds, and 10 percent in cash equivalents. The percentages chosen for each class of investment depend on each investor's objectives and risk tolerance and the climate for various investments at that time. A conservative investor allocates a larger percentage to fixed-income securities; an aggressive individual invests a higher percentage of dollars in stocks.

The ratio that is established must be maintained notwithstanding both the appreciation and depreciation of the securities. In the example in Figure 4.3, an investor has allocated 50 percent of her $60,000 portfolio to stock and 50 percent to bonds. She reviews the ratio of stocks to bonds at the beginning of each quarter and then buys and sells as

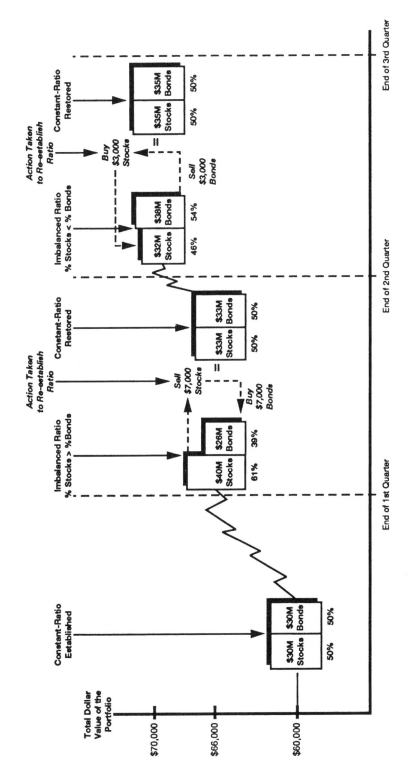

FIGURE 4.3 Constant-ratio plan.

103

appropriate to restore the ratio. During the first quarter, the value of the stocks rises to $40,000, and the bonds decrease in value to $26,000. The total value of the portfolio is now $66,000; however, the ratio of stocks to bonds is no longer 50:50. It is now 61 percent ($40,000 ÷ $66,000) stocks and 39 percent bonds ($26,000 ÷ $66,000). In order to restore the portfolio's value to the 50:50 constant ratio, she sells $7000 of the stocks, reducing the total value of the stock position to $33,000. She uses the proceeds to buy $7000 of bonds, raising their total value to $33,000. Thus, the 50:50 ratio of stocks to bonds is reestablished.

If the bonds had appreciated in value and the stocks had declined, as illustrated during the third quarter of Figure 4.3, the investor would sell the bonds and use the proceeds to buy enough stock to restore the constant ratio.

As with the constant-dollar plan, price risk and time risk are significant factors under the constant-ratio plan. However, the effect of these factors can be minimized by using the same strategy recommended before: setting arbitrary points—percentages, dollar values, or time periods—that trigger buying and selling. Also, prudent investors sell stocks or bonds that do not meet performance expectations over an established period of time.

Significant reinvestment risk is associated with this investment plan. You must carefully select the stocks and bonds that will comprise the portfolio. Short-term fluctuations in the prices of the securities during a general upward trend enhance the results that you will obtain using this strategy.

Keep in mind that the constant-ratio plan, like the constant-dollar plan, is a long-term strategy. The two basic premises are that the prices of stocks and bonds tend to fluctuate and that the values of stocks tend to increase over time. This strategy does not guarantee a gain or maximize your profit, but it does enable you to take profits on an appreciating class of securities and then to reinvest them in another class in which the buying power of the profits is greater. Over the long term, you increase the number of stocks and bonds in the portfolio and thereby expand the gains that can be made from the rise in the value of the securities.

At least annually, investors using the constant-ratio plan should review the percentages allocated to each class of security and to the securities in each class. They need to make certain that the individual securities and the percentages allocated among investments are suitable, given any changes in their objectives as well as the anticipated long-term trend of the stock market.

Many brokerage firms suggest an asset allocation plan suitable to the state of the market at the time. For example, at the writing of this book, Merrill Lynch recommends the following allocation for conservative growth-oriented investors with $100,000 or more: 55 percent stock, 40 percent bonds, and 5 percent cash and equivalents. Other investment advisers have a similar matrix of asset allocation.

BUYING STOCK ON MARGIN

In general, buying on margin is a suitable strategy for only experienced investors. It is a way for these investors, especially those with conservative, growth-oriented goals, to allocate some funds (**never** more than 10 percent) to high-risk–high-growth investments.

Buying stock on margin is buying stock by making a partial payment of its purchase price. You use your own money to make a "down payment," called the *initial margin requirement*. Currently set at 50 percent of a stock's purchase price, the initial margin requirement is set by the Federal Reserve Board under *Regulation T*. The brokerage firm loans you the remaining 50 percent of the stock's value. This loan is called the margin account's *debit balance* and is secured by the stock that you purchase.

As long as you hold the shares, you are charged interest on the debit balance. As with a credit card balance, the interest charge is computed daily and added to the amount of the outstanding loan. Hence, the debit balance increases over your holding period. The rate of interest charged is usually a few percentage points above the *call loan rate*. Also referred to as the "broker loan rate," this is the rate that banks charge brokerage firms for loans collateralized by marginable securities. The firm earns the dif-

initial margin requirement the percentage of a stock's purchase price that must be deposited when initially buying or selling short stock on margin. Set by the FRB under Regulation T.

Regulation T the Federal Reserve's regulation that gives it the power to set the initial margin requirement on most corporate stocks and bonds.

debit balance the balance owed to the brokerage firm by a customer who purchases securities on margin.

call loan rate the interest rate that banks charge brokerage firms for loans collateralized by marginable securities.

ference between the rate it pays to the bank and the rate it charges investors who trade on margin. Like all other short-term interest rates, the call loan rate changes frequently. Figure 4.4 shows the relationship of the broker call loan rate to other interest rates during a period when short-term interest rates were low. Usually the call loan rate is less than the bank's *prime rate*.

prime rate
the short-term interest rate that commercial banks charge their most creditworthy business customers for unsecured loans.

Because shares bought on margin are not fully paid, they are never held in customer name. They are always held in street name. As we shall see later, this situation provides the brokerage firm with some protection should the investor fail to repay the loan.

Treasury Bills	**5.48%**
Discount rate on T-Bills trading in the secondary market	
Discount Rate	**5.50%**
Interest rate the Federal Reserve charges member banks for loans	
Commercial Paper	**5.75%**
Discount rate on unsecured high-quality, short-term debt issued by a corporation	
Certificate of Deposit	**5.75%**
Average yield on negotiable CDs with one month to maturity and in amounts of $1 million or more	
Federal Funds	**5.79%**
Interest rate for overnight loans among commercial banks	
Broker Call Loans	**7.25-8.00%**
Rate banks charge brokerage firms for loans collateralized by securities	
Prime Rate	**8.50%**
Rate banks charge their most creditworthy business customers	

FIGURE 4.4 Short-term interest rates (during a period when rates were considered moderate to low).

The advantage of buying stocks on margin is leverage. You use a relatively small amount of money to control securities that have a much greater value. Any increase in a stock's value results in a greater percentage gain on each dollar invested than would be made if the securities were fully paid. Suppose that two investors buy 100 shares of the same stock that has a market price of $40 per share. Investor A pays in full for the shares, depositing $4000 in his account. Investor B buys the stock on margin, depositing $2000, the 50 percent Regulation T initial margin requirement, in her account. The shares appreciate by $5 each. For investor A, the $500 total price increase ($5 × 100 shares) is a 12.5 percent return ($500 ÷ $4000) on the money invested. For investor B, who bought her shares on margin, the $5 per share increase provides a 25 percent return ($500 ÷ $2000) on each dollar invested. Thus, under the current 50 percent initial margin requirement, buying stock on margin doubles an investor's potential gross return on each dollar invested. Of course, commissions, interest on the margin loan, and taxes must be paid from the gain.

Buying on margin also doubles an investor's price risk. Using the same example, let's examine what would happen if the price of the stock were to fall $5 per share. Investor A, who paid in full for the 100 shares, would lose $500 of his $4000 investment—a 12.5 percent loss ($500 ÷ $4000). Investor B, who purchased the shares on margin, would also lose $500. However, since she put up only $2000—50 percent of the stock's value—her percentage loss would be 25 percent ($500 ÷ $2000), double the percentage loss incurred if the stock had been purchased fully paid. Clearly, leverage can provide investors with a higher percentage gain if a stock's price rises—but it also increases the percentage loss if a stock declines in value. This increased risk makes buying stock on margin more speculative than buying stock fully paid.

When you buy stock on margin, you must deposit the initial margin requirement promptly—within three business days of the trade (regular way settlement). If you do not meet the terms of regular way settlement, Regulation T states that the brokerage firm must either liquidate (sell) your position and freeze the account for at least 90 days or, if warranted, obtain an extension. You are liable for any loss that occurs during the settlement period.

The benefits and risks of buying stock on margin will become clear by following the price fluctuations of a simulated trade using Home Depot, Inc. (HD) common stock. Assume that HD's current price per share is $40. You buy 100 shares of HD on margin and deposit $2000 in your margin account. The brokerage firm lends you the remaining $2000 of the value of the securities. In the firm's *margin department*, your account looks as follows after this transaction:

Current market value (100 at $40)	$4000
− Debit balance	2000
= Equity in the account	$2000

The margin percentage, computed by dividing the equity in the account by the stock's current market value ($2000 ÷ $4000), is 50 percent. Thus, you have met the Regulation T initial margin requirement.

The value of the shares in a margin account is *marked to market* daily. This means that the firm's margin department recomputes the equity in the account at the end of every business day based on the stock's closing price in the market. At the same time, interest on the debit balance accrues daily. Hence, the equity in an investor's margin account changes continuously.

Let's examine what happens in the margin account when the market price of HD shares rises by $10 to $50. Your account would look as follows:

Current market value (100 at $50)	$5000
− Debit balance	2000
= Equity in the account	$3000

Notice that the debit balance does not change, except for the interest added. An increase or decrease in a stock market price does not affect the amount of the loan that you obtained when you initially purchased the stock.

As a result of the price increase from $40 to $50 per

margin department a division of a brokerage firm that computes an investor's equity in a margin account daily and sends out margin or maintenance calls, as appropriate.

mark to market the process by which a brokerage firm computes the value of the shares in an investor's account based on the daily closing price.

share, you have a $1000 *unrealized gain* on the 100 shares of HD. This is a 50 percent gross return ($1000 ÷ $2000) on the money invested—twice as much as it would have been if you had bought the securities fully paid. If you are satisfied with this gain, you can now take your profits, turning them into a *realized gain* by selling long the 100 shares. Part of the proceeds is used to pay off the debit balance and the remainder is released to you.

When you purchase stock on margin, you do not have to sell the securities in order to be able to use the unrealized gains. This feature is one of the benefits of buying stock on margin. The process by which unrealized gains are made usable is simple, although the explanation sounds complex. Careful attention is required to understand how this feature of a margin account works.

As a stock's price rises, a portion of the unrealized gain, called "excess equity," is made available to you as a line of credit—similar to the line of credit that some banks provide to home owners against the appreciated equity of a house. This credit account is called a *special memorandum account*; hence the "excess equity" is commonly referred to by abbreviation for the account—SMA. The amount of the unrealized profits that is made available as a credit line in the special memorandum account is that portion of the account's equity that exceeds what would be the initial margin requirement on the stock at its current market price.

The following example clarifies this point. After the price rise, the current total market value of HD is $5000, and the equity in the margin account is $3000. If you were to purchase 100 shares of HD at the current market value, the initial margin requirement would be $2500. The current equity ($3000) exceeds this requirement ($2500) by $500. The SMA or credit available to you is thus $500. The formula for computing SMA when buying stock on margin is:

$$SMA = Equity - \begin{pmatrix} \text{Stock's current market value} \\ \times \text{ Reg. T margin requirement} \end{pmatrix}$$

How can you use this excess equity or SMA? There are basically two choices, both of which require the broker's approval:

 unrealized gain the profit resulting from an increase in the value of a security position that is still being held.

 realized gain the cash profit resulting from the liquidation of a stock position.

 special memorandum account an account used to show the excess equity or line of credit that an investor has in a margin account.

1. *Withdraw part or all of the SMA as cash.* In the HD example, you can withdraw the $500 of SMA as cash. This is the equivalent of getting a cash advance on a credit card. Your debit balance increases, and additional interest begins to accrue from the first day of withdrawal.

2. *Buy shares of other marginable stocks.* With $500 of SMA, you can purchase shares with a total market value of $1000—two times the amount of SMA. You pay for half of the value of the stock using the SMA credit line, and the firm provides a loan for the remaining value. The account's debit balance therefore increases twice as much as the amount of the SMA used—a good deal for the firm.

The maximum amount of stock that a customer can purchase in a margin account using the SMA (i.e., without depositing any additional cash) is called the *buying power.* With Regulation T currently at 50 percent, this means that an investor's buying power is equal to twice the amount of SMA in the account.

buying power the maximum amount of securities a customer can purchase in a margin account using the SMA and not depositing any additional cash.

Buying power = SMA ÷ Reg. T margin requirement

As SMA is created in a margin account, buying power increases. A customer must call his or her brokerage firm to find out how much buying power the margin account has on any given day. The amount changes as, every business day, the brokerage firm's margin department "marks to market" the stock positions in the account based on the fluctuation in the stock's price.

Keep in mind that SMA is nothing more than a credit line backed by a portion of the unrealized profits on a customer's long stock position in a margin account. And like a credit line on a credit card, every time you use the SMA, your indebtedness increases. Therefore, you cannot use SMA to pay off or reduce your debit balance. The debit is reduced only when you sell stock out of the margin account or deposit cash into the account.

When the price of stock purchased in a margin account declines, recall that your loss on each dollar invested mounts more quickly. In order to protect both the customer and the brokerage firm, the New York Stock Exchange (NYSE) and the National Association of Securities Dealers (NASD) set a *minimum maintenance margin*. This is the lowest percentage to which the equity in the account can fall in relation to the stock's current market value before the firm sends the customer a *maintenance call*. For an account in which a customer buys stock on margin, the NYSE and the NASD currently set the minimum maintenance margin at 25 percent of a stock's current market value. Individual firms often set more stringent requirements, such as 30 percent or 35 percent.

A maintenance call is sent when an account's margin percentage falls below the minimum maintenance margin. In response, the investor usually deposits enough additional cash in the account to return the margin percentage to the minimum requirement. An investor must satisfy this call within three business days; otherwise, the firm liquidates a portion of the person's position. The individual is liable for all losses incurred on the trade during this time.

When the margin percentage in the account is between the initial amount and the minimum, no maintenance call is sent out on existing positions. At this point, you can still buy stock on margin by depositing the required 50 percent initial margin requirement in the account. However, restrictions are placed on the amount of proceeds that can be withdrawn from the account when shares are sold.

Using the HD example, I will illustrate how a price decrease prompts a brokerage firm to send a maintenance call to an investor. You have bought HD on margin at a price of $40 per share; your margin account looks as follows:

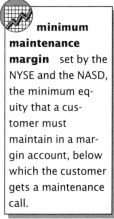

minimum maintenance margin set by the NYSE and the NASD, the minimum equity that a customer must maintain in a margin account, below which the customer gets a maintenance call.

maintenance call a demand from a brokerage firm that an investor deposit enough cash in a margin account to restore the account to the minimum maintenance margin following an adverse price move.

Current market value (100 at $40)	$4000
− Debit balance	2000
= Equity in the account	$2000

The price of HD subsequently drops from $40 to $25 per share; now your margin account looks as follows:

Current market value (100 at $25)	$2500
– Debit balance	2000
= Equity in the account	$ 500

The margin percentage in the account is now 20 percent ($500 ÷ $2500), which is below the 25 percent minimum margin requirement. The brokerage firm immediately sends a maintenance call to you, requesting that you deposit enough cash to restore the account to the required minimum maintenance level of 25 percent. Using the current market value of $25 per share, the margin department would compute the equity necessary to meet the 25 percent minimum. That amount is $625 ($2500 × 25 percent). The current equity in the account is $500. Thus, the amount of the maintenance call sent to you would be $125 ($625 – $500).

At the end of the section explaining the effect of a price increase on a margin account, I noted that all cash deposits in the account are used to reduce the debit balance. Once you meet the $125 margin call, your account would look as follows:

Current market value (100 at $25)	$2500
– Debit balance (*reduced by $125*)	1875
= Equity in the account	$ 625

The margin percentage is now 25 percent ($625 ÷ $2500). Your deposit in response to the maintenance call reduced the debit balance, thereby increasing your equity to 25 percent of the current market value.

People who tend to buy stock on margin are speculators and traders whose investment objectives are usually short-term. They buy on margin in anticipation of a price increase in order to get a bigger bang for each buck. For long-term investors, buying on margin is not nearly as attractive. One reason is the interest charged on the debit balance. It compounds during the holding period. If the dividends do not cover the interest cost, the investor's potential return is steadily reduced by the increasing indebtedness. A second reason that buying on margin is less attractive to long-term investors is the constant risk that a steep price decline could prompt a large maintenance call, and the investor might be forced to sell part or all of his or her stocks in order to meet the call.

For an investor who has previously paid in full for stocks that could have been purchased on margin, a steep price decline can be beneficial. In theory, such a decline is generally interpreted to mean that the price of the stock is at a low point. By now placing the fully paid securities in a margin account, the customer can use additional buying power created by the SMA (special memorandum account) to "double up" on the number of shares owned. When the subsequent price rise occurs, the investor's doubled holdings yield double the profits.

The calculations were presented in this section as a means of clarifying the workings of a margin account and enabling you to understand better the rewards and risks associated with margin purchases. Figure 4.5 shows the various margin requirements and summarizes the effect

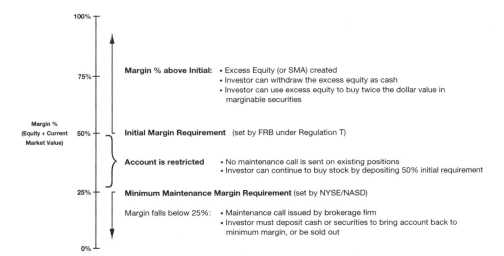

FIGURE 4.5 Effects of fluctuation in margin percentage of a margin account in which a customer buys securities. Note that the typical brokerage firm's minimum maintenance margin requirement is more restrictive (higher) than that set by the NYSE and NASD.

that the rise and fall of a stock's price has on investment activities that you can perform in a margin account.

Margin accounts are available through both full-service and discount brokerage firms. Be aware, however, that a firm's in-house margin requirements, especially the minimum maintenance requirement, may be more restrictive (higher) than those set forth by the New York Stock Exchange and the National Association of Securities Dealers.

SELLING SHORT

Selling short is a strategy investors use to profit during a price decline. Its underlying principle is an inversion of the old "buy low, sell high" axiom. In anticipation of a price rise, you first buy a stock at a low price and later sell it at a higher price—you hope. In anticipation of a price decline, however, you first sell short stock at a high price and later buy it back at a lower price.

For most people, this strategy seems to go against the natural order of investing. The difficulty in understanding short selling is captured in an often-asked question: "How can I first sell a stock when I don't own it?" The answer is that you borrow the shares from a brokerage firm or another investor who has authorized such a loan, and then you sell the shares in the market. Later you repurchase the same number of shares that you borrowed and return them to the lender's account. Although the lender has given permission for such a loan, he or she is unaware of when the loan has been made. The lender continues to receive all the benefits of owning the stock, including dividend payments, voting rights, and preemptive rights.

As Figure 4.6 illustrates, the process of borrowing the shares for a short sale is handled totally by the brokerage firm's operations area and is therefore invisible to you. You simply place the order to sell short stock with the broker, and it is executed. Short sales can be performed only in a margin account, appropriately called a *short margin account*. Furthermore, like an investor who buys stock on margin, a short seller must deposit the 50 percent initial margin required by the Federal Reserve.

short margin account a margin account in which a customer sells stock short.

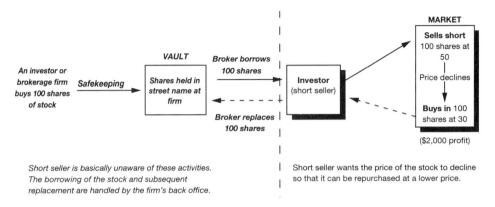

FIGURE 4.6 The mechanics of a successful short sale.

Short sellers hope that a stock's price will decline. If it does, they will profit from the difference between the proceeds from the initial sale and the later cost of repurchasing the shares. Short sellers make their maximum profit if the price of the stock drops to zero.

If the price of the stock rises, however, short sellers lose. They can then repurchase the stock only at a cost that is higher than the proceeds received from the original sale. Also, since short sales are performed only in a margin account, an adverse price move can prompt a maintenance call if the margin percentage falls below the 30 percent minimum maintenance margin set by the New York Stock Exchange (NYSE) and the National Association of Securities Dealers (NASD) for most short positions. (The minimum maintenance margin for an account in which an investor sells short—30 percent—is different from that in which a customer buys securities on margin—25 percent. The greater risk associated with selling short is the reason for its higher minimum maintenance.)

Because the price of a stock can rise an unlimited amount, at least in theory, an investor who sells short faces an unlimited potential loss. In contrast, the most an outright purchaser of stock can lose is the total value of the investment, which would occur only if the price of the stock drops to zero. This potential for unlimited loss makes short selling far riskier than any of the other purchasing strategies that already have been presented.

Because of its highly speculative characteristics, short selling is considered unsuitable for beginning investors. In fact, this strategy is rarely used by the public. It is used primarily by professional traders to hedge existing long stock positions against a price decline or as a tax strategy. (See selling short against the box in Chapter 6.) Investors interested in this strategy should read *Selling Short* by Joseph Walker (Wiley, 1991) for an explanation of its risks and rewards.

HOW MOST PEOPLE INVEST

Most people buy stocks in a cash account, paying the full (i.e., 100 percent) purchase price. They usually make their first purchase based on the recommendation of a relative or friend. This first trade usually is for a small amount of stock. If it is successful, the person typically follows the friend's or relative's next recommendation and buys more shares than the first time. Eventually this cycle comes to an abrupt end when the person loses a substantial portion, if not all, of the money invested. From these types of experiences arise many of the horror stories about investing in stock.

The discipline and research required to develop a rational, long-term investment plan is often undermined by the desire for quick profits. Indeed, investing in stocks is usually less exciting than speculating in them. For the average investor, a long-term view will usually involve less anxiety and less need to follow the investment daily.

"Paper investing" is one good way for those who are deeply skeptical about investing in stock to get started. Select an investment strategy and, using a mock investment portfolio that is in keeping with your financial means, choose stock suitable to your stated objectives. Researching your selections is an essential part of this exercise; there must be a logical basis for making your selections. Follow the investments over a period of time to see how the strategy works and how your choices perform. This is a safe, anxiety-free way for beginners to develop the confidence to invest in stocks.

Chapter

Fundamental Analysis

F undamental analysis is the largely quantitative evaluation of a company's financial condition. It is used to determine the company's intrinsic value and to predict any changes in its anticipated earnings. Fundamentalists hold that any changes in earnings will be reflected in the dividend the company pays to its shareholders and in the market price of the stock. If earnings fall short of expectations and the decline is thought to be long-term or permanent, investors will sell the stock because they anticipate that the company will announce lower dividends at the next dividend declaration date. Thus, the sell-off causes the price of the company's stock to fall. If earnings rise above expectations, more investors will want to buy the stock. They believe that the value of the company and its dividend payments will increase. As a result, the price of the stock rises.

Predicting whether a company will meet its sales, earnings, and growth targets and how this will affect the price of its stock is the job of professional analysts. They examine many of the company's reports that are filed with the Securities and Exchange Commission (SEC), including the quarterly reports (10Qs) and the annual reports (10Ks), paying careful attention to the audited *balance sheet*, audited *income statement*, and *cash flow statement*, and their accompanying footnotes. These statements summarize a company's current financial status. These hard data are analyzed in tandem with more qualitative information, such

 balance sheet a constantly changing snapshot of the company's financial condition that shows all of its assets, liabilities, and stockholders' equity.

income statement a summary of all of the income and expenses of a business for a period of time, usually one year; also called a "profit-and-loss statement."

cash flow statement a statement of the sources and uses of cash by a business for a period of time.

as the effectiveness of the company's management, the company's market share, its research and development (R&D) plans, its marketing efforts, and the economic outlook for that particular industry. The analyst's objective is to predict the long-term growth prospects of the company—its sales, earnings, and dividend payments as well as its assets and liquidation values—and thereby predict the price movement of its stock.

When most beginning investors hear this explanation of fundamental analysis, their almost uniform consensus is that a person needs to know accounting or have a master's degree in business administration (M.B.A.) in order to perform fundamental analysis. This is true only if the individual works as a professional securities analyst. Much of the information that these analysts evaluate, as well as their conclusions, are widely available to the public through such information services as Value Line and Standard & Poor's. Additionally, your broker can provide this information and the brokerage firm's own research to you at no cost.

When a beginning investor first looks at the information published and distributed by these companies (Figures 5.1 and 5.2), it seems overwhelming because of the small, dense type. However, keep in mind that this information is published for individuals with various levels of investment experience. Beginning investors should not feel compelled to perform fundamental analysis per se. Instead, they should learn which information is most essential and attempt to understand the implications of that information on the decision to buy or sell a stock.

Here are six fundamental measures you, as a beginning investor, should examine closely:

1. Earnings per share and earnings growth pattern.
2. Price-earnings ratio.
3. Earnings yield.
4. Sales–to–price per share ratio.
5. Book value.
6. Dividend yield (also called current yield).

Coca-Cola

562

NYSE Symbol **KO**

In S&P 500

04-APR-97

Industry:
Beverages

Summary: Coca-Cola is the world's largest soft-drink company and has a sizable fruit juice business. Its bottling interests include a 45% stake in NYSE-listed Coca-Cola Enterprises.

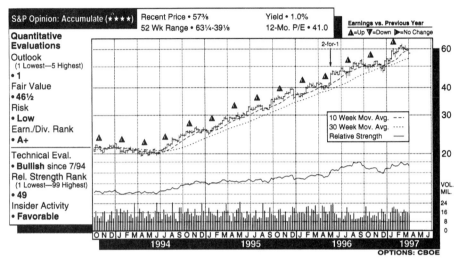

S&P Opinion: Accumulate (★★★★)

Recent Price • 57⅜
52 Wk Range • 63¼-39⅛

Yield • 1.0%
12-Mo. P/E • 41.0

Quantitative Evaluations

Outlook
(1 Lowest—5 Highest)
• **1**

Fair Value
• **46½**

Risk
• **Low**

Earn./Div. Rank
• **A+**

Technical Eval.
• **Bullish** since 7/94

Rel. Strength Rank
(1 Lowest—99 Highest)
• **49**

Insider Activity
• **Favorable**

Earnings vs. Previous Year
▲=Up ▼=Down ▶=No Change

10 Week Mov. Avg. – – –
30 Week Mov. Avg. · · · ·
Relative Strength —

OPTIONS: CBOE

Overview - 04-FEB-97

Operating revenues are projected to grow by approximately 5%-8% in 1997, as an 8% increase in gallon shipments and higher prices are offset in part by possible unfavorable currency exchange translations. Operating profit margins are expected to widen, aided by the recent sale of certain low-margin bottling operations and operating efficiencies derived from recent restructuring actions, and operating profits should advance at a mid-teen rate. Net proceeds realized (approximately $600 million) from the pending sale of the company's 49% interest in its Cadbury Schweppes bottling joint venture should allow for modest debt reduction and further share repurchases. Assuming a modest reduction in the number of weighted shares outstanding, earnings per share of $1.65 are estimated for 1997, up nearly 18% from 1996's $1.40.

Valuation - 04-FEB-97

Despite the stock's rich P/E multiple, which is high relative to that of other companies and to its own past performance, we remain bullish on near-term and long-term prospects. With expectations of continued slow U.S. economic growth, we expect investors to continue to seek companies with dependable earnings growth in both good times and bad, like KO. The company's earnings growth consistency over the years has been bolstered by its vast global reach (in nearly all countries) and well-recognized brand names. We expect KO's rising earnings, consistent high return on equity, dependable dividend growth, and strong balance sheet to continue to make the stock attractive for the long-term for virtually all accounts.

Key Stock Statistics

S&P EPS Est. 1997	1.65	Tang. Bk. Value/Share	2.18
P/E on S&P Est. 1997	34.8	Beta	0.68
Dividend Rate/Share	0.56	Shareholders	22,600
Shs. outstg. (M)	2488.2	Market cap. (B)	$137.8
Avg. daily vol. (M)	3.597	Inst. holdings	47%

Value of $10,000 invested 5 years ago: $ 30,583

Fiscal Year Ending Dec. 31

	1996	1995	1994	1993	1992	1991
Revenues (Million $)						
1Q	4,194	3,854	3,352	3,060	2,770	2,480
2Q	5,253	4,936	4,342	3,899	3,550	3,040
3Q	4,656	4,895	4,461	3,629	3,510	3,170
4Q	4,443	4,333	4,017	3,373	3,240	2,880
Yr.	18,546	18,018	16,172	13,957	13,070	11,570
Earnings Per Share ($)						
1Q	0.29	0.25	0.20	0.17	0.15	0.12
2Q	0.42	0.36	0.29	0.26	0.22	0.18
3Q	0.39	0.32	0.28	0.22	0.21	0.17
4Q	0.31	0.26	0.22	0.18	0.15	0.13
Yr.	1.40	1.18	0.99	0.84	0.71	0.60

Next earnings report expected: mid April

Dividend Data (Dividends have been paid since 1893.)

Amount ($)	Date Decl.	Ex-Div. Date	Stock of Record	Payment Date
0.125	Apr. 18	Jun. 12	Jun. 15	Jul. 01 '96
0.125	Jul. 18	Sep. 11	Sep. 15	Oct. 01 '96
0.125	Oct. 18	Nov. 26	Dec. 01	Dec. 15 '96
0.140	Feb. 20	Mar. 12	Mar. 15	Apr. 01 '97

A Division of The McGraw-Hill Companies

FIGURE 5.1, page 1 Standard & Poor's Stock Report. Reproduced with permission of Standard & Poor's Corporation. All rights reserved.

STANDARD
&POOR'S
STOCK REPORTS

The Coca-Cola Company

562

04-APR-97

Business Summary - 04-FEB-97

Coca-Cola is the world's largest producer of soft drink concentrates and syrups, as well as the world's largest producer of juice and juice-drink products. The company holds a 45% interest in Coca-Cola Enterprises, its largest bottler. Segment contributions in 1995 were:

	Revs.	Profits
Beverages	91%	100%
Foods	9%	Nil

The Beverages division primarily manufactures soft drink and non-carbonated beverage concentrates and syrups, which are sold to independent (and company-owned) bottling/canning operations and fountain wholesalers. Brands include Coca-Cola (best-selling soft drink in the world, including Coca-Cola classic), caffeine free Coca-Cola (classic), diet Coke (sold as Coke light in many markets outside the U.S.), Cherry Coke, diet Cherry Coke, Fanta, Sprite, diet Sprite, Barq's, Mr. PiBB, Mello Yello, TAB, Fresca, PowerAde, Minute Maid, Fruitopia, and other products developed for specific markets, including Georgia ready to drink coffees. KO has equity positions in approximately 32 unconsolidated bottling, canning and distribution operations for its products worldwide, including bottlers representing about 43% of the company's U.S. unit case volume in 1995.

The Foods division is the world's largest marketer and distributor of juice and juice-drink products. Brands include Minute Maid, Five Alive, Bright & Early, Hi-C and Bacardi (under license).

International operations in 1995 accounted for 71% of net operating revenues (34% Greater Europe; 23% Middle East, Far East and Canada; 11% Latin America; 3% Africa) and 82% of operating profits (31% Middle East, Far East and Canada; 28% Greater Europe; 18% Latin America; 5% Africa).

Important Developments

Jan. '97—During 1996, KO realized nonrecurring after-tax gains amounting to $510 million, resulting from a settlement with the U.S. Internal Revenue Service ($320 million), and from certain bottler transactions ($190 million). The gains were offset in part by a $200 million after-tax provision to restructure certain operations at its Minute Maid subsidiary, a $55 million after-tax provision to upgrade its information systems, and a $200 million after-tax provision to adjust concentrate inventory levels held by certain bottlers. Separately, KO received final approval for the sale of its 49% interest in Coca-Cola & Schweppes Beverages Ltd. to Coca-Cola Enterprises.

Capitalization

Long Term Debt: $1,136,000,000 (9/96).

Per Share Data ($)

(Year Ended Dec. 31)	1996	1995	1994	1993	1992	1991	1990	1989	1988	1987
Tangible Bk. Val.	2.18	1.77	1.80	1.55	1.34	1.55	1.31	1.10	1.05	1.06
Cash Flow	1.59	1.36	1.14	0.97	0.84	0.71	0.60	0.49	0.42	0.36
Earnings	1.40	1.18	0.99	0.84	0.71	0.60	0.51	0.43	0.36	0.31
Dividends	0.50	0.44	0.39	0.34	0.28	0.24	0.20	0.17	0.15	0.14
Payout Ratio	36%	37%	39%	40%	39%	39%	39%	39%	41%	46%
Prices - High	54¼	40¼	26¾	22⅝	22¾	20½	12¼	10⅛	5⅝	6⅝
- Low	36⅛	24⅜	19½	18¾	17¾	10¾	8⅛	5⅜	4⅜	3½
P/E Ratio - High	39	34	27	27	32	34	24	24	16	22
- Low	26	21	20	22	25	18	16	13	12	12

Income Statement Analysis (Million $)

	1996	1995	1994	1993	1992	1991	1990	1989	1988	1987
Revs.	18,546	18,018	16,172	13,957	13,074	11,572	10,236	8,966	8,338	7,658
Oper. Inc.	4,394	4,546	4,090	3,485	3,080	2,586	2,237	1,910	1,768	1,514
Depr.	479	454	382	333	310	254	236	184	170	153
Int. Exp.	286	272	199	178	171	185	231	315	239	285
Pretax Inc.	4,596	4,328	3,728	3,185	2,746	2,383	2,014	1,764	1,582	1,410
Eff. Tax Rate	24%	31%	32%	31%	31%	32%	31%	32%	34%	35%
Net Inc.	3,492	2,986	2,554	2,188	1,884	1,618	1,382	1,193	1,045	916

Balance Sheet & Other Fin. Data (Million $)

	1996	1995	1994	1993	1992	1991	1990	1989	1988	1987
Cash	1,658	1,315	1,531	1,078	1,063	1,117	1,492	1,182	1,231	1,468
Curr. Assets	5,910	5,450	5,205	4,434	4,248	4,144	4,143	3,604	3,245	4,136
Total Assets	16,161	15,041	13,873	12,021	11,052	10,222	9,278	8,283	7,451	8,356
Curr. Liab.	7,416	7,348	6,177	5,171	5,303	4,118	4,296	3,658	2,869	4,119
LT Debt	1,116	1,141	1,426	1,428	1,120	985	536	549	761	803
Common Eqty.	6,156	5,392	5,235	4,584	3,888	4,426	3,774	3,185	3,045	3,224
Total Cap.	7,573	6,727	6,841	6,125	5,090	5,611	4,650	4,330	4,376	4,237
Cap. Exp.	990	937	878	808	1,083	792	642	462	387	300
Cash Flow	3,971	3,440	2,936	2,521	2,194	1,872	1,600	1,355	1,208	1,069
Curr. Ratio	0.8	0.7	0.8	0.9	0.8	1.0	1.0	1.0	1.1	1.0
% LT Debt of Cap.	14.7	17.0	20.8	23.3	22.0	17.6	11.5	12.7	17.4	19.0
% Net Inc.of Revs.	18.8	16.6	15.8	15.7	14.4	14.0	13.5	13.3	12.5	12.0
% Ret. on Assets	22.4	20.7	19.9	19.0	17.9	16.6	15.8	15.5	13.6	11.1
% Ret. on Equity	60.5	56.2	52.4	51.8	45.7	39.6	39.3	38.5	33.9	27.7

Data as orig. reptd.; bef. results of disc. opers. and/or spec. items. Per share data adj. for stk. divs. as of ex-div. date. E-Estimated. NA-Not Available. NM-Not Meaningful. NR-Not Ranked.

Office—1 Coca-Cola Plaza, N.W., Atlanta, GA 30313. **Tel**—(404) 676-2121. **Website**—http://www.cocacola.com **Chrmn & CEO**—R. C. Goizueta. **Pres & COO**—M. D. Ivester. **CFO**—J. E. Chesnut. **Secy**—Susan E. Shaw. **Investor Contact**—Gavin A. Bell. **Dirs**—H. A. Allen, R. W. Allen, C. P. Black, W. E. Buffett, C. W. Duncan, Jr., R. C. Goizueta, M. D. Ivester, S. B. King, D. F. McHenry, P. F. Oreffice, J. D. Robinson III, W. B. Turner, P. V. Ueberroth, J. B. Williams. **Transfer Agent & Registrar**—First Chicago Trust Co. of New York, Jersey City, NJ. **Incorporated**—in Delaware in 1919. **Empl**— 32,000. **S&P Analyst:** Kenneth A. Shea

FIGURE 5.1, page 2.

INDUSTRY OUTLOOK

The S&P Beverages (Non-Alcoholic) Index outperformed the major market indices through mid-March, which extends the group's outperformance of the past three years. The gains have been driven principally by strong gains in the shares of Coca-Cola (KO), and to a lesser extent, PepsiCo (PEP), whose performance has suffered recently due to company mishaps in its restaurants and international beverages operations. Although the valuations of these equities are either at or near historically high levels, we expect the S&P Beverages (Non-Alcoholic) index to continue to outperform the market in the near-term, led by rising earnings and positive investor sentiment toward these steady growers in a slow U.S. economy.

Sales and earnings are expected to be in a solid uptrend for U.S. soft drink concentrate producers again in 1997, driven principally by increased unit case volume growth, higher selling prices, quiescent material cost inflation, and consequently wider profit margins. Principal reasons for our optimistic outlook for unit sales volume growth, which is projected at 3%-5% in the U.S., include: increased penetration into non-traditional distribution channels and increasing U.S. consumer demand for non-alcoholic beverage products (particularly for soft drinks, ready-to-drink teas, juices, bottled water and sports drinks), which should continue to raise non-alcoholic beverage per-capita consumption levels. Although PepsiCo has recently experienced weak results in its international beverage segment, S&P expects the U.S. beverage industry to reap long-term rewards in fast-growing international regions, where demand has risen with recent political changes and market openings.

Our near-term outlook for U.S. bottlers is also positive. This consolidating industry is improving its profit margins through higher prices, productivity enhancements, and from favorable packaging and product mix trends. We are especially bullish on the world's largest bottler, Coca-Cola Enterprises (CCE), given its more aggressive acquisition mode. These shares are expected to outperform the market indices in the near-term, driven by consistent, double-digit annual earnings growth and a sizable expansion in its price-to-cash flow multiple.

Industry Stock Performance

Related S&P 1500 Industry Index

Beverages (Non-Alcoholic)

Month-end Price Performance As of 02/28/97

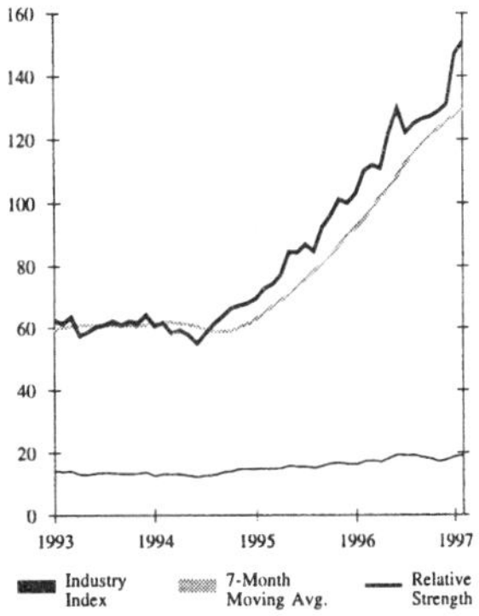

OTHER INDUSTRY PARTICIPANTS

Principal Peer Group	Stock Symbol	Recent Stock Price	P/E Ratio	12-mth. Trail. EPS	30-day Price Chg %	1-year Price Chg. %	Beta	Yield %	Quality Ranking	Stk. Mkt. Cap. (mil. $)	Ret. on Equity %	Pretax Margin %	LTD to Cap. %
Coca-Cola	**KO**	**57 3/8**	**41**	**1.40**	**-8%**	**37%**	**0.58**	**1.0**	**A+**	**142,758**	**60.5**	**24.8**	**14.7**
Buenos Aires Embotelladora	BAE	2 1/8	NM	-12.48	-35%	-87%	NA	Nil	NR	77	NM	NM	141.4
Cadbury Schweppes	CSG	35 3/4	15	2.33	7%	11%	0.94	3.3	NR	8,858	21.3	11.0	33.9
Coca-Cola Bottling Co. Consol.	COKE	43 1/2	25	1.74	0%	27%	0.76	2.3	B	376	42.7	3.3	75.5
Coca-Cola Enterprises	CCE	60 3/4	71	0.85	-5%	98%	1.02	0.2	B-	7,613	8.1	2.4	77.2
Coca-Cola FEMSA	KOF	37 1/4	37	1.02	6%	67%	NA	0.3	NR	1,769	14.9	7.5	75.4
Cott Corp.	COTTF	9 7/8	NM	-0.22	1%	58%	NA	Nil	NR	599	NM	NM	48.5
Embotelladora Andina	AKO	38 1/8	30	1.26	3%	12%	NA	0.8	NR	2,237	20.2	13.4	9.0
Glacier Water Services	HOO	25 1/4	26	0.98	-4%	36%	NA	Nil	NR	82	12.2	10.6	29.0
Grupo Embotellador de Mexico	GEM	10	NM	-0.23	-5%	16%	NA	Nil	NR	5,335	NM	NM	NA
Lancer Corp.	LAN	20 1/4	22	0.94	-3%	85%	0.15	Nil	B	118	14.1	8.8	14.4
National Beverage	FIZ	11 5/8	12	0.96	3%	166%	0.38	Nil	B-	215	17.1	4.1	53.7
Panamerican Beverages	PB	54 3/8	22	2.44	-6%	39%	NA	0.8	NR	2,637	12.3	8.1	22.8
Pepsi-Cola Puerto Rico Bottling	PPO	4 1/4	NM	-3.47	0%	-55%	NA	Nil	NR	91	NM	NM	10.3
PepsiCo	PEP	33 1/4	46	0.72	-2%	4%	1.32	1.4	A	51,656	16.5	6.5	50.1
Whitman Corp.	WH	24 1/4	19	1.31	2%	-2%	0.63	1.7	B	2,476	21.9	8.9	47.5

This report is provided for information purposes only. It should not be considered as a solicitation to buy or offer to sell any security. Neither S&P, its licensors nor any other party guarantee its accuracy or completeness or make any warranties regarding results from its usage. Redistribution or reproduction is prohibited without written permission.

Copyright © The McGraw-Hill Companies, Inc. This investment analysis was prepared from the following Sources: S&P MarketScope, S&P Compustat, S&P Stock Guide, S&P Industry Reports, Vickers Stock Research, Inc., Standard & Poor's, a division of The McGraw-Hill Companies, 25 Broadway, New York, NY 10004.

FIGURE 5.1, page 3.

Coca-Cola Co

SELL | BUY | BUY

AQO = 1.03

WALL STREET CONSENSUS

27-MAR-97

Analysts' Recommendations

Stock Prices

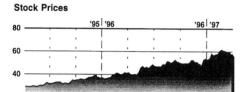

Analysts' Opinions

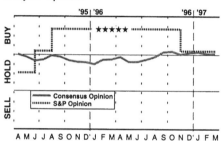

Number of Analysts Following Stock

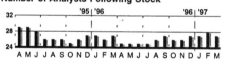

Analysts' Opinion

	No. of Ratings	% of Total	1 Mo. Prior	3 Mo. Prior	Nat'l	Reg'l	Non-broker
Buy	8	30	8	8	5	3	0
Buy/Hold	8	30	9	8	5	1	2
Hold	8	30	8	9	4	4	0
Weak Hold	0	0	0	0	0	0	0
Sell	0	0	0	0	0	0	0
No Opinion	3	11	3	2	0	2	1
Total	27	100	28	27	14	10	3

Stock Evaluation Measures

Average Qualitative Opinion (AQO)   1.03 = Buy

Buy	> 1.00	≤ 2.00	The Average Qualitative Opinion
Buy/Hold	> .75	≤ 1.00	(AQO) summarizes the current
Hold	> .35	≤ .75	investment opinions of the Wall
Weak Hold	> 0	≤ .35	Street analysts who follow the
Sell	≥ -2.00	≤ 0	company.

AQO gives you an average of buy/hold/sell opinions. A buy is greater than one. A sell is less than or equal to zero.

Standard & Poor's STARS   ★★★★
(Stock Appreciation Ranking System)

★★★★★	Buy	Standard & Poor's STARS ranking is
★★★★	Accumulate	our own analyst's evaluation of the
★★★	Hold	short-term (six to 12 month)
★★	Avoid	appreciation potential of a stock.
★	Sell	Five-Star stocks are expected to

appreciate in price and outperform the market.

Analysts' Earnings Estimate

Annual Earnings Per Share

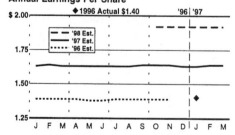

Current Analysts' Consensus Estimates

Fiscal years	Avg.	High	Low	S&P Est.	No. of Est.	Estimated P-E Ratio	Estimated S&P 500 P-E Ratio
1997	1.64	1.68	1.60	1.65	25	35.0	17.2
1998	1.92	2.00	1.85	—	14	29.9	—
1Q'97	0.35	0.40	0.32		12		
1Q'96	0.29 Actual						

A company's earnings outlook plays a major part in any investment decision. S&P organizes the earnings estimates of over 2,300 Wall Street analysts, and provides you with their consensus of earnings over the next two years. The graph to the left shows you how these estimates have trended over the past 15 months.

FIGURE 5.1, page 4.

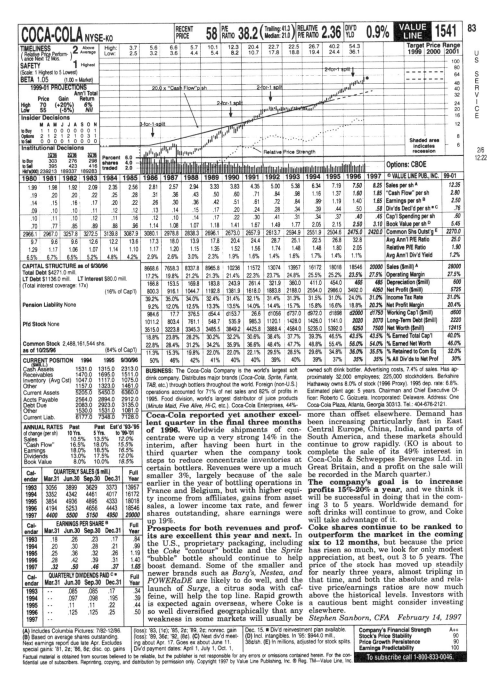

FIGURE 5.2 Value Line Investment Survey analysis sheet. Copyright © 1997 by Value Line Publishing, Inc. Reprinted by permission. All rights reserved.

In explaining how this information is derived and the possible ways of interpreting it, this chapter will try to avoid much of the "number crunching" that most people dread. Only those simple, basic ratios and calculations that are most pertinent to the information that beginning investors need to evaluate are included in this chapter.

Keep in mind at all times that all of the measures cited require interpretations that are relative. There is no totally correct interpretation of their meaning, whether evaluated individually or as a group. As an old saying on Wall Street goes, "If you give 10 different analysts the same information and ask them to interpret it, you'll end up with an argument, not a consensus."

EARNINGS PER SHARE AND EARNINGS GROWTH PATTERN

earnings per share (EPS) the amount of a company's net earnings allocated to each share of outstanding common stock.

Earnings per share (EPS) is perhaps the most widely used and publicized measure of a company's current and future growth. EPS is the amount of the company's net earnings that is allocated to each share of outstanding common stock. Net earnings are those profits that remain after the company has paid, in this order, operating expenses, all interest payments on any outstanding bonds, all taxes, and all dividends on outstanding preferred stock. The formula used for calculating earnings per share (EPS) is:

$$\text{EPS} = \frac{\text{Net earnings for common}}{\text{Number of outstanding common shares}}$$

The number of common shares used in the formula equals the total amount of issued-and-outstanding common stock minus any shares repurchased by the issuer as treasury stock. Additionally, if the company has any common-stock equivalents outstanding—convertible bonds, convertible preferred stock, rights, warrants, and stock options issued to employees—whose conversion could increase the number of common shares outstanding and therefore dilute (lessen) the earnings per share, these must also be included in the calculation. When the conversion of the stock equivalents is included, the resulting earnings figure is called the *fully diluted earnings per share*. When reading any report of a company's earnings, be careful to understand how the number of outstanding shares is calculated.

Analysts spend much time trying to predict (1) what a company's earnings will be for the upcoming quarter, and (2) whether a company's earnings will increase or decrease over the long term. The expectations created by these predictions have a strong effect on the price of a company's stock.

The following examples illustrate two of the many ways that expectations regarding a company's earnings can be a strong price determinant in the stock market.

fully diluted earnings per share the amount of a company's net earnings allocated to already outstanding common shares plus any additional shares that could result from the conversion or exercise of any outstanding stock equivalents.

Example 1: An analyst predicts that a company's earnings for the upcoming quarter will increase over those reported for the same quarter of the previous year. Typically, the price of the company's stock rises in anticipation of the increase. If, however, at the end of the quarter the company reports earnings that are on target with or less than the analyst's prediction, then the price of the stock may often decline. However, if the company's earnings exceed analysts' expectations, then the price of the stock will have a tendency to rise.

Example 2: An analyst predicts that a company's earnings for the upcoming quarter will increase over those reported for same quarter of the previous year. Again, the price of the common shares rises in anticipation of the increase. At the end of the quarter the company reports earnings that far exceed analysts' expectations; however, analysts notice that this increase is due to restructuring within the company instead of increased sales and revenues. The price of the company's stock will usually decline abruptly due to profit taking; investors and analysts conclude that the company will not be able to sustain the earnings growth and therefore sell their shares.

Determining if there is a trend or pattern in the company's EPS over a period of time is an important consideration when making an investment decision. Traditional thought holds that the longer a trend has lasted, the greater is the likelihood that it will continue. For example, the Value Line report in Figure 5.2 (in the table immediately below the graph depicting the price movement of the stock) shows that Coca-Cola's actual earnings from 1980 through 1996 increased steadily from $0.14 to $1.40 per share. Indeed, there were a few years (in the early 1980s) when the earnings were relatively flat; still, the trend has been consistently upward. [**Note:** Page 2 of Figure 5.1 shows the same information from 1987 through 1996 in the section labeled "Per Share Data ($)." The same information showing quarterly earnings amounts for the six years preceding the current year is on page 1 of the figure in the section labeled "Earnings Per Share ($)."] Based on the information presented in the financial statements filed with the SEC, fundamental analysts at both Value Line and S&P predicted that earnings for 1997 would be $1.65 per share. (On the S&P stock report, the projected earnings for 1997 are presented in the section labeled "Key Stock Statistics" on page 1.)

The Coca-Cola example implies that the correlation between increases or decreases in the earnings per share and the company's growth potential is direct. However, other information must be considered when interpreting the significance and implications of the EPS.

Increasing EPS

Steadily increasing earnings per share usually mean that a company is growing or that its financial condition is improving. If the increase is due to a corresponding improvement in sales and profits, then the company is growing. By logical extension, you can expect the market value of the shares that you own to increase accordingly.

Better sales, however, are not the only factor that can cause a rise in EPS. The company may be buying back its stock—turning it into treasury stock. In this case, the number of outstanding shares will decline. Depending on the number of shares repurchased, the net effect could be an increase in EPS even when total sales (and earnings) could be declining. In short, a company's stock repurchase plan can mask the fact that the sales (and earnings) are not improving. Thus, while the EPS may increase, investors may lose confidence in the company's ability to continually increase sales and begin selling their holdings. Thus, the market value of the company's shares will decline.

Decreasing EPS

A decrease in the earnings per share is generally not a good sign. Lower earnings are the result of lower sales or higher costs, and thus lower profits. However, investors are wise to try to determine if the decline is due to internal or external factors.

Internal factors may include a stock split, a stock dividend, the issuance and exercise of rights or warrants, or the forced conversion of outstanding bonds or preferred stock. In each of these cases, the EPS would decline because there are more shares outstanding. Depending on the circumstances, analysts may see this as only a short-term decline, eventually leading to an increase. A decrease in EPS that results from a stock split is usually taken as a bullish sign, especially if the company's total sales and earnings show no decline. In the case of a forced conversion, the company would be eliminating the interest payments on the bonds or dividends on the preferred. This should eventually lead to higher earnings for the common shareholders. Stock dividends are also interpreted as a positive sign. To be sure, the company has more shares outstanding, but typically the earnings (and dividends paid) increase over time. In the case of a stock split or stock dividend, the company and the information services firms adjust their historical data to reflect the change.

External factors generally refer to business conditions

or the state of the overall economy. Perhaps the market sector that is the company's core business is in a temporary slump but will gradually improve, or the overall economy is in a recession and all businesses are experiencing lower earnings. In the latter case, the decrease in EPS may be part of the cyclical character of the business or industry.

"A company's earnings outlook plays a major part in any investment decision." This statement in the "Analysts' Earnings Estimate" section on page 4 of Figure 5.1 underscores the importance of EPS. Standard and Poor's Stock Report gathers earnings estimates of all of the Wall Street analysts that follow a company and summarizes their expectations on the final page of the stock report. This summary shows the number of analysts who made earnings estimates during each fiscal year. The chart on the left side of this section graphically depicts the trend of the estimates for the last two years. On the Value Line page (Figure 5.2), the analyst or analysts explain their earnings expectations in essay form in the analysis section of the page.

Keep in mind that earnings per share is rarely used alone to make an investment decision. Usually EPS is compared to some other factor such as the market price of the stock or company's sales per share. For example, when evaluating a company's EPS, also look at its sales per share to see if they confirm the earnings trend. If they do not, determine why.

PRICE-EARNINGS RATIO

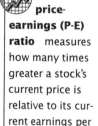
price-earnings (P-E) ratio measures how many times greater a stock's current price is relative to its current earnings per share.

Perhaps the most important ratio to understand is the *price-earnings (P-E) ratio.* The formula is:

$$\text{P-E ratio} = \frac{\text{Current market price of the stock}}{\text{Annual earnings per share}}$$

This ratio, published daily in the financial press, tells how many times greater a stock's current price is relative to its current earnings per share. For example, using the earnings figures shown in the section labeled "Earnings Per Share ($)" on page 1 of Figure 5.1, the Coca-Cola Company (a.k.a. Coca-Cola) reported total earnings per share for the previous four quarters of $1.40. This includes the four quarters of 1996 ($0.29, $0.42, $0.39, and $0.31, respectively). Given that the market price of Coca-Cola common stock was $57⅞ on the day this information was compiled, the company's P-E ratio is close to 41.

$$\text{P-E ratio} = \frac{\$57.375}{\$1.40} = 41$$

This means that Coca-Cola is currently trading at approximately "41 times earnings." Stated another way, the stock's market price is trading at a multiple of 41 times the company's annual earnings.

In the financial press, the annual earnings per share used in the calculation is that which the company reported for the previous year. When computed in this way, the ratio is called the trailing P-E. Information services companies like Value Line and Standard & Poor's use more up-to-date earning figures. Their annual earnings figure may be the total of the reported earnings from the two most recent quarters and the estimated earnings for the next two quarters. This is called the forward P-E. Or, the annual EPS may be the total reported earnings from the most recent 12 months (the previous four quarters). This explains why the P-E ratios that appear in the newspaper differ from those that appear on the stock reports. Also, the P-E ratio is a dynamic measure, changing with the market price of the stock.

It is easiest to think of the P-E ratio as a measure of a stock's relative expensiveness compared to its earnings. A "high" P-E ratio means that the price of the stock is expensive relative to the earnings it provides. A "low" P-E ratio means that the price of the stock is thought to be inexpensive relative to the company's earnings. The adjectives "high" and "low" are relative terms. The standard or "normal" P-E ratio against which a stock is compared varies over time depending on investor sentiment as well as the economic outlook for the company and its industry.

Historically, for example, the long-term P-E ratio for the S&P 500 stocks has been approximately 15 to 1. However, there have been periods (1992, for example) when the P-E ratio for the same group of stocks exceeded 25 to 1. When investors are bullish on the overall market, the prices of stocks tend to rise. Thus, the ratios tend to be higher. On the other hand, when interest rates are high, investors might leave the stock market and invest their money in bonds. As a result, stock prices fall, and P-E ratios tend to be low.

Fundamentalists interpret P-E ratios in various ways. The most common of these are summarized next.

High P-E Ratio

A P-E ratio is considered high when it is above 20 to 1 (although this is more a rule of thumb than an absolute rule). Such ratios have historically been characteristic of growth companies. Established-growth companies like Microsoft, McDonald's, and Coca-Cola may have ratios that are only slightly above or below 20; however, in a strong bullish market (e.g., the mid-1990s) P-E ratios may far exceed this number. This generally reflects investors' belief that new product development or marketing efforts show a strong likelihood of increasing sales and returns to investors. On the other hand, an emerging growth company (such as Amgen) or a penny-stock company may have a P-E ratio that is 40 to 1, 90 to 1, or higher. [**Note**: In Value Line's assessment of Coca-Cola in Figure 5.2, the analyst discusses the company's high P-E ratio, expressing some concern.]

Some analysts believe a high P-E ratio means that investors are bullish on the long-term growth prospects of the company. Hence, they are willing to pay a relatively high price for the stock today in order to benefit from its growth in the future. Others see a high P-E ratio as a bearish indicator. To them it means that the company's stock is overvalued and that the price will soon decline to relatively correct values.

These contradictory interpretations should lead beginning investors to one safe conclusion: High P-E ratios usually indicate greater risk, and greater risk means a greater opportunity for profit. If the company's earnings improve as expected or, even better, exceed expectations, then you have a reasonable chance of making substantial capital gains on the appreciation of the company's stock. [Note the S&P analysts' interpretation of Coca-Cola's high P-E ratio in the section labeled "Valuation" on page 1 of Figure 5.1.] Expectations of growth, however, do not always turn into real growth. When a company fails to meet its earnings target, investors tend to abandon the stock like proverbial rats from a sinking ship. The rush to sell causes the price to fall sharply and quickly. Greater volatility is usually characteristic of stocks with high P-E ratios.

Low P-E Ratio

A P-E ratio is considered low when it is under 10 to 1. Low P-E ratios are characteristic of mature companies with low growth potential (e.g., food companies), blue-chip companies, and companies that are in trouble or heading toward it. A low ratio could indicate a solid investment that is undervalued due to temporary market conditions, such as low sales, a slow economy, or investors' bearish sentiments. Or the low ratio could be the first sign of a Chapter 11 bankruptcy filing. Look at how the information services rank the company's safety and financial stability before deciding to buy stock with a low ratio.

Contrarians, on the other hand, believe that if overall P-E ratios are low, the market as a whole has bottomed out and a moderate- to long-term rally is about to occur. To these analysts, a low P-E ratio for the overall market is bullish, indicating that it is time to buy stocks.

Ultimately, P-E ratios are used to get a relative measure of the price of a company's stock. Do not interpret this measure in isolation. Instead, compare it with the average P-E ratio of companies in the same business sector or industry, with the company's past P-E ratios, as well as with the average ratio of one of the standard measures of the market, such as the Dow Jones Industrial Average, the S&P 500, or the Value Line Index. Much of this information can be found on the Standard & Poor's and Value Line reports illustrated in Figures 5.1 and 5.2, and in various publications available at many public libraries.

EARNINGS YIELD

earnings yield the return that a stock's annual earnings per share represent relative to the stock's current market price.

The *earnings yield* is the inverse of the P-E ratio. The formula for the earnings yield is:

$$\text{Earnings yield} = \frac{\text{Annual earnings per share}}{\text{Market price of the common stock}}$$

yield to maturity a measure of the return on a bond if an investor were to hold the bond to its maturity date; the calculation considers the interest payments (assuming they are reinvested) and any gain or loss that may result from the difference between the bond's purchase price and its redemption price.

Analysts compare this yield to the *yield to maturity* on a long-term bond such as the 30-year U.S. Treasury bond. Looking back over the long term and comparing changes in earnings yield to changes in the yield to maturity on long-term bonds, analysts have concluded that both yields tend to move in tandem. They notice that this is particularly true when comparison is made with the 30-year U.S. Treasury bond yield. When interest rates on 30-year U.S. Treasury bonds are low, investors are willing to accept lower earnings yields from the stock they own. Hence, the prices of stocks rise relative to their earnings per share. When interest rates on long-term bonds are high, investors expect higher yields on their shares. The result is that the prices of the stocks decrease relative to the earnings per share.

Analysts also compare the yield to maturity on long-term bonds to the earnings yield of the overall market as represented by the S&P 500 companies. If the analysis shows that investors expect earnings yields on stocks to exceed comparable yields on bonds, then this is interpreted as being bullish for stock prices in general and individual stocks specifically. If, however, the comparison

shows stronger yields for bonds, then this is a bearish indicator. Investor's will sell their stocks and buy bonds
seeking to lock in the higher yield.

SALES–TO–PRICE PER SHARE RATIO

This ratio is important for evaluating young companies in
new emerging-growth business areas, such as the Internet.
Many of these companies have little or no earnings because of huge start-up expenses. Therefore, their sales
growth becomes an important measure of the potential
growth of the company, as well as of future increases in
the price of its stock. The formula for sales-to-price per
share ratio (also called the revenues-to-price ratio) is:

$$\frac{\text{Sales-to-price}}{\text{ratio}} = \frac{\text{Total annual sales per share}}{\text{Market price of the common stock}}$$

This ratio should not be considered in isolation. It
must be compared with the same ratio of other companies
within the same business sector or growth industry. The
momentum of the quarterly increases or decreases in the
ratio for a specific company is interpreted in light of its
peers, the business sector, and the economy.

Basic interpretations of this ratio and the momentum
of its change are easy to understand. As sales increase, the
sales-to-price ratio increases. If the percentage or momentum of the increase is strong (this is a subjective evaluation that depends upon the particular industry), the price
of the company's stock should also increase. Analysts recommend and investors buy the company's stock, becoming more confident that the sales momentum will
continue. While many hope sales growth will eventually
lead to earnings growth, many others simply buy the
stock because they like the strong and increasing pace at
which the company is able to sell its product in the marketplace.

A slowdown or decline in sales can be quite bearish
for such young companies. This is particularly true if the
decline is due to difficulties within the company (e.g.,

overly optimistic projections, or production and delivery delays) or problems within that particular business sector (e.g., increased competition, pressure to lower prices, or a sector-specific economic downturn). This loss of sales momentum, even in the short term, typically results in analysts downgrading the stock and investors bailing out of the stock in droves. The resulting price decline can be steep and long.

Investors can expect to read or hear analysts' evaluations of the sales-to-price ratios in nascent business areas like the Internet, microbreweries, and specialized retail stores. Because these areas are so new, none of the traditional measures for price valuation—earnings growth, P-E ratio, dividend yield—can be used as meaningful benchmarks to determine the possible price movement of the stock. Investors can also expect these stocks to be quite volatile. When sales remain strong, everyone—analysts, investors, and institutions—just love the stock, snapping it up like tickets to the Super Bowl. But when sales decline, the chorus of adoration quickly turns to "Hit the road, Jack" as nearly everyone sells.

BOOK VALUE

book value
the amount of a company's assets backing each common share after intangibles have been deducted and all outstanding liabilities paid.

In simple terms, *book value* is the amount of money each common shareholder might reasonably expect to receive if a company's assets (not including intangibles such as copyrights, patents, and goodwill) were sold at the value at which they are carried on the balance sheet and all liabilities were paid. An improvement in a company's book value, while not directly related to earnings, could indicate asset growth or a decrease in the company's liabilities.

A company's market price per share is often compared to its book value per share to determine how much above its "real" value the company is selling. This is known as the price–to–book value ratio. There are average book values for each business sector. For example, banks typically have a price–to–book value ratio of 1.5 to 1. Other industries, like technology stocks, may be higher.

Sometimes a company's price-to-book value is below the average for companies in that industry or business sector. Fundamental analysts interpret this as a possible buy signal. In such a case, analysts believe, the company is trading for less than the net value of its assets. By purchasing the stock and holding it, an investor will eventually profit when the price moves up to its "real value."

Companies that grow through leverage (borrowing), such as utilities, tend to have relatively stable book values. These companies have a steady and relatively consistent cash flow (e.g., from bill payments) and use it to borrow heavily. For the most part, the steady influx of cash offsets the increased liability associated with the debt outstanding.

Growth companies tend to have higher price–to–book values. Without the stable cash flow of a larger corporation or a long credit history, borrowing is difficult, so these companies reinvest their net earnings in the company instead of paying them as dividends to investors. Therefore, an investor can usually interpret an increase in book value to mean a growth in the company's assets. Notice that in Figure 5.1 (page 2) and Figure 5.2 Coke's book value has steadily increased. S&P labels the row "Tangible Bk. Val." in the "Per Share Data ($)" section. On the Value Line sheet, the row is labeled "Book Value per sh," and, as the footnote (D) reveals, the number includes intangibles.

Analysts also apply the price–to–book value ratio to the overall market. If the ratio is at historic highs, some analysts will view this as a bearish indicator. They believe that investors are not looking at the fundamental business aspects of the company but instead are buying stock based on hype. Eventually, the price of the company's stock will decline because the underlying fundamentals—delivery of product to the market, growth in market share and earnings—will prove disappointing.

Bullish analysts argue that for some newer industries, like technology and biotech stocks, many of the company's assets are intangibles. Because these are excluded when calculating book value, the price–to–book value ratio cannot be considered a primary tool to determine the value of an investment in many of the newer, non-industrial-based businesses.

DIVIDEND YIELD (CURRENT YIELD)

dividend yield a stock's annual per share dividend (in dollars) divided by its current market price.

Dividend yield, also referred to simply as yield, is the percentage of return that a stock's annual dividend payments represent relative to the stock's current market price. In simple terms, it tells you the return you are making on a stock today. The formula for dividend yield is:

$$\text{Dividend yield} = \frac{\text{Annual per share dividend in \$}}{\text{Stock's current market price}}$$

The importance of the dividend yield depends on the importance that you place on receiving dividend payments. Many investors believe that current and increasing future dividend payments are an indication of a company's financial strength. Logically, steadily increasing dividends should follow increased profits and earnings for a company. This reasoning is not necessarily true. The amount of dividend payments is a reflection of a company's dividend policy, which is determined by its board of directors. Even when a corporation's profits and earnings are down, the board may choose to maintain a relatively steady dividend amount in order to support the company's image as a solid investment. The board may also decide to maintain the same dividend, although the company's profits and earnings have increased. Therefore, like the P-E ratio, there is no absolute correlation between the amount of the dividend payment and the quality of the investment. Indeed, some of the most successful and profitable companies in the United States pay little or no dividends (e.g., Microsoft). Nevertheless, there are some generalizations that beginning investors can use.

High Dividend Yield

A high dividend yield tends to be characteristic of a mature blue-chip company, an income stock, a company in a slow growth industry (e.g., food companies), and regulated industries (e.g., utilities). Such companies usually have substantial earnings and distribute a large portion of them to the shareholders. They pay high dividends because these mature businesses offer little or no opportunity for substantial capital appreciation in the price of their common stock. The market prices of their stocks tend to be relatively stable or to fluctuate in accordance with the general market trend. If you are looking for good, steady current income, buy stock with high dividend yields.

Some fundamentalists track the aggregate dividend yield of a group of stocks like the Standard & Poor's 500 companies as an indication of the future direction of the market. They believe that when the market's aggregate dividend yield is high (again, a relative term), the bottom of a market downtrend is indicated. If stock prices relative to dividend payments have reached a low point, this foretells an uptrend. Investors begin buying stocks because they believe the stocks are undervalued relative to the returns they are now providing.

Low Dividend Yield

Low (or no) dividend yield is characteristic of growth stocks. As both Figures 5.1 and 5.2 show, Coca-Cola has a dividend yield of about 1 percent. Clearly it is considered a growth company. Instead of paying a large part of its earnings as dividends to its shareholders, the company retains most of the earnings and reinvests them in the company. These earnings are usually allocated for research and development and for marketing, in order to build the overall worth of the company. Analysts who are bullish on a stock interpret a low dividend yield as indicating investors' willingness to make a long-term investment in the company and therefore profit from the capital appreciation of the stock's price over time.

Analysts with a bearish outlook see a low dividend yield is a sign that a speculative market may have peaked. In short, the price of a stock is about to reach or has already reached a high and will soon decline—sharply. These analysts believe that investors have been far too willing to chase the short-term price rises instead of earnings or dividend growth. Eventually, the analysts' logic continues, investors will become dissatisfied with the price they are paying for the stock relative to the dividend they receive and will sell their shares. A low dividend yield is, therefore, a bearish indicator.

The weight you give to dividend yield, and therefore to dividend payments, when deciding to invest in a company's stock depends very much on your need for current income or long-term appreciation. To be sure, it is riskier to bet on the future growth of a company than to take your returns as cash dividends today. The choice, however, is hardly ever totally black or white. In almost all investments in stock, you must choose the point along the spectrum of dividend income versus capital gains that is most suitable for your situation.

In making such decisions, also consider total return. A simplified version of the formula for calculating total return follows:

$$\text{Total return} = \frac{\text{Dividends} \begin{cases} + \text{any capital gains} \\ \text{or} \\ - \text{any capital losses} \end{cases}}{\text{Stock's beginning cost basis}}$$

Although historic total yield information should be consulted as a reference, the total annual dividends and the annual capital gain amounts used in the formula are estimates, made when deciding what stock to buy or sell. In relying too heavily on current yield as a reason for all investment decisions, you may be shortchanging yourself on the total return.

KNOW THE COMPANY AND KNOW ITS PRODUCTS

In addition to checking all of the ratios about earnings, sales, growth, book value, and other items, there is another essential bit of advice that applies to any beginning investor who is using fundamental analysis to decide whether to invest in a company: Know the company and know its products. Later in this book, I give an example of a beginning investor who owns a word processing business and decides to invest part of his earnings in the stock of computer- and technology-related companies. He makes this decision based on the fact that he works with different companies' products every day. He therefore has a sense of:

- ✔ Which companies are creating new and innovative products.
- ✔ Which companies are not keeping their products current.
- ✔ Which companies' products are facing increasing competition and price pressure.
- ✔ Which companies are diversifying into new areas that should help to offset any losses due to increased competition.
- ✔ With what products the users are increasingly satisfied (or dissatisfied).
- ✔ What new businesses are being spawned by this industry.

Many people think that "fundamental analysis" is just another term for "financial statement analysis." While it is important to check the ratios, it is equally important to know the company and know its products.

ANALYZING PREFERRED STOCK

As a general statement, an investor interested in buying preferred stock is usually conservative. Typically, this person is looking for a preferred with the highest possible fixed dividend and lowest risk to principal. The process of analyzing and selecting preferred stock is somewhat easier than for common stock because both Moody's and Standard & Poor's rate preferred issues according to the amount of asset protection each issue has and their relative risk of default. The ratings and their meanings are shown in Figure 5.3.

Like a bond, the first four ratings of preferred stock

Moody's	S&P	Meaning
aaa	AAA	Superior quality preferred stock with excellent asset protection and the least risk of divdend nonpayment.
aa	AA	Excellent quality preferred stock with good earnings and asset protection and little risk of dividend nonpayment.
a	A	Very good quality preferred stock with adequate levels of earnings and asset protection. Dividend nonpayment risk is somewhat greater than the preceding rating.
baa	BBB	Adequate quality preferred stock with sufficient earnings and asset protection for the short term. Long-term prospects of dividend payment involve some risk.
ba	BB	First speculative rating for preferred stock. Asset protection for stock may be sufficient at present, but insufficient to withstand long-term adversity.
b	B	This rating (and those that follow) denote an undesirable issue of preferred stock.
caa	CCC	Preferred stock may have defaulted on dividend payments.
ca	CC	Very risky and likely to be in default and in arrears on dividend payments. Little likelihood that back payments will be made up.
c	C	Lowest rated and most risky preferred stock. Issue has extremely poor prospects of achieving higher investment rating.

FIGURE 5.3 Ratings of preferred stock by Moody's and Standard & Poor's.

are considered investment grade. At and below BB (S&P) and ba (Moody's), the stock is considered speculative. While the investment grade ratings will invariably pay the lower dividend, as the interpretations indicate, there is reasonable certainty that the stock will continue to pay its preferred dividend for the long term. The speculative ratings offer a higher stated return; however, there is some doubt as to the company's ability to pay over the long or short term.

Chapter 6

Technical Analysis

echnical analysis is the study of the market's or a stock's past movement as a means of predicting its future price movement. Three premises form the foundation of this approach. First, all information necessary to forecast the movement of the market is contained in the market itself. Outside information—usually meaning such fundamental factors as a company's earnings, its sales, and the demand for its products—is discounted by the market. Second, price movements in the market tend to repeat themselves. And, third, investors tend to have the same reactions to the changes each time they occur. A good analyst has charted or studied charts of the market's past movement and has been able to determine consistencies in investors' buying and selling patterns during certain periods. When he or she sees similar circumstances in the present, the analyst uses this information as a basis for predicting the market's future movement. Not only will the analyst be able to forecast the direction of the market, he or she can also predict the strength and duration of the price movement. Often, but not always, the predictions of a knowledgeable analyst are accurate.

The market indicators with which analysts are most concerned are *price* and *volume*. Price is the point at which a trade occurs—the point at which a buyer, seeking the lowest price, and a seller, seeking the highest price,

technical analysis research that seeks to predict the future price movement of a stock or the overall market by using price and volume as indicators of changes in the supply and demand for a stock; best used to predict short- and intermediate-term price movements.

price in technical terms, the point at which supply (sellers) and demand (buyers) meet and a trade occurs.

volume the total number of shares traded in a given period of time.

charting capturing the patterns of a stock's price and volume movements on a line, bar, point-and-figure, or moving average graph.

chartist a technical analyst who uses charts to capture a stock's price and volume movement and then analyzes this information as a basis for making buy and sell recommendations.

sentiment indicators statistics used to measure the bullish or bearish mood of the market and its investors.

agree to conduct a transaction. Volume is the number of shares traded in a given period of time. The interaction of these forces in the market provides the clues to the short-term to intermediate-term price movement of the security. Analysts base their predictions and time their buying and selling on these indicators. The four basic interactions between price and volume and how they are interpreted by technical analysts are summarized in Figure 6.1.

Technical analysts' primary tool is *charting*; hence, they are sometimes called *chartists*. For most investors, the terms "technical analysis" and "charting" are virtually synonymous. Charting is used to create a picture of the market's movement, which the analyst then interprets. Charts, however, are only one of the factors a technician considers when seeking to forecast the direction of the market. Others include *sentiment indicators* and *flow of funds indicators*. Sentiment indicators measure whether investors and their advisers feel bullish or bearish about the market. These measurements are usually determined by surveying the recommendations made in newsletters published by various *investment advisory services*. Importantly, sentiment indicators are usually interpreted as *contrary indicators*. When investors feel very bullish, technicians interpret this as a signal that the market is about to decline. Conversely, a strongly bearish sentiment prefigures an upturn in the market.

The flow of funds indicators show where both individual and institutional investors are investing their money. In short, these indicators measure the demand for securities. Depending on market conditions, investors may decide to invest in common stocks or fixed-income securities (preferred stock or bonds), or to maintain a high degree of liquidity by placing cash in money market accounts.

Given all the factors that a chartist considers, it is easy to understand why technical analysis is best suited for forecasting the short-term or intermediate movement of stock prices. Technicians are not interested in the dividend income to be made from an investment in an equity security. They are most interested in the capital gains that can be made from short-term price moves. Long-term price fore-

Price	Volume	Indication
↑	↑	**Bullish.** Price will continue to rise. The increasing trading volume reflects growing demand to buy the security, which adds momentum to or supports the upward direction of the market.
↓	↑	**Bearish.** Price will continue to decline. Increasing volume indicates more and more investors are selling, leading to greater downward momentum.
↑	↓	**Moderately Bearish.** The price increase is losing momentum, as indicated by the decline in trading volume. The price rise is unsupported and will soon reverse itself, becoming a decline.
↓	↓	**Moderately Bullish.** The decreasing trading volume indicates that the price decline is losing some of its steam. Demand is still relatively low. Soon, however, the market will reach its bottom, the price will again be attractive to new investors, and the resulting increased demand will cause the price to rally.

↑ = Rising ↓ = Falling

FIGURE 6.1 Technical analysts' interpretations of the four basic interactions of price and volume.

casting is better served by fundamental analysis, although some people use technical analysis for this purpose.

Since charting is the primary tool of the technical analyst, this chapter will look at some of the information that an analyst charts, the theories about market movement, the ways a chartist may depict this information, and how a chartist interprets some of the basic formations that the market's movement creates.

STOCK MARKET AVERAGES AND INDEXES

The charts that most people are familiar with are the market *averages* or *indexes*: the Dow Jones Industrial Average, the Standard & Poor's 500 Index, the New York Stock Exchange Composite Index, the NASDAQ Index, the Russell 2000 Index, and others (Figure 6.2). These indicators chart the broad movement of the overall market. Each average or index is structured and calculated differently, using different numbers of stocks, different divisors, and

flow of funds indicators statistics that enable analysts to determine in which markets—money markets, stock, bonds, savings accounts— individual and institutional investors are most likely to invest their money during given economic conditions or periods of time.

investment advisory services companies or individuals registered with the Securities and Exchange Commission who, for a fee, provide investment advice or money management, usually in specific types of investments.

contrary indicators information used to establish the bullish or bearish sentiment of the market to which an investor responds by taking the opposite position (e.g., if a contrary indicator is bullish, this is a sign for an investor to sell).

average a composite measure of the movement of the overall market or of a particular industry that consists of a small number of stocks and is usually not weighted.

STOCK MARKET DATA BANK   4/7/97

MAJOR INDEXES

—†12-MO— HIGH	LOW		—DAILY— HIGH	LOW	CLOSE	NET CHG	% CHG	†12-MO CHG	% CHG	FROM 12/31	% CHG
DOW JONES AVERAGES											
7085.16	5346.55	30 Industrials	6589.14	6526.07	6555.91	+ 29.84	+ 0.46	+ 961.54	+17.19	+ 107.64	+ 1.67
2469.59	1965.73	20 Transportation	2429.67	2401.16	2427.36	+ 26.82	+ 1.12	+ 259.42	+11.97	+ 171.69	+ 7.61
240.85	204.86	15 Utilities	215.62	214.57	214.64	− 0.21	− 0.10	+ 6.63	+ 3.19	− 17.89	− 7.69
2190.18	1720.66	65 Composite	2075.62	2056.47	2068.38	+ 11.91	+ 0.58	+ 253.11	+13.94	+ 42.55	+ 2.10
769.96	591.10	DJ Global-US	722.03	715.07	719.62	+ 4.55	+ 0.64	+ 110.66	+18.17	+ 19.06	+ 2.72
NEW YORK STOCK EXCHANGE											
427.70	336.07	Composite	401.79	398.02	400.68	+ 2.66	+ 0.67	+ 55.03	+15.92	+ 8.38	+ 2.14
534.70	425.12	Industrials	506.20	502.15	504.71	+ 2.56	+ 0.51	+ 64.66	+14.69	+ 10.33	+ 2.09
275.80	236.63	Utilities	256.58	253.74	256.28	+ 2.54	+ 1.00	+ 16.56	+ 6.91	− 3.63	− 1.40
381.37	304.75	Transportation	364.54	361.81	363.92	+ 2.11	+ 0.58	+ 44.38	+13.89	+ 11.62	+ 3.30
404.51	278.77	Finance	367.10	361.96	365.88	+ 3.92	+ 1.08	+ 77.11	+26.70	+ 14.71	+ 4.19
STANDARD & POOR'S INDEXES											
816.29	626.65	500 Index	764.82	757.90	762.13	+ 4.23	+ 0.56	+ 117.89	+18.30	+ 21.39	+ 2.89
950.96	740.97	Industrials	897.42	889.86	894.53	+ 4.67	+ 0.52	+ 130.79	+17.12	+ 24.56	+ 2.82
205.00	184.66	Utilities	186.90	186.15	186.17	− 0.30	− 0.16	− 0.07	− 0.04	− 12.64	− 6.36
269.05	214.34	400 MidCap	255.07	252.06	255.06	+ 3.00	+ 1.19	+ 27.37	+12.02	− 0.52	− 0.20
148.60	121.57	600 SmallCap	138.86	136.73	138.81	+ 2.08	+ 1.52	+ 10.91	+ 8.53	− 6.67	− 4.58
174.72	135.01	1500 Index	163.89	162.33	163.40	+ 1.07	+ 0.66	+ 23.99	+17.21	+ 3.59	+ 2.25
NASDAQ STOCK MARKET											
1388.06	1042.37	Composite	1256.12	1236.73	1251.35	+ 14.62	+ 1.18	+ 145.69	+13.18	− 39.68	− 3.07
925.52	598.34	Nasdaq 100	839.86	822.40	832.31	+ 9.91	+ 1.21	+ 221.70	+36.31	+ 10.95	+ 1.33
1193.13	960.06	Industrials	1032.09	1025.70	1031.26	+ 11.30	+ 1.11	− 2.53	− 0.24	− 78.37	− 7.06
1506.29	1196.03	Insurance	1414.66	1405.20	1414.66	+ 12.53	+ 0.89	+ 123.47	+ 9.56	− 50.77	− 3.46
1451.21	1034.81	Banks	1364.84	1353.88	1364.67	+ 11.91	+ 0.88	+ 317.39	+30.31	+ 91.21	+ 7.16
583.50	371.51	Computer	517.41	511.36	511.73	+ 6.77	+ 1.34	+ 127.54	+33.20	− 7.06	− 1.36
232.57	189.64	Telecommunications	204.25	202.80	203.61	+ 1.18	+ 0.58	− 11.12	− 5.18	− 12.30	− 5.70
OTHERS											
617.61	524.20	Amex Composite*	560.84	556.71	560.44	+ 3.71	+ 0.67	− 12.40	− 2.16	− 11.90	− 2.08
431.09	331.94	Russell 1000	403.20	399.23	401.98	+ 2.75	+ 0.69	+ 58.10	+16.90	+ 8.23	+ 2.09
370.65	307.78	Russell 2000	344.94	340.84	344.91	+ 4.07	+ 1.19	+ 14.20	+ 4.29	− 17.70	− 4.88
456.03	353.85	Russell 3000	426.39	422.11	425.22	+ 3.11	+ 0.74	+ 57.23	+15.55	+ 5.78	+ 1.38
394.31	325.44	Value-Line(geom.)	373.19	369.83	373.03	+ 3.18	+ 0.86	+ 29.37	+ 8.55	− 2.29	− 0.61
7792.57	6099.34	Wilshire 5000	...	...	7272.99	+ 59.03	+ 0.82	+ 920.03	+14.48	+ 74.70	+ 1.04

†-Based on comparable trading day in preceding year. *-Replaced previous index eff. 1/02/97.

FIGURE 6.2   Stock Market Data Bank showing major indexes. Reprinted by permission of *The Wall Street Journal*, © 1997 Dow Jones & Company, Inc. All rights reserved worldwide.

different *weightings*. As a result, the price movements of different groups of stock have a greater or lesser influence on the index. These averages move in the same direction about 90 percent of the time but occasionally move in opposite directions because of the mix of securities and their weightings. Technical analysts are aware of these differences and take them into consideration when using a specific index to forecast the market's movements.

Like the market they seek to represent, these indexes are not static. Their compositions, divisors, and weightings are affected by corporate mergers, business failures, stock splits, stock dividends, and other changes in a company's capitalization or financial status. The companies that calculate the indexes and averages must be constantly watchful and adjust their measurements to incorporate these effects.

Let's examine the most widely used averages and indexes.

Dow Jones Industrial Average

On any given day anyone listening to an evening news program will hear a report of the level at which "the Dow" closed and the number of points that day's close is up or down over the previous day's—for example, "The Dow Jones Industrial Average closed at 6555.91 today, up 29.84 points." The Dow Jones Industrial Average (DJIA) is the oldest, most popular, and most widely reported indicator of the stock market's performance. It was developed in 1884 by Charles Dow, founder of the Dow Jones Company, which publishes *The Wall Street Journal*. At that time the average consisted of 11 stocks. Today, the industrial average is actually one segment of a larger composite measure known as the Dow Jones Average, comprising 65 companies' stocks: 30 industrial companies, 20 transportation companies, and 15 utilities. As Figure 6.2 shows, there is an average for each of the three business segments.

The Dow Jones Industrial Average consists of 30 blue-chip industrial companies whose stocks trade on the New York Stock Exchange. These companies are thought to represent the broad spectrum and character of industry in America. Their collective price movement is one of the most accurate leading indicators of the state of the economy. Currently, the following 30 companies are contained in the DJIA:

index a composite measure of the movement of the overall market or of a particular industry that consists of a large number of stocks and is usually weighted by other factors, such as capitalization.

weighting the method for determining the worth of each company's stock relative to the value of the overall index.

1. Alcoa (Aluminum Co. of America).
2. Allied-Signal.
3. American Express.
4. AT&T.
5. Boeing.
6. Caterpillar.
7. Chevron.

8. Coca-Cola.
9. Disney.
10. DuPont.
11. Eastman Kodak.
12. Exxon.
13. General Electric.
14. General Motors.
15. Goodyear.
16. Hewlett-Packard.
17. IBM.
18. International Paper.
19. Johnson & Johnson.
20. McDonald's.
21. Merck.
22. 3M (Minnesota Mining & Manufacturing).
23. J. P. Morgan.
24. Philip Morris.
25. Procter & Gamble.
26. Sears.
27. Travelers Group.
28. Union Carbide.
29. United Technologies.
30. Wal-Mart.

As you can see from the list, not all of the companies in the average are strictly industrials. There are services companies (American Express), health-care companies (Johnson & Johnson), retail companies (Sears), communications companies (AT&T), and technology companies (Hewlett-Packard).

Because the DJIA consists of only 30 blue-chip stocks that trade on the New York Stock Exchange, it has been criticized as being too narrow—not truly representative of the broad spectrum of business in the United States, especially technology companies and smaller, entrepreneurial businesses—and as being too influenced by high-priced stocks. Additionally, its critics believe that the stability of the companies included in the Dow causes the average itself to be too stable. It does not, they assert, reflect the volatile price movements that sometimes characterize the stocks of growth companies, for example. The first criticism leads to a second: that the stability of the DJIA causes its movements to lag behind the overall trend in the market. Changes in the economy tend to affect smaller companies and their stock prices first. Many of these criticisms are logical and valid. Nonetheless, they have not reduced the popularity of the Dow Jones Industrial Average as the most widely followed market indicator.

New York Stock Exchange Composite Index

This index measures the movement of the nearly 2740 common stocks that trade on the New York Stock Exchange. The other types of securities that trade on the exchange are not included in this index. Unlike the DJIA, the movement of this index is not quoted in points; it is quoted in dollars and cents. It is therefore described as a market-valued index. Using an example from Figure 6.2, we would say that the NYSE Composite Index closed at $400.68, up $2.66 from the previous day's close.

Standard & Poor's Composite Index of 500 Stocks

The S&P 500, as this index is more popularly known, is composed of 500 of the largest companies that trade on the New York Stock Exchange and NASDAQ. Like the Dow Jones Average, the 500 stocks that comprise the S&P index are grouped into business segments: 400 industrials, 40 utilities, 40 financial companies, and 20 transportations. Each segment has its own index. (See Figure 6.2.) Also like the NYSE Composite Index, the S&P is a market-valued index and is quoted in dollars.

The S&P 500 Index is very popular with institutional investors (mutual funds, banks, insurance companies) and technical analysts. Over the years, it has become the standard against which these investors measure the performance of their portfolios. The reason is that the stocks that make up this composite index are selected because of their impact on the economy. This is not the basis for selecting the stocks in the NYSE or American Stock Exchange indexes, which are composed of the stocks that trade on the exchanges. The result of the more focused selection is that the S&P 500 is a great leading index. Today many investment managers index their portfolios to match the S&P 500; that is, they construct their portfolios of securities so that they reflect or match the composition and weighting of the S&P. In this way, the total investment returns from their portfolios will keep pace with the performance of the index.

NASDAQ Composite Index

This is an index of all the common stocks of domestic companies that trade on NASDAQ (the National Association of Securities Dealers Automated Quotation system). Stocks from six subindexes representing different business segments make up the composite index: industrial (the broadest), banking, insurance, other finance, transportation, and utilities.

American Stock Exchange Composite Index

The new American Stock Exchange Composite Index, introduced on January 2, 1997, is a market capitalization, price appreciation only index. Market capitalization is computed by multiplying the closing price of the security each day by the number of shares or units outstanding. Price appreciation is the amount by which the price of the stock has changed over the previous day. Dividend reinvestment is not taken into account, as it is with other indexes.

Not only does the index include all of the common stock that trades on the AMEX, it also includes limited partnership units, American Depositary Receipts (ADRs), closed-end fund shares, investment company shares, real estate investment trusts (REITs), and other miscellaneous trusts that trade on the AMEX. Because this new index is calculated quite differently from the previous American Stock Exchange Index, investors should not make comparisons between the old and the new indexes.

Value Line Index

The Value Line Index is composed of about 1700 stocks that trade on the exchanges and NASDAQ. It is structured as if an equal amount of money were invested in each of the 1700 companies. The result is that the same dollar amount buys more shares of lower-priced stock than of higher-priced stock. The movement of the Value Line Index is therefore strongly influenced by changes in the value of the lower-priced stocks, a characteristic that makes it more volatile than either the Dow Jones Industrial Average or the S&P 500 Index.

Russell 2000 Index

Created in 1978 by Frank Russell Company in Tacoma, Washington, this is the principal index of the small-capitalization stocks. The company compiles a list of the 3000 largest capitalized stocks across all securities markets. The top 1000 are used in the Russell 1000 Index. The remaining 2000 "small-cap" stocks are used in the Russell 2000 Index. "Small-cap" defines a broad range of companies. The largest company in the index has a market capitalization of $1.018 billion and the smallest company in the index has a market capitalization of $161.9 million. As this explanation suggests, this index is weighted by capitalization. Once each year, usually in July, the Frank Russell Company reconstitutes the index, adding and deleting companies based on changes in their individual capitalization.

Wilshire 5000 Index

Constructed like the S&P 500 Index and the NYSE Composite Index, the Wilshire 5000 Index is the broadest measure of the market. It consists of more than 7000 common stocks that trade on the NYSE, the AMEX, and the over-the-counter market. It also represents the largest dollar amount of all actively traded securities in the United States. Because it is so broad, this index tends to be less influenced by the stability of the blue-chip stocks. It is therefore, like the Value Line Index, somewhat more volatile than the indicators weighted by large capitalization stock.

Many more averages and indexes exist than the few discussed here and listed in Figure 6.2. These were selected because they are most widely used in technical analysis. Today, in addition to these broad-based indexes, analysts have created and follow sector-specific indexes, such as the technology index, the semiconductor index, the pharmaceutical index, the gold index, and so forth. Still, all indexes serve basically the same purpose: to portray current market activity and provide a basis for predicting future price movements. Investors interested in technical analysis must research the various indexes to find which one or more best fit with individual theories about price movement in the marketplace.

MARKET THEORIES

The Dow Theory

The Dow theory was the first technical theory developed. It divides the movement of the stock market into three groups: primary movement, secondary movement, and daily movement. Figure 6.3 illustrates the difference between primary movement and secondary movement.

The primary movement is the long-term direction of the market. In Figure 6.3, the primary movement shown between points A and B is bullish. The movement from point B to point C is bearish.

The secondary movement is a series of brief reversals that occur during the primary movement, represented by the smaller letters a–g in Figure 6.3. These reversals are normal during any trend in the market. After all, the market moves not straight up or straight down but in a jagged series of rises and falls. The frequency and percentage of the reversals serve to indicate a possible change in the direction of primary market movement. The small letters a–d indicate the secondary market moves during a bull market. Notice that each subsequent secondary decline is

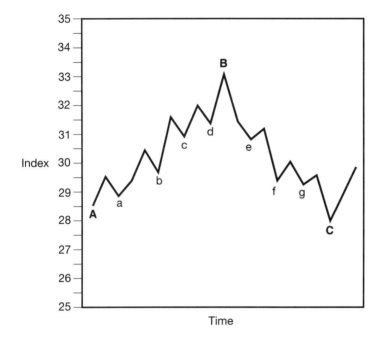

FIGURE 6.3 The Dow theory: primary and secondary market movements.

never lower than the previous reversal. During a bear market, each subsequent secondary price rise—letters *e–g*—is never higher than the previous one.

The market's daily movements are no more than emotional reactions, "Dow-ists" believe, and are not worth considering. They have no effect on either the primary or the secondary movement of the market.

Additionally, the Dow theory states that in order for the direction of the primary movement to be valid, it has to occur in both the industrial average and the transportation average; that is, the movements of the industrial average and the transportation average must confirm each other. Around 1900, when this theory was developed by Charles Dow, S. A. Nelson, and William P. Hamilton, this qualifier made quite good sense. The country's primary industrial production was durable goods. As the demand for these goods rose or was anticipated to rise, there was an increased need for transportation—primarily trains in those days—to deliver the products to the marketplace.

Conversely, decreased demand for durable goods meant a decreased need for transportation. The movement of the industrial sector was therefore validated by the same movement in the transportation sector.

The Dow theory was not designed to help investors "beat the market" by improving their return from investing in the stocks during the primary movements. Nor was it able to estimate the duration of a trend. Its purpose was to predict any change in the market's primary movement, thereby permitting investors to take appropriate actions to protect the value of their holdings.

Today, virtually no one advocates the Dow theory. Historically, it has produced mixed results and has been criticized for being superficial, imprecise, and slow to confirm market direction.

The Advance-Decline Theory

This theory looks at the total number of issues traded during a given session and compares the number of stocks whose prices advanced with the number of those whose prices declined. The total number of shares traded, called the *breadth of the market*, varies from market to market. This is because of the different number of companies' stocks listed on the different exchanges and stock markets. The greater the number of issues traded compared with the number of issues listed, then the greater the breadth of the market.

breadth of the market the number of individual stocks traded out of the number of stocks listed.

Figure 6.4 shows the daily Diaries of trading on the New York Stock Exchange (NYSE), NASDAQ, and American Stock Exchange (AMEX) from *The Wall Street Journal*. Using the NYSE data, you can see that of all of the common and preferred stock listed on the NYSE, 3326 issues traded on Monday. Of the issues traded, 1740 advanced in price, 801 declined, and 785 remained unchanged.

Technical analysts use this information to create an advance-decline line illustrated in Figure 6.5. This line is one of the simplest indicators of the direction of the overall market. At the end of each day, analysts compute the difference between the number of stocks whose prices

DIARIES

NYSE		MON	FRI	WK AGO
Issues traded		3,326	3,303	3,343
Advances		1,740	1,432	552
Declines		801	1,068	2,130
Unchanged		785	803	661
New highs		53	31	26
New lows		45	86	104
zAdv vol	(000)	292,255	321,570	76,424
zDecl vol	(000)	123,487	164,299	452,364
zTotal vol	(000)	453,420	537,237	555,727
Closing tick[1]		+181	+686	−539
Closing. Arms[2] (trin)		.92	.69	1.53
zBlock trades		10,253	12,127	12,760
NASDAQ				
Issues traded		5,750	5,749	5,755
Advances		2,329	2,279	1,397
Declines		1,678	1,657	2,803
Unchanged		1,743	1,813	1,555
New highs		76	43	41
New lows		213	337	247
Adv vol	(000)	352,614	495,911	96,567
Decl vol	(000)	174,263	135,232	437,227
Total vol	(000)	568,274	667,637	583,641
Block trades		9,386	11,508	8,839
AMEX				
Issues traded		712	705	757
Advances		300	254	159
Declines		205	257	426
Unchanged		207	194	172
New highs		15	7	13
New lows		11	24	39
zAdv vol	(000)	12,678	10,984	4,757
zDecl vol	(000)	3,239	7,306	14,596
zTotal vol	(000)	18,375	21,254	21,118
Comp vol	(000)	23,915	26,052	26,252
zBlock trades		n.a.	430	412

FIGURE 6.4 Diary of advancing and declining issues. This diary is published every business day in the Stock Market Data Bank column on page C2 of *The Wall Street Journal*. Reprinted by permission of *The Wall Street Journal*, © 1997 Dow Jones & Company, Inc. All rights reserved worldwide.

advanced and the number of stocks whose prices declined. If there are more advances than declines, then the net difference is added to the previous day's cumulative total. If there are more declines than advances, then the net difference is subtracted from the cumulative total. Figure 6.5 shows an advance-decline line for October

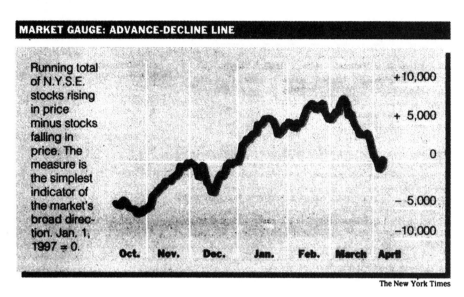

MARKET GAUGE: ADVANCE-DECLINE LINE

Running total of N.Y.S.E. stocks rising in price minus stocks falling in price. The measure is the simplest indicator of the market's broad direction. Jan. 1, 1997 = 0.

+10,000
+ 5,000
0
– 5,000
–10,000

Oct.   Nov.   Dec.   Jan.   Feb.   March   April

The New York Times

FIGURE 6.5 Advance-decline line for NYSE issues. © 1997 *The New York Times.* Reprinted by permission.

1996 to April 1997. Analysts begin calculating the cumulative total from a zero base on January 1 of each year.

Technical analysts' basic interpretation of the advance-decline line is quite straightforward. When advancing issues exceed declining issues, the net difference is added to the cumulative total. As a result, the advance-decline will rise over time. This indicates a bullish market. More declines than advances over a period of time would clearly cause the line to fall, indicating a bearish market.

Analysts also use the advance-decline line's movement to confirm the overall market's direction. For example, if the NYSE Composite Index reaches a new high, an analyst might examine the advance-decline line for NYSE issues to see if the cumulative total has also reached a new high. If it has, then the market's direction is confirmed. If, in the same scenario, the advance-decline line does not also reach a new high, then the lack of confirmation may indicate a possible change in the market's direction.

Some analysts are more selective in the stocks they

use when computing the advance-decline line. For example, the NYSE's total listed issues include both common and preferred stock. Some analysts perform the advance-decline calculation using only the common issues that trade on the NYSE. Other analysts are even more specific. They use only the common stock of operating companies when doing the calculation; hence, they exclude the shares of closed-end funds, REITs, and other common stock equivalents that are included in the exchanges' or NASDAQ's definition of "common stock."

In a slightly more complex application of the same theory, technical analysts use these data to compute a positive or negative percentage figure that represents the strength of the advance or the decline, respectively. Using the New York Stock Exchange data, an analyst would calculate the percentage of the advance or the decline by subtracting the number of declining issues from the number of advancing issues and then dividing the net difference by the total number of issues traded:

$$\frac{+1740 - 801}{3326} = \frac{+939}{3326} = +28\%$$

Continued positive and high net percentages indicate a technically strong bullish market. Increasing negative percentages indicate a technically weak market and are a bearish indicator. During either of these market trends, if the net percentage begins to show a continued and increasing shift in the opposite direction, the analyst interprets the movement as an indication that the market is about to change direction and responds by initiating new positions to take advantage of the change or liquidating existing positions to take profits. Additionally, an increase in the breadth of the market during a bullish market is thought to be a positive sign; conversely, an expansion in negative breadth portends a weak market.

Because of its focus on the breadth of the market instead of just selected issues (as with the Dow theory), the advance-decline theory has been widely used as the basis for developing more complex technical measures and theories about the market's movement, such as the ARMS Index.

Named after its creator, Richard Arms, the ARMS Index is a slightly more complex and accurate application of the advance-decline theory. Popularly called TRIN (Trading Index), it factors into the calculation the volumes associated with both advancing and declining issues, in addition to the number of issues advancing and declining.

The Short Interest Theory

short interest the total amount of a company's outstanding shares that have been sold short and have not been covered or bought in.

Short interest is the number of shares investors have sold short that are still standing open in the market—in other words, the short sellers have not repurchased the borrowed stock and returned it to the lenders. Technical analysts view short selling as a sentiment indicator. As we discussed in Chapter 4, investors sell short when they expect the market price of a security to decline. It would seem logical that large outstanding short interest is a bearish indicator. Indeed, this is true for the short term; however, technical analysts take a different view for the long term. Recall that every short seller borrows the stock that he or she sells short in the market. Eventually this individual must repurchase the stock and return it to the lender. When the short sellers begin to cover their positions—they "buy in" the borrowed stock—because of a reversal in the downward price movement of the stock, the increased demand for the security will cause the price to rise even higher. Large outstanding short interest is therefore considered to be a intermediate-term bullish indicator. Small or moderate amounts of short interest are considered to have little potential impact on a stock's price.

Short interest data are published in *The Wall Street Journal*, usually around the twentieth of the month; this information is compiled around the fifteenth of the month. The information contained in Figure 6.6 shows all the stocks with substantial short interest and those whose

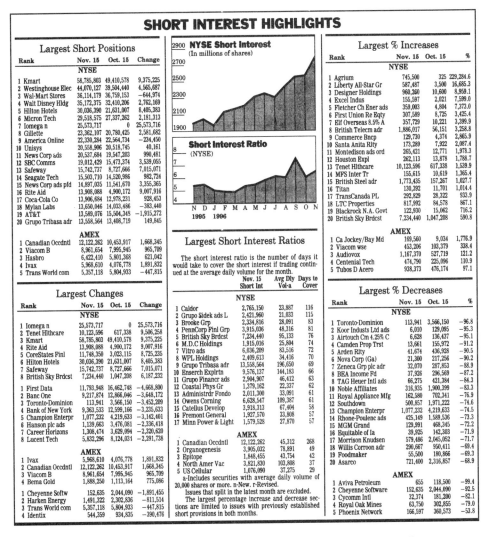

FIGURE 6.6 Short interest data. Reprinted by permission of *The Wall Street Journal*, © 1996 Dow Jones & Company, Inc. All rights reserved worldwide.

short interest changed significantly during the month. By the time this information is available to the public, it is already somewhat out of date; for many analysts, the delay limits the usefulness of the information.

The short interest theory is not thought to be reliable because less than 1 percent of all investors sell short.

Hence, the number of short sellers does not represent a sufficient breadth of the market. The lower percentage is largely due to two factors: Selling short is not popular, and an investor who uses this strategy is subject to unlimited loss. Also, many investors sell short only for tax reasons—specifically to defer paying taxes on a capital gain. This strategy is known as *selling short against the box*. The following example illustrates this strategy.

selling short against the box a strategy used to lock in a gain on securities that an investor owns and defer taxes to the next year. The investor sells short the same security that he or she owns and later uses the long position to cover the short sale.

An investor owns 100 shares of a stock that she purchased early in 1997 at $15 a share. By December 1997, the price of the stock has appreciated to $55 per share. The investor wishes to take profits ($4000), but she also wants to defer paying taxes on the gain until 1998. In order to accomplish this, she establishes a second, but **opposite**, position in the same stock by selling short 100 shares of the stock at the current market price of $55. She now has two positions in the stock: she is long 100 shares at $15 and short 100 shares at $55. In effect, she has locked in the $40 per share gain. If the stock's price appreciates, every dollar she makes on the long position will be lost on the short. If the stock's price declines, every dollar made on the short position will be lost on the long position. With the gain protected, the investor holds both positions open until the first business day of the new tax year or any business day afterward. She then uses the stock held in the "box"—the long position—to replace the stock she borrowed for the short sale. Now that both positions have been liquidated in the new tax year, the investor pays taxes on the gain in that year. This strategy gets its name from a time when a customer's securities were held in a safety deposit box or in the firm's vault (referred to as the "box"), and the customer would sell short against those securities.

The short sales involved in shorting against the box are included in the short interest reported in *The Wall Street Journal*. Also included in this report are the short sales that are part of an arbitrage. These make up an even larger portion of the short interest data than do the short-against-the-box sales. However, these sales do not always represent any eventual demand for the security because the investors and arbitrageurs can or will use the securities that they own to cover their short positions. Again, given the small number of investors who sell short and the purposes for which they do it, tracking the increases and decreases in open short positions may not provide analysts with much useful information.

Technical analysts consider the *short interest ratio* to be a more useful measure of the market's potential movement:

$$\text{Short interest ratio} = \frac{\text{Short interest position}}{\text{Average daily trading volume}}$$

The ratio obtained by dividing a stock's short interest position by the average daily trading volume indicates the number of days it would take to cover the outstanding short positions. Using an example from Figure 6.6, the short ratio for Caldor is 116.

The ratio does not represent a hard-and-fast indicator of a bullish or bearish sentiment, but there are some rule-of-thumb norms against which the ratio is compared. Generally, the short interest ratio is considered to be high when it is greater than 2. This is a bullish indicator because there are a large number of investors in the market who eventually will have to buy back the shares that were sold short.

> **short interest ratio** a calculation (a stock's short interest divided by its average daily trading volume) used to determine the number of days it would take to cover or buy in the number of shares that investors have sold short.

This section has explained some of the more widely applied and basic technical theories that are used to determine the movement of individual stocks, as well as the overall securities market. More in-depth information on technical analysis can be found in other authoritative texts. Keep in mind that few technical analysts use or follow just one theory. Most apply several theories at one time, using one to confirm the indications of another.

THE BASICS OF CHARTING

The terms "technical analysis" and "charting" are virtual synonyms. All chartists hold to the basic theory that past patterns of price movements, properly analyzed, can be used to predict future price movement. In short, all the information necessary to predict reasonably the direction in which the market will move is contained in the chart patterns. Chartists do, however, differ as to which charting method they consider to be most effective. In this section, we will explore the three basic charting techniques.

Line Charting

This is the type of chart that we first learned to construct in elementary school. Many securities analysts use line charts to show the closing prices of an index or a particular stock over a period of days or months. Figure 6.7 is a line chart depicting the price movement of the Dow Jones Industrial Average from October 1995 to April 10, 1997. These charts are also used to show the minute-to-minute and hourly price movement of a specific security or the overall market. Figure 6.8, published daily in most financial newspapers, shows the movement of the Dow Jones Industrial Average at five-minute intervals. (This illustrates how volatile the Dow can be during a single trading session.) Many technicians who use line charts believe that much of the information necessary to

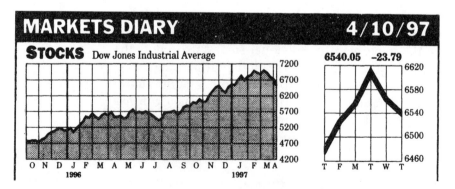

FIGURE 6.7 Line chart showing the movement of the Dow Jones Industrial Average over a number of months. Reprinted by permission of *The Wall Street Journal,* © 1997 Dow Jones & Company, Inc. All rights reserved worldwide.

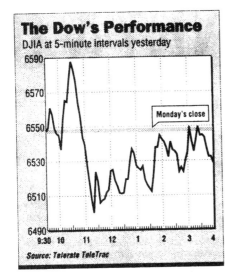

The Dow's Performance
DJIA at 5-minute intervals yesterday

Source: Telerate TeleTrac

FIGURE 6.8 A line chart showing the movement of the Dow Jones Industrial Average in five-minute intervals during a trading day. Reprinted by permission of *The Wall Street Journal*, © 1997 Dow Jones & Company, Inc. All rights reserved worldwide.

judge the market is reflected in the succession of closing prices.

Bar Charting

This is the simplest charting technique used by technical analysts. Price is indicated on the chart's vertical axis, and time is indicated on the horizontal axis. The market or price movement for a given session is represented on one line. The vertical part of the line shows the high and the low prices at which the stock traded or the market moved. A short horizontal tick on the vertical line indicates the price or level at which the stock or market closed.

In the example in Figure 6.9, the first bar shows that the stock represented traded at a high of 26⅝ and a low of 25¼ during the session; its closing price was 26¼. Figure 6.10 is a bar chart showing the movement of the Dow Jones Industrial Average for the same period as depicted in the line chart in Figure 6.7.

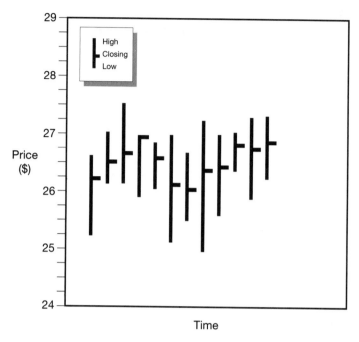

FIGURE 6.9   Vertical lines used in a bar chart.

Point-and-Figure Charting

This charting method uses the boxes on a graph to record the price movements of a stock. When the price rises up, the increase is depicted by a series of x's in a column of boxes. When the stock price reverses downward, the chartist moves over one column and uses a series of o's to denote the decline. Figure 6.11 is an example of a point-and-figure chart.

This chart shows the price movement of the stock in units of one point ($1). (Smaller units may be used depending on the price sensitivity that the technician wishes to monitor.) In the example, the x's in the first column show that the price of the stock rose from $23 to $29. When the price fell by one point ($1), the chartist moved over one column and depicted the price decline from $28 to $24 using o's in the second column. Then it rose again from $25 to $32. Given the type of information this chart contains, an analyst interested in the daily price movement of a security can construct a

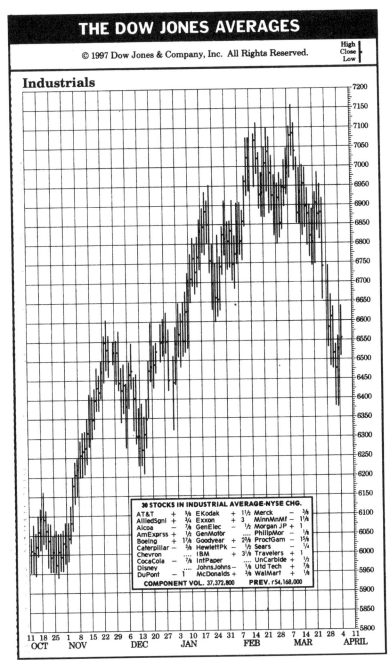

THE DOW JONES AVERAGES

High
Close
Low

Industrials

30 STOCKS IN INDUSTRIAL AVERAGE-NYSE CHG.

AT&T	+	⅝	EKodak	+	1½	Merck	−	⅜
AlliedSgnl	+	¾	Exxon	+	3	MinnMnMf	−	1⅛
Alcoa	−	⅞	GenElec	−	½	Morgan JP	+	1
AmExprss	+	½	GenMotbr		....	PhilipMor	−	⅛
Boeing	+	1⅞	Goodyear	+	2⅜	ProctGam	−	1⅝
Caterpillar	−	⅜	HewlettPk	−	½	Sears	−	¼
Chevron		....	IBM	+	3⅛	Travelers	+	1
CocaCola	−	⅞	IntPaper		....	UnCarbide	+	½
Disney		....	JohnsJohns	−	⅛	Utd Tech	+	⅞
DuPont	−	1	McDonalds	+	⅜	WalMart	+	⅛

COMPONENT VOL. 37,372,800   PREV. r54,168,000

11 18 25 | 1 8 15 22 29 | 6 13 20 27 | 3 10 17 24 31 | 7 14 21 28 | 7 14 21 28 | 4 11
OCT | NOV | DEC | JAN | FEB | MAR | APRIL

FIGURE 6.10 Bar chart showing the movement of the Dow Jones Industrial Average. Reprinted by permission of *The Wall Street Journal*, © 1997 Dow Jones & Company, Inc. All rights reserved worldwide.

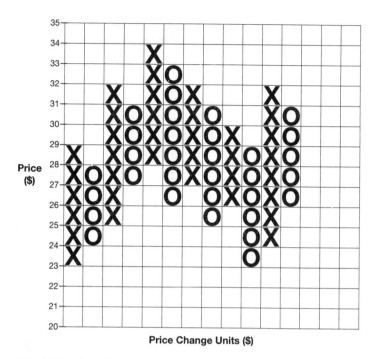

FIGURE 6.11 Point-and-figure chart.

point-and-figure chart from information contained in newspapers.

The time at which the price rises or falls is not recorded; nor is the volume recorded. Analysts who use point-and-figure charts are interested only in recording the fact that price changes occur. The degree or percentage of the change, as an indicator of continued movement in a direction or of a potential shift in direction, is more important than when it occurs. Buy and sell signals may be more easily discerned from a point-and-figure chart than from the other types of charts.

Once you decide which charting method you prefer, you can create your own charts, buy them from a charting service, or get them from your broker at a full-service brokerage house. You must then learn to analyze the charts, looking for certain formations to emerge as the stock's price movement is recorded. Keep in mind that the formations occur as the market moves in its usually jagged pattern—a series of peaks (high points) and troughs (low points). (See Figures 6.7 and 6.10.) With bar charting, the most common formations are illustrated and interpreted below.

Formations

A *trend* can be defined simply as the direction in which the market is moving. However, the market does not move straight up or straight down. Instead, it moves in a series of peaks and troughs that form a jagged pattern. If the succession of highs (peaks) and lows (troughs) occurs at increasingly higher prices, then the market is clearly in an *uptrend* (Figure 6.12). This trend is bullish, indicating a good time to buy securities. But if the peaks and troughs occur at successively lower prices, the market is in a *downtrend* (Figure 6.13). This trend is bearish, indicating a good time to sell securities.

Many investors think that the market moves only

trend in technical terms, the up, down, or sideways movement of the overall market (as reflected in an average or index) or a stock's price over a period of time, usually longer than six months.

uptrend the upward movement of a stock's price or of the market as measured by an average or index over a period of time.

downtrend the downward movement of a stock's price or of the market as measured by an average or index over a period of time.

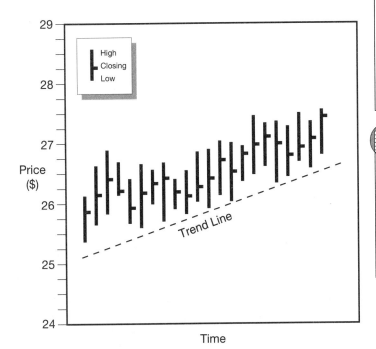

FIGURE 6.12 Bar chart showing an uptrend.

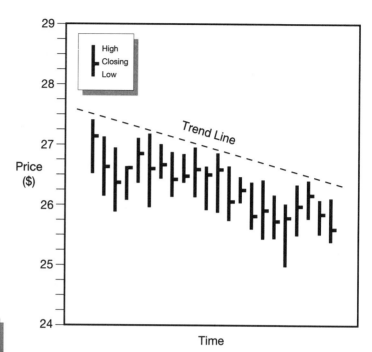

FIGURE 6.13 Bar chart showing a downtrend.

resistance level a price level to which a stock or the market rises and then from which it falls repeatedly; selling increases as the stock's price approaches this level.

support level a price level to which a stock or the market falls or bottoms out repeatedly and then bounces up again; demand for the security increases as the price approaches a support level.

up or down. This is a misconception. At least a third of the time, according to technical analysts, the market moves sideways. A sideways trend is characterized by stock prices trading in a range where successive peaks occur at similar price levels and successive troughs occur at similar price levels (Figure 6.14). The two levels create parallel horizontal trend lines. This trend often thwarts technical analysts because there are no clear buy or sell signals. During this time, many investors react cautiously and prudently. They sit on the sidelines and wait for more definite indicators of the market's future movement.

A *resistance level* occurs during an uptrend or a sideways trend. It is a price point to which the market rallies repeatedly but cannot break through. Each time the stock approaches the identified price level, investors begin selling the stock, which causes the price to fall.

A *support level* occurs during a downtrend or a sideways trend. It is a price point to which the market declines repeatedly but cannot fall below. At the identified

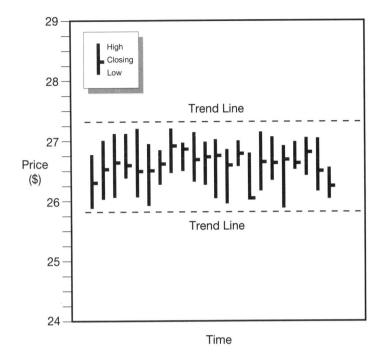

FIGURE 6.14   Bar chart showing a sideways trend.

price level, the stock's downward movement is stopped because investors begin buying the stock. This buying pressure or demand supports the price of the stock, preventing it from going lower. (See Figure 6.15.)

Technical analysts have two theories about resistance and support levels:

1. If the market breaks through a resistance level, the price will continue upward, reaching a new high.
2. If the market breaks through a support level, the price will continue downward, falling to a new low.

Chartists therefore try to identify the *breakout*, the point at which the market penetrates a support or resistance level, indicating the beginning of a new short-term uptrend (in the case of resistance levels) or a downtrend (in the case of support levels). When the breakout occurs in an uptrend, the old resistance level often becomes the

breakout a price rise above a resistance level that results in a substantial advance, or a price decline below a support level that results in a substantial price decline; breakouts usually establish new support and resistance levels.

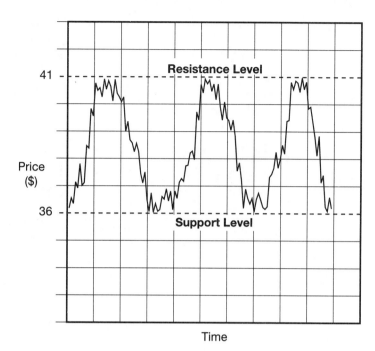

FIGURE 6.15 Line chart showing support and resistance levels.

new support level. In a downtrend, the old support level sometimes becomes the new resistance level.

The head-and-shoulders pattern indicates the reversal of an uptrend. Figure 6.16 contains an example of this formation. The formation begins with a strong price advance (A), which is supported by a high volume of trading. (Volume changes are depicted at the bottom of the graph.) A pause or slight decline (B) follows. The price then advances to a higher level (C) but supported by a lighter trading volume. A price decline follows (D) but to a level no lower than the first price decline (B), forming what is called the "neckline" of the formation. This pause is then followed by a rally to a lower peak (E) than the previous one (C) but still on decreasing volume.

The head-and-shoulders bottom pattern, shown in Figure 6.17, is an inverted version of the head-and-shoulders top formation. It indicates the reversal of a downtrend.

Two other basic patterns also indicate the reversal of

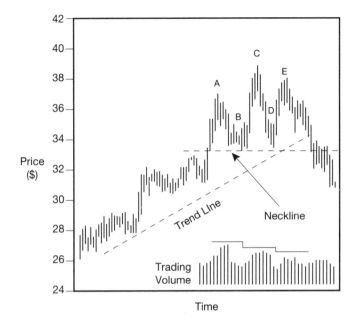

FIGURE 6.16   Head-and-shoulders top formation indicating a reversal of an uptrend.

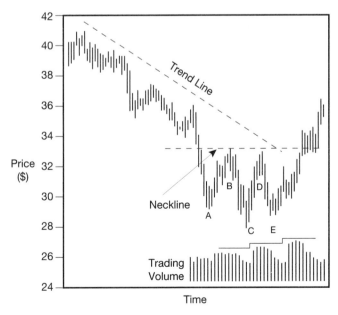

FIGURE 6.17   Head-and-shoulders bottom formation indicating a reversal of a downtrend.

a trend. The double-top (Figure 6.18), sometimes referred to as the "m" formation, occurs as an uptrend is about to reverse itself. In addition to indicating that a security's price has reached a peak, the second top is supported by substantially less volume than the first, indicating an upcoming price decline.

In the double-bottom (Figure 6.19), sometimes called the "w" formation, the second decline is supported by substantially more volume, indicating that the price is about to rise.

The kinds of formations identified by chartists—rising bottoms, saucers, pennants, flags, and others—and their indications are as varied as the flag symbols seamen

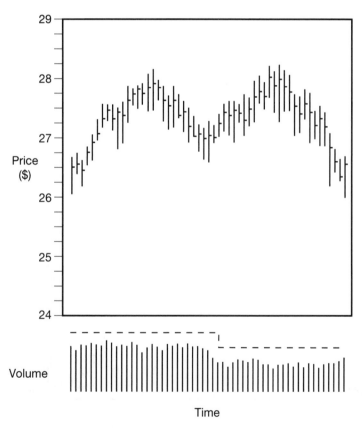

FIGURE 6.18 Double-top formation indicating a reversal of an uptrend.

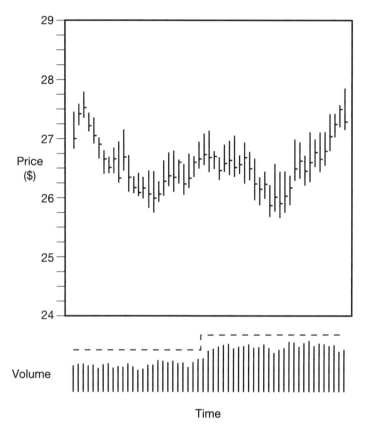

FIGURE 6.19 Double bottom formation indicating a reversal of a downtrend.

use. And they are also as confusing to beginning investors as the flags are to first-time sailors. Investors must study the logic of each formation carefully before they can successfully apply them in analyzing the market.

CONCLUSION

The basic attraction of technical analysis is its belief that all information necessary to forecast the movement of the market is in the market itself. This information is contained in the interaction of price and volume, which tends to repeat itself over time. Investors interested in technical analysis soon discover that there is no shortage of theories that have been developed from this simple premise. Some can be used by all investors; some are used only by traders; still others can be applied to only certain industries. The numerous variations and interpretations make using technical analysis difficult. Nonetheless, it remains popular among securities traders and of keen interest to serious students of the securities markets.

Technical analysis is not without its detractors. It has been compared to reading tea leaves and to the ancient Greek practice of reading goat entrails as a method of predicting the future. Other investors and traders view technical analysis as a self-fulfilling prophesy. They argue that there is only a fixed and limited amount of price information about each security that each analyst uses to make forecasts. Thus, the "group" actions of these analysts, not "real" supply and demand forces, cause the "technical rises" and "technical declines" in the markets.

moving average an average of a stock's or the market's closing prices over a fixed period (e.g., 20 days, 30 days), which is recomputed each day to include the current day's closing price within the fixed period.

Today, technical analysis is easier, more accurate, and more efficient than in the past because it is performed using computers. Analysts also use *moving averages* as a way of smoothing out the chart patterns. These enable analysts to keep the big picture of the market's movement in view without getting lost in the day-to-day movement. This has not necessarily brought about increased accuracy in the predictions made using these data. But at the very least, the technical approach organizes information about the movement of price and volume, showing where the market is today. At its best, technical analysis offers clues that prefigure where the market will move tomorrow, becoming a useful tool for profiting from the short-term and intermediate-term movements of the stock market.

The Random Walk Theory

Having discussed fundamental analysis in the previous chapter and technical analysis is this chapter, we will now look at a market theory that says that all stock analysis is essentially useless. This theory is known as the Random Walk Theory. In simple terms, it states that the movement of a stock's price is generally unpredictable in the short term, not unlike a person who, while taking a walk, flips a coin to decide whether to turn left or right at each intersection. The ultimate implication of this theory is that an investor does not need analysts' recommendations to make successful investments. Instead, he or she can choose the companies' shares totally at random and these shares will have an equal chance of performing as well as the analysts' recommendations over the long term.

The Random Walk Theory is more popularly known as the Dart Board Theory. *The Wall Street Journal* tests this theory periodically by setting up a contest between the dart board and a group of investment professionals (analysts, mutual fund managers, and money managers). The dart board selections are made by having any available *Wall Street Journal* employees throw darts at stock tables that have been randomized and tacked to a wall. The performances of these random stock picks are compared to recommendations of the investment professionals over a six-month period.

Since the inception of the contest in 1990, the recommendations of the investment professionals have beaten the Dart Board about 60 percent of the time. During this time, the professionals' average six-month performance has been +10.8 percent, while the dart board has been +5.5 percent and the Dow Jones Industrial Average (the performance benchmark for the contest) has been +6.5 percent.

So what do these statistics suggest? As we said earlier, the predictions of an insightful analyst can often come true and prove profitable. However, keep in mind that at any given time the stock market can be cruel to even the most experienced, successful analyst.

7

Chapter

Building a Stock Portfolio or Investing in Mutual Funds

S hould you build your own portfolio, buying shares of individual companies, or should you buy mutual fund shares, whose professional staff organizes and manages portfolios? The answer to this question can be found in the answer to another question: How actively do you want to become involved in stock selection and portfolio management?

BUILDING AND MANAGING YOUR OWN PORTFOLIO

Recently a young businessman who owns a growing word processing and computer design firm told me proudly, "I've just opened a discount brokerage account and bought my first stock—200 shares of Dell Computer. I wish I had bought more." He added, "This is just the first step to building my own portfolio of investments. Good things are ahead as I learn to make money from stocks." This person works long days—12 to 14 hours—in order to keep his business growing. And his business is becoming successful; but when will he find the time to do the necessary research and devote his attention to building a portfolio?

Some investors, this businessman included, believe

that the best way to learn about stocks and how to make money from them is to "try their hand," getting directly involved. They want to do the research, select the stocks, follow the fluctuations in each stock's price, and decide when to buy or sell. These individuals want to be fully responsible for the profits and losses that result from their trades.

Other factors that may increase a person's desire to select individual stocks by himself or herself can be (1) the perceived financial sophistication associated with directing one's own portfolio, (2) the belief that brokers, who make commissions on every transaction, do not always have a customer's best interest in mind, and (3) the desire to keep investment costs (i.e., commissions and other fees) as low as possible.

Two significant developments in the securities industry have made it much easier for an individual investor to "do it yourself." First, the proliferation of discount brokerage firms and the competition among them for individual investors have driven commission costs to all-time lows. And second, the implementation of now-commonplace technological capabilities such as 24-hour on-line order entry (i.e., entering buy and sell orders via a telephone keypad or using a computer) means that an individual investor no longer needs a "real person" to handle his or her orders.

Discount and Deep-Discount Brokerage Firms

Since 1975, when commissions on securities transactions became negotiable, discount brokerage firms have offered investors order-execution-only services at the lowest possible commission rate. You can call up the brokerage firm, typically using an 800 telephone number, and tell the customer service representative what security to buy or sell. If you don't want to talk to a person, many discount firms offer you the ability to enter your orders using a Touch-Tone phone or a computer. These discount brokers do not offer their customers any frills like research, investment advice, or hand-holding during uncertain, volatile market conditions. In short, you are the captain of your own ship.

Competition among discount firms has resulted in their being divided into two groups: discount firms and deep-discount firms. The first term is commonly used to refer to the Big Three discounters: Charles Schwab & Co., Fidelity Investments, and Quick and Reilly, Inc. These firms' commissions on securities transactions are lower than those of full-service brokerage firms; however, to attract and keep customers with substantial amounts of investable assets, they now offer a variety of premium services. Ironically, these additional services result in discount brokers looking more and more like full-service firms. For example, while a discount firm does not perform its own research, it may offer investors on-line access to the Value Line Investment Survey or Standard & Poor's Stock Reports. Other discount brokers have begun to offer customers "investment help." While these firms make no specific recommendations, upon request they will provide a customer with a list of the top-rated mutual funds that meet his or her investment objectives.

Deep-discount brokerage firms are the industry's equivalent of the no-frills airlines. Technology, however, has made placing orders much easier than it was in the past. These firms offer order execution only at the lowest possible commissions. A daily scan of various investment publications, advertisements, or television programs shows firms offering commissions as low as $17 per 100-share trade.

Keep in mind that few things in the investment community are ever totally free or really inexpensive. To be eligible for the lowest commission charge, customers of some deep-discount firms must meet certain minimum deposit requirements and adhere to various restrictions. For example, some brokerage firms require a customer to deposit and maintain at the firm a minimum cash balance, usually $10,000, in order to pay the lowest commissions. In other cases, additional fees for postage and handling are added to the commission charges. When selecting a deep-discount firm, be sure to find out any requirements and restrictions before you open the account.

Direct Stock Purchase Plans (No-Load Stocks)

Some investors feel they should have the right to buy stocks without paying **any** commission. They reason that if they are making all of the investment decisions themselves they should not pay commissions to anyone, even the lowest-priced deep-discount brokerage firm.

It is now possible for an individual investor to avoid paying all commissions when buying certain stocks. A person can buy a company's common stock directly from the company itself, without using a broker. These shares, bought through a company's *direct stock purchase plan*, are called *no-load stocks*. (The name is borrowed from the term used to describe a mutual fund that does not charge investors a sales load.)

direct stock purchase plan a company-sponsored program that enables individuals to buy common shares directly from the company itself without using a broker.

To open a direct purchase plan account, call the company's shareholder services department or its direct purchase plan clearinghouse. Both usually have an 800 number that can be obtained from directory assistance for toll-free numbers. Figure 7.1 lists the names and the phone numbers of many of the popular and recognizable companies that have no-load stock plans.

no-load stocks common shares bought directly from a company through that company's direct stock purchase plan without using a broker and therefore without paying a commission.

If, for example, you call McDonald's toll-free number, you would be connected to the company's direct purchase plan clearinghouse. (Notice that several companies on this list use the same toll-free number.) An automated system informs you, in accordance with SEC rules, that you can order the company's prospectus. The system then gives you directions for ordering prospectuses of any domestic and foreign companies that participate in that clearinghouse's direct stock purchase plan. Once you have received the prospectus, you can open an account and buy stock through the program.

All direct stock purchase plans set minimum (ranging from $50 to $1000) and maximum investment amounts. Your first shares purchased are placed in the company's dividend reinvestment plan (DRIP). The frequency with which you can invest additional cash depends upon each company's plan. Some permit additional cash contributions weekly, others monthly, and others quarterly. Each plan sets a specific date on which it purchases the stock for your account; this date is commonly referred to as the cutoff date. If your contribution arrives after this date, then your money will not be invested in the company's stock until the next designated purchase

NO-LOAD STOCK PURCHASE PROGRAM

ABT Building Products	800-774-4177	Dominion Resources	800-552-4034
Advanta	800-774-4117	DQE	800-247-0400
Adeco	800-774-4177	DTE Energy	800-774-4117
Aflac	800-227-4756	Duke Realty	800-774-4117
Air Products & Chem.	888-233-5601	Eastern Co.	800-774-4117
AirTouch Communications	800-233-5601	Empresa Nac. de Electricidad	800-711-6475
Amer. Recreation Centers	916-852-8005	Energen	800-774-4117
Ameritech	800-774-4117	Enron	800-662-7662
Amoco	800-774-4117	Entergy	800-225-1721
Arrow Financial	518-745-1000	Equitable Cos.	800-774-4117
Atlantic Energy	609-645-4506	Exxon	800-252-1800
Atmos Energy	800-774-4117	Fiat	800-711-6475
Augat	617-575-3400	First Commercial	501-371-6716
Banco de Santander	800-711-6475	First USA	800-524-4458
Barclays Bank Plc	800-774-4117	Food Lion	800-232-9530
Bard (C.R.)	800-828-1639	General Growth Properties	800-774-4117
Barnett Banks	800-328-5822	Gillette	800-730-4001
Benetton Group S.P.A.	800-774-4117	Grand Metropolitan	800-711-6475
Bob Evans Farms	800-774-4177	Guidant	800-537-1667
British Airways	800-711-6475	Hawaiian Electric Industries	808-543-5662
British Teleco mmunications	800-711-6475	Hillenbrand Industries	800-774-4117
Cadbury Schwepps	800-711-6475	Home Depot	800-774-4117
Capstead Mortgage	214-874-2323	Home Properties	716-546-4900
Carpenter Technology	800-822-9828	Houston Industries	800-774-4117
Central & South West	800-774-4117	Illinova	800-750-7011
Chevron	800-774-4117	Imperial Chemical Industries	800-711-6475
CMS Energy	800-774-4117	Integron	910-770-2000
Coastal	800-788-2500	Interchange Fncl Services	201-703-2265
Comsat	301-214-3200	Invesco Plc.	800-774-4117
Conrail	800-243-7812	Johnson Controls	800-524-6220
C.R. Bard	800-828-1639	Lucent Technologies	888-582-3686
Crown American Realty	800-278-4353	Kellwood	314-576-3100
Dean Witter, Discover	800-228-0829	Kerr-McGee	800-395-2662
DeBartolo Realty	800-850-2880	Madison Gas & Electric	800-356-6423
Dial	800-453-2235	Mattel	888-909-9922
Disney	818-560-1000	McDonald's	800-774-4117

FIGURE 7.1 Companies with direct stock purchase programs. These are some of the nearly 300 U.S. and foreign companies that sell their shares directly to investors. These stocks are called no-load stocks because investors can buy them without paying commissions to brokers. Some of the phone numbers listed above are for individual companies' shareholder services departments, and other numbers are for direct purchase plan clearinghouses, the companies that handle no-load plans for certain issuers. All direct purchase plans set a minimum investment amount ranging from $50 to $1000.

NO-LOAD STOCK PURCHASE PROGRAM (cont.)			
Merck	800-774-4117	Santos Ltd.	800-774-4117
MidAmerican Energy	800-247-5211	Scana	800-774-4117
Mobil	800-648-9291	Sears, Roebuck & Co.	888-732-7788
Morton International	800-774-4117	Sierra Pacific Resources	800-662-7575
National Westminster Bank	800-711-6475	Sony	800-711-6475
Nippon Telegraph	800-711-6475	Southern Co.	800-774-4117
NorAm Energy	800-843-3445	Stone Container	800-346-9979
Norsk Hydro	800-711-6475	TAG Heuer	800-774-4117
Norwest	800-774-4117	TDK	800-711-6475
Novo Nordisk	800-711-6475	Telecom Argentina S.A.	800-774-4117
Oklahoma Gas & Electric	800-395-2662	Telefonica del Peru S.A.	800-774-4117
Oneok	800-395-2662	Telefonos de Mexico Series L	800-711-6475
Owens Corning	800-472-2210	Tenneco	800-446-2617
Pacific Dunlop	800-711-6475	Texaco	800-774-4117
Penney (J.C.)	800-565-2576	Tyson Foods	800-822-7096
Peoples Energy	800-774-4117	Unilever NV	800-774-4117
Pharmacia & Upjohn	800-774-4117	Unilever Plc	800-774-4117
Philadelphia Suburban	800-774-4117	Urban Shopping Centers	800-774-4117
Piedmont Natural Gas	800-774-4117	US West Comunications	800-537-0222
Pinnacle West	800-774-4117	US West Media Group	800-537-0222
Portland General	503-464-8599	Wal-Mart Stores	800-438-6278
Proctor & Gamble	800-764-7483	Waterford Wedgewood Plc	800-774-4117
Public Service Ent.	800-242-0813	Western Resources	800-774-4117
Public Service of New Mex.	800-774-4117	Westpac Banking	800-774-4117
Public Service of NC	800-774-4117	Whitman	800-660-4187
Questar	800-729-6788	Wisconsin Energy	800-558-9663
Reader's Digest	800-242-4653	WPS Resources	800-236-1551
Regions Financial	800-446-2617	York International	800-774-4117
Reuters Holdings	800-711-6475		

FIGURE 7.1 Continued.

date. Again, you must read the plan's prospectus for details.

Currently nearly 300 companies offer direct stock purchase programs, and the number is growing rapidly. However, keep in mind that nothing is ever free in the securities industry. Some direct stock purchase plans charge participants an annual account maintenance fee or a small handling fee for every share purchased through the program. Fees may also apply when you sell shares purchased through the program. The specific details and fees of each program are disclosed in the information that you receive from the company's shareholder services department or its direct stock purchase plan clearinghouse.

Choosing Your Stocks

For many small and beginning investors, selecting individual stocks and self-managing a portfolio can be risky. In addition to the time needed, two other factors—the lack of diversification (stock-specific risk) and high transaction costs—have direct effects on the risk these investors face and the investment return that the portfolio yields.

Given that most people begin by investing a modest amount of money in the stock market, it is difficult for small investors to acquire stocks in enough different business sectors to protect themselves against stock-specific risk—the risk of putting too much of your investment dollars in too few stocks. As investors add different stocks to their portfolios, this risk decreases as the holdings become more diversified. How many stocks must they own before stock-specific risk is neutralized? Numerous studies have confirmed that a portfolio consisting of only 8 to 10 stocks in diverse industries from the Standard & Poor's 500 will achieve 90 percent of the benefits of a portfolio diversified across the entire market.

Diversification can be costly for investors who wish to establish a portfolio. If, for example, the average price of a stock in the S&P 500 is $50 per share and the customer buys one round lot of 8 to 10 different stocks as required for sufficient diversification, the total cost of establishing a portfolio would be $40,000 ($50 per share × 8 stocks × 100 shares) excluding commissions. In order to lower the initial cost, the investor could buy the shares on margin. The initial out-of-pocket costs would be $20,000 (the 50 percent Regulation T initial margin requirement); however, interest would be charged on the broker's loan used to pay in full for the securities. The investor could also buy odd lots, but the commission cost per share is higher for these transactions than for round lot transactions. Hence, the percentage of an investor's overall costs increases. Even if the investor uses a discount brokerage firm, the total initial investment and associated costs are substantial. Furthermore, if the investor plans to trade actively in the account—or even change the stocks in the portfolio only occasionally—transaction costs increase even more. As a result, the price points at which the stock positions will become profitable are higher.

Time commitment, stock-specific selection risk, and high transaction costs are just a few of the adverse factors that investors must consider in establishing their own portfolio. Others (all discussed in Chapter 1) include knowledge of various investment instruments, asset allocation, diversification, timing risk, transaction costs, and, perhaps least often spoken of, expertise. Clearly the businessman cited at the beginning of this section has tried to lower his transaction costs by using a discount broker. Nonetheless, he still remains vulnerable to many other investment risks.

What can he do to lower the number of risks his investment is subject to and at the same time try his hand at direct investing in stock? He could allocate a certain percentage—say 10 percent, 20 percent, or 30 percent—of his investment dollars to direct investing and purchase a *mutual fund* with the remaining money. (Mutual funds and other types of investment companies are discussed in the next section of this chapter.) The advantage of this approach is that the larger portion of his capital is in an investment vehicle that, by definition, provides diversification, professional management, and relatively low fees. He can use the remainder for riskier investments. Individual stocks, which are generally more risky than diversified mutual funds, have the potential to provide much higher returns on every dollar invested. Combining individual stocks and mutual funds in a portfolio may provide higher returns than if the investor put all of his assets in mutual funds.

 **mutual fund** common name for an open-end management company that establishes a diversified portfolio of investments; these companies issue new shares and redeem old shares representing ownership in the portfolio.

In what areas should this entrepreneur choose to invest? The old adage first written by Pliny comes to mind: "The cobbler should stick to his last." The businessman who owns the word processing firm decided to invest in computer stocks because he works with computers every day. For him, this is a sound decision: He is aware of innovations being made in hardware and software, and he assists companies in setting up word processing systems. His work experience has become the basis for his investment decision.

In choosing a specific computer company's stock to buy, he went through a rudimentary version of fundamental analysis. He observed that many of the companies for which he works are ordering Dell Computers and are pleased with the price relative to the quality of the machine. He concluded that demand would increase as more people became aware of the excellence of the company's product and its quite reasonable price. On a technical level, he noted that the company's quality control is good because there are few problems with the product when it is delivered. And finally, he believed that the firm's customer service department works hard to support the products it has sold. His conclusion was that a quality product sold at a reasonable price, combined with increased awareness, will turn into increased sales, and good product support will enable the company to sustain its growth. His optimism is not without some concerns, however; he worries that the company may be unable to sustain its success if it expands too fast and that stiff price competition could result in lower profits.

The point of recounting this businessman's decision-making process is to illustrate and emphasize that he is choosing to invest in a product area or business sector in which he has some first-hand knowledge. Using your own work experience—in computers, medical research, building, printing, or some other field—is a good starting point for choosing your first investment in stocks. Other places from which to begin include your interests (e.g., motorcycles) and hobbies (e.g., electronics). You already have some knowledge of the reputations, products, services, and growth potential of the companies in these areas. Therefore, in making your investment decision, whether you use a full-service broker or a discount broker, you are not completely a novice.

Putting all of your investment dollars in only a few stocks is usually not a prudent decision for beginners. However, by using some of your money to purchase mutual funds and then allocating the remainder to invest directly in the market, you decrease the overall risk exposure without totally sacrificing the direct investment experience.

MUTUAL FUNDS

index fund
a mutual fund that invests in a group of securities whose performance replicates the performance of a particular stock market index, such as the Standard & Poor's 500 Index or the New York Stock Exchange Composite Index.

special situation fund a mutual fund that invests in companies that are candidates for takeover or those that are emerging from bankruptcy.

country fund
a mutual fund that invests in the equity securities of a particular foreign country.

Mutual funds are the means by which most people invest in stocks. In all of the mutual funds together (stock funds, bond funds, and money market funds), the public has invested over $3.5 trillion. Increasingly, financial newspapers are devoting more columns to articles about investing in and the performance of mutual funds. Bookstores are allocating more and more shelf space in the finance/business section to publications on the subject. And new types of funds are being created in response to the development of new financial instruments (*index funds*), new investment opportunities (*special situation funds*), world political events (the *country funds* of Eastern Europe), and social concerns (the *socially responsible funds*). Industry statistics estimate that at least one new mutual fund is launched in the United States every business day. Currently, the total number of mutual funds available is greater than the total number of different companies' stocks that trade on all of the U.S. stock exchanges.

In many ways, investing in a mutual fund is investing in the stock market for most small and beginning investors. The reasons for the popularity and growth of investing in mutual funds can be summarized in three phrases: convenience, perceived safety, and reasonable return. The first item, convenience, is an inherent feature of this type of investment. The second and third features are variables, although they are widely perceived by most investors as being built-in characteristics of mutual funds.

This section presents an overview of mutual fund investing. It will clarify and explain many of the issues related to the convenience, perceived safety, and anticipated returns of mutual funds. While much of the information presented will apply to all mutual funds, emphasis will be placed on items to consider when choosing and investing in an *equity or stock fund.*

Overview

"Mutual fund" is the commonly used name for an *open-end management company*—a company that pools the money of many investors who have essentially the same investment objective and uses it to establish a portfolio of securities, which is then managed by a financial professional, called an *investment adviser* or portfolio manager. At some mutual funds, the investment adviser is a team of financial professionals rather than an individual. This person or team chooses the specific securities and the allocations of each that will constitute the fund's investment portfolio. The portfolio manager is also responsible for determining the best times to buy securities into or sell securities out of the portfolio in order to take advantage of investment opportunities. The manager's decisions depend strongly on two items: the individual's investment philosophy or style, and the fund's investment objectives.

Investment Philosophy or Style

In today's market, a portfolio manager employs, either alone or in combination, one of four investment philosophies listed below when analyzing and selecting a specific company's stock to buy into a mutual fund.

Value Investing. The portfolio manager invests in a company's common stock whose market value appears to be a bargain—i.e., the price is below the company's "real" worth or earnings power, or below the value of comparable companies in the same business sector. The manager uses such fundamental measures as price-earnings (P-E) ratio and price–to–book value ratio to find such bargains. As soon as the stock becomes "fully valued" based on the same measures, the manager will typically sell the stock out of the portfolio. This philosophy focuses on long-term investing.

socially responsible fund a mutual fund that does not invest in any company that has holdings in politically or environmentally incorrect sectors of the world.

equity or stock fund a mutual fund that invests primarily in common and/or preferred stocks; in practice, the term is used for both stock-and-bond funds, such as balanced funds.

open-end management company an investment company that, after the initial public offering of shares to the public, continually issues new shares and redeems outstanding shares; legal name for a mutual fund.

investment adviser the financial professional who manages the investment portfolio of a mutual fund and charges a management fee for these services; often called a portfolio manager.

Growth Investing. The investment adviser selects a company in which to invest based on expectations of strong growth in earnings. The underlying belief is that if the earnings keep growing, then the price of the stock will follow.

Momentum Investing. The manager selects and invests in the common stock of companies whose market value he or she expects to increase rapidly. The fund manager ignores value when selecting a stock for the fund's portfolio. Hence, some of the stocks purchased may be overpriced and others underpriced; nonetheless, the manager believes that as long as earnings are increasing strongly and on target with expectations, then the market price of the company's shares will continue to rise.

Investing Based on Insider Trading Activity. A mutual fund manager or investment adviser follows the trading patterns of a company's senior executives, members of its board of directors, and large shareholders, many of whom own shares or stock options in the company. These insiders are required to report all trading in their company's stock to the SEC by the tenth day of the month after the month in which the activity occurred. Also, every week *The Wall Street Journal* publishes a column and table showing recently reported insider activity. The fund manager reviews the reports of insiders' purchases and sales and interprets them as indicators of the company's future performance.

Mutual Funds' Investment Objectives

A portfolio manager's investment selections must be in keeping with the mutual fund's stated investment objectives. A fund's objective indicates the types of stocks and classes of asset in which the portfolio manager can invest, as well as the method (i.e., dividends, capital gains) by which he or she tries to make money for the shareholders. The investment objectives are established when the fund is created and can be changed only with a majority vote of the shareholders.

The risk associated with a specific mutual fund corresponds to the collective character of the securities in the portfolio. It is therefore important for you to choose a fund whose objectives and level of risk are suitable to your goals. (Figure 7.2 shows those investment objectives specifically associated with stock mutual funds.)

The most common fund objectives with descriptions are explained in order of increasing risk. Those discussed

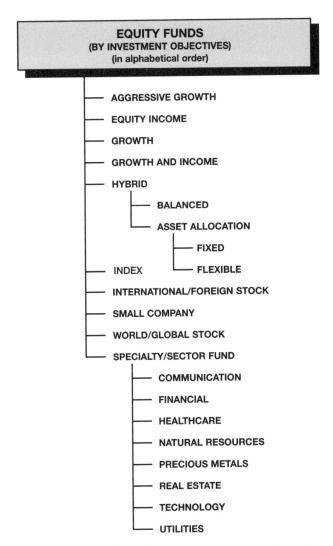

FIGURE 7.2 This chart shows the investment objectives of the most widely held types of stock or equity mutual funds.

first are considered the safest. They offer the highest potential for steady current income, yet the lowest potential for capital appreciation. Those near the end of the list offer the greatest potential for capital appreciation but little, if any, opportunity for current steady income. They are considerably more speculative. Additionally, those at the bottom of the list tend to be less diversified than those at the top. For the beginning investor, one of the funds in the middle of the list is probably an appropriate first selection.

Money market mutual fund. Invests in safe, short-term debt securities—such as Treasury bills and high-rated commercial paper—and pays a yield that reflects short-term interest rates.

U.S. government/agency bond fund. Invests in long-term U.S. government or agency debt securities such as T-bonds and Fannie Maes. Because many of these bonds are backed by the full faith, credit, and taxing power of the U.S. government, they are very safe—and offer a low yield.

Municipal bond fund. Invests in high-grade municipal bonds. Some funds are triple-tax-exempt and therefore offer a lower yield than U.S. government/agency bond funds. This type of fund is sometimes called a tax exempt fund.

Balanced fund. Emphasizes preservation of capital as a main objective and invests in bonds, preferred stock, and common stock. In a typical balanced fund, 60 percent of the assets are invested in stocks and 40 percent in bonds.

Income fund (debt and equity). Conservative income funds invest in blue-chip stocks that have high dividend payout ratios and bonds with modest interest rates; more speculative income funds have a mix of blue-chip and speculative stocks and high-yield bonds in the investment portfolio.

Income fund (equity). Invests at least 65 percent of its assets in common and preferred stocks that pay high dividends.

Index fund. Invests in a group of common stocks whose performance closely replicates that of one of the market indexes such as the Standard & Poor's 500 Index.

Asset allocation fund. A variation on the balanced fund that invests in stocks, bonds, and cash equivalents. There are two types of asset allocation funds: fixed and flexible. A fixed asset allocation fund maintains a fixed percentage of its assets in each of the three asset classes: stocks, bonds, and cash equivalents. This type is therefore quite similar to a balanced fund except that the fixed percentages differ. A flexible asset allocation fund adjusts the mix of its assets in response to changing market conditions and investment opportunities. This flexibility is this fund's major advantage. The disadvantage, however, is that its success depends almost entirely upon the fund manager's skill.

Income/growth fund. A fund with two investment objectives that invests in a combination of high-yield common stocks (e.g., utilities) and established-growth stocks.

Growth/income fund. A dual-purpose fund that, in emphasizing growth over income, invests in established-growth companies that pay steady and increasing dividends.

Growth fund. Invests in the common stock of new companies in new industries that have a high potential for capital appreciation. In the short term, this fund typically provides no income, and its price tends to be volatile. A growth fund is often further categorized according to the market capitalization of the companies whose stocks are bought into the portfolio. Capitalization, also known as market capitalization, is the value of a corporation determined by multiplying the number of issued-and-outstanding common shares by the current market price of a share.

> *Large capitalization.* More than $5 billion of common stock outstanding.

Mid capitalization. Between $1 billion and $5 billion of common stock outstanding.

Small capitalization. $1 billion or less of common stock outstanding.

Micro capitalization. Less than $100 million of common stock outstanding.

Aggressive growth fund. Invests in small companies or emerging industries whose market value is expected to rise rapidly. This type of fund is more likely than other funds to invest in initial public offerings (IPOs) and in companies with high price/earnings and price/book value ratios. This fund may or may not be diversified, investing heavily in one sector of the market.

Small-company fund. Invests primary in stocks of companies with market capitalization of $1 billion or less. These companies tend to provide great opportunity for capital appreciation; however, this potential reward is always accompanied by high volatility and risk. Income from dividends is unlikely.

High-yield fund. Also called a junk bond fund, it invests in high-yield bonds with lower than investment-grade ratings.

World/Global fund. Invests primarily in equity securities of issuers located throughout the world, usually maintaining a percentage of assets (normally 25 percent to 50 percent) in U.S.-based companies that have large international operations and sales (e.g., Coca-Cola, Ford Motor Company, Gillette).

International/Foreign fund. Invests primarily in equity securities of issuers located outside the United States. Some of the more common concentrations include:

European Stock. Invests at least 65 percent of its total assets in equity securities of European companies.

Diversified Emerging Markets. Invests primarily in equity securities issued by companies in emerging markets worldwide. The investments are not typically concentrated in any one region.

Pacific Stock. Invests primary in equity securities of issuers located in countries in the Pacific Rim, including Japan, China, Hong Kong, Malaysia, Singapore, New Zealand, and Australia.

Specialty/Sector fund. Invests in companies in a single industry or geographical area whose stock prices are expected to appreciate. Popular sectors include technology, communications, financial services, banking, healthcare, utilities, natural resources, precious metals, and real estate.

Hedge fund. Highly leveraged mutual fund that uses some of the most speculative trading strategies, such as trading on margin and short selling.

In reality, the distinction between some objectives is rather fuzzy. The actual stocks that constitute a specific mutual fund portfolio depend on the analysis and perspective of the fund's manager. A generic investment objective (e.g., growth, income) can be interpreted and executed differently by different managers; hence, one company's aggressive growth fund may look like another company's specialty fund. It is important to read the fund's prospectus before making the final investment decision.

Understanding Mutual Fund Prices and Fees

Each share of a mutual fund represents an undivided interest in the investment portfolio. Unlike the common or preferred stock distributed by a corporation, there is not a fixed number of mutual fund shares issued and outstanding in the market. After the initial public offering, a mutual fund continually issues new shares and redeems already outstanding shares. (This is why mutual funds are described as "open-end.") Hence, the fund's capitalization changes constantly depending on whether investors purchase more shares or redeem more shares.

Unlike equity securities, there is no secondary trading market for mutual fund shares. These shares are not listed on a stock exchange and they are not traded over NASDAQ. You can buy them only from the fund itself,

net asset value (NAV) the market value of each share of a mutual fund, computed by subtracting the fund's liabilities from its total assets and dividing the remainder by the total number of outstanding shares.

redemption fee a flat fee that some mutual funds sometimes charge investors when they liquidate their shares.

public offering price (POP) the price at which a mutual fund share is purchased; also called the asked price, it may or may not contain a sales charge.

sales charge a fee that an investor may pay when buying or redeeming a mutual fund share; also called a "load."

from the fund's own in-house salespersons, or from a securities firm, bank, or insurance company that is an authorized sales agent. Each share that you buy is a **new** share of the fund, **not** a redeemed share that is being resold.

Since there is no secondary trading market for mutual fund shares, what determines the price at which each share can be bought or sold? It is not the supply and demand for the mutual fund shares. Rather, the price is determined by the demand for the securities that make up the investment portfolio. Each day, based on the closing price of each individual security, the fund calculates the total value of the portfolio. After deducting its operating expenses (management fees, commissions, legal fees, 12b-1 fees if appropriate, etc.), the net amount is divided by the number of outstanding shares. This resulting dollar amount, called the *net asset value (NAV)*, is the unit value of one share of the mutual fund. (It is also called the fund's "bid price.") The NAV is the price at which you, the investor, can redeem (i.e., sell) your mutual fund shares. An additional *redemption fee* may or may not be charged when you cash in your shares.

When you want to buy mutual fund shares, you do so at the fund's *public offering price (POP)*, also called the asked price. A mutual fund's POP may be equal to its NAV, or its POP may be greater than its NAV. (*Note:* The public offering price of a mutual fund can never be lower than the fund's net asset value.) Remember that each mutual fund must compute its NAV daily; hence a fund's POP also changes daily. The relationship between a fund's NAV and POP depends on how the fund's sponsor or management chose to structure certain *sales charges* and fees associated with buying, redeeming, and holding mutual fund shares. While these fees are usually determined when the mutual fund is created, they can change or be amended by a majority vote of the fund's shareholders.

Front-End Load. A *front-end load* is a sales charge that is incorporated into a mutual fund's public offering price (POP) when an investor buys a fund share. Anytime a mutual fund's POP is greater than its NAV, the fund charges a front-end load. All of the funds under the Franklin Class I illustrated in Figure 7.3 have front-end

MUTUAL FUND QUOTATIONS

NAV	Net Chg	Fund Name	Inv Obj	Ytd % ret	4 wk % ret	Total Return			Max Init Chrg	Exp Ratio
						1 yr	3 yr	5 yr		
		AIM Funds:								
42.48	-0.17	Agrsv p	SC	-0.9	-2.7	+11.4 D	+22.4 A	+14.0 A	5.50	1.08
25.72	+0.04	Const p	GR	+1.8	+0.4	+13.0 D	+16.6 B	+15.8 A	5.50	1.20
29.86	+0.03	Valu A p	GR	+2.4	+1.0	+15.2 C	+16.3 C	+16.3 A	5.50	1.12
29.61	+0.04	Valu B t	GR	+2.4	+1.0	+14.3 D	+15.4 D	NS	0.00	1.94
		Dean Witter:								
28.49	+0.05	AmVl t	GR	+5.5	+2.8	+13.7 E	+15.1 D	+14.1 C	0.00	1.61
45.82	+0.06	DivGr t	GI	+2.8	+1.2	+18.3 D	+16.5 D	+14.1 D	0.00	1.31
9.45	...	DivIn t	GT	-0.5	-0.4	+6.5 D	+5.6 D	NS	0.00	1.42
		Fidelity Invest:								
14.48	...	Balanc	MP	+2.8	+1.9	+11.0 D	+6.3 E	+9.3 D	0.00	0.79
28.43	+0.08	Egldx	GI	+5.5	+3.5	+23.1 B	+21.1 A	+16.3 B	0.00	0.28
83.18	+0.11	Magln	GR	+3.1	+1.1	+12.9 E	+14.8 D	+15.1 B	3.00	0.95
33.07	+0.01	OTC	MC	+1.1	-0.9	+22.7 A	+18.8 A	+14.6 B	3.00	0.83
18.17	+0.02	Real E	SE	+0.8	+1.4	+34.9 A	+16.0 B	+14.4 B	0.00	0.00
15.66	+0.01	Wrldw	GL	+1.8	+1.4	+16.4 B	+7.8 D	13.4 A	0.00	1.19
		Franklin Class I:								
12.78	-0.01	Gold p	SE	-3.8	+1.3	-21.6 E	-2.4 E	+4.4 E	4.50	0.95
23.87	+0.04	Grwthl p	GR	+1.9	+1.3	+13.8 E	+19.3 B	+13.3 C	4.50	0.87
9.62	...	Utilsl p	SE	-0.1	-0.2	0.0 E	+7.2 D	+8.5 D	4.25	0.71
		Franklin Class II:								
12.75	...	Goldll p	SE	-3.8	+1.3	-22.1 E	NS	NS	1.00	1.74
23.64	+0.03	Grwthll p	GR	+1.8	+1.2	+12.9 E	NS	NS	1.00	1.63
9.60	-0.01	Utilsll p	SE	-0.2	-0.2	-0.5 E	NS	NS	1.00	1.23
		Vanguard:								
18.62	+0.03	Asset A	MP	+3.8	+2.6	+15.4 B	+16.3 A	+14.5 A	0.00	0.47
19.02	+0.04	Eqlnc	EI	+3.8	+2.5	+18.2 C	+18.1 A	+15.7 A	0.00	0.42
72.96	+0.19	Indx 500	GI	+5.5	+3.5	+23.3 B	+21.3 A	+16.0 A	0.00	0.20
16.76	-0.01	Idx Eur	IL	+1.1	+2.0	+21.1 A	+13.4 A	+13.4 A	0.00	0.35
22.80	-0.25	SPEnrg r	SE	+1.2	-3.1	+35.2 A	+16.7 B	+18.0 B	0.00	0.51
11.12	+0.22	SPGold r	SE	-4.4	+0.9	-24.3 E	-4.9 E	+5.6 E	0.00	0.60
60.53	+0.34	SPHlth r	SE	+3.7	+3.7	+20.4 B	+25.4 A	+17.3 B	0.00	0.46

FIGURE 7.3 Mutual fund quotations. A typical newspaper listing of mutual fund quotations summarizes information about individual funds' net asset value (NAV), the price at which an investor can redeem a mutual fund share; sales charges and expenses indicated by the letters "p" (12b-1 fees), "r" (back-end load), and "t" (both letters "p" and "r" apply); investment objective; performance (four weeks to five years); maximum initial sales charge; and expense ratio. Notice that the public offering price (POP), the price at which an investor can purchase a fund share, is not published. For a fund with no front-end load (i.e., initial sales charge), the POP will be the same as the NAV. For a fund with a front-end load, the POP will be greater than the NAV, reflecting the applicable sales charge or breakpoint percentage. This price is calculated by a broker's or customer service person's computer.

**front-end
load** a sales
charge that is incor-
porated into the
public offering price
when an investor
buys a mutual fund
share.

breakpoint
a quantity discount
on the front-end
load or sales charge
an investor pays
when buying mu-
tual fund shares.

**right of
accumulation** a
reduction in the
front-end sales
charge on all sub-
sequent purchases
when the value of
an investor's shares
and current pur-
chases reaches a
breakpoint.

loads. The percentage of the load is shown under the column "Max Init Chrg" (maximum initial charge).

To many investors, the sales charge or load is a commission. While this is conceptually correct, the use of the
word "commission" is actually incorrect. By definition a
commission is a charge that is added to a security's purchase price, not included in its market price.

Notice that the definition of the term "front-end
load" does not say that the sales charge is added to the
fund's NAV. Instead, the sales charge is defined as an
amount that is **incorporated into** the fund's public offering price when a person buys fund shares. Why is this
careful distinction made? Because the NASD-approved
formula for computing a fund's POP actually calculates
the sales charge as a percentage of the public offering
price, **not** as a percentage of the net asset value (NAV). Industry regulation mandates that mutual funds with front-
end loads must contain a chart in the fund's prospectus
showing the sales charge as a percent of the fund's public
offering price and as a percent of the net amount invested.

The NASD sets the maximum sales charge on a mutual fund at 8.5 percent. However, few front-end load
funds charge the maximum. Increased competition
among mutual funds combined with investors' reluctance
to buy funds with high loads have caused mutual fund
companies to reduce the front-end sales load and the
number of funds that have them. Today, the typical sales
charge percentage of a mutual fund with a front-end load
ranges from 4.5 percent to 5.5 percent.

If a mutual fund has a front-end load, industry regulations mandate that under certain circumstances, the
fund must offer *breakpoints* to investors. A breakpoint is a
reduction in a mutual fund's front-end load for large-dollar
purchases. While each front-end load fund has its own
breakpoint schedule (see an example in Figure 7.4), mutual fund regulations set a minimum breakpoint schedule.

Front-end load funds usually reduce their sales
charges to investors under two situations: for lump-sum
purchases and under the *right of accumulation*. Using the
sample breakpoint scale in Figure 7.4, an investor who
makes a lump-sum purchase of $40,000 of the fund's

Front-End Load Breakpoint Schedule

Amount of Purchase	Sales Charge (as a % of Offering Price)
0 - $24,999	5.50%
$25,000 - $49,999	4.25%
$50,000 - $99,999	3.25%
$100,000 - $199,999	2.50%
$200,000 - $399,999	2.00%

FIGURE 7.4 Example of a breakpoint schedule for a mutual fund with a front-end load.

shares would be entitled to a reduced sales charge of 4.25 percent on the entire amount. Under the right of accumulation, when the greater of either the total amount of an investor's purchases or the total market value of an investor's mutual fund shares reaches a breakpoint, all subsequent purchases receive the lower sales charge. For example, the total current market value of an investor's shares in a mutual fund is $23,000. She is going to invest $5000 in the same fund. Her sales charge for this purchase will be 4.25 percent because the total of both the current market value and the amount of the purchases is $28,000, which places her above the $25,000 breakpoint.

Breakpoints are not only available for individual mutual funds; they also apply when you buy funds within the same mutual fund family, called a *family of funds*. Breakpoints encourage individuals to invest more in a mutual fund or family of funds in order to reduce the front-end load.

Contingent Deferred Sales Charge (also called a Back-End Load). Instead of charging a front-end load, many funds assess a sales charge when you redeem shares within a relatively short period of time (usually from one

 family of funds a group of different funds with portfolios made up of different securities or having different investment objectives, all managed by the same investment adviser.

to six years) after purchasing them. The percentage of the load decreases over time. Figure 7.5 illustrates a declining schedule of *contingent deferred sales charges (CDSCs)*.

When you redeem a mutual fund that has CDSCs, the charge is usually calculated by multiplying the applicable percentage by the lesser of the original purchase price of the shares or net asset value of the shares at the time you redeem them. In the newspaper listings in Figure 7.3, the letter "r" next to the mutual fund name (see the Vanguard Energy, Gold, and Healthcare specialty funds) indicates that the fund has a back-end load. Whether a fund charges a front-end load, back-end load, or both, the maximum percentage of the sales load cannot exceed 8.5 percent.

Redemption Fee. This fee is often confused with a contingent deferred sales charge or back-end load. They are not the same. (*Note*: Many newspapers use the term "redemption fee" to describe a back-end load. This usage is inaccurate and confusing.) A redemption fee is a flat fee

Declining Back-End Load Schedule

Redemption During	Contingent Deferred Sales Charge
1st Year Since Purchase	5.00%
2nd Year Since Purchase	4.00%
3rd Year Since Purchase	3.00%
4th Year Since Purchase	3.00%
5th Year Since Purchase	2.00%
6th Year Since Purchase	1.00%
7th Year (or Later) Since Purchase	None

FIGURE 7.5 Example of a contingent deferred sales charge schedule.

(e.g., 0.5 percent) that is charged anytime a customer redeems certain mutual fund shares. Unlike a CDSC, redemption fees do not reduce over time. Few funds today charge this type of redemption fee; instead many charge back-end loads.

12b-1 Fee. More than 50 percent of all mutual funds charge existing shareholders distribution fees and a portion of costs associated with attracting new shareholders. The charges are called *12b-1 fees*, named after the regulation that permitted funds to assess them.

> **12b-1 fees**
> a mutual fund may charge investors distribution fees and a portion of advertising costs; otherwise these costs are borne by the fund.

There are two types of 12b-1 fees: an asset-based 12b-1 fee and a service 12b-1 fee. An asset-based 12b-1 fee is charged against the total value of the assets in a particular mutual fund portfolio. Regulations set the maximum asset-based fee at .75 percent; however, it typically declines as the fund's assets increase. Service 12b-1 fees are ongoing compensation to the broker who advised you to invest in the mutual fund. The maximum service fee set by regulation is .25 percent. The combined maximum of both 12b-1 fees cannot exceed 1 percent. In Figure 7.3, the letter "p" after a fund's name (see the Franklin Class 1 funds) indicates that it assesses 12b-1 fees. The letter "t" following a fund's name (e.g., the Dean Witter funds) indicates that it charges both 12b-1 fees and a back-end load.

The impact of 12b-1 fees may surprise many investors. These are not one-time charges like a front-end load or a back-end load. They are ongoing annual fees, charged to the investor during the entire time he or she holds the shares. (*Note:* When a fund computes its NAV at the end of each day, one of the deductions is for 12b-1 fees.) If you buy shares in a fund with these fees and hold the shares over a long period, the cumulative total percentage of the ongoing 12b-1 fees may exceed the maximum NASD-mandated sales charge of 8.5 percent. The SEC mandates that this fact must be clearly stated in the fund's prospectus. Additionally, these fees can be a drag on a fund's performance.

> **no-load fund**
> a mutual fund that does not charge its purchasers a sales charge, but may have a 12b-1 fee of less than .25 percent.

No-Load and Pure No-Load Funds. When the SEC permitted mutual fund companies to charge shareholders

12b-1 fees, it also redefined how the term *no-load fund* can be used. Traditionally, a no-load mutual fund assessed no front-end load, no back-end load, and no 12b-1 fees. Today, the term "no-load" can be used by a fund that charges 12b-1 fees as long as the percentage of the fee does not exceed .25 percent. A fund that has no front-end load, no back-end load, and no 12b-1 fees is now referred to as a *pure no-load fund.*

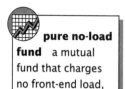

pure no-load fund a mutual fund that charges no front-end load, no back-end load, and no 12b-1 fees.

All money market mutual funds are pure no-load funds. Approximately 40 percent of all equity funds are no-load. The remaining 60 percent have either a front-end load or a back-end load. However, an increasing number of stock mutual funds that describe themselves as simply "no-load" incorporate 12b-1 fees into their ongoing charges.

Classes of Mutual Fund Shares

Not so long ago, each mutual fund issued only one class of shares. A mutual fund's share would charge either a front-end load or a back-end load, or a no-load fund. Those simpler days have disappeared as mutual fund companies have become more savvy at marketing the same fund to investors with differing sensitivities to costs and differing time horizons. Now one mutual fund portfolio can offer its different classes of shares—Class A, Class B, and even Class C shares—all backed by the same or a substantially similar portfolio of securities. (See the AIM Value A and Value B as well as Franklin's Class I and Class II funds in Figure 7.3.)

The major difference among the various classes is how the front-end load, back-end load, and 12b-1 fees are allocated among each. Figure 7.6 and the discussion that follows illustrate some of the general differences among the three most common classes. Keep in mind, however, that a specific fund may choose to "slice and dice" these fees in different ways and different percentages.

Class A shares usually have a low to moderate front-end sales load, no contingent deferred sales charges, and low or no 12b-1 fees. If Class A shares do have 12b-1

Classes of Mutual Fund Shares	Usual Fees Charged and the Relative %
Class A	• front-end sales charge: low to moderate • back-end load: none • 12b-1 fees: low (typically .25%) or none
Class B	• front-end sales charge: none • back-end load: 5% the first year scaled down to 0% over 6 years • 12b-1 fees: high (near the 1% maximum)
Class C	• front-end sales charge: none • back-end load: typically 1% on share sold within 1 year of purchase • 12b-1 fees: high (usually near the 1% maximum)

FIGURE 7.6 Chart showing the three most common classes of mutual fund shares and the usual fee structures associated with each.

fees, they are usually .25 percent or less. Class B shares have no front-end load, but typically have contingent deferred sales charges and moderate to high 12b-1 fees (near the maximum 1 percent). Class C shares are usually sold only through a financial planner or financial adviser who charges the customer an annual fee based on the total amount of assets under management. In addition to the fee that the individual pays the investment adviser for his or her services, the mutual fund also pays the adviser. This second fee, sometimes called a trailing commission, is the 12b-1 service fee paid for the services (i.e., advice) that the investment adviser provides the customer.

The fee structures for the different classes of shares make it difficult for an investor to decide which shares to purchase. When most investors are asked to choose between buying Class A or Class B shares, most immediately select the B shares because there is no up-front sales charge. Bargain-savvy, outlet-shopping Americans have become skillful at looking for the best price on everything from appliances to unmentionables. And, generally, buying a security without paying a "commission" is a better deal; in the case of mutual funds, however, an old adage comes to mind: "Cheap is dear."

If you plan to hold the shares for the long term, it may be better to buy the Class A shares than Class B shares. The high 12b-1 fees on B shares will prove to be a drag on the fund's performance over time. You can prove this to yourself by looking in the newspaper listings in Figure 7.3 for AIM Value A and B, and Franklin's Class I and II. Notice that the B shares and Class II shown have a lower NAV and a lower return over time when compared to the same fund's A shares. The longer you hold the B shares, the greater the cumulative effect of the 12b-1 fees will be.

When buying Class A shares, Class B shares, Class C shares, or one of the new classes that mutual funds are creating to further reallocate the fees, it is important to read the prospectus. The NASD mandates that fund companies place a comparative chart near the front of the prospectus that shows the impact of the fees on a $1000 investment in the fund over 1, 5, and 10 years for each class of shares.

Mutual Fund Performance

When a person looks at investing in a mutual fund, he or she is really seeking answers to two questions:

"How much money can I possibly earn by investing in a particular fund?"

"Could I earn more money in another fund or other type of investment?"

There are three ways that investors earn money in mutual funds:

1. *Increase in the fund's NAV.* Like a stock, a mutual fund share can be bought and the price may appreciate. This rise or fall in the NAV is based on the unrealized gains or losses of the securities that the manager still holds in the portfolio. (Unrealized gains or losses are commonly referred to as "paper profits or losses.")

2. *Dividend distributions.* Dividends paid on common and preferred stocks as well as interest paid on bonds in the investment portfolio are distributed to investors as mutual fund "dividends." Technically, these dividends are referred to as investment income and may be paid monthly, quarterly, or annually, as described in the fund's prospectus.

3. *Capital gains distribution.* When a portfolio manager sells a security out of the fund's portfolio that has appreciate in value, he or she has a realized capital gain. Again, these gains are distributed to the shareholders; however, under IRS regulations, a mutual fund can distribute capital gains only once per year, although the fund may have realized the gain six months earlier.

The most frequently published measure of a mutual fund's performance is its total return. This measure includes any changes in the fund's NAV (i.e., any unrealized capital gains or losses), as well as the reinvestment of any dividend and capital gains distributions over a specific period of time (one year, three years, etc.). (See "Total Return" column in Figure 7.3.)

The total return gives the best indication of how much a person's invested dollars have grown or declined. This is, of course, no guarantee of future performance. However, it is a good yardstick by which to compare funds with similar objectives. After having selected the type of fund whose risk-to-reward profile best suits your investment objectives, you can then choose the specific fund whose total return has been consistently better than its peers over time.

While we have discussed many of the differences between mutual funds and equity securities, there is one area in which they have much in common: shareholders' rights. Like most common stockholders, all mutual fund shareholders have the right to vote. They elect the board of directors of the fund, approve the fund's annual contract with the investment adviser or portfolio manager, and by a majority vote approve any changes in the investment objectives of the fund. Mutual fund shareholders can vote by proxy, voting in absentia, or give someone else the right to vote on their behalf. Mutual funds are required by law to send semiannual reports (including an audited financial statement) to shareholders in the same way that the Securities and Exchange Commission requires reporting corporations to provide reports to their shareholders.

Conveniences of Investing in Mutual Funds

Professional management is one of the conveniences that a mutual fund provides individual investors. Because they are usually quite large, mutual funds try to hire the best investment advisers available. However, hiring the best people does not always result in the funds providing the best investment return. More than any other factor, the expertise of the portfolio manager is pivotal to the return that you receive from investing in a mutual fund. This is especially true for common stock funds, which have greater price fluctuation and greater potential for capital appreciation, just as the equity securities that make up the investment portfolio do.

In addition to professional management, a mutual fund provides small or beginning investors with other conveniences that could not be easily obtained if they chose to invest directly in individual stocks: diversification and low transaction costs. All of these are a result of the *economy of scale* that the large pool of investors' funds creates.

 **economy of scale** a reduction in the ratio of expenses to assets as the size of a mutual fund increases.

Diversification is an inherent feature of mutual funds. It also provides a relative amount of safety against the substantial losses that could result from having too much money in only a few stocks. Because the fund's portfolio is made up of a variety of different securities, the decline of a single company's stock will have less impact on the total value of the mutual fund's portfolio. Also, as some securities in the portfolio are declining in value, others are appreciating. Thus diversification provides some protection against stock-specific risk.

Additionally, you can sell part of your mutual fund holdings and the sale will not reduce the diversification of the remaining shares. Remember that each mutual fund share represents an undivided interest in an investment portfolio. Selling part of the shares reduces the percentage ownership in the overall portfolio but does not affect the remaining shares' diversification among the securities that make up the fund's portfolio.

A typical beginning investor who wants to invest in individual stocks will be able to buy only a small number of shares. Consequently, the commission cost per share will be high. However, when many small investors' funds are pooled, as they are in a mutual fund, the collective buying power increases. In effect, the fund manager is able to buy more shares at a substantially lower commission cost per share. Hence, diversifying the investment portfolio as well as making changes in it can cost each investor a fraction of a cent per share.

There are other conveniences that mutual funds offer purchasers that are designed to make investing relatively easy:

1. *Smaller amount of capital required for investment.* Whereas stock purchases are made for a given number of shares, mutual fund purchases are made for a given dollar amount. Also, you can purchase fractional shares of a mutual fund. This feature makes it easy (and effective) to use dollar-cost averaging as an investment strategy. Individuals can invest small amounts of money ($25, $50, or $100) on a regular basis. (See Figures 7.7 and 7.8.) Some funds set no minimum on the amount you can invest.

2. *Liquidity.* You can buy mutual fund shares or redeem them with the same ease as buying and selling shares of a stock—in some cases, more easily. You can purchase mutual fund shares regularly through automatic deductions from your checking account, thereby relieving you of having to write a check. If you use dollar-cost averaging, this option makes investing even more passive. You can place buy orders for mutual funds with any securities firm that is authorized to offer them. You can place orders to redeem shares directly with the mutual fund or with the securities firm from which you bought the shares. Also, by law, a mutual fund must be ready to redeem its outstanding shares on any day the securities markets are open. Most mutual fund buyers hold their shares in street name in order to avoid the bother of safekeeping. As with stock transactions, this makes selling (i.e., redeeming) the shares easy.

3. *Automatic reinvestment.* Most mutual funds permit shareholders to reinvest dividends and capital gains automatically at the fund's net asset value. Thus, the purchaser of a front-end load fund is able to reinvest without paying a sales charge. Over the long term, the compound-

ing that results from automatic reinvestment will tend to benefit the shareholder—if the NAV does not fall.

4. *Exchange feature.* Many mutual funds are grouped into a family of funds—different funds with different investment objectives but all managed by the same investment adviser or team of investment advisers. Investors in a given fund within a family can usually exchange their shares for an equal dollar amount of another fund within the same family. If a fund has different classes of shares, then investors can only exchange them for the same class of shares of another fund in the same family. This feature gives investors the flexibility of switching their holdings to different funds should their investment objectives or their outlook on a particular segment of the market change. If, for example, you expect stock prices to be bullish over the long term, you might switch from a bond fund to an equity fund within the same family. Parents who have invested money in a bond fund to pay for their children's education may switch to a stock fund during periods of low interest rates in order to protect the value of the investment against inflation. An investor who is approaching retirement and wants a steady source of income may switch from a growth fund to an income fund within the same family. Usually you can switch from one fund to another at the new fund's net asset value with no additional charges or only a modest transfer fee.

5. *Withdrawal plans.* Once you have accumulated a certain amount of money in a mutual fund, you can begin making regular withdrawals. The terms of the withdrawal, including how dividend payments and capital gains distributions will be handled during this period, are detailed in the fund's prospectus. There are four withdrawal plans that a mutual fund can offer investors:

Fixed dollar. You specify a fixed-dollar amount that you want to receive at each payment period, and the fund regularly liquidates as many shares as necessary to pay the stated amount.

Fixed shares. You specify a fixed number of mutual fund shares that you want the fund to liquidate at each regular payment period. The proceeds, which will vary with the net asset value of the shares, are paid to you.

Fixed percentage. You specify a fixed percentage of your total mutual fund holdings that will be liquidated at each payment period. The amount of each payment will vary with the net asset value of the shares at the time of liquidation.

Fixed time. You specify the number of years over which your total holdings in the fund will be liquidated. This withdrawal method may be chosen for a fund set aside to pay for education.

If you choose one of the first three withdrawal plans, it is generally recommended that you withdraw no more than 6 percent of your entire holdings in the fund each year. Large withdrawals can reduce your holdings more rapidly than anticipated and result in the total depletion of your investment.

Once you have chosen a particular withdrawal plan, you are not locked into it for life. You can change the time (monthly, quarterly, annually) at which the payments are made; switch from one withdrawal plan to another; increase or decrease the number of shares, dollar amount, percentage, or time period that applies to the plan; or discontinue the withdrawal plan at any time.

6. *Simplified record keeping.* For record-keeping purposes, a mutual fund investment is treated as if it were an investment in a single security. At year end, the fund provides a detailed statement of all purchases, sales, dividends, and capital gain distributions, as well as all reinvestments. The fund provides a single tax statement early in the calendar year so that you can file your tax return simply and accurately. Thus, you are spared the bookkeeping problems that often face individual investors—tracking down the dividend distributions and realized capital gains from a number of different stocks.

Most mutual funds even have 24-hour toll-free telephone numbers assigned to their shareholder services departments. You can place an order to buy, sell, or switch funds at your leisure any time of day or night. At most funds, however, your order is executed at the close of the business day when the fund computes its NAV.

Selecting a Mutual Fund

As with individual stocks, your interest in investing in a mutual fund must first be determined by your investment objectives. Always keep in mind that, with the exception of money market funds, a mutual fund is a long-term investment. You must clearly decide the amount of risk that you are willing to accept in pursuit of the objectives.

Once you have determined the objectives, you must choose the fund in which to invest. Comparing funds with similar investment objectives is not easy. Recall that the skill of the investment adviser or portfolio manager is key to the returns that a fund provides its investors. Therefore, it is wise and prudent to examine the quality of the fund's management and its investment policies while at the same time examining the fund's past performance.

Some of the questions you should ask before investing in a mutual fund are listed below. Most of the answers can be obtained from the fund's prospectus as well as other sources such as Morningstar, Value Line and *The Wall Street Journal.*

✔ **What is the fund's performance track record over 1-year, 3-year, 5-year, and 10-year periods?**
This historic performance information—the fund's total return—must be summarized in the fund's prospectus for the periods cited above or for the period that the fund has been in existence. Also, most major newspapers publish a detailed summary table of the performance of most mutual funds once a week—typically on Friday or Sunday. (See Figure 7.3.) This information helps an investor determine how the fund might continue to perform in the future; but is no guarantee of future performance. The total return information is perhaps most useful as a comparative tool now that there are so many mutual funds from which to choose. By comparing the fund's

performance to its peers (i.e., those mutual funds with the same investment objectives) and to a benchmark index (typically the Standard and Poor's 500 index), an investor can better gauge the fund's potential return and risk, especially in a bear market, relative to similar funds. A beginning investor may discover that there are other funds with the same objective that provide consistently better returns with lower risks.

✔ **How long has the portfolio manager been handling the fund?**
Good fund managers tend to stay with a mutual fund company for a long period of time—through bull and bear markets. The prevailing wisdom states that you want to find a fund run by a manager with a good long-term record at that fund or another fund within the same company. This commonly held point of view is changing. Younger fund managers tend to change jobs more often, looking for a fund or company that gives them greater investment flexibility or that offers them a higher payout. Therefore, when evaluating a fund manager, you should look at other funds the individual has managed and how they performed under his or her tenure. The fund prospectus provides a summary of the manager's employment and educational background. Also, Value Line and Morningstar surveys tell how long the manager has run the fund and discuss the individual's investment philosophy and strategy.

✔ **What is the minimum amount required for the initial investment?**
Many people who are considering investing for the first time think they need thousands of dollars to get started. This is not true. The minimum amount required for initial investment is set by the fund and varies widely. The Franklin Growth Fund, for example, has an initial minimum of $100, while the Vanguard Index 500 Portfolio has a minimum initial investment of $3000. Also, many mutual funds waive their minimum initial requirement if the shares is being purchased in an Individual Retirement Account (IRA).

✔ **What is the minimum purchase amount the fund will accept after the initial investment?**
In order to make mutual fund investing more attractive—and easier—for a broader range of individuals, funds permit shareholders to invest as little as $25 per month. When the amount is this low, many funds require the contribution to be transferred automatically from your bank account, money market fund, payroll, and social security checks. The restrictions and minimum amounts of the transfers vary from fund to fund. Automatic monthly investment plans have proved enormously popular, primarily for two reasons: First, for the investor, the money is invested before you can spend it and, as discussed earlier, you benefit from dollar-cost averaging. And second, for the fund, an automatic plan reduces administrative and operations costs associated with check clearing.

✔ **Does the fund permit automatic reinvestment of dividends, interest, and capital gains at the net asset value?**
This is a common feature among funds. Automatic reinvestment enables compounding of investors' interest, dividends, and capital gains so they work more effectively for them.

✔ **What are the fund's annual expenses—management fee paid to the investment adviser, the cost of providing various services to the shareholder, audit fees, legal fees?**
A mutual fund's expenses are deducted a little each day when it computes the shares' net asset value (NAV). When a fund reports and publishes its total return, these expenses have already been deducted. Excessive expenses can, therefore, substantially reduce any gain a fund yields. As a rule of thumb, a total expense ratio of 1 percent or less is considered reasonable for domestic stock funds. This percentage is typically higher for more aggressive funds, for international/global funds, and for funds with star portfolio managers. (See the "expense ratio" column in Figure 7.3.) Other companies, such as the Van-

guard Group and the Franklin Group of Funds, specialize in offering mutual funds with some of the
lowest expense ratios in the industry.

✔ **What other fees (front-end load, back-end load,
12b-1 fees) does the fund charge?**
As discussed earlier in this chapter, multiple fee
charges have become quite popular among funds. Industry regulations set the maximum sales charge on
a mutual fund at 8.5 percent. This limit applies to
the total front-end load and back-end load. It does
not, however, apply to 12b-1 fees, which is an annual cost that never goes away. Depending on how
long an individual holds shares of a fund with this
fee, the total may exceed the 8.5 percent maximum
sales charge. A statement in the prospectus must in-
form the investor of this fact.

    Like the expenses cited in the previous question,
a little of the 12b-1 fee is deducted each day when the
fund computes its NAV. Therefore, if a fund has multiple classes of mutual fund shares—Class A, Class B,
Class C—with different fees and expenses, the total return will differ over time. The SEC requires that the
amount of these fees on a $1000 investment in each
share class be shown in table format in the front part of
a mutual fund's prospectus. The table, which is used
only as an example and assumes an annual return of 5
percent, shows the projected expenses over 1-, 3-, 5-,
and 10-year periods. It is important to be aware of
what additional fees you may be paying because fees
reduce your overall return.

✔ **How varied are the offerings of your mutual fund
family and do they have an exchange feature permitting you to buy and sell funds within the family
without any additional sales charges?**
Choosing a company with a large number of funds
in the family benefits an investor. It allows an investor to apply the principles of asset allocation as
investment goals and economic conditions change.
This is especially useful if the investor is not charged
additional fees to make the changes.

✔ **What are the most important things to know about redeeming shares of a mutual fund?**
Some of the issues surrounding this question are timing, tax consequences, and fees depending on whether the fund has a back-end load and you are selling before the time limit.

Statement of Additional Information an addendum to a mutual fund's prospectus that includes more detailed information, such as the calculation methods used for computing the fund's results and the fund's audited financial statements.

Where can you find the information necessary to compare and select an appropriate mutual fund? Start with the fund's prospectus and its *Statement of Additional Information*. Both will show the performance record of the fund over at least 10 years. Included in the data is a table that shows what a typical investment of $10,000 would be worth today had it been invested in the plan in a certain year. Also, several independent publications and services, such as Morningstar (Figure 7.7), Value Line Mutual Fund Survey (Figure 7.8), Lipper Analytical Services, and Wiesenberger Investment Company Service, provide useful and easy-to-understand summaries about investment companies. Each of the figures (7.7 and 7.8) shown provides the fund's investment objective; lists the composition and specific contents of the investment portfolio; ranks the fund's performance and risk; answers shareholders' questions about minimum initial investment, automatic investment, systematic withdrawal, telephone exchanges, and so forth; gives the name (and sometimes an assessment) of the investment adviser; and provides other important information that can help an interested investor to select the fund most appropriate for his or her investment objectives.

Money, Business Week, Forbes, Barron's, Consumer Reports, and other magazines publish rankings of the performances of mutual funds. As part of its daily listing of mutual fund quotations, *The Wall Street Journal* publishes a "Mutual Fund Scorecard" by type of fund (equity income, growth, balanced, convertible securities, international, etc.). The scorecard states the investment objectives of funds in this group and then lists the 15 top performers and the 10 worst performers, ranked by the 12-month return (Figure 7.9).

Be aware that 12-month performance can be quite deceptive. Mutual funds are meant to be long-term invest-

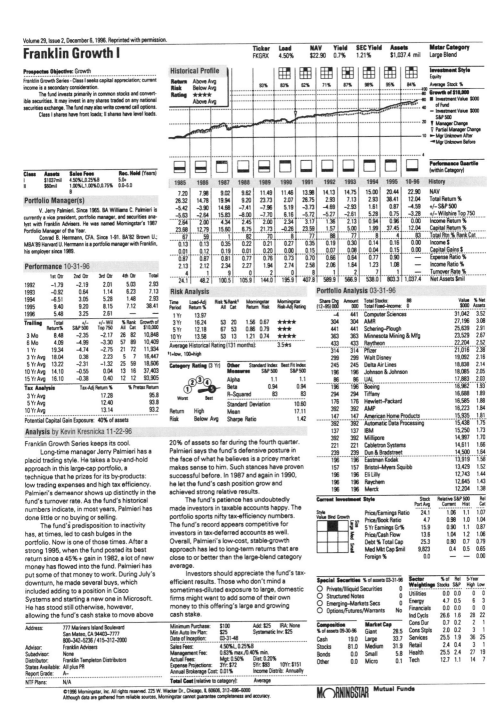

FIGURE 7.7 Morningstar Mutual Funds report for the *Franklin Growth Fund* and the *Vanguard Index 500 Portfolio*, with a diagram explaining key terms and information found on a typical page. The former fund is managed, while the latter is an unmanaged index fund. Reprinted by permission of *Morningstar Mutual Funds*, Morningstar, Inc., 225 W. Wacker Drive, Chicago, IL 60606. 312-696-6000.

Volume 29, Issue 3, December 20, 1996. Reprinted with permission.

Vanguard Index 500

	Ticker	Load	NAV	Yield	SEC Yield	Assets	Mstar Category
	VFINX	None	$71.39	1.7%	1.95%	$27,715.9 mil	Large Blend

Prospectus Objective: Growth and Income

Vanguard Index Trust 500 Portfolio seeks investment results that correspond with the price and yield performance of the S&P 500 index.

The fund allocates the percentage of net assets each company receives on the basis of the stock's relative total-market value: its market price per share multiplied by the number of shares outstanding.

Shareholders are charged an annual account-maintenance fee of $10. Prior to Dec. 21, 1987, the fund was named Vanguard Index Trust. Prior to 1980, it was named First Index Investment Trust.

Historical Profile

Return	Above Avg	
Risk	Average	
Rating	★★★★ Above Avg	

Investment Style: Equity
Average Stock %

	1985	1986	1987	1988	1989	1990	1991	1992	1993	1994	1995	11-96	History
			97%	97%	100%	99%	100%	99%	99%	100%			Investment Value $000 of Fund
NAV	22.99	24.27	24.65	27.18	33.64	31.24	39.32	40.97	43.83	42.97	57.60	71.39	NAV
Total Return %	31.23	18.06	4.71	16.22	31.37	-3.33	30.22	7.42	9.89	1.18	37.45	25.33	Total Return %
	-0.51	-0.62	-0.55	-0.39	-0.32	-0.21	-0.26	-0.20	-0.17	-0.14	-0.09	-0.10	+/- S&P 500
	-0.72	0.64	0.60	-0.98	-0.06	0.76	-2.25	-0.78	0.16	3.53	-0.21	1.56	+/- Wilshire Top 750
	4.54	3.69	2.42	4.56	4.33	3.54	3.87	2.96	2.83	2.69	3.02	1.29	Income Return %
	26.69	14.37	2.28	11.66	27.04	-6.86	26.35	4.46	7.06	-1.52	34.42	24.04	Capital Return %
	.29	.34	.35	.36	.21	.52	.49	.43	.50	.19	8	.18	Total Rtn % Rank Cat
	0.91	0.89	0.69	1.10	1.20	1.17	1.15	1.12	1.13	1.17	1.22	0.66	Income $
	1.61	2.02	0.17	0.32	0.75	0.10	0.12	0.10	0.03	0.20	0.13	0.04	Capital Gains $
	0.28	0.28	0.26	0.22	0.21	0.22	0.20	0.19	0.19	0.19	0.20	—	Expense Ratio %
	4.09	3.40	3.15	4.08	3.62	3.60	3.07	2.81	2.65	2.72	2.38	—	Income Ratio %
	36	29	15	10	8	23	5	4	8	8	4	—	Turnover Rate %
	394.3	485.1	826.3	1,055.1	1,803.8	2,173.0	4,345.3	6,517.7	8,272.7	9,356.4	17,371.8	27,715.9	Net Assets $mil

Performance Quartile (within Category)

Portfolio Manager(s)

George U. Sauter. Since 10-87. BA'76 Dartmouth C.; MBA'80 U. of Chicago. Sauter joined Vanguard in 1987. As vice president of core management, he is responsible for the management of all Vanguard's index funds. He previously spent two years as a trust-investment officer with FNB Ohio.

Performance 11-30-96

	1st Qtr	2nd Qtr	3rd Qtr	4th Qtr	Total
1992	-2.57	1.87	3.08	5.00	7.42
1993	4.33	0.43	2.52	2.30	9.89
1994	-3.84	0.40	4.86	-0.05	1.18
1995	9.71	9.49	7.94	6.01	37.45
1996	5.36	4.44	3.05	—	—

Trailing	Total Return%	+/- S&P 500	+/- Wil Top 750	% Rank All Cat	Growth of $10,000
3 Mo	16.72	-0.01	0.95	4 11	11,672
6 Mo	14.34	-0.03	1.71	5 17	11,434
1 Yr	27.75	-0.09	2.28	7 14	12,775
3 Yr Avg	20.83	-0.11	1.72	5 9	17,642
5 Yr Avg	18.05	-0.15	0.99	11 16	22,923
10 Yr Avg	14.96	-0.26	0.32	12 9	40,312
15 Yr Avg	16.37	-0.36	0.48	11 10	97,220

Tax Analysis	Tax-Adj Return %	% Pretax Return
3 Yr Avg	19.62	94.2
5 Yr Avg	16.85	93.3
10 Yr Avg	13.37	89.4

Potential Capital Gain Exposure: 24% of assets

Analysis by Russel Kinnel 12-06-96

Vanguard Index Trust 500 Portfolio is in the unlikely role of hot fund.

Investors are sinking $600 million into the fund every month, making it one of the hottest selling funds this year. It's a surprising development for a rather bland fund that critics called "guaranteed mediocrity." After all, accepting returns that are certain to be slightly below the S&P 500's is a rather sober investment strategy. The fund won't ever top the charts, and its manager won't likely win a seat at the Barron's roundtable.

Now that the fund is nearing its third straight year of exceptional relative performance, critics have dropped the mediocrity charge in favor of the "trendy" label. It's true that many of the largest stocks in the S&P 500 have reached such extreme valuation levels that they might be in for a big fall. They're mistaken, however, when they explain the tremendous rally in the S&P 500 on trend-hopping individuals who are buying

index funds. Funds that track the S&P 500 and are open to individual investors have taken in about $10 billion this year, and they have $32 billion in total net assets. The index itself has a market value of greater than $1 trillion, however, and has appreciated by a sum that dwarfs the index funds. Thus, this year's move toward index funds is an effect of the index's rally—not a cause. (Pension funds that have switched to indexing and individuals who are buying actively managed funds no doubt have boosted the S&P, because much greater sums are involved.)

Although buying a hot fund is usually a bad idea, this one is quite capable of handling huge inflows. While it would tax the best of fundamental investors, manager Gus Sauter can easily put the money to work through purchasing futures and buy programs. In the long run, greater assets will drive down this fund's costs thus assuring its competitive advantage over other index funds.

Address:	Vanguard Financial Ctr. P.O. Box 2600 Valley Forge, PA 19482 800-662-7447 / 610-669-1000
Advisor:	Vanguard Core Management Group
Subadvisor:	None
Distributor:	Vanguard Group
States Available:	All plus PR,VI,GU
Report Grade:	B
NTF Plans:	N/A

Minimum Purchase:	$3000	Add: $100	IRA: $1000
Min Auto Inv Plan:	$3000	Systematic Inv: $50	
Date of Inception:	08-31-76		
Sales Fees:	No-load		
Management Fee:	Provided at cost., at cost%A		
Actual Fees:	Mgt: 0.00%	Dist: —	
Expense Projections:	3Yr: $81	5Yr: $61	10Yr: $124
Annual Brokerage Cost: 0.02%		Income Distrib: Quarterly	
Total Cost (relative to category):		Below Avg	

Risk Analysis

Time Period	Load-Adj Return %	Risk % Rank[1] All Cat	Morningstar Return Risk	Morningstar Risk-Adj Rating
1 Yr	27.75			
3 Yr	20.83	58 36	1.65 0.72	★★★★★
5 Yr	18.05	61 27	1.32 0.71	★★★★
10 Yr	14.96	63 48	1.39 0.84	★★★★

Average Historical Rating (132 months):   3.9★s

[1]=low, 100=high

Category Rating (3 Yr)		Other Measures	Standard Index S&P 500	Best Fit Index S&P 500
1 2 ③ 4 5 Worst Best		Alpha	-0.1	-0.1
		Beta	1.00	1.00
		R-Squared	100	100
Return	High	Standard Deviation	11.19	
Risk	Average	Mean	19.51	
		Sharpe Ratio	1.62	

Portfolio Analysis 09-30-96

Share Chg (08-96) 000	Amount 000	Total Stocks: 508 Total Fixed-Income: 0	Value $000	% Net Assets
189	8,295	General Electric	754,889	2.87
351	12,524	Coca-Cola	637,165	2.42
181	6,239	Exxon	519,372	1.98
122	6,109	Merck	429,895	1.63
261	8,096	AT & T	423,033	1.61
79	2,693	Royal Dutch Petroleum (NY)	420,466	1.60
109	3,005	Microsoft	395,963	1.51
127	4,132	Intel	394,046	1.50
67	4,113	Philip Morris	369,121	1.40
197	6,695	Johnson & Johnson	343,113	1.30
99	3,444	Procter & Gamble	335,801	1.28
-2	2,650	IBM	329,918	1.25
338	11,522	Wal-Mart Stores	303,895	1.16
120	3,227	Pfizer	255,356	0.97
164	5,136	Hewlett-Packard	250,393	0.95
86	2,819	El duPont de Nemours	248,744	0.95
68	2,520	Bristol-Myers Squibb	242,856	0.92
51	2,359	American International Group	237,652	0.90
55	1,979	Mobil	229,030	0.87
225	7,869	PepsiCo	222,311	0.85
44	2,415	Citicorp	218,833	0.83
99	3,407	Walt Disney	215,950	0.82
97	3,279	Chevron	205,364	0.78
110	3,195	American Home Products	203,689	0.77
121	3,252	cisco Systems	201,607	0.77

Current Investment Style		Stock Port Avg	Relative S&P 500 Current Hist	Rel Cat
Style Value Blend Growth (Large Med Small)	Price/Earnings Ratio	24.1	1.00 1.0	1.01
	Price/Book Ratio	4.9	1.00 1.0	1.06
	5 Yr Earnings Gr%	17.5	1.00 1.0	0.96
	Price/Cash Flow	13.9	1.00 1.0	1.02
	Debt % Total Cap	31.4	1.00 1.0	1.00
	Med Mkt Cap $mil	24,974	1.0 1.0	1.54
	Foreign %	1.7	— —	0.29

Special Securities % of assets 09-30-96			Sector Weightings	% of Stocks	Rel S&P	5-Year High Low
○ Private/Illiquid Securities		0	Utilities	3.5	1.0	9 4
○ Structured Notes		0	Energy	9.2	1.0	11 8
○ Emerging-Markets Secs		0	Financials	14.1	1.0	14 8
● Options/Futures/Warrants		Yes	Ind Cycls	16.9	1.0	19 17
			Cons Dur	3.7	1.0	5 3
Composition % of assets 09-30-96		**Market Cap**	Cons Stpls	11.6	1.0	15 10
		Giant 47.7	Services	13.2	1.0	18 10
Cash	0.0	Large 40.1	Retail	5.7	1.0	9 5
Stocks	100.0	Medium 11.7	Health	10.9	1.0	13 8
Bonds	0.0	Small 0.5	Tech	11.2	1.0	12 5
Other	0.0	Micro 0.0				

M**O**RNINGSTAR Mutual Funds

FIGURE 7.7 Continued

The Morningstar Mutual Fund report:
An explanation of key terms and information found in each report

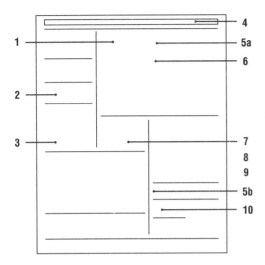

4 Yield
Yield represents a fund's income return on capital investment. There are two yield measures on the page, distributed yield and SEC yield. Morningstar computes distributed yield by summing all income distributions for the past 12 months and dividing by the previous month's NAV (adjusted for capital gains distributions). SEC yield is a standardized figure that the Securities and Exchange Commission requires funds to use when mentioning yield in advertisements.

5 Style Box
This propriety tool reveals a fund's true investment strategy, which may or may not match its stated objective. For equity funds, the vertical axis categorizes funds by size: Funds with median market capitalizations of less than $1 billion are small cap: $1 billion to $5 billion, medium cap: and more than $5 billion, large cap. The horizontal axis denotes investment styles: value-oriented, growth-oriented, or a blend of the two. A stock-fund portfolio's average price/earnings and price/book ratios are computed relative to the combined averages of the S&P 500 index set at 2.00). Funds with a combined relative P/E and P/B figure of less than 1.75 are considered value funds; 1.75 to 2.25, blend funds; and more than 2.25, growth funds. The style box located in the lower right **(5a)** of the page represents the fund's investment style as of the most recent month-end. The style boxes located above the performance graph **(5b)** represent the fund's investment style at the beginning of each calendar year.

6 Performance Graph
The top line of this graph expresss the growth of a $10,000 investment as of the most recent date: the fund's inception or the earliest date indicated on the graph. The horizontal dotted line shows the fund's performance relative to a benchmark (the S&P Index for equity funds). When the dotted line slopes pward, the fund has outperformed its index; when it slopes downward, it has underperformed its index.

7 Morningstar Return
Morningstar Return rates a fund's performance relative to other funds within the same class. The average figure for any investment class is set at 1.00.

8 Morningstar Risk
Morningstar Risk evaluates a fund's downside volatility relative to that of other funds in its class. The average Morningstar Risk rating for any class is set equal to 1.00.

9 Morningstar Risk-Adjusted Ratings
These star ratings represent a fund's historical risk-adjusted performance compared with the other funds in its class. If the fund scores in the top 10% of its class it receives 5 stars; the next 22.5%, 4 stars; the middle 35% 3 stars; the next 22.5%, 2 stars: and the bottom 10%, 1 star. Ratings are recalculated monthly.

10 Special Securities %
Here we show whether a fund can and does hold a variety of complex or illiquid securities, including derivatives. * indicates that a fund holds the securities; O indicates that the fund may but doesn't currently hold them: — means that the fund cannot own the securities. Percentages held in each category also appear.

1 Historical Profile
This provides an overall assessment of a fund's historical returns and risk, and its overall risk-adjusted star rating. The three time periods (three-, five-, and 10 year) are combined as a weighted average, with more weight given to the longer periods. The same bell curve used in the calculation of the risk-adjusted rating is used for a fund's historical risk and return profiles.

2 Total Return
Total return is calculated by dividing the change in a fund's net asset value, assuming reinvestment of income and capital gains distributions, by the initial net asset value. Total returns are adjusted for management, administrative, and 12b-1 fees, and other costs automatically deducted from fund assets. Total returns indicated here are not adjusted for sales load. (Load-adjusted total returns are located in the Risk Analysis section.) Total returns for periods longer than one year are compounded average annual returns.

3 Tax Analysis
Tax-adjusted historical returns show the fund's average annualized after-tax total return for three-, five-, and 10 year periods. It is computed by diminishing each income and capital-gain distribution by the maximum tax rate in effect at the time of the distribution. The highest possible score is 100% for funds with no taxable distributions. Potential capital-gain exposure gives an idea of an investment's potential tax bite. This figure shows what percentage of a fund's total assets represent capital appreciation, either unrealized or realized. If unrealized, the fund's holdings have increased in value, but the fund has not sold these holdings; taxes are not due until the fund does so. Realized gains represent actual gains achieved by the sale of holdings, on which taxes must be paid. Unrealized appreciation may turn into realized gains at any time if the fund's management decides to sell profitable holdings.

FIGURE 7.7 *Continued*

FIGURE 7.8 Value Line Mutual Fund Survey sheet for the Franklin Growth Fund and Vanguard Index 500 Portfolio with a diagram explaining key terms and information found in the report. The Franklin Fund is a managed fund while the Vanguard is an unmanaged index fund. © 1997 by Value Line Publishing, Inc. Reprinted by permission. All rights reserved.

THE VALUE LINE MUTUAL FUND SURVEY

VANGUARD INDEX 500 PORTFOLIO VFINX

	PEER GROUP	DIV YLD	SEC YLD	NAV	TNA(Mil)	VALUE LINE
	Growth/Inc/LB	1.8%	–	69.16	26293.4	**606**

108

OVERALL RANK	RISK RANK	5-YR RETURN
1 (Highest)	**3** (Average Risk)	**15.1%** (Annualized)

PAST MARKET CYCLE PERFORMANCE

	Fund	Peer	S&P 500
Bull 10/90 - 11/96	+192.9%	+166.9%	+196.8%
Bear 5/90 - 10/90	-14.7%	-14.4%	-14.7%
Bear 8/87 - 11/87	-29.8%	-25.4%	-29.5%

FUND INFORMATION

Address: PO Box 2600, Valley Forge, PA 19482
Distributor: Vanguard Group Inc.
Advisor: Vanguard's Core Mgmt Group

Sub-Advisor: None | Telephone: 800 662-7447
Shareholders: 896,563 | Began Operations: 8/31/76
Fiscal Year-End: December | # Funds in Family: 65

Min. Initial Invest: $3,000 | Syst. Withdrawal: Yes
Min. Subsequent Invest: $100 | Auto. Investing: Yes
Telephone Exchanges: No | Last Capital Gain: 12/20/96
Tel. Redemption: Yes | Dividends Paid: Quarterly

PORTFOLIO INFORMATION

SECTOR WEIGHTINGS

As of 11/29/96

	Port. %	Rel. S&P500
Consumer Durables	4.5	0.98
Energy	8.4	1.01
Finance	14.4	0.96
Industrial Cyclical	15.8	1.04
Non-Durable	14.2	0.97
Retail Trade	5.6	1.11
Health	10.2	1.00
Services	1.1	1.21
Technology	20.7	0.97
Utilities	4.0	0.96

COMPOSITION %

As of 9/30/96

Stock	100
Preferreds	-
Convts.	-
Bonds	-
Other	-
# Stocks	506

STATISTICS

As of 11/29/96

	Port. Avg.	% Stock	Rel. S&P 500	Rel. Peer
Price/Earnings	21.67	93	1.01	1.09
Price/Book	4.56	96	0.99	1.20
5-Yr.Earn.Growth %	11.37	83	0.99	1.07
Avg.Mkt.Cap.($Mil.)	38,367	99	1.00	1.64

PORTFOLIO HOLDINGS

Top 20 Equity Holdings — As of 9/30/96

	VL Rank*	Shares Held	Value ($000)	%Net Assets
GENERAL ELEC CO	3	8295485	754889	2.87
COCA COLA CO	2	12524134	637165	2.42
EXXON CORP	4	6238698	519372	1.98
MERCK & CO INC	2	6108632	429895	1.63
AT&T CORP	-	8096324	423033	1.61
ROYAL DUTCH PETE CO	4	2693135	420466	1.60
MICROSOFT CORP	1	3005412	396339	1.51
INTEL CORP	1	4131540	394306	1.50
PHILIP MORRIS COS INC	2	4112766	369121	1.40
JOHNSON & JOHNSON	2	6694884	343113	1.30
PROCTER & GAMBLE CO	3	3444117	335801	1.28
INTERNATIONAL BUSINESS MACHS	2	2649943	329918	1.25
WAL MART STORES INC	3	11522065	303895	1.16
PFIZER INC	1	3227246	255356	0.97
HEWLETT PACKARD CO	2	5136268	250393	0.95
DU PONT E I DE NEMOURS & CO	2	2818625	248391	0.94
BRISTOL MYERS SQUIBB CO	3	2519906	242856	0.92
AMERICAN INTL GROUP INC	2	2358828	237652	0.90
MOBIL CORP	4	1978665	229030	0.87
PEPSICO INC	4	7869419	222311	0.85

*Latest available Timeliness ™ rank from Value Line Investment Survey.

PORT. MGR. George U. Sauter 10/87 | **%RATING** 0.5 | **TAX STATUS 9/30/96** Unrealized Apprec. % 22

Style/Perf. Quintile

DIVIDENDS PAID

Year	1st Q	2nd Q	3rd Q	4th Q
1992	0.22	0.22	0.22	0.46
1993	0.22	0.22	0.22	0.47
1994	0.22	0.22	0.22	0.51
1995	0.22	0.22	0.22	0.58
1996	0.22	0.22	0.22	0.62

ISSUE DATE 2/4/97

EXPENSE STRUCTURE

Management Fee 0.17%

12b-1 Fee — None
1st Yr. Red. Fee — None

Sales Load — Pct.
Maximum — None
at $25K — None
at $100K — None
at $500K — None
Minimum — None

HISTORICAL ARRAY

	1982	1983	1984	1985	1986	1987	1988	1989	1990	1991	1992	1993	1994	1995	12/96	
	17.56	19.70	19.52	22.99	24.27	24.65	27.18	33.64	31.24	39.32	40.97	43.83	42.97	57.60	69.16	Bid Price (NAV)
	0.83	0.87	0.88	0.91	0.89	0.69	1.10	1.20	1.17	1.15	1.12	1.13	1.17	1.22	1.28	Dividends ($)
	4.66	4.26	4.40	3.69	3.38	2.78	4.00	3.48	3.73	2.91	2.72	2.57	2.71	2.11	1.84	12-Mo. Div. Yield (%)
	0.25	0.71	0.48	1.61	2.02	0.17	0.32	0.75	0.10	0.12	0.10	0.03	0.20	0.13	0.25	Cap. Gains ($)
		.28	.27	.28	.28	.26	.22	.21	.22	.20	.19	.19	.20	.20	Expense Ratio (%)
		0.30	0.26	0.28	0.27	0.22	0.18	0.17	0.18	0.17	0.16	0.18	0.17	0.18	0.19	Exp.Ratio Rel. to Peer
		35	14	36	29	15	10	8	23	5	4	6	6	4	6	Turnover (%)
		233.7	289.7	394.2	485.0	826.4	1055.0	1804.0	2172.9	4345.9	6547.5	8273.0	9356.3	17371	26293	Net Assets ($Mil.)
	21.0	21.3	6.2	31.2	18.1	4.7	16.2	31.4	-3.3	30.2	7.4	9.9	1.2	37.4	22.9	Total Return (%)
	-0.4	-1.2	-0.1	-0.9	-0.4	-0.5	-0.6	-0.1	-0.2	-0.3	-0.4	-0.2	-0.1	-0.1	-0.4	+/- S&P 500 (%)
	-2.4	-0.6	2.3	4.4	2.0	2.5	0.6	7.9	1.3	1.4	-1.3	-1.5	2.4	6.9	3.0	+/- to Peer (%)
																Quintile Perf. Rel. to Peer

PERFORMANCE (12/31/96)

	Total Return	+/- % S&P 500	+/- % Peer	Percentile Rank Peer	Value $10,000 Investment	Est. Taxes on $10,000 Investment	Value $10,000 +$100/Mo.
3 MONTHS	8.3	-0.1	1.4	31	10,834	36	11,038
6 MONTHS	11.7	-0.2	1.5	31	11,165	47	11,708
1 YEAR	22.9	-0.4	3.0	25	12,285	75	13,520
3 YEAR	19.5	-0.2	3.9	9	17,084	283	22,058
5 YEAR	15.1	-0.2	1.7	26	20,168	507	29,665
10 YEAR	15.0	-0.3	2.1	11	40,588	1,891	67,660
15 YEAR	16.4	-0.4	1.8	13	98,015	6,692	164,805
20 YEAR	14.1	-0.4	0.5	36	140,868	10,677	284,138

MPT vs. S&P 500

	Fund	Peer
Beta	1.00	0.88
Alpha	-0.2	-1.8
R²	99	96
Std. Dev.	9.65	9.44

RANKINGS (1 (best) to 5 (worst))

	Fund	Peer
Overall	1.9	2.5
Risk	3.3	3.0
Growth 5Yr.	2.8	3.0
Persistence 1Yr.	2.3	2.7

Recent Developments and Strategies

Vanguard Index 500 Portfolio benefited last year from its emphasis on large-cap companies, as the market favored these issues through the second half of 1996. With large stakes in blue chip stocks such as General Electric, Coca-Cola, Exxon, Intel, and IBM, it outperformed its Growth/Income peers by approximately 300 basis points through December. Also of note is the fact that the fund's average market capitalization has continued to swell–its now nearly $39 billion– due to the strong gains in the market since our last review in September.

Management Style

The fund seeks to replicate the price and yield performance of the Standard & Poor's 500 Composite Stock Price Index, which emphasizes large-capitalization stocks. The correlation between the performance of the fund and the S&P 500 is expected to be at least 0.95. By investing in all 500 stocks in the index in approximately the same proportions as they are represented in the index, the portfolio will at all times be close to fully invested. As a result, the fund's returns have tracked the S&P 500 with a high degree of accuracy. It maintains a low expense ratio relative to its peers (an advantage associated with passively managed funds) and doesn't charge a sales load.

Under normal circumstances, management will invest at least 95% of the fund's assets in the common stocks of the index. In addition, the portfolio is allowed to invest up to 20% of its assets in stock futures contracts and options in order to invest uncommitted cash balances. Lastly, the fund may invest in certain short-term, fixed-income securities such as cash reserves, although cash or cash equivalents are normally expected to represent less than 1% of the portfolio's assets.

Conclusion

This offering has been a strong performer relative to its peers: This passively managed fund has consistently outpaced the Growth/Income group over the long term. Additionally, it has lagged its S&P 500 benchmark slightly, which is attributable to its minimal management costs. With average volatility, this fund is recommended to investors seeking long-term growth and additional income in a portfolio of blue-chips.

FIGURE 7.8 *Continued.*

Value Line Mutual Fund Page:
An explanation of key terms and information found on each page

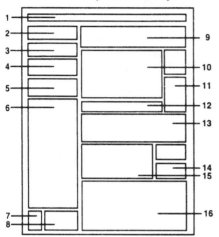

horizontal axis reflects the growth-value continuum as measured by the overall price/earnings and price-to-book value ratios of the portfolio's securities.

8 Dividends Paid
Quarterly dividend totals are shown for the past five years. The information provides an indication of the reliability of the fund's income stream.

9 Fund Description
The basic objectives and policies of the fund are explained.

10 Performance Graph
This graph illustrates the results of a $10,000 investment over the past 15 years (or life of the fund). For comparative purposes, results also are shown for the relevant index. For front-end load funds, the investment is assumed to be made at the current sales charge. The index assumes no sales charge. These data enable an investor considering a load fund to evaluate the effects of the sales charge on an actual investment over a long time period.

11 Expense Structure
A synopsis of the fund expenses, including maximum and minimum management fees, sales charges, etc.

12 Relative Performance
This graph shows the fund's performance relative to its peer group on a cumulative basis over the past 15 years (or the life of the fund, for younger funds). This relative-performance graph shows how well the fund has done over time compared to its peers. A rising curve indicates that a fund is outperforming its peers; a declining curve reflects underperformance.

13 Historical Array
Price per share, dividends, capital gains, expenses, assets, and performance are included for each of the past 15 years. The bottom row documents how well the fund has performed, on a relative basis.

14 Rankings
The fund's position within the rank. The number to the left of the decimal point represents the fund's broad rank on Value Line's scale of 1 (best) to 5 (worst), while the number to the right of the decimal point denotes the fund's position within that rank. For example, a fund that falls within the top tenth of all funds ranked 1 will show a rank of 1.0; a fund in the bottom tenth of all rank-1 funds will show a rank of 1.9.

15 Performance
The fund's total returns over various periods are shown in the first column. Results for periods longer than one year are expressed as average annualized rates. The second and third columns shows the percentage difference between the fund's performance and those of the relevant index and peer group, respectively. The fourth column indicates the percentile rank versus the fund's peers, with 1 the Highest and 100 the Lowest. The final three columns show what return a shareholder would have realized from a $10,000 investment. The first $10,000 illustration assumes that a lump sum was invested at the beginning of the period, at the current sales charge, and that no subsequent transactions were made. The last column shows the results of a $10,000 initial investment with subsequent investments of $100 at the end of each month during the entire period. This provides an illustration of dollar-cost averaging.

16 Analyst Commentary
A concise report on the fund's performance, management strategies, and future prospects.

1 Highlight Bar
The fund's name, ticker symbol, investment objective, dividend yield, latest NAV (net asset value) or price per share, and net assets.

2 Ranks
The Risk Rank shows each fund's level of risk relative to that of all other mutual funds. The fund's total-return performance (dividend and interest plus capital appreciation) is shown for the latest five years and is expressed as an average, annualized rate.

3 Past Market Cycle Performance
The fund's total return during the latest bull and bear stock markets. Total returns for the fund's peer group (those with a similar investment objective) and for the S&P 500 Index over the same periods.

4 Shareholder Information
Details about fees, minimum investments, special services, etc.

5 Fund Information
Companies servicing the fund, number of shareholders, when the fund began operations, the fund's address and telephone number, etc.

6 Portfolio Information
These details start with the percentage of assets in each of 10 broad equity-market sectors. The composition box shows the percentage of the fund's assets invested in common stocks, preferred stocks, other assets categories, and cash. The list of the 20 largest holdings of the fund is also listed. Concluding this section are the name and starting date for the individual(s) managing the fund and the fund's tax status, which includes "unrealized appreciation." This item indicates the percentage of the fund's current portfolio value that represents gains on securities. If and when these gains are realized through sale of the securities, the distributions to shareholders become taxable as capital gains.

7 Management Style
A representation of the fund's major orientation, within a two-axis grid. For equity fund, the vertical axis represents market capitalization of equities in which the fund invests; the

FIGURE 7.8 *Continued.*

Mutual Fund Scorecard/Growth

INVESTMENT OBJECTIVE: Capital growth without regard for income; usually characterized by moderate portfolio turnover. Bull/Bear ratings are figured over the latest two rising and two falling market cycles

ASSETS DEC. 31 (in millions)	PAST PERFORMANCE BULL MKTS	BEAR MKTS	FUND NAME	TOTAL RETURN[1] IN PERIOD ENDING FEB. 27 4 WEEKS	52 WEEKS	5 YEARS*
TOP 15 PERFORMERS						
1.1	**	**	VanKamp Am Growth;A[2,4]	−0.23%	56.22%	**%
1978.0	Med	Low	Legg Mason Val Tr;Prm[2,4]	2.22	44.36	21.58
17.0	**	**	Hudson Capital Apprec[3]	1.15	42.32	14.16
61.8	**	**	VanKamp Am Exchange[2]	−3.73	40.75	17.97
397.5	**	**	Fidelity Export[3]	−4.83	39.00	**
131.5	**	Med	Sound Shore[2]	2.03	36.86	18.96
10.2	**	**	Weitz:Hickory[2]	3.08	35.83	**
1.9	**	**	Texas Cap:Value & Growth	1.17	35.63	**
24.2	**	**	Thompson Plumb:Growth[2]	−1.62	34.28	14.11
90.9	**	**	Legg Mason Am Ld;Prm[2,4]	0.65	33.80	**
100.6	**	**	Glenmede:Equity Fund[2,5]	0.70	33.11	16.86
277.5	Med	Low	Pioneer Growth Shrs;A[4]	−0.47	32.65	13.43
30.5	**	**	Transam Prem:Eqty;Inv[2,4]	1.26	32.52	**
7.2	**	**	Kenilworth Fund[2]	−1.56	32.51	**
303.2	**	**	Chestnut St Exch LP[2]	0.35	32.26	18.16
AVG. FOR CATEGORY				−0.53%	18.80%	13.44%
NUMBER OF FUNDS				791	698	260
BOTTOM 10 PERFORMERS						
0.4	Low	Low	Steadman Tech & Growth[2]	−14.63%	−42.15%	−26.07%
1.2	**	**	Frontier:Equity Fund	−8.22	−19.28	**
137.4	**	**	Calvert Fd:Strat Gro;A[4]	−14.81	−9.24	**
1.8	Low	Low	Steadman Investment[2]	−8.33	−8.33	−10.82
3.1	**	**	American Heritage Growth[2]	−6.25	−5.83	**
51.2	Low	Low	Dreyfus Spc Growth;Inv[2,4]	−5.52	−5.74	7.30
26.6	**	**	Dominion:Insight Growth[3]	−15.09	−3.62	**
230.2	**	**	Masterworks:Growth Stk[2,5]	−9.87	−2.91	**
5.4	**	**	Reserve Prv:Inf Inv;A[3,4]	−4.47	−2.83	**
243.4	**	**	Waddell&Reed:Growth;B[2,4]	−3.41	−1.33	**

[1] Change in net asset value with reinvested dividends and capital gains
[2] No initial load
[3] Low initial load of 4.5% or less
[4] Fund has other share classes
[5] Fund may not be open to all investors
** Fund track record is too short

Hi = Top third
Med = Middle third
Low = Bottom third
* Annualized

Source: *Lipper Analytical Services Inc.*

FIGURE 7.9 Mutual fund scorecard. Reprinted by permission of *The Wall Street Journal*, © 1997 Dow Jones & Company, Inc. All rights reserved worldwide.

ments. The Securities and Exchange Commission requires all funds to give 1-, 2-, 5-, and 10-year performance summaries in their sales literature. Thus, this year's hot fund may not be a good long-term investment.

Closed-End (or Publicly Traded) Funds

closed-end fund an investment company has a one-time offering of a fixed number of shares to the public and then does not issue new shares or redeem old shares; the fund's shares are bought and sold like stock; also called a "publicly traded fund."

While there are over 6000 mutual funds available in the market, there are only about 1000 *closed-end funds*. Called "publicly traded funds," these companies assemble an investment portfolio and then issue shares to the public. The portfolio may or may not be diversified. After the initial public offering, a closed-end fund does not issue new shares or redeem old shares. The fund's shares thereafter trade on stock exchanges and in the over-the-counter market. Unlike mutual fund shares, closed-end fund shares are not redeemed by the sponsor. Instead, investors buy and sell them through brokers in the same way that common and preferred stocks are traded. They also pay a commission for each trade.

The relationship between a closed-end fund's market value and its net asset value is different from that of a mutual fund share. As Figure 7.10 shows, each closed-end fund share has an NAV. Like a mutual fund, this value changes daily depending on the market value of the shares that make up the investment portfolio. However, the fund's NAV is not the basis for computing the market value of the fund's shares. Because the shares trade like stock, their market value (labeled "market price" in the listing) is determined by demand for the fund's shares themselves and not directly by the supply and demand for the stocks that constitute the portfolio. As a result, the market value of a closed-end fund may be higher than the NAV (trading at a premium), equal to the NAV, or lower than the NAV (trading at a discount).

Traditionally, the shares of a closed-end fund (especially closed-end equity funds) trade at a discount to their net asset value. This is true of newly issued funds also. After most new shares are sold in the primary market at their net asset value, they almost immediately trade at a discount in the secondary market to reflect the start-up

CLOSED-END FUNDS

Friday, February 14, 1997

Closed-end funds sell a limited number of shares and invest the proceeds in securities. Unlike open-end funds, closed-ends generally do not buy their shares back from investors who wish to cash in their holdings. Instead, fund shares trade on a stock exchange. The following list, provided by Lipper Analytical Services, shows the ticker symbol and exchange where each fund trades (A: American; C: Chicago; N: NYSE; O: Nasdaq; T: Toronto; z: does not trade on an exchange). The data also include the fund's most recent net asset value, its closing share price on the day NAV was calculated, and the percentage difference between the market price and the NAV (often called the premium or discount). For equity funds, the final column provides 52-week returns based on market prices plus dividends. For bond funds, the final column shows the past 12 months' income distributions as a percentage of the current market price. Footnotes appear after a fund's name. a: the NAV and market price are ex dividend. b: the NAV is fully diluted. c: NAV, market price and premium or discount are as of Thursday's close. d: NAV, market price and premium or discount are as of Wednesday's close. e: NAV assumes rights offering is fully subscribed. v: NAV is converted at the commercial Rand rate. w: Convertible Note-NAV (not market) conversion value. y: NAV and market price are in Canadian dollars. All other footnotes refer to unusual circumstances; explanations for those that appear can be found at the bottom of this list. N/A signifies that the information is not available or not applicable.

Fund Name (Symbol)	Stock Exch	NAV	Market Price	Prem /Disc	52 week Market Return
General Equity Funds					
Adams Express (ADX)	♣N	25.20	20 7/8	– 17.2	16.8
Alliance All-Mkt (AMO)	N	27.94	22 7/8	– 18.1	18.8
Avalon Capital (MIST)	O	12.80	11 1/2	– 10.2	18.0
Baker Fentress (BKF)	♣N	22.53	18	– 20.1	15.9
Bergstrom Cap (BEM)	A	146.26	122 5/8	– 16.2	11.4
Blue Chip Value (BLU)-f	N	9.78	9	– 8.0	29.4
Central Secs (CET)	A	26.09	28	+ 7.3	34.8
Corp Renaissance (CREN)-c	O	8.82	7 1/2	– 15.0	–20.0
Engex (EGX)	A	16.49	11 1/2	– 30.3	–7.1
Equus II (EQS)	♣A	24.81	17	– 31.5	20.4
Gabelli Equity (GAB)	N	10.08	9 1/4	– 8.2	7.9
General American (GAM)	N	25.84	21 3/4	– 15.8	20.5
Inefficient-Mkt (IMF)	A	12.74	12 1/4	– 3.8	39.5
Librty AllStr Eq (USA)	♣N	12.94	11 7/8	– 8.2	17.2
Librty AllStr Gr (ASG)	♣N	12.05	10 1/4	– 14.9	21.4
MFS Special Val (MFV)-a	N	14.05	18 3/8	+ 30.8	27.4
Morgan FunShares (MFUN)-c	O	11.78	9	– 23.6	12.5
Morgan Gr Sm Cap (MGC)	N	12.09	10 5/8	– 12.1	23.5
NAIC Growth (GRF)-c	C	19.16	22 1/2	+ 17.4	51.9
Royce Value (RVT)	♣N	14.64	12 3/8	– 15.5	12.7
Royce,5.75 '04Cv-w	N	111.00	100 1/4	– 9.7	3.0
Salomon SBF (SBF)	N	18.44	16 7/8	– 8.5	39.1
Source Capital (SOR)	N	46.54	45 1/2	– 2.2	14.7
Tri-Continental (TY)	♣N	31.12	25 3/4	– 17.3	20.8
Zweig (ZF)	♣N	11.61	11 1/4	– 3.1	11.0
World Equity Funds					
ASA Limited (ASA)-cv	N	34.74	35 3/4	+ 2.9	–22.4
Anchor Gold&Curr (GCT)	C	6.13	6 1/4	+ 2.0	–3.9
Argentina (AF)	N	14.90	13 1/2	– 9.4	5.4
Asia Pacific (APB)	N	14.83	12 1/2	– 15.7	–16.1
Asia Tigers (GRR)	N	13.44	10 7/8	– 19.1	–18.5
Austria (OST)	N	11.54	9 1/8	– 20.9	1.4
BGR Prec Metals (BPT.A)-cy	T	21.72	17 1/4	– 20.6	–6.1
Brazil (BZF)-c	N	N/A	25 5/8	N/A	4.7
Brazilian Equity (BZL)-c	♣N	18.30	15 1/2	– 15.3	13.2
Cdn Genl Inv (CGI)-cy	♣T	17.89	14 3/4	– 17.6	35.1
Cdn Wrld Fd Ltd (CWF)-cy	♣T	5.94	4 45/64	– 20.9	19.0
Central Eur Eqty (CEE)	♣N	27.48	22 7/8	– 16.8	41.6
Chile (CH)	N	26.13	24 1/8	– 7.7	1.6
China (CHN)	N	16.30	13 3/8	– 17.9	–5.4
Clemente Global (CLM)-c	N	10.83	8 1/4	– 23.8	3.4
Czech Republic (CRF)	N	17.65	15 1/2	– 12.2	14.7
Economic Inv Tr (EVT)-cy	T	119.98	82	– 31.7	21.2
Emer Mkts Grow (N/A)	z	N/A	N/A	N/A	N/A
Emerging Mexico (MEF)-c	N	9.70	8 1/8	– 16.2	21.8
Europe (EF)	N	18.71	17 1/8	– 8.5	34.7
European Warrant (EWF)-c	N	17.96	14 5/8	– 18.6	66.3
F&C Middle East (EME)-c	N	19.25	16 7/8	– 12.3	40.6
Fidelity Em Asia (FAE)	N	16.84	14 1/2	– 13.9	3.8
Fidelty Ad Korea (FAK)	N	8.83	9 3/8	+ 6.2	–14.1
First Australia (IAF)	A	10.70	8 7/8	– 17.1	–0.2
First Iberian (IBF)	A	14.17	11 1/8	– 21.5	36.1
First Israel (ISL)	♣N	16.22	14 3/8	– 11.4	14.3
First Philippine (FPF)	N	20.04	16 5/8	– 17.0	8.2
France Growth (FRF)	N	13.82	10 7/8	– 21.3	17.4
GT Devel Mkts (GTD)	N	15.03	12 1/8	– 19.3	10.8
GT Glbl Estn Eur (GTF)	N	18.46	15 7/8	– 14.0	25.6
Germany Fund (GER)	♣N	15.97	12 3/4	– 20.2	18.6
Germany, Emer (FRG)	N	10.82	8 1/4	– 23.8	6.7
Germany, New (GF)	♣N	17.46	13 5/8	– 22.0	20.2
Global Small Cap (GSG)	A	15.32	12 1/4	– 20.0	21.0
Greater China (GCH)	N	19.12	15 1/2	– 18.9	3.9
Growth Fd Spain (GSP)	♣N	15.54	12 1/2	– 19.6	21.4
Herzfeld Caribb (CUBA)	O	5.74	5 15/16	+ 3.4	–3.7
India Fund (IFN)	N	8.08	8 1/4	+ 2.1	–15.3
India Growth (IGF)-d	N	11.03	12 3/8	+ 12.2	–16.3
Indonesia (IF)	N	11.97	10 3/4	– 10.2	–14.9
Irish Inv (IRL)	N	17.25	14 3/4	– 14.5	12.5
Italy (ITA)	N	11.58	9 7/8	– 14.7	21.6
Jakarta Growth (JGF)	N	10.80	9 1/4	– 14.4	–9.8
Japan Equity (JEQ)	♣N	8.13	9 3/4	+ 19.9	–23.6
Japan OTC Equity (JOF)	N	6.38	6 7/8	+ 7.8	–23.2
Jardine Fl China (JFC)	N	14.34	11 3/4	– 18.1	–2.9
Jardine Fl India (JFI)-c	N	8.01	8	– 0.1	–21.0
Korea (KF)	N	14.62	16 3/8	+ 12.0	–25.8
Korea Equity (KEF)	N	6.52	6 7/8	+ 5.4	–26.7
Korean Inv (KIF)	N	7.96	8	+ 0.5	–24.7
Latin Amer Disc (LDF)	N	17.40	15 3/4	– 9.5	36.4
Latin Amer Eq (LAQ)	N	18.78	16 5/8	– 11.5	7.7
Latin Amer Growth (LLF)	N	13.19	11 1/4	– 14.7	1.3
Latin Amer Inv (LAM)	N	21.18	18 3/8	– 13.2	4.8
Malaysia (MF)	N	19.86	18 3/8	– 7.5	3.4
Mexico (MXF)-c	N	20.39	16 3/4	– 17.9	16.5
Mexico Eqty&Inc (MXE)-c	N	12.84	10 1/2	– 18.2	22.2
Morgan St Africa (AFF)	N	19.78	16	– 19.1	17.8
Morgan St Asia (APF)	N	11.81	9 7/8	– 16.4	–21.4
Morgan St Em (MSF)	N	17.77	16 5/8	– 6.4	0.2
Morgan St India (IIF)	N	9.12	10 1/4	+ 12.4	–2.4
Morgan St Russia (RNE)	N	28.26	25 5/8	– 9.3	N/A
New South Africa (NSA)	N	17.69	14 1/8	– 20.2	–15.2
Pakistan Inv (PKF)	N	5.84	5 5/8	– 3.7	–23.7
Portugal (PGF)	N	19.13	15 1/4	– 20.3	27.8
ROC Taiwan (ROC)	N	12.90	11 3/8	– 11.8	11.0
Royce Global Trust (FUND)-c	♣O	5.59	4 9/16	– 18.4	17.7
Schroder Asian (SHF)-c	N	13.62	12 1/8	– 11.0	–10.2
Scudder New Asia (SAF)	N	15.79	13 5/8	– 13.7	–20.1
Scudder New Eur (NEF)	N	18.22	15	– 17.7	31.0
Singapore (SGF)-c	♣N	14.08	12 7/8	– 8.6	–9.4
Southern Africa (SOA)	N	19.69	16	– 18.7	0.4
Spain (SNF)	N	14.69	11 5/8	– 20.9	25.7
Swiss Helvetia (SWZ)	♣N	24.83	20 3/8	– 17.9	3.1
TCW/DW Emer Mkts (EMO)	♣N	15.30	13 1/8	– 14.2	9.8
Taiwan (TWN)-c	N	27.77	24 1/4	– 12.7	10.3
Taiwan Equity (TYW)-c	♣N	13.29	10 7/8	– 18.2	7.4
Templeton China (TCH)-c	N	15.93	13 3/8	– 16.0	13.9
Templeton Dragon (TDF)	N	18.80	15 5/8	– 16.9	10.2
Templeton Em App (TEA)-c	N	15.39	13 7/8	– 9.8	2.6
Templeton Em Mkt (EMF)	N	19.81	21 5/8	+ 9.2	8.9
Templeton Russia (TRF)-c	N	30.78	36	+ 17.0	177.4
Templeton Vietnm (TVF)	N	14.31	11 3/4	– 17.9	–9.5
Thai (TTF)	N	13.51	15 1/2	+ 14.7	–40.3
Thai Capital (TC)	♣N	8.19	9 3/8	+ 14.5	–40.0
Third Canadian (THD)-cy	T	19.28	19	– 1.5	32.6
Turkish Inv (TKF)	N	7.09	6 7/8	– 3.0	14.6
United Corps Ltd (UNC)-cy	T	58.96	39 57/64	– 32.3	29.2
United Kingdom (UKM)	N	16.67	14	– 16.0	20.4
Worldwide Value (VLU)	N	N/A	22 3/8	N/A	40.4
Z-Seven (ZSEV)	O	17.35	19	+ 9.5	7.3

FIGURE 7.10 Closed-end funds (publicly traded funds) price quotations. This table shows the current market prices of domestic and international (e.g., Asia Pacific, Brazil, First Australia, Irish Investment, Jakarta Growth) closed-end funds that invest primarily in equity securities. The list is published every Monday in *The Wall Street Journal*. It states the name of the fund, the market (exchange or over-the-counter [OTC]) in which it trades, the NAV per share, and the current market price of each share. The next column—"Prem/Disc"—indicates whether the fund's current price is at a discount (–) or premium (+) to its current net asset value. Notice that the majority of closed-end funds in the listing are trading at a discount. Reprinted by permission of *The Wall Street Journal*, © 1997 Dow Jones & Company, Inc. All rights reserved worldwide.

costs of the fund. Thus, the purchaser has an immediate paper loss. It should be kept in mind that closed-end funds are long-term investments. Over the long term, the market value of the portfolio should rise, thereby enabling investors to sell shares at a gain. Another strategy is to research the discount at which a fund usually trades. If the discount deepens appreciably, it may be a signal that the time is right to buy shares of the fund.

Closed-end funds can trade at a premium. This is particularly true when the stocks that make up the investment portfolio are those of foreign companies in countries with bright economic futures and restrictive rules governing foreign investment, such as many emerging markets. The Templeton Emerging Market Fund listed under "World Equity Funds" is a good example. Notice in Figure 7.10 that it is trading at a 9.2 percent premium over its net asset value. The combination of a limited number of shares and the anticipated economic growth of the country or countries frequently results in the shares' trading at a premium. This can be interpreted in one of two ways: Either the premium anticipates or indicates investor sentiment about the fund's future growth, or the fund provides an investment return that is higher than the current market rate of return.

Beginning investors should evaluate the possibilities of investing in closed-end funds just the same as they would investing in any other type of security, keeping in mind that each fund is essentially a package deal. Most international closed-end funds are either country funds or regional. It is rare that you will like the entire package of securities in the fund. On the other hand, if a fund has invested in an area or country where you may not be able to invest directly or obtain enough data to make an informed investment decision, then closed-end funds may be the only investment option.

Chapter

Indirect Investing in Stock: Rights, Warrants, and Options

Not all investors are interested in making money through the dividends that stocks pay. Many want only to profit from the rise and fall of a stock's price. They want to do this, however, without owning the stock and at the lowest possible cost. Rights, warrants, and options are appropriate investment vehicles for these individuals. Called *stock derivatives*, each of these securities can be thought of as a contract that offers its owner the right to buy (or sell) the underlying stock if he or she chooses. (Strictly speaking, rights and warrants are stock equivalents and options are stock derivatives. For the sake of simplicity throughout this chapter, I will refer to all three as stock derivatives.)

These derivatives have none of the traditional benefits of equity ownership. None entitles the owner to receive dividends. The holder has no voting rights or preemptive rights and no priority in the liquidation of a company. The primary benefit is that the market price movement of each of these derivatives tends to parallel the price movement of the stock that underlies the contract while the cost of purchasing them is usually a fraction of what it would cost to purchase the actual stock.

The owner of one of these stock derivatives typically

stock derivative a security that offers an investor some but not all of the benefits of stocks, particularly the capital gains potential, usually at a lower cost per unit.

has the right to purchase (or sell) the underlying stock for a predetermined price but only for a fixed period of time. Most equity derivatives do not have indefinite lives like the stocks they represent. On a designated expiration date, the security becomes worthless. During the period that an individual holds a right, warrant, or option, its market value varies depending on the relationship between the derivative's fixed *exercise price* and the market value of the underlying stock. If, for example, a stock-derivative security gives its owner the right to buy the underlying common stock at $15 per share (the exercise price) and the market value of that common stock is $25 per share, then the equity derivative has a built-in profit, or intrinsic value, of $10 per share. If the market price of the stock is equal to or less than the derivative's fixed price, then the stock-derivative security would clearly have no intrinsic value for its owner—although it could have time, or speculative, value.

exercise price the pre-determined, fixed price at which the owner or holder of a derivative security can buy (or sell) the underlying common stock.

The holder of any of these stock-derivative securities has a choice of three actions to take:

1. Exercise the contract by buying (or selling) the underlying stock. This is the choice if the investor wants the underlying stock or there is a built-in profit due to the difference between an equity derivative's fixed price and the underlying stock's market price.

2. Trade the equity derivative. This action takes advantage of the fact that the market price of the derivative tends to move in the same direction as the price of the underlying stock. As the price of the underlying security increases, so does the price of the derivative security. (The same price movement relationship holds for price decreases.) An investor who buys an equity-derivative security can sell it at a profit when its market value increases. An investor who sells short a derivative can later cover the short position profitably by purchasing it.

3. Hold it to the expiration date, at which time it becomes worthless.

Like the common stocks that underlie them, equity derivatives offer investors a high degree of liquidity. Rights and warrants trade on stock exchanges and in the over-the-counter market—on the same exchange or in the same market where the underlying stock trades. Options trade on exchanges: the Chicago Board Options Exchange, the American Stock Exchange, the Philadelphia Stock Exchange, the Pacific Stock Exchange, and others. Unlike rights and warrants, most options do not usually trade on the same exchange where the company's stock is listed.

As the basic uses of rights, warrants, and options are explained in this chapter, we will look at different scenarios to illustrate how each works. The discussions and the accompanying examples are designed to provide beginning investors with a clear understanding of the rewards and risks associated with each security and strategy.

RIGHTS

A preemptive right is a short-term security that gives existing common shareholders the first opportunity to purchase any additional common shares that a company may issue. This privilege, known as the "preemptive right" and granted in a company's charter, permits each common shareholder to maintain his or her proportionate ownership in a company. Unlike the common stock they represent, however, rights do not have an indefinite life. Usually you have 30 to 60 days to decide if you want to subscribe to the new shares or sell the rights to another investor.

It is customary to distribute one right for each share of a company's outstanding common stock. If you own 1000 shares of a company's stock, then you will receive 1000 rights during a rights offering. The number of rights needed to buy each new share of a company's stock is set by the board of directors. The ratio is determined using a simple calculation:

$$N = \frac{\text{Number of outstanding shares}}{\text{Number of new shares to be offered}}$$

where

N = *number of rights needed to buy one new share*

If, for example, a company has 100,000 common shares outstanding and it plans to issue 20,000 new shares, then the number of rights needed to buy each new share is 5 (100,000 ÷ 20,000). An investor who owns 1000 shares (1 percent) of the company's stock would have enough rights to buy 200 (1000 ÷ 5) of the new shares. Upon subscribing to the new issue, the investor would own 1200 shares, or 1 percent of the total 120,000 shares now outstanding. The investor's proportionate ownership is maintained.

In order to be eligible to acquire the additional shares at the subscription price, you must own the stock on or before a specified date set by the board of directors. This date is known as the record date. Once the record date is announced, the exchange or the National Association of Securities Dealers uses this information to establish an appropriate *ex-rights date*. If you buy the stock at any time prior to the ex-rights date, you are buying the stock with the right included. In technical terms, the stock is described as trading *cum-rights* (literally, *with* rights). After the ex-date and until the end of the subscription period, the stock trades *ex-rights*. From this day forward, anyone purchasing the stock no longer receives the rights with the stock.

In a rights offering, the company's board of directors does not expect the existing shareholders to subscribe to (i.e., buy) the new shares at the same price at which the already outstanding shares are trading. Instead, they offer the shares to the stockholders at a *subscription price*, which is lower than the current market price. This is done primarily to make the new shares so attractive to the shareholders that they will buy all of the issue. It is the difference between the outstanding shares' current market price and the new shares' subscription price that gives the rights their value.

The theoretical value of one right when it is trading with the stock or separate from the stock can be determined using two different formulas. The first, known as the cum-rights value, is determined using the following formula:

$$\text{Cum-rights value} = \frac{M - S}{N + 1}$$

where

ex-rights date by industry practice, the first business day after the distribution of the rights; the bid price of the stock is reduced by an amount equal to the value of the right.

cum-rights literally, *with* rights; describes transactions in which the preemptive rights accompany the purchase (or sale) of common stock; their value is included in the market price of the shares.

M = *current market price of the outstanding shares*
S = *subscription price of the new shares*
N = *number of rights needed to buy one new share*

The following example shows how this formula can be used if you own 1000 shares (or 1 percent) of a company's outstanding 100,000 shares. The company has announced that it will issue 20,000 additional common shares. Each existing shareholder needs five rights (100,000 ÷ 20,000) in order to be able to purchase each new share. The stock, which is trading at $50 per share, is offered at a subscription price of $35 per share. Using the cum-rights formula, the value of a right in this example is $2.50:

$$\text{Cum-rights value} = \frac{\$50 - \$35}{5 + 1} = \frac{\$15}{6} = \$2.50$$

After the stock goes ex-rights, its price is reduced by an amount equal to the value of one right. This is done because an investor who buys the stock on or after the ex-rights date does not get a right with it and therefore should not pay for it. The stock, whose price on the previous business day was $50.00, is reduced to $47.50 ($50.00 − $2.50) on the ex-rights date. Now the rights trade separately from the stock. As shown in Figure 8.1, the right (rt) now has its own separate entry in the stock listings. Any investor who wants the rights can purchase them in the market just as he or she would buy the stock. Its ex-rights value is computed using a slightly different formula:

$$\text{Ex-rights value} = \frac{\text{Adjusted M} - S}{N}$$

where

Adjusted M = *adjusted market price of the outstanding shares after the stock "goes ex"*
S = *subscription price of the new shares*
N = *number of rights needed to buy one new share*

 ex-rights
literally, *without* rights; describes transactions in which the preemptive rights do not accompany the purchase (or sale) of common stock; the rights, at this time, trade separately from the stock in the market.

 subscription price usually lower than a stock's current market price, the fixed price at which a company's existing shareholders can purchase new shares during a rights offering.

NEW YORK STOCK EXCHANGE

52 Weeks Hi	52 Weeks Lo	Stock	Sym	Div	Yld %	PE	Vol 100s	Hi	Lo	Close	Net Chg
31	11 ¼	BankBost pfA		3.51e	12.5	...	3	28 ¼	28	28	- ⅜
30 ⅛	10 ¾	BankBost pfB		3.39e	12.8	...	5	26 ½	26 ¾	26 ½	- ⅜
52	16	BankBost pfC		6.15	12.7	...	z860	48 ⅜	48 ¼	48 ⅜	- ⅜
39 ¼	13 ¼	BankNY	BK	1.52	4.8	20	3711	32 ⅛	31 ¼	3	+ ⅜
37	24 ⅛	BankNY adj pfA		3.35e	9.3	...	9	36	36	36	...
40 ⅜	17 ½	Bank Amer	BAC	1.20	3.0	10	5091	40 ¼	39 ⅜	39 ⅝	- ⅝
88 ¾	54 ¾	BauschLomb	BOL	1.44	1.7	19	613	86 ¼	85 ⅜	85 ¾	+ ¼
15 ¾	7 ⅛	BearSterns	BSC	.60b	3.8	13	3291	15 ¾	15 ½	15 ⅝	...
56 ¼	39 ½	BellAtlantic	BEL	2.52	5.6	13	5929	45 ⅝	44 ⅝	4 ⅝	- ⅝
32550	30550	BerkHathwy	BRK		...	25	z270	32575	31425	32500	-50
23 ¼	12 ½	Berlitz	BTZ	.50	2.9	31	8	17 ⅜	17 ⅜	17 ⅜	- ⅛
21	10 ½	BirmghamSti	BIR	.50	3.1	29	376	16 ⅛	15 ¾	15 ⅞	...
7 ⅝	5 ⅛	BluChipValFd	BLU	.74e	10.0	...	150	7 ⅜	7 ¼	7 ⅜	...
68	47 ¾	BritTelcom	BTY	3.23e	5.0	11	243	65 ¼	64 ⅞	65	...
12 ½	6 ⅛	BrookeGp	BGL	.56b	6.2	6	127	9	8 ¾	9	+ ⅛
2 ⅜	**½**	**BrookeGp rt**			**...**	**...**	**179**	**2 ⅜**	**2 ¼**	**2 ⅜**	**...**
6 ⅝	3 ⅜	Playboy B	PLA		...	65	4	6	5 ⅞	5 ⅞	...
43 ¼	19 ⅝	Polaroid	PRD	.60	2.4	13	1305	25 ¾	25 ⅛	25 ¼	- ½
14 ¾	8 ½	PortugalFd	PGF	.12e	1.2	...	205	9 ⅞	9 ⅝	9 ⅝	- ¼
37 ¾	16 ⅞	Primerica	PA	.40	1.3	9	3502	31 ⅝	30 ⅝	30 ⅝	-1
91 ¼	70 ⅛	ProctGamb	PG	2.00	2.4	17	5079	84	82 ⅞	83	- ¾
8 ½	6 ½	PropTram	PTR	.64	8.1	23	47	7 ⅞	7 ¾	7 ⅞	...
25/64	**3/32**	**PropTrAm rt**			**...**	**...**	**418**	**⅛**	**3/32**	**3/32**	**- 1/32**

FIGURE 8.1 Typical rights listing in a financial newspaper. Rights, highlighted in gray, are represented by the abbreviation "rt" in the listings. Notice that rights trade in fractions like the common shares they represent. Typically the minimum fluctuation is 1/8 ($.125); however, as the second example shows, they can also trade in units as small as 1/32 ($.03125) or less. Rights and the common stock they represent trade in the same market.

Using the same information from the previous example, we find that the ex-rights value is $2.50, the same as the cum-rights value:

$$\text{Ex-rights value} = \frac{\$47.50 - \$35.00}{5} = \frac{\$12.50}{6} = \$2.50$$

This theoretical value is important for investors who want to sell their rights instead of exercising them. During the subscription period when the rights are being bought and sold by investors, their market value changes constantly with the value of the outstanding shares. In reality, the rights market value remains close to the theoretical value. The formula, therefore, calculates the approximate price at which an investor can sell his or her rights. If, as in our example, you choose to sell the 1000 rights you own, your total proceeds would be approximately $2500 ($2.50 × 1000). A person who holds an odd number of rights can sell those that he or she cannot use to subscribe to the issue. However, usually enough rights are lost by shareholders so that the company will permit holders of odd numbers of rights to round up to the next whole share number.

When selling rights, investors are faced with the classic investment timing question: "When do I sell my rights so that I get the highest price?" The prevailing sentiment regarding the best time to sell rights is captured in the saying, "The early bird captures the worm." The logic behind this belief is that by disposing of the rights early in the subscription period, an existing shareholder gets a higher price because he or she sells before the other investors have decided what they will do. Once everyone begins to sell, usually near the end of the subscription period, the price almost invariably declines. This theory would certainly hold true if the stock is in a downtrend or even a sideways trend. In an uptrend, however, the value of a right will increase during the subscription period, and investors would get the best price by selling near the end of the period.

In the past, companies like AT&T used traditional rights offerings, like the one discussed, as a means of raising capital. Today, however, rights offerings are rarely issued by U.S. companies. When they are issued, they are usually associated with the recapitalization of a highly leveraged company following a takeover or merger. Some companies issue *long-dated rights*. These so-called poison pills are automatically exercised when, during a hostile takeover, a company or an investor acquires a certain percentage of the shares, thereby diluting the takeover. When a traditional rights offering does appear in the financial news, it is most often being made by a British firm or by closed-end management companies.

long-dated rights a dilutive, anti-takeover device in which rights are automatically distributed to existing stockholders during a hostile takeover.

Beginning investors are probably best advised to use rights to subscribe to the new shares. This means depositing additional funds to pay for new shares; however, the profitability that trading rights seems to offer is reduced by the commission costs charged for these transactions. In reality, investors would have to hold a large number of rights in order to make a reasonable profit after commissions have been paid.

WARRANTS

warrant a long-term security, usually attached to a bond or preferred stock, that gives the holder the right to buy a fixed number of a company's common shares at a price that is higher than the stock's current market price.

unit term used for a common or preferred stock or bond issued with one or more warrants attached; the combined products trade as one in the stock market.

A *warrant* is a long-term security that gives its owner the right to buy a specified amount of common stock at a fixed price for a fixed period of time. The fixed price at which the stock can be purchased is at a substantial premium to the market value of the stock at the time the warrant is issued. There is usually a waiting period—typically a year—before the owner can exercise the warrant. Most warrants expire within 10 to 20 years, although some companies have issued perpetual warrants.

Warrants are seldom issued to the public as stand-alone securities. Most often, they are issued by a company attached to its new common stock, preferred stock, or bond. The combination of the new stock and the warrant is often referred to as a *unit* and is designed to "sweeten" or increase the marketability of the speculative new issue. In essence, when you buy the new security, you get the warrant for free.

When it is issued, a warrant usually has no intrinsic worth. It becomes valuable only when and if the market price of the common stock moves above the fixed price (the exercise price) at which the warrant permits the investor to buy the stock. For example, a company has common shares outstanding that are trading in the market at $20 per share. The company issues a preferred stock with a five-year warrant attached. The warrant gives each purchaser of the new preferred the right to purchase one additional common share at $35. If the price of the common stock rises to $50 per share during the five-year period, the warrant has an intrinsic value of

$15 per share($50 − $35). In cases where the warrant can be detached from the security, you can sell the warrant in the market and take the profit. In this case the warrant trades separately in the market as shown in Figure 8.2. You retain the security to which the warrant was originally attached.

You can also exercise your warrant, buying the shares at the specified price and depositing the required cash in your brokerage account. Sometimes in order to exercise the warrant, you must surrender the bond or the preferred stock. In this case, no additional money is required

NEW YORK STOCK EXCHANGE

52 Weeks Hi	Lo	Stock	Sym	Div	Yld %	PE	Vol 100s	Hi	Lo	Close	Net Chg
7 ⅜	3 ¾	**Hanson wt**			...	...	250	5 ¾	5 ⅝	5 ¾	+ ⅛
23 ¼	17	Hanson	HAN	1.54e	7.9	10	6378	19 ⅝	19 ⅜	19 ½	...
3 ⅝	¹⁵/₃₂	HarBrJ	HBJ		...	...	773	⅝	⁹/₁₆	⁹/₁₆	−¹/₁₆
2 ¾	¹¹/₃₂	HarBrJ pf			...	...	3137	¹³/₁₆	¾	¹³/₁₆	+¹/₁₆
41 ⅛	29 ⅜	Heinz	HNZ	.96	2.5	18	2963	38 ⅜	37 ⅝	37 ⅝	−¼
57 ¼	37	KnghtRidder	KRI	1.40	2.5	21	597	57 ½	56 ⅞	57	...
27 ⅜	11 ⅜	KoreaFd	KF	2.20e	16.6	...	84	13 ½	13 ¼	13 ¼	− ⅛
23 ⅛	12 ⅜	LaZBoy	LZB	.56	2.4	18	67	23 ⅛	22 ⅞	23	...
26 ¾	17 ⅝	MfrsHan pf	MHC	2.74	10.4	...	36	26 ⅜	26 ¼	26 ⅜	− ⅛
2	⁹/₁₆	**Manville wt**			...	...	73	2 ⅛	2 ⅛	2 ⅛	+ ⅛
7 ½	4	Manville	MVL		...	9	316	7 ½	7 ¼	7 ⅜	...
38 ½	25	McDonalds	MCD	.37	1.1	16	7575	35 ⅛	34 ⅜	34 ⅝	− ⅜
33 ⅝	17 ⅝	Mellon BK	MEL	1.40	4.6	11	786	31 ⅜	30	30 ⅜	−1
28 ⅝	25	Mellon Bk pf		2.80	10.1	...	54	27 ⅞	27 ½	27 ⅝	− ¼
19 ⅝	15 ½	Mellon Bk pf		1.69	8.8	...	4	19 ⅛	19 ⅛	19 ⅛	− ⅛
122 ⅞	72 ⅜	Merck	MRK	2.24	1.9	24	5347	117	115 ⅝	116 ¼	− ⅜
95 ⅝	73 ⅝	MinnMngMfg	MMM	3.12	3.3	16	3606	96 ¼	93 ¾	93 ⅞	−1 ⅛
91 ¾	47 ⅛	MorganStan	MS	1.50	1.7	11	503	89 ⅛	88 ½	88 ½	− ½
25 ⅛	24 ½	MorganStan pf			...	...	611	24 ¾	24 ⅝	24 ⅝	...
44 ¼	16 ⅞	NCNB	NCB	1.48	3.5	13	2258	42 ¼	41 ½	41 ¾	− ¾
9	3	NtlSemi	NSM		...	...	1845	7 ⅜	6 ⅞	6 ⅞	− ½
⅝	¹/₁₆	**NtlSemi wt**			...	...	66	⅛	⁷/₆₄	⅛	...
40 ½	20	NtlSemi pf		4.00	10.1	...	31	39 ½	39	39 ½	...

FIGURE 8.2 Typical warrants listing in a financial newspaper. Warrants for several stocks are highlighted in gray. The symbol "wt" denotes warrants in financial newspapers. The minimum fluctuation is usually $1/8$ ($.125), the same as the underlying stock. However, they can also trade in units as small as $1/64$ ($.0156). Warrants and the common shares that underlie them trade in the same market.

strike price
the fixed price at which stock can be bought or sold when a call or put is exercised. Also known as the "exercise price."

call option
a security that gives its holder the right to buy 100 shares of a stock at a fixed price for a fixed period of time.

put option
a security that gives its holder the right to sell 100 shares of a stock at a fixed price for a fixed period of time.

from you unless you must buy full shares to compensate for any fractional shares that result when the warrant is exercised. In effect, such "nondetachable" warrants are the equivalent of convertibles.

OPTIONS

An option is a contract representing the right or obligation to buy or sell 100 shares of a stock at a specified price (called the *strike price*) at any time during a specified period. There are two types of options contracts: a *call option* and a *put option* (Figure 8.3). A transaction involving either type always involves two parties. The person who purchases the option contract is referred to as the "buyer," the "holder," or someone who is "long" the option. The person who sells the contract is referred to as the "seller," the "writer," or someone who is "short" the option.

The other terms of an options contract can be found by examining a typical newspaper listing such as the one illustrated in Figure 8.4. Using Boeing options as an example, we see that beneath the stock's name, the price

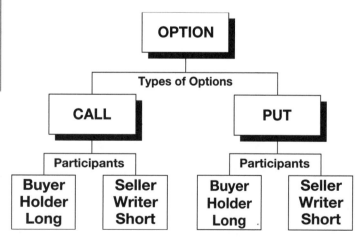

FIGURE 8.3 Types of options and participants in each transaction.

47⅛ is repeated. This is the price at which Boeing's common shares closed on the New York Stock Exchange (or another stock market) on the previous day. The next column shows the different strike prices of the option contracts. The strike price is the fixed price at which the option can be exercised. In this case, they occur in $5 intervals—$35, $40, $45, $50, and so on. This interval may be smaller ($2.50) or larger ($10) depending on the market price of the underlying security. The next column,

CALL ◄
1 Boeing Jun 45 Call @ 3 ¼

PUT ◄
1 GE May 165 Put @ 5⅜

LISTED OPTIONS QUOTATIONS

Option/Strike		Exp.	- Call -		- Put -	
			Vol.	Last	Vol.	Last
Baxter	22 ½	May	30	12 ⅛	...	...
34 ⅞	25	May	20	9 ½	4	¹⁄₁₆
34 ⅞	25	Aug	22	9 ¾	...	...
34 ⅞	30	May	40	4 ½	...	...
34 ⅞	30	Jun	15	5	...	...
34 ⅞	30	Aug	8	5	2	½
34 ⅞	35	May	4	½	5	⅝
34 ⅞	35	Jun	12	1 ¼	16	1 ⅞
34 ⅞	35	Aug	26	2 ½	24	2 ⅜
34 ⅞	40	Aug	7	⅝	...	...
Boeing	35	Aug	...	...	24	1 ⅝
47 ⅛	40	May	60	7 ⅜	...	...
47 ⅛	40	Aug	106	8	19	⁷⁄₁₆
47 ⅛	45	May	64	2 ⅜	17	³⁄₁₆
47 ⅛	45	Jun	120	3 ¼	26	¾
47 ⅛	45	Aug	90	4 ¼	30	1 ¾
47 ⅛	50	May	181	⅛	86	3 ⅛
47 ⅛	50	Jun	21	¹³⁄₁₆	...	...
47 ⅛	50	Aug	21	¹³⁄₁₆	197	4 ⅛
47 ⅛	55	May	76	¹⁄₁₆	207	8 ⅛
47 ⅛	55	Aug	479	8 ⅛	...	...
Coke	40	May	47	14 ⅞	...	...
54 ⅝	45	May	67	9 ½	...	...
54 ⅝	45	Aug	...	...	14	⅜
54 ⅝	50	May	122	5 ⅛	16	¹⁄₁₆
54 ⅝	50	Aug	356	10 ⅜	...	...
54 ⅝	55	May	166	¾	42	1 ⅛
54 ⅝	55	Jun	338	2 ¼	21	2 ⅛
54 ⅝	55	Aug	351	2 ¾	76	2 ⅜
54 ⅝	60	May	...	...	26	6 ⅛
GE	150	Aug	...	...	238	4 ⅞
159 ⅞	160	May	196	1 ¹⁵⁄₁₆	267	2
159 ⅞	165	May	47	⁹⁄₁₆	200	5 ⅜
159 ⅞	165	Jun	50	4 ¼	...	...
159 ⅞	165	Aug	40	8 ⅝	...	...
159 ⅞	170	Jun	50	2 ⅞	...	...
159 ⅞	190	Aug	20	2	...	...

FIGURE 8.4 Typical options listing in a financial newspaper.

premium
the market price of a call or a put option.

labeled "Exp.," shows the expiration month of the option contract. The columns with the headings "–Call–" and "–Put–" show, respectively, the trading volume and the closing market price (called the *premium*) of the option contract whose strike price and expiration month are presented at the beginning of the line. The premium prices are always stated per share. An investor wishing to buy the June call with the 45 strike price would pay $3\frac{1}{4}$ per share, or a total of $325. (Remember that each option represents 100 shares of the underlying stock.) Conversely, the investor who sells the same call would receive $325.

Throughout this discussion on options, we will use the terms "holder" and "writer" to describe the two parties involved in each type of option contract in order to reduce potential confusion. We assume you are the holder most of the time although you can be either party in reality.

Call Option

You as the holder of a call have the right, but not the obligation, to buy 100 shares of the underlying stock at the option's strike price at any time until the option's expiration date. You pay the total amount of the option's premium for this right. The writer of a call is obligated, on demand, to sell 100 shares of the underlying stock to you at the strike price if and when you exercise the option. For assuming this obligation, the writer receives the premium that you paid. Importantly, the premium is a one-time, nonrefundable payment by the holder of the option to the writer. The premium is not part of the exercise price. (Figure 8.5 shows the rights and obligations of the holder and writer of a call.)

Using the Boeing call cited in Figure 8.4, 1 Boeing Jun 45 Call @ $3\frac{1}{4}$, we will discuss both parties' potential risks and potential rewards. When you as the holder buy this call, you pay the total premium, $325 ($3.25 × 100 shares), for the right to buy 100 shares of Boeing at $45 per share any time up through the option's expiration date. You want the price of the underlying stock to rise

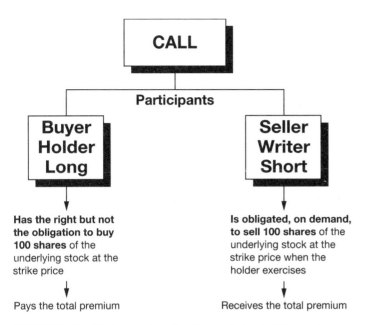

FIGURE 8.5 Rights and obligations of the holder and writer of a call.

above a total cost per share equal to the strike price plus the premium you paid for the option. At any point above this amount, you make a profit. You can then exercise the call, buying the stock at the call's strike price, when the market price is higher.

If the market price of Boeing common stock rises to $65 per share, you can exercise the option, buying 100 shares at $45. This action produces an immediate gain of $20 per share ($2000 total) on the stock transaction. However, you paid a $325 premium for the call; therefore, your net profit on the entire trade is $1675. (Commission costs are not included in these examples because the amount charged varies among brokerage houses.)

If the price of Boeing common falls below the call's strike price ($45), then you would not exercise the option because it would be unprofitable to do so. You would let the option expire, losing $325, the total premium paid for the contract.

The writer of an option receives the premium that you as holder paid. The writer cannot exercise the call.

(For the purposes of exercising, think of the relationship of the holder and the writer in psychological terms. The writer is in a "passive" position, while the holder is in an "active" position.) The writer of a call wants the market price of Boeing stock to stay flat or decline, so that you as the holder would not exercise the option, and the writer would keep the premium—$325 in our example.

If the price rises to $65 per share and you as holder exercise, the writer is obligated, under the terms of the options contract, to deliver or sell 100 shares of Boeing to you at $45 per share. If the writer does not already own the stock, then he would have to buy it at its current market price of $65, incurring a loss of $20 per share ($2000 total). Remember, however, that the writer received the premium when he or she wrote the option. The loss would therefore be partially reduced by the amount of the premium received, leaving the writer with a net loss of $1675. (Figure 8.6 summarizes these expectations, rewards, and risks for the holder and writer of a call option.)

Most of these investors are not interested in owning the stock that underlies the option. They simply want to profit from the rise and fall of the stock's value. Given this objective, most holders are not interested in exercising the option. Nor are writers interested in being exercised. Neither party wants to incur the additional transaction fees and margin calls that must be paid when an option is exercised. Instead, each wants to trade the contracts: to buy and sell them based on changes in the premium. A holder of a call wants to buy the option at a low premium and later sell it at a higher premium. The writer of a call wants to sell the option at a high premium and then buy it back at a lower premium. This is possible because the value of a call's premium changes in direct relationship to several factors, including the market price of the underlying security and the time remaining to expiration.

A call is profitable to a holder only when the market price of the underlying security is above the option's strike price. As the stock's market price increases, it becomes more and more profitable for the holder to exercise

```
                    ┌──────────────┐
                    │     Call     │
                    └──────────────┘
              ┌───────────┴───────────┐
    ┌──────────────┐         ┌──────────────┐
    │   Holder     │         │   Writer     │
    │   Buyer      │         │   Seller     │
    │   Long       │         │   Short      │
    └──────────────┘         └──────────────┘
```

- EXPECTATION: Wants the market price of the underlying stock to *rise.*

- REWARD: Potentialy unlimited gain when the price of the underlying stock appreciates.

- RISK: Loses only the total premium paid for the call when the market price of the underlying stock declines.

- EXPECTATION: Wants the market price of the underlying stock to *stay flat* or *decline.*

- REWARD: Gain limited to the total premium received when the option was written. Keeps the premium when the market value of the stock stays flat or declines.

- RISK: Potentially Unlimited loss when the market price of the underlying stock rises.

FIGURE 8.6 Summary of rewards and risks for the holder and writer of a call option.

in the money the relationship between the market price of the underlying security and the strike price of the option is such that exercising would yield a profit to the holder.

a call. When this occurs, the option is described as being *in the money.* The amount by which the call is in the money is known as the *intrinsic value.* A call's intrinsic value is computed using the following formula:

Intrinsic value = Stock's market price − Call's strike price

intrinsic value part of the value of an option's premium reflecting the amount by which an option is in the money.

Returning to our Boeing example (Figure 8.4) we can see that the market price of the common stock, $47\frac{1}{8}$, is above the call's strike price, 45. This call is in the money and has intrinsic value of $2\frac{1}{8}$, or $2.125 per share.

When the market price of the stock equals the strike price of the option, a call is said to be *at the money.* When a stock's market price is below a call's strike price, the option is described as being *out of the money.* Both at the money and out of the money options have no intrinsic

at the money the market price of the underlying security and the option's strike price are the same.

out of the money the relationship between the market price of the underlying security and the option's strike price is such that the holder (buyer) would not exercise the option because it would result in a loss.

time value the amount of an option's premium that exceeds its intrinsic value, representing the price investors place on the time an option has until its expiration; if an option is out of the money, all of the premium represents time value.

value. (The concept of negative intrinsic value does not exist.)

Time value is the price that investors pay for the likelihood that the option will move in the direction they want before the expiration date. Time value can be computed using the following formula:

Time value = Call's premium − Call's intrinsic value

The premium on the June 45 call is $3\frac{1}{4}$, and the intrinsic value, which we just computed, is $2\frac{1}{8}$. The time value is thus $1\frac{1}{8}$, or \$1.125 per share. The more time an option has until its expiration, the greater the time value. As an option approaches its expiration date, this value decreases. On the expiration date, no time value remains. Thus, options are said to be "wasting assets." If an option has any value on this date, it will be solely intrinsic value. The typical life of a listed option is about eight months; however, there are long-term options with one-year, two-year, and three-year expirations. These long-term options are called LEAPs—the acronym for Long-term Equity Anticipation Products. These are available only on the most actively traded stock options.

As the price of the security underlying a call increases in value—that is, moves more and more in the money—the increasing intrinsic value is directly reflected in the premium, sometimes almost dollar for dollar. Rather than exercising the call as we showed earlier, you as the holder can sell or offset it on an exchange at close to its intrinsic value. Your net profit will closely equal what you would have obtained by exercising the option, and the total transaction costs will be substantially less. If the stock's price moves below the strike price, you simply let the option expire, losing only the total premium paid.

The writer of a call profits only when the option remains at the money or moves more and more out of the money. The option will not be exercised, and the writer keeps the premium. When the option moves in the money, the writer begins to lose. This investor cannot exercise the option but can buy it back at a higher premium, incurring perhaps a smaller loss than he would if he were forced to wait until you as holder exercised.

Strategies for Buying Calls. There are two basic strategies that beginning investors in stocks can use for buying call options. We will use an example to illustrate how each of these strategies works.

   1. *Buying calls to profit when a stock's price is rising.* Our example using Boeing illustrates this strategy. Rather than buying 100 shares of the stock and paying $4712.50 if they were paid in full or $2356.25 if they were bought on margin, you buy one Boeing call for substantially less—$325 for the total premium. If the market price of Boeing shares appreciates, so will the market value of the Boeing call. In theory, when the stock advances from $47\frac{1}{8}$ per share to $65, the option would move in the money by an additional $17\frac{7}{8}$ per share and this would be reflected in the premium. In reality, the premium would probably increase by a bit more if the upward price momentum of the underlying stock were strong. You as holder would be able to sell the call at a higher premium than you paid for it, earning a profit. If, however, the market price of the stock declines, your total loss is limited to the price paid for the option contract.

   2. *Buying calls to protect profits on a short stock position.* You sold short 100 shares of IBM when the price of the stock was $96 per share. The price has declined to $75 per share, and you are worried that the price may turn around and wipe out the $21 per share gain. To protect the profit, you buy one IBM call option with a $75 strike price. If the price of IBM shares rise, your profits are protected. Every dollar lost on the short stock position is offset by every dollar gained on the long call. Also, you can exercise the call, buying 100 shares at $75 each, and then use the shares to cover the short sale. On the other hand, if the market continues downward, you continue to make money on the short position. The call moves out of the money, and you lose only the premium paid for the call.

In technical terms, this is one of many hedging strategies. An investor uses the call as insurance to protect the profits on an existing short stock position without liquidating the position.

Strategies for Writing Calls. Strategies involving writing options are commonly called *income strategies* because the writer of a call receives the premium. This terminology does not consider the fact that when writing an option, an investor may have to deposit margin approximately equal to 20 percent of the market value of the underlying security. The writer of an *uncovered option*—a call or a put—must deposit the required margin. The writer of a *covered option* deposits no margin. Instead, he or she owns enough of an offsetting position to eliminate the risk that a naked writer faces. The covering position can include:

1. Owning the underlying common shares.
2. Owning a preferred stock or bond that can be converted into the underlying common shares.
3. Owning enough warrants that can be used to acquire the underlying common shares.

These are sophisticated strategies and should be attempted only after you have a solid understanding of the risks associated with them.

The two basic income strategies involve writing uncovered calls and writing covered calls. As before, examples will be used to illustrate both scenarios.

1. Writing uncovered calls to profit in a flat or declining market. This is one of the most speculative option strategies because the investor is exposed to unlimited risk. You must deposit margin with the broker in order to establish this position. Recall that in our initial example, an investor wrote 1 Boeing Jun 45 Call, receiving a premium of $325. As long as the price of the stock remains at or below the option's strike price, you, as the holder, will not exercise the option, and the writer will keep the premium. If the price rises, the writer will be exercised,

income strategy in options, any strategy in which the investor receives more options premium than he or she pays.

uncovered option term used to describe a call or put writer who is unprotected against the maximum possible loss on a short option position.

covered option term used to describe the writer of a put or a call who holds another security position that protects against or offsets the risks of a short option position.

forced to deliver or sell 100 shares to you (the holder) at $45 per share, the call's strike price. Since the writer does not own 100 shares of Boeing common, he is forced to go into the market and buy the stock at whatever the prevailing market price is at the time, which could be $65 per share, $85 per share, or $105 per share. Since a stock's price can rise potentially an unlimited amount, the writer of an uncovered or naked call is subject to unlimited risk. The writer's gain is limited to the premium received for selling the option.

2. *Writing covered calls to increase returns from stock during a flat market.* There is much less risk for an investor who writes covered calls. This strategy is used to increase income and to protect a stock position. Covered call writing is a popular strategy among investors who hold portfolios of blue-chip stocks, whose prices are reasonably stable. It is used to increase total returns from the portfolio. In addition, the customer does not have to deposit any margin on the option positions because there is little or no risk.

The following example demonstrates how this strategy works. (In this case, you, the reader, are the writer of the call, not the holder.) Say you own 500 shares of Commonwealth Edison (CWE) stock that you originally purchased at $25 per share and that is currently trading at $40 per share. The stock's price is relatively stable, offering you little opportunity for capital gains. Although you are reasonably satisfied with the dividends the company pays, you want to increase your return from the shares you own. You write 5 CWE Jun 40 Calls @ 3, receiving a total premium of $1500. As long as the price of Commonwealth Edison remains relatively flat (i.e., the stock does not rise above $40 per share) you will not be exercised and will get to keep the total premiums. If the price rises above $40, the option will be exercised (by the holder) and the stock called away from you. But you still profit. Because the price at which you are obligated to sell the shares—the call's $40 strike price—is higher than the price you originally paid for Commonwealth Edison ($25), you make $15 per share on the share transaction. Additionally, you keep the

$3 per share earned for writing the call. The total profit is $9000 ($18 × 500 shares). If you wanted to keep the stock, you could go back into the marketplace and repurchase it.

If the price drops below $37 per share, then you lose because the total loss on the value of the 500 shares of Commonwealth Edison exceeds the premiums received for writing the call. There would still be a gain on the 500 common shares that you own; however, you would not have achieved your goal of generating additional income by writing covered options.

Put Option

The holder of a put has the right, but not the obligation, to sell 100 shares of common stock at the option's strike price at any time through the option's expiration date. The holder pays the premium for this right. The writer of a put is obligated, on demand, to buy 100 shares of the underlying stock at the strike price if and when the holder exercises the option. (Remember that only the holder can exercise the put.) For taking on this obligation, the writer receives the total premium paid by the holder. (Figure 8.7 summarizes the rights and obligations of both parties.)

Using the General Electric (GE) put cited in Figure 8.4, 1 GE May 165 Put @ $5^3/_8$, let us examine the rewards and risks of the holder and the writer. You as holder of this GE put pay a total premium of $537.50 ($5.375 × 100 shares) when you purchase the option. You want the market price of GE common shares to decline. If this occurs, you can exercise the put, selling short 100 shares of General Electric common stock at the strike price, knowing that you can cover the position by purchasing the shares at the lower market price. Before you can make any profit, the price of the stock must fall below the strike price by an amount that exceeds the premium paid for the option.

If, for example, the price of GE common stock falls to $140 per share, you as holder of the put can exercise the option, selling short the stock at $165 per share. You can then cover this short sale by purchasing the stock in the

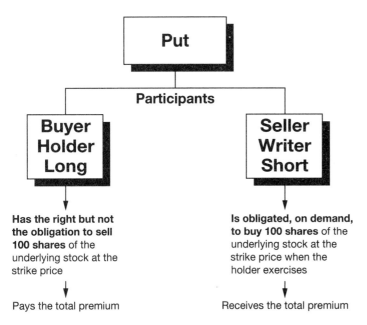

FIGURE 8.7 Rights and obligations of the holder and writer of a put.

market at $140 per share. The result is a gain of $25 per share or $2500 total on the stock transaction. However, you had already paid $537.50 for the option, so your net profit on the transaction is $1962.50. The firm's commission would be deducted from this gain. The further a stock's price declines, the more it profits the holder of a put.

If the price of the stock rises after you have purchased the put, then it would be unprofitable for you to exercise it. If you did, you would sell 100 shares at a price lower than you could buy it in the market—not a prudent action. You would probably hold the put until it expires, losing the total premium paid—$537.50 in the GE example. This is the maximum risk for you, the holder of this put.

The writer of a put profits only when the price of underlying stock stays flat or rises. When this occurs, it is not profitable for the holder to exercise the put. Hence, the writer does not have to fulfill the contractual obligation to buy 100 shares of GE from the put holder at the strike price. The option expires, and the writer keeps the premium that was paid to him or her. In the General Electric example, the writer of a put would make $537.50 if the price of the common shares stays at or above $165.

The writer loses when the price of the underlying shares declines. As we have shown, when the price of General Electric common stock declines below the strike price, you as holder of the GE put will force the writer to buy 100 shares at the option's strike price—$165 per share. Since the market price of GE stock is only $140 per share when the option is exercised, the writer has an immediate loss of $25 per share, for a total of $2500. This loss is then partially reduced by the total premium that the writer received ($537.50) when the put was sold. The writer's net loss is therefore $1962.50. The brokerage house's commissions are added to this loss. (Figure 8.8 summarizes the expectations, rewards, and risks for the holder and writer.)

As with calls, the holder and writer of a put are not interested in exercising the options or being exercised. They too prefer to trade the option based on the rise and fall of its premium. Like a call, a put's premium is influenced by the option's intrinsic value and its time value. The intrinsic value is the amount by which an option is in the money. A put is in the money when it is profitable for the holder to exercise the option. This occurs when the market price of the underlying stock is below the option's strike price. The formula for computing the intrinsic value of a put is:

Intrinsic value = Put's strike price – Stock's market price

Using the General Electric put in Figure 8.4, we see that the market price of the stock is $159^7/_8$, and the put's strike price is $165. This put is clearly in the money with an intrinsic value of $5^1/_8$. As the price of the underlying stock decreases, the put's intrinsic value will increase by almost the same amount. The put's premium will also increase. Instead of exercising the put, you as holder can simply trade it—sell the put—and reap close to the same amount of profit. By trading the put instead

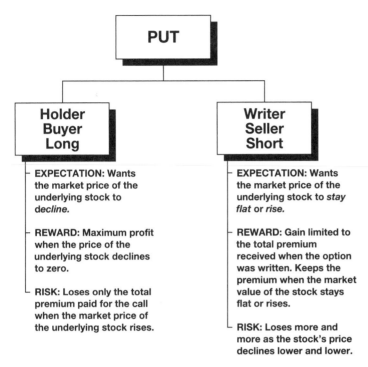

FIGURE 8.8 Summary of rewards and risks for the holder and writer of a put option.

of exercising it, you also save on transaction costs and do not have to meet the initial margin call on the short stock position. If the market price of the common stock moves above the option's strike price, the put is described as being out of the money. The option would have no intrinsic value and it would not be profitable for you to exercise. You would let the put expire, losing only the total premium paid.

The holder loses as the option moves out of the money or stays at the money; the writer profits in both situations. The holder will most likely let the put expire, and the writer will keep the premium. As the put moves in the money, the writer, knowing that there is increasing likelihood that the option will be exercised, can buy it back at a higher premium prior to being exercised. Not only would her obligation to the holder be removed, but the writer may, depending on the price at which the position was closed out, retain part of the premium originally received or sustain a smaller loss than she would have if she had to waited for the holder to exercise.

Strategies for Buying Puts. Investors can buy puts to profit from the underlying stock's price decline or to protect the profits on an existing long stock position. Two basic strategies are described below.

1. *Buying puts to profit when a stock's price is falling.* Instead of selling short a stock to profit from a price decline, you can buy a put. As the example using General Electric showed, the holder of a put makes money when the price of the underlying stock falls. More important, the investor's risk is substantially reduced. When you sell short a stock and the price of the stock increases, you are potentially subject to an unlimited loss and a maintenance margin call. If you do not liquidate the position, you will have to deposit more and more money in the account as the stock's price appreciates. If you buy a put, the only risk you face is the loss of the premium paid. An adverse price move would not result in a margin call.

2. *Buying puts to protect profits on a long stock position.* Known as hedging, this strategy permits investors to lock in profits that have been made on an investment and still maintain the stock position. For example, you purchased 200 shares of GE common stock when the price was $125 per share. At a current price of $160 per share, you have a $35 per share gain. You believe that the price of GE shares is about to fall. You want to protect the $7000 profit ($35 × 200 shares) but do not want to sell off the stock. You buy two GE puts with a $160 strike price. You have now locked in the profit. The price of this insurance is the premium you pay for the put. If the price of GE common stock falls, as you believe it will, then every dollar lost on the long stock position is offset by every dollar made on the put. If the price of GE increases, you continue to make money on the 200 shares of GE common stock and lose the premium on the put. Perhaps of equal importance, you have been able to maintain hold-

ings in General Electric common stock, benefiting from any dividends that may be paid during this time.

Strategies for Writing Puts. Like the writing strategies for calls, these are also called income strategies because the investor receives the premium. They are equally complex and should be attempted only after you have a clear understanding of the risks involved.

1. *Writing uncovered puts to profit in a rising market.* In our initial example, involving an investor who wrote 1 GE May 165 Put @ $5^3/_8$, the person profited when the price of General Electric common shares rose above the option's strike price or stayed close to it. The writer kept the premiums. There is, however, substantial risk for the writer when the price of the stock declines. Once she is forced to buy GE when you as holder exercise, she may be able to sell the stock in the market only at a price less than what she has paid for it.

2. *Writing uncovered puts as a means of buying a stock at a lower price.* This is a conservative strategy. Normally when you want to buy a stock at a price that is lower than its current market price, you would use a buy limit order. (This was discussed in Chapter 3.) The same objective can be accomplished by writing a put whose strike price is at or near the price you wish to buy the stock. Imagine that General Electric common stock is trading at $160 per share. You believe the price will decline and want to buy 300 shares of the stock only when the price is at $150 or lower. You write 3 GE Jun 150 Puts and receive the premium. If the price declines below $150, the holder of the put will exercise it, forcing you as writer to buy 300 shares of GE at $150 per share. The cost of buying the stock is further reduced by the premiums that you received when the option was sold. If the price of the stock rises, you keep the premium. This is a decided advantage over simply using a limit order, which would not be executed if the price of the stock rises and you would not receive the premium as compensation. You are still subject to the risk that the price of the stock will continue to fall after you have been forced to purchase it when the put was exercised.

3. *Writing covered puts.* An investor who writes a put is covered only by simultaneously holding another put whose strike price is the same or higher and whose expiration date is the same or later than the one written. This strategy is done primarily so that the investor will have to deposit no margin. Because stocks or other equities are not directly involved in this strategy, it is not appropriate to the scope of this book and will not be discussed here. Investors interested in covered put writing strategies should consult another book in this series, *Getting Started in Options*, or one of the many advanced books on options available in bookstores.

THE EFFECT OF STOCK SPLITS AND STOCK DIVIDENDS

When a company chooses to split its stock or pay its common shareholders a stock dividend (not a cash dividend), the holders or owners of a warrant or an option are also affected. (Because the life of a right is usually very short-term, that derivative security is usually not trading long enough to be affected by stock splits or stock dividends.)

Warrants and options have an "antidilutive" feature. If there is any increase (or decrease) in the number of a company's outstanding common shares, then the number of shares underlying the derivative security (i.e., the warrant or option) must be adjusted so that the holder maintains the right to buy (or sell) the same proportionate number of shares.

If you are the holder of a warrant and the company splits its stock or pays a stock dividend, then the warrant's exercise price is reduced in proportion to the percentage of the stock split or dividend. The result is that if you exercise the warrant, you end up getting more shares in the company. Specifically, you can acquire enough additional shares to compensate for the change. This adjustment protects the warrant holder against dilution (i.e., a decrease in the percentage of ownership of a company's total outstanding shares).

With options, the adjustment depends on whether

the split or dividend results in a round lot or an odd lot. Splits or dividends resulting in a round lot cause an increase in the number of option contracts and a proportional reduction in the option's strike price. If you own 1 Boeing Jun 60 Call and the underlying stock splits two for one, you will own 2 Boeing Jun 30 Calls afterward.

If a split or dividend results in an odd-lot number of shares, then the number of options contracts remains the same, but the number of shares underlying it increases. The strike price is decreased proportionately to the percentage of the change. For example, Boeing declares a 20 percent stock dividend, and you own 1 Boeing Jun 60 Call. After the dividend, the number of shares underlying the one option would be 120 instead of 100. The option's strike price would decrease. Recall that the total value of the shares underlying the original option is $6000 (strike price × 100 shares). After the split, the total value of the shares remains the same ($6000); however, there are now more shares underlying the option. By dividing the total value by the new number of shares, you get the adjusted strike price: $6000 ÷ 120 = $50. After the dividend, you will own 1 Boeing Jun 50 Call. In all cases, the fixed prices at which these equity-related securities can be exercised are unaffected by the payment of cash dividends.

Your brokerage firm's operations area, specifically the reorganization ("reorg") department, keeps track of any changes in total quantity of stocks, bonds, and other securities that a company has outstanding. It also records the effect that stock dividends, stock splits, or any such actions have on any outstanding derivative securities. All adjustments automatically appear on your statement at the end of the month.

International Investing in Stocks

The Pacific Rim, Eastern Europe, Latin America, and the republics that were once part of the Soviet Union have been cited as markets having great potential for economic growth and investment profit. Most investors who hear these predictions on news reports or read them in various financial and investment publications assume that investing abroad is beyond their financial means and, perhaps more important, far beyond their risk tolerance. Another widely held belief is that this type of investing is only for experts or big players. Both of these ideas are incorrect and serve only to limit the gains that investors—small or large—can make as investment opportunities become increasingly international.

Today, you cannot ignore the gains in market share, product development, and profits that some international companies have made during the past several years— many of them greater than gains posted by the largest and most successful U.S. companies. A handful of these companies' names are familiar to many U.S. households: Honda, Sony, Gucci, Daimler-Benz, Nissan, Samsung, British Petroleum, British Airways, Nestlé, Royal Dutch, and Bayer, for example. In the 1970s the United States was the largest issuer of stock in the world. During the 1980s, the balance shifted. Now more than 60 percent of the total dollar value of all stock in the world is issued by non-U.S. companies. In practical terms, this shift means that more and more investment opportunities lie in the growth of markets outside the United States. In fact, over the past two decades, investments in many of these foreign markets have yielded greater gains than investments in U.S. stock markets.

Remember that where there is potential for great gains, there are always greater risks to bear. What are the risks associated with investing in foreign markets? How do you go about investing in these foreign companies and markets? What percentage of your investment portfolio should be in foreign stock? This chapter answers these questions and serves as a primer for beginning investors who are interested in this increasingly important part of the equities market.

One important distinction must be clarified at the outset: the difference between international investing and global investing. "International investing" denotes the buying and selling of the securities of foreign companies—those located outside the United States. "Global investing" refers to trading the securities of any company with a broad international presence (in other words, a multinational corporation), whether its primary office or headquarters is located outside or within the United States. Thus, an "international" portfolio might consist of Glaxo-Wellcome, TelMex, British Airways, Toyota, and Sony stock. A "global" portfolio could consist of the same companies but might also include Coca-Cola, GM, IBM, and Gillette—U.S. multinational companies that earn a substantial part of their revenues in foreign markets.

WHAT ARE THE RISKS ASSOCIATED WITH INVESTING ABROAD?

Three primary risks face anyone who invests in the international markets: foreign exchange fluctuation, political instability, and lack of disclosure.

Foreign exchange risk (also called "currency risk") is that risk associated with a change in the value of the foreign currency relative to the dollar. When the value of the dollar rises on the foreign exchange market, a foreign currency is worth less. Conversely, when the value of the dollar declines, a foreign currency is worth more. A foreign company pays dividends in its home currency. If the value of the dollar rises relative to the foreign currency, the dividends (and capital gains) an investor earns will result after conversion in fewer dollars for the investor. In response, the price of the foreign company's securities falls because there will be a decline in demand for the securities by U.S. investors. However, when the exchange rate for the dollar declines, the foreign currency becomes more valuable. In this case, the dividends and capital gains will result in more dollars after conversion. The demand for the foreign securities increases, and so do the prices.

Another risk associated with foreign investment is political turmoil. When investing overseas, particularly in countries with histories of political instability, there is always the risk that a change in government could bring about a change in the investment climate. The threat of a civil war, for example, could devastate the business investments in a country. Also, although some governments favor foreign investments and try to make the path easier, others impose restrictions. The greatest risk that investors face is the possibility that a new government could nationalize all businesses, which generally would leave U.S. and other foreign investors with no legal recourse. They would lose all of their investment dollars.

A third risk is a lack of disclosure about both the foreign company's financial performance and its management. Great differences exist among countries in their regulation of and attitudes about insider trading, and the disclosure of financial information to investors. It is incorrect to assume that the frequency and uniformity of information provided by U.S. corporations (quarterly reports, annual reports with audited financial statements, and so on) is the norm around the world. This lack of consistent standards, especially in accounting practices, puts the individual who wishes to invest directly in these foreign markets at a disadvantage.

Other risks resulting from differences in language, trading and settlement practices, and general securities industry regulations are also significant. It is therefore important to have access to good information when investing overseas. For beginning investors, this type of information is most easily obtained from a full-service brokerage firm, an investment advisor, or an investment advisory firm that has direct access to these markets.

INVESTING IN INTERNATIONAL COMPANIES AND MARKETS

There are four ways to invest in companies located abroad. Figure 9.1 lists these investment vehicles in order of the easiest to the most complicated.

U.S. Multinational Corporations

Many large U.S. companies actually sell more of their products in foreign markets than they do in the United States. Coca-Cola is one of the best examples of this. (See the second page of Figure 5.1.) Perusing several of the company's annual reports, one discovers that a substantial portion—more than 50 percent—of its sales and profits comes from its operations in Europe, Asia, and Latin America. Gillette is another company with a huge international presence and sales. If you are traveling overseas, you can find Gillette razor blades in any pharmacy or department store in the world, except in the most remote or closed countries. As new markets open in other countries, Gillette will not only promote its basic shaving products but will doubtlessly make strong marketing efforts for its other lines, such as the Oral-B dental products.

These large multinational companies are often the first to establish trade and sales agreements in the emerging markets of newly accessible countries. As each country's economy improves, it becomes increasingly receptive to sales of the multinational companies' products. For beginning investors, this is perhaps the least risky way to invest abroad. Of course, investing in multinational, publicly held corporations is not what most people have strictly in mind when they think about investing overseas.

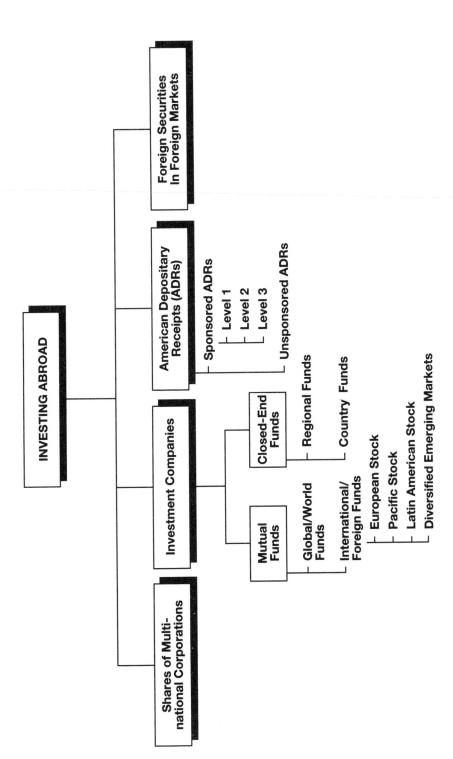

FIGURE 9.1 Four means of investing abroad.

253

This approach is decidedly indirect. Usually the companies that have substantial visibility and sales in foreign markets are among the largest and most successful in the United States—3M, IBM, GM, Coca-Cola, McDonald's, Exxon (known as Esso abroad), and Procter & Gamble, to name just a few. For the average investor, many of these companies' names are synonymous with blue-chip investments. Hence, the risks associated with buying their common stock are substantially lower than the risks associated with buying the stock of a company located in a foreign country.

Two simple facts illustrate this reduced risk. First, because U.S. multinational companies pay dividends in dollars and not a foreign currency, the investor who buys these shares does not directly experience the effects of the fluctuations in the exchange rate. Second, because the multinational corporation's shares trade in the U.S. stock markets, the performance of these securities closely follows the movement of the U.S. markets, not the market in the foreign country. The seemingly beneficial effect of being shielded from the direct effects of the currency movement and volatility of the local market means that the investor is also shielded from the potential profits that such volatility offers.

Although the connection between buying the shares of multinational U.S. corporations and investing abroad is more tenuous than the other methods discussed here, this strategy offers beginning investors an opportunity to learn about the international markets as they read through the quarterly or annual reports of these companies. In short, purchasing stock in United States-based multinationals exposes investors to the international investment marketplace in a very limited and protected way.

American Depositary Receipts or Shares

Investing in *American Depositary Receipts* (ADRs) or *Shares* (ADSs) is the easiest way for U.S. residents to invest directly in the stock of non-U.S. companies. An ADR or ADS is a negotiable receipt representing the common stock of a foreign corporation. An ADR is not a common stock. Rather, it is backed by those common shares of a

American depositary receipts (or shares) negotiable securities traded in the United States representing ownership of the common or preferred stock of a non-U.S. company that is being held in trust; commonly known as ADRs or ADSs.

foreign company held for this purpose in trust by a bank in the corporation's home country. In essence, each ADR is a certificate representing a percentage ownership of the securities being held in trust. The ADR is priced in U.S. dollars and trades like U.S. stock.

Importantly, one ADR does not always represent one share of the common stock held in trust. Each ADR can be backed by any number of the foreign corporation's common shares or even a fraction of a share. These terms are negotiated at the time that the trust is established and the ADRs issued.

ADRs are divided into two groups: *sponsored* and *unsponsored*. An ADR is said to be sponsored if the foreign company is directly involved in its issuance in the U.S. markets. In this case, the issuer chooses a bank to serve as the depository for its shares. (The three largest depository banks in the United States are Citibank, Bank of New York, and J. P. Morgan.) The foreign company is responsible for registering the ADRs (and/or the underlying shares held at the depository bank) with the Securities and Exchange Commission and with the securities agencies in the states in which the ADRs will be offered and sold to U.S. residents. It also selects the U.S. brokerage firms that will be involved in the distribution of the ADRs. Like shareholders of publicly held U.S. corporations, holders of sponsored ADRs have all of the usual rights of common shareholders, including the rights to receive dividends and to vote (including by proxy). The depository bank is responsible for converting the company's dividend payments into U.S. dollars and distributing them to shareholders. Additionally, the foreign corporation must provide U.S. shareholders with quarterly and annual reports in English. Sponsored ADRs trade on the exchanges (e.g., Sony, Gucci, Honda, British Airways, Telefonos de Mexico, Daimler-Benz, and Glaxo-Wellcome) or in the over-the-counter market (De Beers, Fuji, Toyota). (Increasingly the term "American depositary share" is being used to denote a sponsored ADR.)

The description of sponsored ADRs in the preceding paragraph is accurate; however, the actual characteristics of a given sponsored ADR will depend on whether it is a

 sponsored ADR an American depositary receipt created by the non-U.S. company working directly with a depository bank.

 unsponsored ADR an American depositary receipt created usually by a bank without the participation or consent of the non-U.S. company; unsponsored ADRs trade only over the counter, not on U.S. stock exchanges.

Level 1, Level 2, or Level 3 sponsored ADR. To understand the different levels, it is important to know that an ADR (whether sponsored or unsponsored) consists of two components. The first component is the foreign company's shares that are held at the depository bank (i.e., the underlying shares). These deposited shares may be already trading in the foreign company's domestic market or they may be new shares issued specifically to back the ADR. The second component is the receipts themselves (i.e., the ADRs) which trade on the U.S. stock markets.

In a Level 1 ADR program, the receipts (i.e., the ADRs) issued in the United States are registered with the SEC, but the underlying shares held at the depository bank are not registered with the SEC. Also, the underlying shares at the depository bank already trade in the foreign company's domestic market. Because these underlying shares are not registered with the SEC, the foreign company issuing the Level 1 ADRs is not subject to many of the SEC's registration and reporting requirements, and not subject to the Generally Accepted Accounting Principles (GAAP) used in the United States. Therefore, the information provided to the shareholder by the foreign issuer will most likely be sketchy and the financial statements may be difficult to decipher. Level 1 ADRs trade in the over-the-counter market. Specifically, their prices are listed only on the Pink Sheets and on the OTC Bulletin Board (see Chapter 3), which are the two least liquid over-the-counter markets. Figure 9.2 shows the Pink Sheet listing for Nestlé, one of the largest Level 1 ADRs.

Level 2 ADRs are those in which both the ADRs and the underlying shares (that already trade on the foreign company's domestic exchange) are registered with the SEC; therefore, the non-U.S. issuer is subject to the ongoing registration and reporting requirements of the SEC. Because both securities are registered with the SEC, the ADRs can trade on U.S. stock exchanges (e.g., NYSE and AMEX) and on NASDAQ. Importantly, Level 2 ADRs must partially adhere to GAAP accounting practices used in the U.S. Under GAAP, not only must the foreign company provide more complete disclosure about the company's finances and management, it must also present this

NEOLENS INC	NEOL	WK VOL- 1569 HB- 1 3/16	LB- 1	1/32	1 1/16	1 1/8
M- NEOPROBE CORP	NEOP	WK VOL- 1494 HB- 6 5/8	LB- 6	1/4	6 1/4	6 3/8
M- NEOPROBE CORP 97 E WTS	NEOPW	WK VOL- 650 HB- 1 7/8	LB- 1	1/2	1 1/2	1 11/16
M- NEORX CORP $2,4375 EX PR1	NERXP	WK VOL- 9 HB- 23 3/4	LB- 22	3/4	22 3/4	23 3/4
		O ' CONNOR & ASSOCIATES CG	800 641	2509		
		BEAR STEARNS & CO NY	800 964	6403		
		ROBERTSON STEPHENS&CO SF	415 693	3215		
NEORX CORP	NERX	WK VOL- 988 HB- 8 1/2	LB- 8	1/4	8 1/4	8 3/8
NEOSPORT INC		HERZOG HEINE GEDULD NY	800 221	3600		
NEOTERIK HEALTH TECH INC	*NTRK	DATKB ,01FO,11FPGONB,02FO, 20FTSCOB,02FO,10F				
M- NEOZYME II CRP/ 98 UTS	NIIUF	WK VOL- 341 HB- 36 5/8	LB- 36	1/2	36 1/2	37
NEPTUNE ORIENT LINES ADR		ARNHOLD&S BLEICHROEDER NY	212 943	7518		
NESTLE'S.A. ADR		SMITH NEW CRT CRL MRKS NY	800 221	7420		
		HERZOG HEINE GEDULD NY	800 212	3600		
		DEUTSCHE BK CAPTAL CRP NY	212 474	7472		
		MERRILL LYNCH PFS NY	800 937	0507		
		UBS SECURITIES INC NY	800 446	8732		
		MORGAN STANLEY & CO NY	212 703	4663		
		CS FIRST BOSTON CORP NY	212 909	3441		
		BEAR STEARNS & CO NY	212 272	4569		
		MERRILL LYNCH PFS NY	212 449	4093		
		S G WARBURG & CO INC NY	212 459	7075		
		HERZOG HEINE GEDULD NY	212 962	0300		
		SWISS BK CRP INV BNKNG NY	212 335	1059		
		KIDDER PEABODY & CO NY	212 510	4643		
NESTLE'S.A. SPONS ADR	*NSRGY	SWISS BK CRP INV BNKNG NY	212 335	1059		
		CS FIRST BOSTON CORP NY	212 909	3441		
		S G WARBURG & CO INC NY	212 459	7075		
		MERRILL LYNCH PFS NY	212 449	4093		
		BEAR STEARNS & CO NY	212 272	4569		
		GOLDMAN SACHS & CO NY	212 902	1115		
		SMITH NEW CRT CRL MRKS NY	800 221	7420		
		DEUTSCHE BK CAPTAL CRP NY	212 474	7472		
		MORGAN STANLEY & CO NY	212 703	4663		
		KIDDER PEABODY & CO NY	212 510	4643		
		UBS SECURITIES INC NY	800 446	8732		
		CJD88485/8049FAHNB453/80457/8KPC0B395/80397/8MASHB37038 RGILB385/8039				
NESTOR INC	*NEST	ALFRB23/4FO31/2FFRANB3FO4FHILLB3FO33/4FHRZGB3FO31/2F MASHB3FO33/4FPGONB31/8FO35/8FTSCOB3FO33/4F				
NET HOLDING INC SPONS ADR	*NETHY	ARNHOLD&S BLEICHROEDER NY 212 943 9214 FAHNB7/8011/4				
NET/TECH INTL INC	*NTTI	ALFRB21/2FO4FHILLB3FO41/2FPGONB3FO41/2FQUINB3FO41/2F				
NET/TECH INTL INC UTS	*NTTIU	HRZGB3F				

STOCK	PAGE 91	FEB. 16, 1994	NATIONAL DAILY QUOTATION SERVICE

FIGURE 9.2 Listing of ADRs on the Pink Sheets. The listing for Nestlé, a Level 1 sponsored ADR, includes the names of the brokerage firms that are market makers in the stock and their telephone numbers. In order to get the current Bid-Asked quote for a Level 1 ADR, a broker must call one of the market makers.

information in a format that is consistent with that prepared by U.S.-based companies. These requirements make understanding and evaluating the non-U.S. company somewhat easier for U.S. citizens. Partial adherence to GAAP can mean that disclosure of the company's financial performance will be more informative than Level 1, but still somewhat incomplete. Ericsson LM Telephone Company ADR Class B is an example of a Level 2 sponsored ADR. Headquartered in Sweden, Ericsson is most familiar to U.S. investors as a maker of mobile telephones and telecommunications systems. Its ADRs trade over NASDAQ, one of the National Market Issues.

Level 3 ADRs are similar to Level 2 ADRs in that the issuer registers both the ADRs and the underlying shares with the SEC, and is subject to the SEC's ongoing registration and reporting requirements. However, there are two important differences: First, Level 3 ADRs must adhere to all GAAP accounting rules. And second, the underlying shares held at the depository bank are typically new shares, not those already trading in the foreign company's domestic exchange. In other words, the foreign company issues Level 3 ADRs to raise additional capital outside its domestic markets. These ADRs typically trade on the U.S. stock exchanges. Daimler-Benz and British Sky Broadcasting, both NYSE-listed issues, are examples of Level 3 sponsored ADRs.

If the foreign company is not directly involved in the issuing of its ADRs, then the issuance is described as unsponsored. In this case, a bank, acting for itself, is the depository and issuer. After first determining that there is sufficient interest in the foreign company's stock in the United States to warrant the issuance of ADRs, a bank purchases a predetermined number of the foreign company's common shares and places them in trust. The bank handles all of the U.S. registration requirements, including paying all of the associated expenses, and then offers and sells the ADRs to the public through U.S. brokerage firms. Because the foreign company is not involved in the issuance of the ADRs, the bank is considered to be the owner of record of the common shares. The holders of the unsponsored ADRs have only the right to receive dividends, which are converted into dollars and distributed by the bank. These shareholders have no voting or proxy rights. As the owner of the shares, the bank has the right to vote. If there is a rights offering, the bank sells the rights and distributes the proceeds to the ADR owners. Additionally, the bank is not required to provide shareholders with quarterly and annual reports in English. Instead, they receive only an annual report in the language of the issuer's home country. Unsponsored ADRs do not trade on stock exchanges. They trade solely in the over-the-counter market, mostly on the Pink Sheets.

Today, nearly 1200 sponsored and unsponsored ADRs trade in the U.S. stock markets, of which approximately 30 percent trade on the stock exchanges. Purchasing an ADR is as easy as purchasing the common stock of a publicly held U.S. corporation. When you buy an ADR, it is usually held in street name, although a stock certificate in your name may be requested. Current trading and price information is widely available in the financial press. In fact, the information is included in the same column and format as the reports on U.S. stocks. In the NYSE and AMEX listing, no special notation is usually used to highlight or distinguish ADRs, although the listing for Glaxo-Wellcome in Figure 9.3 does have the abbreviation "adr" next to the name. In the NASDAQ listings, ADRs are given a separate area, usually at the end of the NASDAQ Small-Cap listing, as shown in Figure 9.4.

The market value of an ADR is determined not only by analysts' and investors' expectations of the company's growth, but, more importantly, by the market price of the foreign company's shares in its domestic market and by changes in the value of the company's home currency. The Telefonos de Mexico SA (TelMex) scenario illustrates how these forces can provide great gains and then suddenly prove quite risky. From the day it began trading on the NYSE until late 1994 the price of TelMex ADRs moved, with minor downturns, in only one direction—up. This lulled many investors into a false sense of expectation and confidence. In December of 1994, the Mexican government devalued the Mexican peso. At the same time, uncertainty about TelMex's future growth in a new political environment caused a huge sell-off of its common shares at the Bolsa in Mexico City. The devaluation and the sell-off in Mexico prompted an even bigger sell-off of TelMex ADRs on the New York Stock Exchange. Within days, the value of TelMex ADRs had hit all-time lows. The effect of the currency risk and the political risk

NEW YORK STOCK EXCHANGE

	52 Weeks Hi	52 Weeks Lo	Stock	Sym	Div	Yld %	PE	Vol 100s	Hi	Lo	Close	Net Chg
	8¼	3⅛	BrillAuto	CBA	.08	1.7	...	317	4⅝	4⅜	4⅝	...
	19	11⅞	Brinkerint	EAT		...	31	2742	15¼	14⅜	14⅝	– ⅝
n	32½	22⅛	♣BrisHotel	BH		...	...	65	29¾	29⅝	29¾	...
	90⅜	66¾	BrisMyrsSqb	BMY	3.00	3.4	24	9917	89½	88¾	89⅛	...
	88	**65¾**	**BritAir**	**BAB**	**2.61e**	**3.1**	**...**	**108**	**85**	**84¼**	**84⅜**	**– ⅜**
	47¼	**26**	**BritGas**	**BRG**	**2.78e**	**9.5**	**...**	**1220**	**29**	**29**	**29⅛**	**– ⅛**
	113⅝	**86**	**BritPetrol**	**BP**	**3.70e**	**3.3**	**25**	**2973**	**113⅛**	**112⅝**	**113**	**...**
	44	**29⅜**	**BritSkyBdcst**	**BSY**	**.58e**	**1.3**	**...**	**250**	**44¼**	**43⅞**	**43⅞**	**+ ⅜**
	31½	**23¼**	**BritSteel**	**BST**	**1.93e**	**7.4**	**...**	**1134**	**26⅝**	**26¼**	**26¼**	**...**
	65½	**49¼**	**♣BritishTele**	**BTY**	**5.67e**	**10.3**	**...**	**520**	**55⅝**	**55**	**55**	**+ ⅝**
	11/16	⅛	BrdwyStore wt			...	...	63	9/32	¼	¼	...
s	31¾	26⅜	BrokenHill	BHP		...	...	160	27⅞	27½	27¾	– ¼
	14	4	BrookeGp	BGL	.30	5.0	1	69	6⅛	5⅞	6	– ⅛
	29⅞	23¼	♣BklynUnGas	BU	1.42	5.3	14	1059	27¼	26¾	26¾	– ½
	12⅛	6⅞	BrownShrp	BNS		...	22	95	10	10	10	+ ⅛
	25¾	12⅛	BrownGp	BG	1.00	6.0	36	185	16⅝	16¼	16⅝	...
	⋯											
	15¾	11	GettyPete	GTY	.12	.8	29	51	15½	15	15	– ½
	10⅞	6⅝	GIANT Gp	GPO		...	dd	5	7 ¾	7¾	7¾	...
	15⅞	7⅞	GiantInd	GL	.20	1.3	17	104	15	14⅝	15	+ ¼
	62½	40½	Gillette	G	.72f	1.2	32	9442	60⅝	59⅞	60½	+ ⅜
	8⅞	5½	GlamisGld g	GLG	.06	...	...	798	7¼	7⅛	7⅛	...
	29⅝	**22⅜**	**GlaxoWell adr**	**GLX**	**1.35e**	**4.9**	**21**	**7822**	**27¾**	**27½**	**27½**	**+ ⅛**
	43	22½	♣Gleason	GLE	.50	1.3	6	47	38¾	37⅞	37⅞	– ⅝
n	15¼	12	Glenborough	GLB	1.20	8.4	...	59	14¼	13¾	14¼	...
	20	12⅛	GlendaleFed	GLN		...	68	3595	18	17½	17¾	– ⅛
	50¼	34	GlendaleFed pfE		2.19	4.7	...	19	47	46¾	47	+ ⅛
	22⅜	15⅛	GlimchRlty	GRT	1.92	11.5	13	245	16⅞	16⅝	16¾	– ⅛
	48⅛	21	Globl Drctml	GML		...	42	560	41⅛	40	41⅛	+ ⅞
	19⅝	12⅛	GloblHlth	GHS		...	...	1563	17¼	16¾	16⅞	– ½

FIGURE 9.3 Listing of New York Stock Exchange–traded ADRs. Most NYSE listings do not distinguish ADRs (highlighted in gray) from other equity securities; however, Glaxo-Wellcome has the abbreviation "adr" following its name.

on U.S. investors was immediate, wiping out many investors' gains.

Currency risk and political risk vary depending on the foreign company's home country. Therefore, you should investigate ADRs of companies in a country or countries appropriate to your risk tolerance. When considering buying an ADR for the first time, it is probably prudent to look at conservative companies with long histories of consistently increasing earnings and dividends. As in the United States, foreign companies that meet this profile will be grocery stores, utility companies, and pharmaceutical companies. It is usually not prudent to buy ADRs of the company that's

NASDAQ SMALL-CAP ISSUES

TchSv wt	222	1¾₆	+ ¹⁄₁₆	Zila	142	7⅝	+ ¼
TelCTV	138	7	− ½	Zonagen	815	6½	− ⅜
TelCTV wt	40	1⅛	...	ZydecoE n	80	6⅝	− ⅛
TelC pfB 6.00	9	59¼	− ¼	ZydcoE wt	14	2¼	− ⁵⁄₁₆
Telechps n	27	2 7/8	− ⅛	Zynaxis	13	6¹⁄₆₄	+ ⁷⁄₆₄
Telech wt	30	7/8	− ⅛				
Telmn wt	30	20	+1½		**ADRS**		
Telepad n	486	4¾	...		Friday, Aug. 2, 199–		
Tlepd wtA	6	1⅝	...				
Tiepd wtD	941	2⁷⁄₃₂	...	ABB AB	2.33e	282	102⅝ + ⅝
Telepanel	8	1²³⁄₃₂	− ⁵⁄₃₂	AngSA	1.34e	252	55⅛ + ⅞
Telescan	469	7⅛	+ ¼	AngAG	.28e	50	9 + ¼
Telesft	13	4⅛	+ ¾	Blyvoor	.10e	75	2 + ¹⁄₃₂
Teletek	1053	5³⁄₁₆	+ ⁷⁄₁₆	BurmhC	1.30e	27	30½ − ⅞
Teletouch	39	3³⁄₁₆	...	CSK	.11e	18	28⅜ − ⅞
Teltron	140	6⅛	− ⅛	CPcMn		380	6¼ − ¼
TeraCo n	100	4½	+ ¼	Dai Ei	.31e	1	23½ ...
TeraCo wt	45	1⅜	...	DBeer	.83e	606	30⅛ + ⅝
Terrace n	692	3⅞	...	DriefC	.36e	597	13¼ + ³⁄₆₄
Tescrp	46	2⅞	− ¼	FreSCn	.38e	491	10⅜ ...
Texoil	135	1¹⁄₁₆	...	FujiPh s	.20e	239	31¼ + ⅞
ThrmTch	2415	1⁷⁄₁₆	+ ¹⁄₁₆	Futrmdia		109	⁹⁄₃₂ ...
ThmoMz n	72	1³⁄₃₂	...	GrtCtrl		66	8¹¹⁄₁₆ + ³⁄₁₆
ThmoM wt	67	³⁄₁₆	...	Highvld	.09r	3	4½ + ³⁄₁₆
Thrmogn	165	3⁹⁄₁₆	+ ³⁄₁₆	InstruCp	.29e	18	16¼ + 1
3 CI	193	1⅝	+ ⅜	JapnAr	.10e	190	16⅜ − ⁵⁄₁₆
TimbLdg	44	4⅛	+ ¼	KirinBr	1.14e	31	18½ − 1
Timeline	94	5½	− ⅜	KloofG	.25e	986	10⅛ ...
Timeln wt	200	2	...	Minorc	.63e	218	22 + ½
Tinsley	20	12⅝	− ⅜	Nissan	.13e	294	16½ − ⅛
TitanPh un	84	14½	+ ⅜	RankOrg	.60e	120	15 − ⅜
Tivoli	187	1⅝	− ¹⁄₁₆	Rexam	.27e	22	5¹¹⁄₁₆ + ³⁄₁₆
Tivoli wtB	5	¼	− ¹⁄₆₄	SfHlGd	.33e	86	5¾ ...
Toporo wt	5	⅝	...	Santos	.70e	6	14¹¹⁄₁₆ − ¼
TotalRs	90	1⅜	...	Sanyo	.34e	83	27¾ − ¼
TouTone n	257	6½	...	Sasol	.28e	21	10¼ + ⅛
TouTne wt	547	3⅜	+ ⅜	Senetek		249	1⁵⁄₁₆ − ¹⁄₁₆
TchApid	630	⅞	− ⅛	SoPcPt		918	2⅝ − ¹⁄₁₆
TowrRch	23	10½	− ¼	Telemex	.05e	1337	1¹⁷⁄₃₂ + ¹⁄₃₂
TracrPt	1007	¹⁷⁄₃₂	...	Toyota	.36e	444	49¾ − ⅜
TracrP wt	61	³⁄₁₆	− ¹⁄₁₆	TrnBio		506	4¹¹⁄₁₆ − ¹⁄₁₆
TrnsEn	20	4⅜	...	TrnB wtA		27	3⅝ + ⅜
TrnsGlbl	76	1⁷⁄₁₆	+ ¹⁄₃₂	TrnBi wtB		72	2 + ³⁄₁₆
TrnsWste	1532	2¼	− ⅛	VaalRf	.39e	179	8⅜ + ³⁄₁₆
TrWst wtA	150	½	− ¹⁄₁₆	Wacoal		6	68¹¹⁄₁₆ +1⁵⁄₁₆
TrWst wtB	50	¼	− ¹⁄₁₆	WDeep	1.31e	298	38⅝ +1¾

FIGURE 9.4 Listing of NASDAQ-traded ADRs. In the listings for NASDAQ Small-Cap Issues, ADRs are grouped separately. Some of the best-known non-U.S. companies' ADRs trade over NASDAQ (e.g., Toyota, Nissan, De Beers, and Japan Airlines).

the hottest fad. Chances are you will be left with losses when the fad cools—as they generally do. You must determine your tolerance for currency risk and political risk.

Also, the information (e.g., annual reports) about the foreign company and the timeliness with which you receive it (if at all) will vary depending on the type of ADR you buy. Beginning investors who are interested in the international markets and who can tolerate the risks discussed would probably be prudent to consider only

Level 2 or Level 3 sponsored ADRs. Not only are you likely to get more information about the foreign company, you also have greater liquidity.

Investors researching the possibility of buying an ADR are likely to encounter another product, *global depositary receipts* (GDRs). Domestically, the two products are similar, except a GDR permits the non-U.S. company to issue depositary receipts simultaneously in two or more markets outside the issuer's home country through a global offering. In the U.S., the terms ADR and GDR are often used as synonyms.

global depositary receipts (GDRs) negotiable depositary receipts issued simultaneously in two or more countries other than the issuer's home country; GDRs issued in the United States are essentially the same as ADRs.

International Investment Companies: Mutual Funds and Closed-End Funds

Like investment companies that buy and sell domestic securities, investment companies that invest in the common stock of corporations located abroad provide investors with many of the same advantages: convenience, professional management, diversification, and lower costs. The foreign stocks that comprise a portfolio are selected by professional portfolio managers who research and evaluate the individual companies, as well as the economies of the countries or regions in which they are located. All that you have to do is select the fund that best meets your investment objectives. (The process of selecting the appropriate investment company was discussed in Chapter 7.)

Investment companies that buy and sell foreign securities can be divided into two types: mutual funds and closed-end funds. Within these types are funds with varying investment objectives or strategies.

global or world fund a mutual fund or closed-end fund that invests in the negotiable securities of corporations located in the United States and abroad.

Mutual Funds. Mutual funds that invest abroad can be divided into two major categories: global or world funds and international or foreign funds.

1. *Global or world fund.* This mutual fund's investment portfolio consists of shares of both U.S. multinational corporations and foreign corporations. Typically 25 percent to 50 percent of the fund's assets are invested in U.S. multinational corporations. It is perhaps the most diversified type of mutual fund available. The combination of domestic and international securities enables investors to diversify across stocks on a global scale.

   2. *International or foreign fund.* This mutual fund invests in foreign corporations whose share trade only outside the United States. This fund is appropriate for you if your current investment portfolio consists solely of domestic securities. By placing some of your investment dollars in an international fund, you can achieve the diversification that is already built into a global fund.

   Under the broad heading of international funds is a subcategory known as *regional funds.* Each of these is described according to the specific region, specific country, or even investment focus.

- ✔ *Europe Stock Fund.* This international mutual fund invests at least 65 percent of its total assets in equity securities of European companies.

- ✔ *Latin America Stock Fund.* At least 65 percent of this international fund's total assets are invested in equity securities of companies located Mexico, Central America, and South America.

- ✔ *Pacific Stock Fund.* This international fund invests primarily in equity securities of companies located in the Pacific Rim, including Japan, China, Hong Kong, Malaysia, Singapore, New Zealand, and Australia.

- ✔ *Diversified Emerging Markets Fund.* This fund invests primarily in equity securities issued by emerging markets worldwide. Typically the manager does not concentrate the fund's investments in any one region. The portfolio manager selects equity securities whose price he or she expects to rise over the short or long term.

Regional funds offer investors an opportunity to focus their investment dollars in one or more regions they believe will grow more than others. Keep in mind that they are also less diversified than broad-based international funds and are, therefore, more risky.

international or foreign fund a mutual fund or closed-end fund that invests only in the negotiable securities of companies located outside the United States.

regional fund a mutual fund or closed-end fund that invests in the negotiable securities of companies located in a specific geographical area.

Like most domestic mutual funds, most international and global funds are actively managed by a professional portfolio manager. While you avoid the hassles of doing all of the research about a foreign company or market yourself, you must remember to investigate the skills and track record of the portfolio manager. It is, after all, the manager's expertise and access to information that ultimately determines the returns that the fund will provide.

The popularity of domestic index funds has spread to the international markets. Like all index funds, international index funds are unmanaged and seek only to reflect the performance or returns of markets in a specific region or specific country. For example, you can buy shares in an Asia-Pacific Index fund that tracks the performance of a combination of markets in Asia. The fund's investment portfolio consists of a "basket" of equity securities whose market value changes in tandem with the designated stock markets in Asia. Once the portfolio is established, there is no manager to buy securities into it or sell them out of it; the portfolio follows the ups and downs of the designated market. In contrast, actively managed mutual funds offer the opportunity for returns that exceed the performance of the designated market.

In general, global or international mutual funds—whether actively managed or indexed—are the cheapest and most convenient way for beginners to invest directly in foreign markets. Because many of the funds are diversified across several different countries, the currency risk and political risk associated with a specific country is diminished. However, at any given time a portfolio manager may have the fund's assets heavily invested in one country; as a result, these risks increase. You will usually not know about any such concentrations or changes until the next quarterly reporting period. Also keep in mind that some mutual fund companies (e.g., Templeton and GT Global) specialize in international and foreign funds, while others offer these types of funds as part of a larger group of mostly domestic mutual funds.

Closed-End Funds. The names for closed-end funds that invest in international stocks are similar to those of mutual funds—global or international fund, European fund, Latin American fund, and Pacific fund. As discussed in Chapter 7, closed-end funds trade on a stock exchange or NASDAQ just like common stocks. Figure 7.6 shows a listing of World Equity Funds under the Closed-End Funds listing published in *The Wall Street Journal* every Monday near the end of Section C. Peruse the list and you will see that all of the names of the closed-end funds enumerated at the beginning of this paragraph are under the one heading.

Traditionally, most international closed-end funds tend to be *single-country funds* or regional funds. Today some closed-end funds may be industry-specific—for example, investing in telecommunications companies in emerging nations. Figure 7.6 shows many of the country and regional funds—among them the Chile Fund, the Indonesia Fund, the India Growth Fund, and the Greater China Fund. Many countries restrict foreign investment in local corporations. The result is that only a small number of shares may be available to U.S. investors. Closed-end funds may represent the only vehicle for investors outside the country to benefit from the economic growth of businesses located within the country.

 country fund usually a closed-end fund that invests in the securities of companies located in one country whose name the fund bears.

In addition to the currency risk and political risk of the country or regional closed-end fund, you also have a third totally unpredictable risk: investor sentiment. This makes single-country closed-end funds perhaps the riskiest of the investment companies that buy and sell securities abroad. Remember that a closed-end fund issues a fixed number of shares that trade on a stock exchange just like common stock. If U.S. investors panic because of bad news (the devaluation of the peso, for example) and begin to sell the closed-end fund shares, the market price of the fund shares falls to a deep discount below the net asset value (NAV) of the foreign companies' stocks in the fund's underlying portfolio. On the other hand, if investors begin to buy closed-end fund shares in anticipation of good news, the market price of the fund shares may rise to a steep premium above the NAV of the stock in the underlying portfolio. In short, investor sentiment may tend to increase the volatility of closed-end fund shares, giving investors roller-coaster-like price swings.

The less diversified the closed-end fund, the more volatile the price movements will be. If you get nervous or nauseous on roller-coaster-like price swings, then a country closed-end fund is probably not a good place to begin. Regional closed-end funds, with their built-in diversification, are a more reasonable starting point. The difficult part is identifying the region or country in which you want to invest. Regions have cycles of being hot and cold. Access to good information, usually from an investment professional, is indispensable. Once the decision has been made, the prevailing wisdom for selecting a specific fund is the same as for selecting domestic closed-end funds discussed in Chapter 7. First, look for an international closed-end fund with good long-term returns. Both Morningstar and Value Line provide this information. It is also available from your broker or through libraries that subscribe to these information services. Second, select a fund whose market price is at a discount to the net asset value (NAV) of the underlying portfolio. Over time as the economy and market prospects in the region improve, more U.S. investors may want to invest in the region. As a result, the market value of the closed-end fund shares may rise, trading equal to or at a premium to the NAV of the underlying portfolio. Keep in mind, however, that a very deep discount may be no bargin. It may indicate poor prospects for the future performance of the fund.

Like mutual funds, closed-end funds must be viewed as long-term investments. However, the added emotional element of investor sentiment means that the return from a closed-end fund may be even more uncertain.

Buying Foreign Company Shares on Foreign Exchanges

Trading shares on foreign exchanges is probably not suitable for beginning investors. Although the types of investment risks are the same as for the other investment tools, the degree of risk is much greater. Many factors—the differences in language, trading regulations and procedures, and reporting systems; different (and high) fee structures; often no degree of investor protection or legal recourse; and many, many others—could place small investors at a disadvantage and also in serious danger of losing all of their investment.

Having become alert to the risks associated with buying shares directly in a foreign market, investors should be aware that it is getting easier to purchase stocks that trade in these markets through U.S.-based brokerage firms. Three developments have contributed to this: First, several U.S. brokerage firms have acquired or merged with non-U.S. brokerage firms. These U.S. firms now have direct access to local markets where the non-U.S. firms are located and also to the stocks for which the non-U.S. firms are market makers (if the shares trade over-the-counter) or in which they invest directly. Second, a handful of boutique and discount brokerage firms specialize in handling orders for foreign stocks. And third, technology has made it easier to direct trades to the local markets. Today, a beginning or small investor willing to take the risk can, usually using his or her own broker, invest directly in thousands of shares that trade on foreign exchanges.

Increased availability does not mean that executing the trade will be easier or that information about the company will be more available, more clear, or more timely. Price information about foreign companies' shares available in the United States can be found on the Pink Sheets. Finding accurate and timely information about the foreign company is more difficult. Several full-brokerage firms have begun to offer their institutional research on foreign investment to their retail clients. Without such a resource, you will have to spend a good amount of time (and phone calls) to get the information you need to make an informed investment decision.

WHAT PERCENTAGE OF A PORTFOLIO SHOULD I INVEST IN FOREIGN SECURITIES OR MARKETS?

Consider investing abroad only if you are willing to take the heightened risk for a chance to obtain a better return. It is definitely not suitable for risk-averse investors. Experts recommend that no more than 10 percent of an investment portfolio be allocated to foreign securities. Figure 9.5 shows how the traditional asset allocation mix looks when the recommended percentage of international investments is included. However, if you refer to the footnotes to the asset allocation recommendations shown in Figure 1.3, you will notice that the percentages vary among brokerage firms. While the lowest is 10 percent, the highest is 15 percent that firms suggest should be allocated to international stocks.

For most beginning investors, the best way to invest in international stocks is to use mutual funds. A more aggressive investor may increase the percentage above the generally accepted 10 percent allocation. An index fund, specifically a European index fund or an Asia-Pacific index fund, is probably a good first step. The built-in diversification, passive management, and low expenses combined with ease of selection make an international index fund an attractive choice for a beginning investor. If, however, you are looking for a return that will exceed the

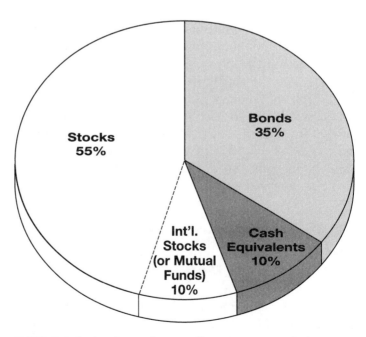

FIGURE 9.5 Traditional asset allocation mix including investing abroad.

specified market, then a managed fund is more appropriate. A managed fund also gives you access to the skills and expertise of a specific fund manager.

The fund you select depends, of course, on how you think the markets in a certain part of the world will perform relative to the U.S. markets. Your choices include investing in an established-markets international fund, an emerging-markets international fund, or both. Clearly, emerging markets involve more risk and the potential for higher returns because the currency movements and politics yield wider price fluctuations. Also, instead of allocating part of your available assets to an emerging market fund, you may want to buy shares in a fund that invests in a specific region or country in which you have particular knowledge or interest. Keep in mind that as the market in which you choose to invest becomes more specific (and less diversified), both your risk of loss and potential for high returns increase.

Because of the increased risk associated with investments in the international market, you must watch your investments more carefully. Experts recommend that investors occasionally rebalance their international portfolios using the constant-ratio plan described in Chapter 4. (See Figure 4.3.) If, for example, your emerging-markets or single-country mutual fund outperforms your established-markets index fund, experts suggest pulling some of the money out of the risky fund and reallocating it to safer securities. This is called "rebalancing." Periodic rebalancing enables you to reestablish the designated percentage of your portfolio in the foreign markets. You therefore avoid exposing a larger percentage of your investment portfolio to greater risk.

Epilogue

The Psychology
of Investing

T he long-term performance of the stock market has shown that stocks are indeed appropriate investment vehicles for most people. Rationally, then, almost everyone should allocate some of his or her investment dollars to stocks or equity mutual funds. However, the way each of us handles or invests our money is seldom a paradigm of reasonable thinking. Emotions are, more often than not, the strongest influence on our decisions.

Now that you have a basic knowledge of stocks—the different types, how they work, what investment opportunities each provides—you must now ask yourself this question: "Do I have the temperament to invest in stocks?"

Accurately answering this question is essential. Knowing that stock and equity mutual funds are volatile is not the same as knowing whether or not you are able to handle that volatility. You need to determine whether you are able to endure emotionally the stock market's periodic declines—some of which are more precipitous and last longer than others. Can you keep your long-term goals in focus through a relatively short period of sharp volatility? Will every rise and fall result in a sleepless night or knots in your stomach? Will the pain of losing money overshadow the joy of making gains?

As the three investor profiles in the Introduction demonstrate, individuals' attitudes toward their money and the stock market are as varied as their investment goals. To

271

begin determining how you feel about money, ask yourself—and answer honestly!—the following questions:

- ✔ How and on what do I spend my extra money?
- ✔ Do I save regularly, and how much do I save?
- ✔ In what vehicles—certificates of deposit, securities, or objects (art, coins, baseball cards, furniture, pottery, and other collectibles)—do I "invest" my extra money?
- ✔ Do I believe that money and other financial matters simply "take care of themselves" or that "the less time I think about money, the better"?
- ✔ Do I frequently worry when buying anything—clothing, furniture, a computer, or securities—that "it won't be the right or perfect" use of the money?
- ✔ Am I so concerned about every penny, nickel, or dime that I feel more secure knowing exactly where my money is and what it is worth?
- ✔ Do I make my money work for me—to let me enjoy life, to treat myself well occasionally, to live today and plan for the future?

To gain some insight into how you feel about the stock market, ask yourself:

- ✔ Do I have a healthy respect (and skepticism) for the investment markets or do I think I can consistently outsmart them?
- ✔ Do I have the discipline to take the profits in hand or will I want more and hold a stock too long?
- ✔ Do I have the discipline to sell an investment on which I have lost money, or will pride prevent me from doing it?
- ✔ Do I tend to focus on lost opportunities ("the ones that got away") instead of new opportunities that exist every day?
- ✔ Do I want someone else to make the investment decisions for me through a mutual fund or a managed account?

While these questions are somewhat touchy-feely, their purpose is simply to lead you toward a clearer—not a perfect—statement of your investment goals, in terms of your comfort level with money and the stock market, as well as your financial suitability for investing. Not surprisingly, the answers or insights you seek may be found by examining your past behavior in any situation where your money was at risk. The clearer your thinking and your self-assessment, the better you will be able to choose stocks and mutual funds that are appropriate for you, and communicate your financial goals to the investment professional who recommends individual stocks or mutual funds to you.

Also keep in mind that your ability to tolerate the ups and downs of the market is not static. It is influenced by such factors as age, employment status, and the performance of the market itself. Generally speaking, people believe they are more risk-tolerant during a prolonged bull market. However, a severe downturn causes this belief to evaporate quickly, and suddenly everyone is risk-averse. It is important to assess periodically how much risk you are willing to accept and adjust the allocation of your assets appropriately.

Having now read the entire book and determined your attitude toward your "hard-earned dollars" or your "nest egg" and the stock market itself, **go back and reread Chapter 1**. With your new knowledge and understanding of the points you must consider before investing, you will undoubtedly see the information and questions presented in sections of this chapter from a slightly different vantage point—one that is better informed and based on greater self-awareness. It should be easier for you to state clearly your investment objectives, set the time frame of those objectives, and determine the amount of risk you are willing to take—and can tolerate—to achieve those objectives.

Always remember: Understanding how various stock investments work and how each matches your personal "money characteristics" is an essential component in your becoming a successful investor.

account executive an individual who is employed by a broker/dealer to give advice to the public about investing in securities, to solicit buy and sell orders for securities, and to handle customer accounts. This person must be registered with the National Association of Securities Dealers or an exchange and be licensed to sell securities in the state. Also known as a broker or registered representative.

adjustable rate preferred (ARP) a preferred stock whose dividend is adjusted periodically to reflect changing interest rates.

aftermarket a collective term for the markets—exchange and over-the-counter—in which stocks are bought and sold after they are issued to the public. Proceeds from trades in this market go to the investors. Also called the secondary market.

agent *See* **broker**; **account executive**.

American Depositary Receipt (ADR) a negotiable receipt traded in the United States representing ownership of a foreign company's stock that is being held in trust by a U.S. bank. ADRs give the holder the right to receive dividends and capital gains. *See also* **sponsored ADR**; **unsponsored ADR**.

American Depositary Share (ADS) usually synonymous with American Depositary Receipt, but the term is evolving to denote those ADRs whose issuance is sponsored by the foreign company that issued the common stock rather than by the bank that holds the shares on deposit.

annual report an abbreviated version of Form 10K, which all reporting corporations (those with 500 or more shareholders) are required by the Securities and Exchange Act of 1934 to print and distribute to their shareholders annually. Contains audited financial statements, as well as other information about the company's performance and business plans. *See also* **Form 10K**.

arbitrage the simultaneous purchase and sale of securities in different markets in an attempt to profit from short-term price disparities.

asked price the price at which a market maker offers to sell stock to a buyer; also known as the offer price.

asset allocation the systematic and thoughtful placement of investment dollars into various classes of investments, such as stocks, bonds, real estate, insurance, and cash equivalents.

275

asset allocation fund mutual fund that invests in stocks, bonds, and cash equivalents. A flexible asset allocation fund adjusts the mix in response to changing market conditions. The advantage of this type of fund is diversification and flexibility. The disadvantage is that its success depends almost entirely upon the fund manager's skill. A fixed asset allocation fund maintains a fixed percentage of its money in each of the three asset classes. *See also* **asset allocation**.

at the money the market price of the underlying security and an option's strike price are the same.

auction market a phrase used to describe how trading is performed on a stock exchange. In reality, the exchange is a "double auction" market in which buyers call out successively higher bids and sellers call out successively lower offers until a trade is arranged at a price satisfactory to the successful buyer and seller.

auction rate preferred adjustable rate preferred stock whose dividend is adjusted periodically by the issuer; however, the shareholders (usually large institutions) must agree to the rate before it goes into effect. If they do not, the issuer continues to offer other rates until one is accepted. The term "Dutch auction" is also used. *See also* **adjustable rate preferred.**

authorized shares the maximum number of common and preferred shares that a company is authorized to issue by its corporate charter.

average a composite measure of the movement of the overall market or of a particular industry that consists of a small number of stocks and is usually not capitalization weighted.

averaging down a strategy in which an investor lowers the average price paid for each share of stock by purchasing more shares as the price declines.

back-end load the fee charged when an investor redeems mutual fund shares within a short time (e.g., one to six years) after purchasing them. It is also called a contingent-deferred sales charge (CDSC). *See also* **contingent-deferred sales charge**.

balance sheet a constantly changing snapshot of a company's financial position that shows all of its assets, liabilities, and net worth (stockholders' equity).

bear market a period during which the overall prices of common stocks are falling. The term is less frequently used for bond prices.

below-investment grade bond *See* **junk bond**.

beneficial owner term used to describe an investor who owns securities held in street name. (*Compare* **holder of record**.)

beta the relative volatility of a particular stock relative to the overall market as measured by the Standard & Poor's 500 Index. If a stock's beta coefficient is 1, it means that its price rises and falls in direct relationship to the movement of the S&P index. A beta that is less than 1 indicates a stock is less volatile than the overall market; a beta greater than 1 indicates that a stock is more volatile.

bid price (1) for stocks, the price at which a market maker offers to purchase a stock from a seller; (2) for mutual funds, the net asset value.

Big Board stocks a popular name for stocks that trade on the New York Stock Exchange.

blue-chip stock the shares of stable, profitable, and well-known public companies that have a long history of consistent revenue and earnings growth, as well as increasing dividend payments.

Blue-sky laws commonly used name for the state laws that govern the securities industry under the Uniform Securities Act.

board of directors individuals elected by a company's shareholders to set the firm's management policies, including setting the amount of the dividend that common shareholders will receive.

bond a long-term debt security in which the issuer (a corporation, a municipality, or the U.S. government) promises to pay the holder a fixed rate of interest at regular intervals and to repay the face value of the security at maturity. *See also* **zero-coupon bond**.

book entry a term describing securities for which no certificates are issued. The names, addresses, and holdings of investors are listed only in the records of the issuer or registrar. However, a certificate can be issued upon request from a customer. The customer is charged a fee for the certificate.

book entry only a term that describes securities, primarily bonds, for which certificates are not issued and therefore are not available to the customer. An investor's name, address, and the number of shares owned are held in the computer records of the issuer, registrar, or transfer agent. The confimation that the brokerage firm sends to the investor is his or her proof of ownership of the securities. *See also* **book entry**.

book value the theoretical value of the company that remains if all the assets of the company were liquidated at the values carried on the balance sheet and then all liabilities paid off. Intangible assets such as goodwill, patents, and copyrights are excluded from the total assets.

box the physical location where securities are held for safekeeping at a brokerage firm. The term evolved from a time when firms held certificates for securities in a large box.

breadth of the market the number of individual stocks traded during a given session compared with the total number of stocks listed in a particular market or on a specific exchange.

breakout a price rise above a resistance level that results in a substantial advance, or a price decline below a support level that results in a substantial price decline; breakouts usually establish new support and resistance levels.

breakpoint the dollar level at which a mutual fund investor qualifies for a lower front-end sales charge on either a lump-sum purchase or under the right of accumulation.

broker a registered person who acts as the intermediary in the purchase or sale of a security for the account of a customer and charges a commission for the service. The term is used for both the member firm acting as an agent and for the registered representative or account executive acting as an agent. *See also* **account executive**; **agent**.

bull market a period during which the overall prices of securities are rising.

buying power the maximum amount of securities a customer can purchase in a margin account using SMA and not depositing any additional cash.

cabinet stock exchange-listed stock, usually preferred, that trades in 10-share round lots and does not have an active trading market.

call feature a provision that permits the issuer to repurchase preferred stock, usually at a premium to its par value.

call loan rate the interest rate that banks charge brokerage firms for loans collateralized by marginable securities.

call option a security that gives its holder the right, but not the obligation, to buy 100 shares of common stock at a fixed price (the option's strike price) for a fixed period of time.

call protection a period of time following the issuance of a security when it may not be called by the issuer.

capital appreciation an increase in the market value of a security or the overall market.

capital gain the profit that results when the proceeds from the sale of a security are higher than the security's cost basis. (*Compare* **capital loss**.)

capital loss the loss that results if the proceeds from the sale of a security are less than the security's cost basis. (*Compare* **capital gain**.)

capital risk the risk that an investor can lose the money invested in a security. This risk is made up of several different types of risks, including business risk, liquidity risk, systematic risk, inflationary risk, and political risk.

capitalization (1) market capitalization is the total market value of a company's issued-and-outstanding common shares; (2) capitalization for accounting purposes is the value of all sources of long-term capital for a company, consisting of common shares, preferred shares, and bonds.

cash account an account in which an investor buys securities by paying for them in full or sells securities that he or she owns fully paid.

cash balances cash deposits in an account at a brokerage firm that are uninvested or awaiting investment.

cash dividends part of a company's after-tax earnings that its board of directors decides, usually quarterly, to distribute to the shareholders.

cash equivalents short-term investments (such as money market mutual funds and Treasury bills) that are like cash because of their high liquidity and safety.

cash flow statement a statement of the sources and uses of cash by a business for a period of time.

charting capturing the patterns of the overall market's or of a stock's price and volume movements on a line, bar, point-and-figure, or moving average graph.

chartist a technical analyst who uses charts to capture a stock's price and volume movements and then analyzes this information as a basis for predicting the future price movement of a stock or the market.

churning excessive trading in a customer's account by a broker in order to generate commissions. Churning is illegal.

closed-end fund an investment company that has a one-time offering of a fixed number of shares to the public and then does not issue new shares or redeem old shares; the fund's shares are bought and sold like stock on the exchanges and in the over-the-counter market. Also called a "publicly traded fund." *See also* **publicly traded fund**.

closed-end management company legal name for a **closed-end fund**.

commercial paper short-term unsecured debt issued by a corporation. It is issued at a discount and redeemed at face value. While commercial paper can have a maximum maturity of 270 days, it is most commonly issued with a 30-day maturity.

commission the fee charged by a broker or agent for executing an order for a customer.

common stock an equity security that usually gives the holder the right to receive dividends and vote on company issues.

confirmation a notice sent from a broker to the customer on the day after the trade date that gives the details of the execution of an order, including price, number of units, and commission.

consolidated tape an electronic display of trades of all listed securities on all exchanges and in the over-the-counter market. Currently, the consolidated tapes consist of two networks. Network A displays trades of all New York Stock Exchange–listed stocks, and Network B displays trades of all American Stock Exchange–listed issues.

constant-dollar plan an investment method in which a person maintains a fixed-dollar amount of a portfolio in stocks, buying and selling shares periodically to maintain the fixed-dollar amount.

constant-ratio plan an investment method in which a person maintains a fixed ratio between stocks and bonds throughout the investment period, with regular adjustments made to compensate for different levels of price increases and decreases.

contingent-deferred sales charge a fee that is charged when an investor redeems shares within a relatively short period of time after purchasing them; also called a **back-end load**.

contrary indicators information used to establish the bullish or bearish sentiment of the market to which an investor responds by taking the opposite position (e.g., if the indicators are bullish, this is a sign for an investor to sell). In general, the indicator provides an opposing insight. For example, the put/call ratio is a classic contrary indicator because it measures index options, the typical instrument professional money managers use to hedge portfolio positions. If the managers are bullish, they buy stocks and buy puts to hedge. Therefore, an increase in the put/call ratio is bullish. If they are bearish, they sell short stocks and buy calls to hedge. A decrease in the put/call ratio is therefore bearish.

conversion ratio the number of common shares that an investor receives when converting a preferred stock or convertible bond. The conversion ratio is set when the convertible security is first issued.

convertible preferred preferred stock that shareholders can convert into a fixed number of common shares.

cost basis the price, for tax purposes, paid for a security, including commissions, markups, and other cost adjustments.

country fund usually a closed-end fund that invests in the securities of companies located in one country, whose name the fund bears. Mutual funds can also be country funds.

covered option term used to describe the writer of a put or a call who holds another security position that protects against or offsets the risks of a short option position. For example, the writer of a call option is covered if he or she owns the stock that underlies the option.

covering eliminating a short position by buying the shares that have been sold short and delivering them to the lender.

cum-rights literally, *with* rights; describes transactions in which the pre-emptive rights accompany the purchase (or sale) of common stock—the value of the rights is included in the market price of the shares.

cumulative preferred if dividend payments are missed, holders of these shares have a right to receive all back dividends (called "arrearages") before any dividend payments can be made to common shareholders.

cumulative voting method a procedure whereby a shareholder can place his or her votes on directorships or other issues in any combination he or she chooses.

curb market an anachronistic name for the American Stock Exchange (AMEX) that is still used today. It refers to the fact that the AMEX was called the New York Curb Exchange until 1921.

current ratio a measure of a company's ability to pay its current expenses and obligations from its current assets. The formula is current assets divided by the current liabilities.

current yield a security's annual dividend or interest amount divided by its current market price; synonym for a stock's **dividend yield**.

day order an order to buy or sell securities without a time notation; if it is not executed or canceled, it expires at the end of the trading session during which it was placed.

dealer an NASD member firm that makes a market in an over-the-counter stock by buying shares into and selling securities out of its own inventory; also called a principal or a **market maker**.

debenture an unsecured corporate bond that is backed by the full faith and credit of the issuer.

debit balance the balance owed to the brokerage firm by a customer who purchases securities on margin.

debt ratio a measure of the percentage of bonds that comprise a company's total capitalization.

declaration date the day on which the board of directors announces the terms and amount of a dividend payment, rights offering, or stock split.

depository a place, usually a bank or trust company, where securities are held and where the day-to-day movement of securities is handled by computer. The Depository Trust Company (DTC) in New York is the largest repository of securities in the United States and is the central depository facility for most brokerage firms and banks.

direct stock purchase plan a company-sponsored program that enables individuals to buy common stock directly from the company itself without using a broker. Purchases, which may include fractional shares, can be made at times specified in the company's written plan. While no commissions are charged on these transactions, there may be small fees assessed for holding the shares in the plan or for selling the shares. Stocks bought through a direct stock purchase plan are called no-load stocks. *See* **no-load stock**.

discount the amount by which the market value of a preferred stock or a bond is below its par value.

diversification investing in different securities, different industries, or a mutual fund portfolio containing various securities in order to diminish the risk associated with investing in too few securities.

dividend that portion of a corporation's after-tax earnings that its board of directors distributes to stockholders. Dividends are usually distributed quarterly.

dividend reinvestment plan a plan whereby a company's existing shareholders choose to have their cash dividend payments automatically reinvested in additional shares of the company's stock; often abbreviated DRIP.

dividend yield a stock's total annual dividend divided by its current market price. It tells an investor what percentage of the stock's current market price the dividend represents; also called the current yield, particularly in the bond markets. *See also* **current yield**.

dollar-cost averaging a strategy whereby a person invests the same amount of money at regular intervals in a stock or a mutual fund without regard for the price fluctuations of the security.

downtrend the downward movement of a security's price, or of the market, as measured by an average or index over a period of time.

earnings per share (EPS) the amount of a company's profit allocated to each share of outstanding common stock after operating expenses, bond interest, taxes, and preferred dividends have been paid. A company's board of directors decides what portion of the EPS is distributed as a dividend.

earnings yield the return that a stock's annual earnings per share represent relative to the stock's current market price.

economy of scale a reduction in the ratio of expenses to assets as the size of a mutual fund increases.

EPS *See* **earnings per share**.

equity fund a mutual fund that invests primarily in common and/or preferred stocks. In practice, the term is used for funds that invest in both stocks and bonds, such as a balanced fund. Funds that invest only in stocks tend to be called stock funds.

equity security more commonly called a share or a stock, it is a security representing ownership of a corporation and the right to receive dividends.

ex-dividend date the day, set by the National Association of Securities Dealers or an exchange, on which the bid price of a stock is reduced by the dividend amount. Anyone purchasing the stock on this day or later will not be eligible to receive the upcoming cash dividend.

exercise price the predetermined, fixed price at which the owner or holder of a warrant, option, or right can buy or sell the underlying common stock; also called the **strike price**.

ex-rights literally, *without* rights; describes transactions in which the preemptive rights do not accompany the purchase (or sale) of common stock; the rights, at this time, trade separately from the stock in the market.

ex-rights date by industry practice, the first business day after the distribution of the rights; the bid price of the stock is reduced by an amount equal to the value of the right.

family of funds a group of mutual funds created by the same company with portfolios made of different securities or having different investment objectives. This group is typically managed by different investment advisers.

financial profile an assessment of an investor's assets, liabilities, investment objectives, and willingness to bear risk.

floor broker an exchange member and an employee of a member firm who executes buy and sell orders on the trading floor of an exchange; sometimes called a commission house broker.

flow of funds indicators statistics that enable analysts to determine in which markets—money markets, stocks, bonds, savings accounts—individual and institutional investors are most likely to invest their money during given economic conditions or periods of time.

foreign fund *See* **international fund**.

Form 10K the detailed, audited report that all companies with 500 or more shareholders must file annually with the Securities and Exchange Commission. The information contained in the report is made public so that investors can use it to evaluate their investments. *See also* **annual report**.

forward P-E ratio the P-E (price-earnings) ratio calculated using the earnings per share reported from the two most recent quarters plus the estimated earnings for the next two quarters. (*Compare* **trailing P-E ratio**.)

front-end load a sales charge that is incorporated into the public offering price when an investor buys a mutual fund share.

fully diluted earnings per share a calculation of the earnings per share using all of the common shares currently outstanding plus any additional shares that could result from the conversion or exercise of any outstanding convertible preferred stock, convertible bonds, rights, or warrants.

fundamental analysis evaluation of a company's balance sheet, income statement, management, marketing and sales efforts, and research and development (R&D) efforts as a means of predicting the future, long-term price movement of its stock.

global depositary receipt (GDR) a negotiable depositary receipt issued simultaneously in two or more countries other than the issuing corporation's home country; GDRs issued in the United States are essentially the same as ADRs. *See also* **American depositary receipt**.

Global fund a mutual fund or closed-end fund that invests in the negotiable securities of corporations located in the United States and abroad; also called a **World fund**.

good 'til canceled *See* **GTC**, **open order**.

growth investing selecting a company in which to invest based on expectations of strong growth in earnings.

growth stock stocks of new, expanding companies whose market values are expected to appreciate rapidly. These stocks typically pay little or no dividends.

GTC a time notation on an order meaning "good 'til canceled." Subject to periodic renewal, the order remains in the market until it is executed or expires. *See also* **open order**.

hedging protecting against or limiting losses on an existing stock position or portfolio by establishing an opposite position in the same or an equivalent security.

high-yield bond a more attractive, less emotionally charged synonym for a junk bond. *See also* **junk bond**.

holder buyer of an option contract.

holder of record the name of the owner of a security as it is recorded in the records of the transfer agent or issuer. For securities held in street name, the brokerage firm is listed as the holder or owner of record, and the specific investor is listed as the beneficial owner. (*Compare* **beneficial owner**.)

hot issue a newly issued stock that immediately begins trading in the secondary market at a price higher than its public offering price.

hypothecation agreement *See* **margin agreement**.

illiquid market *See* **thin market**.

in the money in option trading, a phrase that describes an option that has intrinsic value. Specifically, an option is in the money when the relationship between the market price of the underlying security and the strike price of the option is such that exercising would yield a profit to the holder (buyer).

income statement a summary of all of the income and expenses of a business for a period of time; also called a profit-and-loss statement.

income stock the shares of companies that make regular and substantial dividend payments to investors.

income strategy in options, any strategy in which the investor receives more options premium than he or she pays.

index a composite measure of the movement of the overall market or of a particular industry that consists of a large number of stocks and is usually weighted by other factors, such as capitalization.

index fund a mutual fund that invests in a group of securities whose performance reflects the performance of a particular stock market index, such as the Standard & Poor's 500 Index or the New York Stock Exchange Composite Index.

initial margin requirement the percentage of a stock's market price that must be deposited when initially buying or selling short stock on margin; set by the Federal Reserve Board (FRB) under Regulation T.

initial public offering (IPO) the first time that a company issues or sells its stock to the public.

insider an officer, director, principal, or large shareholder of a company, as well as any person with material, nonpublic information that could affect the market price of a security.

"insider-trading" investing a method of stock picking whereby a mutual fund manager follows the trading patterns of company's senior executives and members of its board of directors, most of whom own shares or stock options in the company. Insiders are required to report all trading in their company's stock to the SEC shortly after the end of each month. The fund manager reviews the reports of insiders' purchases and sales as an indication of the company's future performance.

international fund a mutual fund or closed-end fund that invests only in the negotiable securities of companies located outside the United States. Also called a **foreign fund**.

intrinsic value the amount by which an option is in the money. Also, that portion of an option's premium reflecting the profit that exists from the difference between the market price of the underlying security and the strike price of an option. *See also* **in the money**.

investment adviser the financial professional who manages the investment portfolio of a mutual fund and charges a management fee for these services; often called a portfolio manager.

investment advisory services companies or individuals registered with the Securities and Exchange Commission who, for a fee, provide investment advice or money management, usually in specific types of securities.

investment banker a securities firm or individual at a securities firm that assists businesses in raising capital through issuing securities. Also called an underwriter. *See also* **underwriter**.

investment company generic name for one of the many companies whose primary business is investing and reinvesting in securities for the accounts of others. These companies include mutual funds, closed-end funds, variable annuities, and unit trusts. Neither banks nor holding companies are included in this definition.

investment planning defining an investment objective and establishing a systematic approach to achieve it.

IPO abbreviation for **initial public offering**, a company's first-time issuance of common stock to the public.

issued and outstanding authorized shares that have been distributed to investors and that may trade in the market.

junk bond low-quality, high-risk, long-term debt security rated BB by Moody's, Ba by S&P, or lower. To avoid the negative associations of the word "junk," the investment community uses synonyms such as high-yield bond, noninvestment-grade bond, and below-investment-grade bond.

large-cap stock a large company whose outstanding common shares have a total market value of $5 billion or more. [NOTE: The dollar amount cited is generally accepted and subject to change over time.]

leverage the purchase (or sale) of a large amount of a security using a small amount of an investor's money. The rest of the money is borrowed from the brokerage firm.

limit order an order to buy stock (buy limit) at a specified price or lower, or to sell stock (sell limit) at a specified price or higher.

liquid market a market in which it is easy for an investor to buy and sell securities. Such a market typically contains a large number of investors willing to buy and sell.

listed stock a company whose stock meets the listing requirements of one of the exchanges and has been accepted by the exchange to trade on its floor.

load the sales charge that an investor may pay when buying mutual fund shares or redeeming shares within a short period after the purchase. *See* **front end load** and **back-end load**.

load fund a mutual fund that charges its purchasers a front-end sales charge or a back-end load. (*Compare* **no-load fund**.)

long margin account a margin account in which a customer buys stock or other marginable securities.

long position phrase denoting ownership of a security, which includes the right to transfer ownership and to participate in the rise and fall of its market value.

long-dated rights a dilutive, anti-takeover device in which rights are automatically distributed to existing stockholders during a hostile takeover. *See also* **poison pill**.

maintenance call a demand from a brokerage firm that an investor deposit enough cash or securities in a margin account to restore the account to the minimum maintenance margin requirement *See also* **minimum maintenance margin** and **margin call**.

management company one of the three types of investment companies defined under the Investment Company Act of 1940. This investment company manages by objectives and, depending on its structure, is described as either an **open-end management company** (a mutual fund) or a **closed-end management company** (a closed-end fund).

management fee a percentage of a mutual fund's total assets that the fund's portfolio manager charges for his or her services. It is typically the largest expense of a mutual fund.

margin account an account in which an investor buys (or sells short) securities by depositing part of their market value and borrowing the remainder from the brokerage firm.

margin agreement a document an investor must sign when opening a margin account. By signing it, the investor pledges the securities purchased as collateral for the margin loan. The agreement also details the terms of the margin loan, including the interest rate and how it will be computed. Also called a hypothecation agreement.

margin call a demand from a brokerage firm for an investor to deposit cash (or securities) in a margin account. If the call is to meet the Regulation T initial margin requirement, it is commonly referred to as a "Fed call." If the demand is to restore the account to the minimum maintenance margin requirement after an adverse price move, it is referred to as a "maintenance call." *See also* **maintenance call**.

margin department a division of a brokerage firm that computes an investor's equity in margin and cash accounts daily and sends out margin or maintenance calls, as appropriate.

marginable security a security that can be bought or sold in a margin account. These include all stocks registered (listed) on exchanges, all NASDAQ National Market Issues and any over-the-counter stock that appears on the Federal Reserve Board's OTC margin list.

mark to market the process by which a brokerage firm computes the value of the shares in an investor's account based on the daily closing price.

markdown the amount or percentage subtracted from the bid price when the customer sells over-the-counter stock to a market maker or principal firm.

market maker an NASD member firm that disseminates bid and ask prices at which it stands ready to buy stock into and sell stock from its own inventory at its own risk; synonymous with **dealer**.

market not held order abbreviated MKT (NH), a market order in which an investor gives the floor broker discretion as to the time and price at which the order may be executed. The broker is not held liable for the execution price. These orders are used typically for large or complex trades.

market order an order to buy or sell stock immediately at the best available market price. No price is specified by a customer placing this order.

market value the price of a stock determined in the marketplace by expectations of a company's earnings.

markup the amount or percentage added to the ask price when a customer buys an over-the-counter stock from a firm acting as a principal or market maker in the transaction.

merger the joining of two companies, under either friendly or hostile terms.

micro-cap stock a company whose outstanding common shares have a total market value of $100 million or less. These stocks tend to be characterized by high volatility, illiquidity, and wide spreads (i.e., a large difference between the stock's bid and asked prices). [NOTE: The dollar amount cited is generally accepted and subject to change over time.]

mid-cap stock a company whose outstanding common shares have a total market value of between $1 billion and $5 billion. [NOTE: The dollar amounts cited are generally accepted and subject to change over time.]

minimum maintenance margin set by the New York Stock Exchange and the National Association of Securities Dealers, the minimum equity that a customer must maintain in a margin account. When the account's equity falls below this percentage or amount, the customer gets a call to restore equity in the account to the maintenance margin level. *See also* **maintenance margin call**.

momentum investing investing in the common shares of a company whose market price is expected to increase rapidly over time. The fund manager ignores value when selecting a stock for the fund's portfolio. Hence some of the stocks may be overpriced and others underpriced; however, the manager believes that as long as the company's profits are increasing strongly and on target with expectations, then the market price of the share will continue to rise.

money market fund a mutual fund that invests in high-grade and very liquid short-term debt securities. Cash—i.e., dividend payments and sales proceeds—in a customer's brokerage account is typically invested in a money market mutual fund.

money market preferred adjustable rate preferred whose dividend is adjusted to reflect short-term interest rates of money market instruments such as Treasury bills and commercial paper. The dividend rate is usually reset every quarter.

moving average an average of a stock's or the market's closing prices over a fixed period (e.g., 20 days, 30 days), which is recomputed each day to include the current day's closing price within the fixed period.

mutual fund common name for an open-end management company that establishes a diversified portfolio of investments; these companies continually issue new shares and redeem old shares representing ownership in the portfolio.

NASD abbreviation for the National Association of Securities Dealers, the self-regulatory organization of the over-the-counter market.

NASDAQ acronym for National Association of Securities Dealers Automated Quotation system, the electronic trading system that enables brokers and dealers that trade NASDAQ-listed stocks to get real-time quotes and execute orders directly with each other. *See also* **NASDAQ Stock Market**.

NASDAQ National Market Issues the approximately 4000 best-capitalized and most active OTC stocks that meet NASDAQ's most stringent listing requirements and trade on the NASDAQ Stock Market.

NASDAQ Small-Cap Issues the second tier of stocks that trade on the NASDAQ Stock Market, consisting of approximately 1400 companies whose shares are less active, lower-priced, and more speculative. Listing requirements for these stocks are much lower than those for NASDAQ National Market Issues.

NASDAQ Stock Market the completely electronic stock market in which market makers, traders, and brokers execute buy and sell transactions for the approximately 5400 securities that meet the National Association of Securities Dealers Automated Quotation system's tiers of listing requirements. This market consists of two major groupings—NASDAQ National Market Issues and NASDAQ Small-Cap Issues.

negotiable security a security whose ownership is readily transferred when it is bought or sold.

net asset value (NAV) (1) the price at which a mutual fund shareholder can redeem shares; (2)the market value of each share of a mutual fund computed by subtracting the fund's liabilities from its total assets and dividing the remainder by the total number of outstanding shares. A mutual fund must calculate its NAV at the end of each business day. (*Compare* **public offering price**.)

net transaction a trade, such as the purchase of a new issue, in which the buyer or seller is not charged a commission, markup, or markdown.

net worth (1) also called **stockholders' equity**, the amount of a company's total assets that exceeds its total liabilities on the balance sheet; (2) the difference between the total value of a person's assets and possessions (e.g., home, land, savings accounts, investments) and the person's total indebtedness (e.g., mortgage, credit cards, car loan, student loans).

new issues securities offered for sale for the first time by an issuer in the primary market (for example, an **initial public offering**).

no-load fund a mutual fund that charges no front-end sales charge and no back-end sales charge; however, it may charge a 12b-1 fee as long as the amount is less than 0.25 percent of the fund's total net assets. (*Compare* **pure no-load fund**.)

no-load stock common shares bought directly from a company through that company's direct stock purchase plan. Because these shares are purchased without using a broker, the customer pays no commission. *See also* **direct stock purchase plan**.

noninvestment-grade bond *See* **junk bond**.

not held order *See* **market not held order**.

OCC (1) in the securities industry, abbreviation for the Options Clearing Corporation, a clearing organization owned by the exchanges that issues all option contracts and guarantees the performance or obligation of both the option buyer and seller under the terms of the contract; (2) in the banking industry, abbreviation for the Office of the Controller of the Currency.

odd lot trade a stock trade involving between 1 and 99 shares. (*Compare* **round lot trade**.)

offer price synonym for **asked price**.

open order order that remains valid until it is executed or canceled. Same as a **good-'til-canceled (GTC) order**.

open-end management company legal name for a **mutual fund**; an investment company that, after the initial offering of shares of the public, continually issues new shares and redeems outstanding shares.

OTC common abbreviation of the **over-the-counter market**.

out of the money the relationship between the market price of the underlying security and the option's strike price is such that the holder (buyer) would not exercise the option because it would result in a loss; a phrase that describes an option with no intrinsic value.

overbought market a technical term used to describe a stock (or market) whose value has risen quickly and unexpectedly and thus may represent a price far above its actual worth; usually an indication of a future price decline.

oversold market a technical term used to describe a stock (or market) whose value has fallen quickly and sharply, far below its real value; usually interpreted as an indication of an impending price rise.

over-the-counter (OTC) market a decentralized, negotiated market in which many dealers in diverse locations execute trades for customers over an electronic trading system or telephone lines. The market is currently segmented into two main groups. The first, containing approximately 5400 of the highest quality over-the-counter stocks, is called the NASDAQ Stock Market. The second is called the Pink Sheets and consists of approximately 8000–10,000 lesser quality stocks. *See also* **NASDAQ Stock Market**; **Pink Sheets**.

par value (1) for common stock, an arbitrary (and meaningless) value assigned the stock at the time it is issued; (2) for preferred stock, the fixed value—$100, $50, or, more common today, $25—upon which dividend payments are based.

parity when the total market value of the common shares into which a security can be converted equals the market value of the convertible security.

participating preferred a rarely issued stock that pays the shareholder a fixed dividend and part of the earnings that are distributed to common shareholders.

payable date the date on which a cash dividend or stock is paid to an investor who has purchased the stock before the appropriate ex-date.

P-E ratio *See* **price-earnings ratio**.

penny stock traditionally, any stock with a market value of less than $5. However, increasingly the term is used to refer to any stock listed on the Pink Sheets that has a market value of less than $5. *See also* **Pink Sheets**.

Pink Sheets sheets listing the bid and ask prices of certain thinly traded over-the-counter stocks, mostly low-priced stocks, foreign issues, and unsponsored ADRs. Named for the color of the paper and published each business day by the National Quotation Bureau.

point the price movement on an individual stock equal to one dollar. On bonds, a point represents 1 percent of face value.

poison pill jargon used to describe a security whose features are specifically designed to defend against a hostile takeover. *See also* **long-dated rights**.

preemptive right an entitlement giving existing stockholders the right to purchase a proportional amount of new common shares before they are offered to other investors.

premium (1) the amount by which the market value of a preferred stock or a bond exceeds its par value; (2) the market price of a call or a put option.

price in technical terms, the point at which supply (sellers) and demand (buyers) meet and a trade occurs.

price-earnings (P-E) ratio computed by dividing a stock's current market price by its annual earnings per share, this ratio measures the number of times a stock's price exceeds its earnings. Stated another way, the P-E ratio measures how expensive a stock's market price is relative to the earinigs per share. Traditionally, this ratio is used by fundamental analysts to determine when the share price of a company, a sector, or the overall market is overvalued or undervalued, hence indicating a time to sell or buy, respectively. Analysts sometime refer to this ratio as "the multiple."

primary issue another name for a new issue of securities.

primary market the market in which the issuer and underwriter first offer and sell securities to the public, with the proceeds from the sale going to the issuing corporation. (*Compare* **aftermarket**.)

prime rate the short-term interest rate that commercial banks charge their most creditworthy business customers for unsecured loans.

principal *See* **dealer**.

prior preferred sometimes called a senior preferred, it receives dividends before all other preferred stock.

prospectus a printed summary of the Securities and Exchange Commission–filed registration statement that discloses the details of a particular offering of securities, including the company's business history and that of its management, its future business plans, and its intended use of the proceeds from the issue. The prospectus must contain enough material information for the investor to judge the merits of the issue. *See also* **registration statement**.

proxy a form by which an investor votes in absentia. Proxies may also be used to transfer voting authority to another party.

public offering price (1) for stocks, the price at which new shares are sold to the public by its underwriters; (2) for mutual funds, the price at which a mutual fund share is purchased which may or may not contain a front-end load; also called the **asked price**.

publicly traded fund *See* **closed-end management company**.

pure no-load fund a mutual fund that charges no front-end sales charge, no back-end sales charge, and no 12b-1 fees. (*Compare* **no-load fund**.)

put option a security that gives its holder the right to sell 100 shares of common stock at a fixed price for a fixed period of time.

Random Walk Theory also called the Dart Board Theory, this classic stock market theory states that there are no predictable patterns in the movement of stock prices; hence, using either technical or fundamental analysis to choose a stock in which to invest is useless.

realized gain the cash profit resulting from the liquidation of a security position.

record date the deadline date, set by a corporation's board of directors, on which an investor must be recorded as an owner of the stock in order to be eligible to receive the dividend payment or stock distribution.

red herring jargon for the preliminary prospectus, an abbreviated version of the final prospectus, which is often used to get an indication of the public's interest in a security before the price is set and the security is issued.

redemption fee a flat fee that some mutual funds charge an investor when he or she sells (i.e., redeems) shares. (*Compare* **contingent-deferred sales charge**.)

regional fund a mutual fund or closed-end fund that invests in the negotiable securities of companies located in a specific geographical area.

registered securities (1) securities that are registered and held in customer's name at a brokerage firm; (2) securities that are registered with the Securities and Exchange Commission.

registrar a firm, usually a commercial bank or trust company appointed by the issuer of a security, that is responsible for maintaining an accurate list of all stockholders' names and addresses.

registration statement the disclosure document that companies planning to offer non-exempt securities to the public are required to file with the Securities and Exchange Commission under the Securities Act of 1933. The registration statement must be filed before the securities can be issued, and it must contain full and fair disclosure of the company's business history, financial status, management, and planned use for the proceeds from the sale of the new securities. *See also* **prospectus**.

regular way settlement the normal settlement method for stock transactions in which the securities must be paid for or delivered no later than three business days after the trade date.

Regulation T the Federal Reserve's regulation that gives it the power to set the initial margin requirement on most corporate stocks and bonds and thereby governs the amount of credit that brokerage firms can extend to their customers.

resistance level a price level to which a stock or the market rises and then falls from repeatedly; selling increases as the stock's price approaches this level.

retained earnings the portion of the earnings per share that the board of directors does not pay out as dividends to the common stockholders. Retained earnings are reinvested in the company. *See also* **dividend**; **earnings per share**.

right of accumulation a reduction in a mutual fund's front-end sales charge on all subsequent purchases when the market value of an investor's shares or the current amount of a purchase reaches a **breakpoint**.

rights offering an offering of new shares to existing shareholders. The method and terms by which preemptive rights are distributed to existing shareholders are explained in the prospectus that accompanies the offering. *See also* **preemptive right**.

risk arbitrage the simultaneous purchase of one company's shares and the short sale of another company's shares in anticipation of or upon the announcement of a merger or acquisition between the two companies.

round lot trade a trade involving 100 shares of common stock. (*Compare* **odd lot trade**.)

sales charge a fee that an investor may pay when buying fund shares or redeeming fund shares shortly after purchase. Also called a sales load. *See also* **load**; **load fund**; **back-end load**.

secondary market *See* **aftermarket**.

Securities and Exchange Commission established in 1934 as the regulatory authority of the securities industry, the SEC is responsible for interpreting, supervising, and enforcing compliance with the provisions of the various securities acts.

selling long selling securities or liquidating stock positions that an investor owns.

selling short strategy investors use to profit from a price decline; involves selling securities that the investor has borrowed with the intention of repurchasing them later at a lower price.

sentiment indicators statistics used to measure the bullish or bearish mood of the market and its investors.

settlement date the date on which cash and securities are exchanged following a purchase or sale.

short against the box an end-of-the-year tax strategy used to lock in a gain on securities that an investor owns and, at the same time, defer taxes to the next year. The investor sells short the same security that he or she owns and later uses the long position to cover the short sale on a business day early in the new tax year.

short interest the total amount of a company's outstanding shares that have been sold short and have not been covered or bought in.

short interest ratio a calculation (a stock's short interest divided by its average daily trading volume) used to determine the number of days it would take to cover or buy in all of the shares that investors have sold short.

short margin account a margin account in which a customer sells stock short.

sinking fund provision a feature that permits the issuer of preferred shares or bonds to deposit funds regularly into an escrow account that will eventually be used to redeem or repurchase the outstanding preferred issue or bond.

SIPC acronym for Securities Investors Protection Corporation, a government-sponsored private corporation created in 1970 that provides insurance protection for the customers of broker/dealers that go bankrupt. Each customer's account is covered for up to $500,000 of securities, of which no more than $100,000 may be for cash.

SMA abbreviation for **special memorandum account**.

small-cap stock a company whose outstanding common shares have a total market value of $1 billion or less.

socially responsible fund a mutual fund that does not invest in any company that has holdings in politically or environmentally incorrect sectors of the world.

SOES acronym for Small Order Execution System, NASDAQ's automated order routing, execution, and reporting system that executes orders for 500 shares or less.

special memorandum account (SMA) an account used to show the excess equity or line of credit that an investor has in a margin account.

special situation fund a mutual fund that invests in companies that are candidates for takeover or those that are emerging from bankruptcy.

specialist an exchange member firm located at the trading post, responsible for maintaining a fair and orderly market in the stock(s) assigned to it. The term is used to refer to both the company (i.e., a specialist firm) and the individual who actually handles the trades.

sponsored ADR an American depositary receipt created and issued in the United States by the foreign company whose stock is being held in trust, usually at a U.S. depository bank. Increasingly referred to as American depositary shares, sponsored ADRs offer holders all of the rights of a common shareholder, including the right to vote. Only sponsored ADRs can trade on the New York Stock Exchange. (*Compare* **unsponsored ADR**.)

spread (1) the difference between the bid and asked prices for a security; (2) the compensation that an underwriter receives for distributing a new issue; (3) in options, the simultaneous purchase and sale of the same type of option (calls or puts), with the options having different expirations and/or different strike prices, but involving the same stock.

statement a summary of all transactions in an investor's account, as well as the current value of all long and short positions being held in the account. Statements are sent monthly for active accounts and quarterly for inactive accounts.

Statement of Additional Information an addendum to a mutual fund's prospectus that includes more detailed information, such as the fund's audited financial statements, the methods used for computing the fund's results, the holdings in the fund's portfolio, and the names of the fund's board of directors.

statutory voting method a procedure whereby a shareholder must divide his or her total votes equally among the directorships or issues being decided; the standard voting method in most corporations.

stock a security representing ownership of a company and entitling its owner to the right to receive dividends. *See also* **equity security**.

stock derivative a security that offers an investor some but not all of the benefits of stocks, particularly the capital appreciation potential, usually at a lower cost per unit.

stock exchange an auction market in which exchange members meet in a central location to execute buy and sell orders for individual and institutional customers.

stock option *See* **call option**; **put option**.

stock power usually a separate document attached to a stock or bond certificate and signed by the stockholder, it is a power of attorney giving the brokerage firm the right to transfer ownership to another party, such as to the securities firm when the securities are pledged or to another individual when the securities are sold.

stock split an increase or decrease in the number of a company's authorized shares that results in no change in the total value of the investor's holdings. A positive stock split causes the customer to own more shares at a lower price per share. A negative stock split causes the shareholder to own fewer shares of a higher price per share.

stockholders' equity a synonym for **net worth**, the equity that remains after a company's total liabilities have been subtracted from its total assets.

stop order an order that becomes a market order to buy (buy stop) or to sell (sell stop) when the stock trades at a specified price, known as the stop price. Also called a **stop-loss order**.

stop-loss order *See* **stop order**.

straight preferred a synonym for nonconvertible preferred.

street name industry term describing securities owned by an investor but registered in the name of the investor's brokerage firm.

strike price the fixed price at which stock can be bought or sold when a call or put is exercised. Also known as the **exercise price**.

subscription price usually lower than a stock's current market price, the fixed price at which a company's existing shareholders can purchase new shares during a rights offering.

SuperDOT acronym for Designated Order Turnaround, the NYSE's automated order routing and reporting system. Orders for up to 30,099 shares are routed to the appropriate trading post on the floor of the exchange where a specialist executes the order, typically matching one customer's buy order with another customer's sell order.

support level a price level to which a stock or the market falls or bottoms out repeatedly and then bounces up again; demand for the security increases as the price approaches a support level.

technical analysis (1) research that seeks to predict the future price movement of a stock or the overall market by using price and volume as indicators of changes in the supply and demand for a stock; (2) using charts of a stock's past price and volume movements to predict its future short-term or intermediate-term price movements.

tender offer a limited-time offer by a company to purchase its own shares or another company's outstanding shares, usually at a premium to their current market value.

thin market a situation in which there are few buyers or sellers of a security and that is characterized by increased price volatility; also called an illiquid market.

tick the minimum price movement of a stock. On most stocks, a tick is $1/8$ of a point, or $0.125, although many active over-the-counter stocks trade in $1/16$ of a point, or $0.0625.

ticker the electronic display that continuously shows the stock symbol, volume, and price at which each successive trade occurs; also called the ticker tape or the **consolidated tape**.

time value the amount of an option's premium that exceeds the option's intrinsic value, representing the price investors place on the time an option has until its expiration; if an option is out of the money , all of the premium is considered to be time value. *See also* **out of the money**.

timing attempting to buy or sell a security at the optimum moment in its price movement.

tombstone an advertisement published in financial newspapers and periodicals announcing as a matter of record the public offering of securities by its underwriters.

total capitalization the total long-term debt, preferred stock, and common stock that makes a company's capital structure.

total return the percentage gain or yield on an investment that considers both the income made from dividends and the capital gain made on the stock's (or mutual fund's) price appreciation.

trading post the designated place on an exchange floor where a particular stock trades. It is also referred to as the specialist's post.

trailing P-E ratio the P-E (price-earnings) ratio calculated using the previous year's earnings per share. (*Compare* **forward P-E ratio**.)

transfer agent usually a commercial bank or trust company, a firm appointed by an issuer of a security that is responsible for canceling old certificates and issuing new certificates; also responsible for mailing dividends, proxies, and other important information and documents to the shareholders.

treasury stock outstanding stock that has been repurchased by the corporation that issued it.

trend in technical terms, the up, down, or sideways movement of the overall market (as reflected in an average or index) or a stock's price over a period of time, usually longer than six months.

12b-1 fees an annual percentage of a mutual fund's total net assets assessed to existing shareholders that enables the fund to recover part of the costs, such as advertising, associated with attracting new investors to the fund. The two types are: (1) asset-based 12b-1 fees, a charge based on the total assets that the fund has under management, and (2) service-based 12b-1 fees, ongoing compensation to the agent or brokerage firm that advised the customer to buy the shares.

uncovered option term used to describe a call or put writer who is unprotected against the maximum possible loss on a short option position. (*Compare* **covered option**.)

underwriter a brokerage firm that assists the issuer of a new security in setting the offering price and in marketing the securities to the public; also known as an **investment banker**.

unit a term used for a common stock, preferred stock, or bond issued with one or more warrants attached; the combined products, usually issued by small, very speculative companies, trade as one in the stock market. The warrant is added to the issuance to "sweeten" the purchase for new investors (i.e., to make buying the stock or bond more attractive with a free warrant attached). *See also* **warrant**.

unlisted stocks virtually synonymous with over-the-counter stocks; a term used to describe any stock or other security that does not trade—is not listed—on an exchange. (*Compare* **listed stock**.)

unrealized gain the profit resulting from an increase in the value of a security position that is still being held.

unsponsored ADR an American depositary receipt created and issued in the United States by a bank or other financial services firm that had no relationship with the foreign company whose common stock backs the ADR.

Unsponsored ADRs do not trade on the NYSE; instead they trade in the over-the-counter markets. (*Compare* **sponsored ADR**.)

uptrend the upward movement of a stock's price or of the market as measured by an average or index over a period of time.

value investing investing in a company's common stock whose market value appears to be a bargain (i.e., the price is below the company's "real" worth or earnings power, or below the value of comparable companies in the same business sector). The managers use such fundamental measures as price-earnings (P-E) ratio and price-to-book-value ratio to find such bargains. As soon as the stock becomes "fully valued" based on the same measures, the manager will typically sell the stock out of the portfolio.

venture capital money invested in a new, unproved, and risky business or enterprise.

volatility the relative amount or percentage by which a stock's price rises and falls during a period of time.

volume the total number of shares traded in a given period of time.

voting trust a trust, usually having a maximum life of 10 years, established to control the voting shares of a corporation.

voting trust certificate (VTC) negotiable certificates showing that common shares have been deposited into a voting trust and that shareholders have forfeited their right to vote.

warrant a long-term security, usually attached to a bond, preferred stock, or common stock, that gives the holder the right to buy a fixed number of a company's common shares at a price that is set higher than the stock's current market price at the time of issuance. *See also* **unit**.

wasting asset a security that becomes worthless on a predetermined expiration date. Rights, standard warrants, and options are securities that are wasting assets.

wealth building an investment strategy designed to increase one's net worth over time.

weighting the method for determining the worth of each company's stock relative to the value of the overall index.

when-issued security a security that is sold to the public and trades in the market before the physical certificates are available for distribution.

World fund *See* **Global fund**.

writer seller of an option contract.

yield the percentage or rate of return that an investor makes on capital invested in a security or in a portfolio of securities.

zero-coupon bond a bond sold at an original issue discount that pays interest in a lump sum at maturity. *See also* **bond**.

Index